CBSE ACCOUNTANCY

[Class XII]

M Hanif • A Mukherjee

New Central Book Agency (P) Ltd

LONDON

HYDERABAD ERNAKULAM BHUBANESWAR

NEW DELHI KOLKATA PUNE GUWAHATI

NCBA

REGD OFFICE
8/1 Chintamoni Das Lane, Kolkata 700 009, India
email: ncbapvtltd@eth.net

OVERSEAS
NCBA (UK) Ltd, 149 Park Avenue North, Northampton, NN3 2HY, UK
email: ncbauk@yahoo.com

EXPORT
NCBA Exports Pvt. Ltd, 212 Shahpur Jat, New Delhi 110 049
email: ncbaexports@ncbapvtltd.com

BRANCHES

2/27 Ansari Road, 1st Floor
Daryaganj, **New Delhi** 110 002
email: ncbadel@ncbapvtltd.com

Shop Nos. 3 & 4, Vinayak Towers
681/B Budhwar Peth, Appa Balwant Chowk
Pune 411 002
email: ncbapune@ncbapvtltd.com

Shop No. 15, Bharati Towers, Ground Floor
Forest Park
Bhubaneswar 751 001
email: ncbabub@ncbapvtltd.com

House No. 3-1-315, 1st Floor
Nimboliadda, Kachiguda, **Hyderabad** 500 027
email: ncbahydb@ncbapvtltd.com

GSS Shopping Complex, 1st Floor
Opposite College Post Office, Convent Road
Ernakulam 682 035
0484-4021054/53

Radhamayee Complex (Second Floor)
Opp. SBI, Panbazar, Jaswanta Road
Guwahati 781 001
email: ncbaguwahati@ncbapvtltd.com

CBSE ACCOUNTANCY [XII] SUPPLIMENT • M Hanif • A Mukherjee

First Published: January 2016

PUBLISHER
New Central Book Agency (P) Ltd
8/1 Chintamoni Das Lane, Kolkata 700 009

PRINTER
New Central Book Agency (P) Ltd
Web-Offset Division, Dhulagarh, Sankrail, Howrah

COVER DESIGNER
Soumen Paul

COVER PRINTER
Techno Process, Kolkata

Contents

How to tackle Multiple Choice Questions

Multiple Choice type Questions will have **three / four** options for each question. One option will be right, and others wrong. You will have to choose the right option as your answer.

Following are few tips on correctly tackling these questions :

(1) Go through the paper carefully and identify the questions you are absolutely sure about. Attempt those questions first.

(2) First look at the question, think of the possible answer, or work out the answer (for numerical questions). Then look at the options given. If one of those matches your answer, probably that is the correct option. Still, go through the solution once more.

(3) At times questions are ambiguous. More than one option might seem to be the right answer. Go through the question again carefully for exact requirement.

(4) At times none of the option seems right. In those cases, first eliminate the obviously wrong option. Then consider remaining option for the most possible right choice.

(5) Finally, as in all exams, some questions will be tricky, or options are designed to match common mistake. So revise all the answers carefully. There is no harm in being cautious and careful.

Preface

In this book, 'Accounting for Companies' has been discussed as per the format incorporated in the Companies Act, 2013. The different different aspects have been dealt with, starting from a very basic level to a higher level with sufficient illustrations, examples and real life scenarios. Proper care had to been taken to explain various ideas and concepts lucidly.

Relevant sections of the Companies Act, 2013 have been discussed in details as per the requirement of the syllabus for 2015-16 onwards. I have observed that the CBSE has introduced a new pattern of questions from curriculum year 2015-16 for class XII. Thus, special emphasis has been given to provide enough illustrations following this new pattern for the benefit of the young learners.

Suggested answers for the question papers of 2014 and 2015 (Part-A:Accounting for Partnership and Companies) have been given for assistance of the students.

I thank Mr. Rangarajan for typesetting and formatting of this book.

Special thanks goes to Mr. Amitabha Sen of New Central Book Agency (P) Ltd. for his initiative and untiring efforts to make this book a reality.

I believe that there is always a scope for improvement in the quality of the book. I have taken utmost care to eliminate any error or mistake. However, I will be very happy to get feedback and suggestions for improving the quality of the book.

Author

Author can be reached at —
Email : pmhanif@gmail.com

Accountancy (Code 055)
Class-XII (2015-16)

One Paper | | 3 Hours
Theory : 80 Marks

Units	Periods	Marks
Part A: Accounting for Partnership Firms and Companies		
Unit 1. Accounting for Partnership Firms	90	35
Unit 2. Accounting for Companies	60	25
	150	60
Part B: Financial Statement Analysis		
Unit 3. Analysis of Financial Statements	30	12
Unit 4. Cash Flow Statement	20	8
	50	20
Part C: Project Work	**40**	**20**
Project work will include:		
Project File: 4 Marks		
Written Test: 12 Marks (One Hour)		
Viva Voce: 4 Marks		
OR		
Part B: Computerized Accounting		
Unit 3. Computerized Accounting	60	20
Part C: Practical Work	**26**	**20**
Practical work will include:		
File 4 Marks		
Practical Examination 12 Marks (One Hour)		
Viva Voce 4 Marks		

Part A: Accounting for Partnership Firms and Companies **60 Marks 150 Periods**

Unit 1: Accounting for Partnership Firms **90 Periods**

Units / Topics	Learning Outcomes
• Partnership: features, Partnership deed. • Provisions of the Indian Partnership Act 1932 in the absence of partnership deed. Fixed v/s fluctuating capital accounts. Preparation of Profit & Loss Appropriation Account – division of profit among partners, guarantee of profits. • Past adjustments (relating to interest on capital, interest on drawing, salary and profit sharing ratio). • Goodwill: nature, factors affecting and methods of valuation - average profit, super profit and capitalization. **Scope :** *Interest on partner's loan is to be treated as a charge against profits.* **Accounting for Partnership firms - Reconstitution and Dissolution.** • **Change in the Profit Sharing Ratio** among the existing partners - sacrificing ratio, gaining ratio. Accounting for revaluation of assets and re-assessment of liabilities and distribution of reserves and accumulated profits. Preparation of revaluation account and balance sheet. • **Admission of a partner** - effect of admission of a partner on change in the profit sharing ratio, treatment of goodwill (as per AS 26), treatment for revaluation of assets and re - assessment of liabilities, treatment of reserves and accumulated profits, adjustment of capital accounts and preparation of balance sheet. • **Retirement and death of a partner**: effect of retirement /death of a partner on change in profit sharing ratio, treatment of goodwill (as per AS 26), treatment for revaluation of assets and re-assessment of liabilities, adjustment of accumulated profits and reserves, adjustment of capital accounts and preparation of balance sheet. Preparation of loan account of the retiring partner. Calculation of deceased partner's share of profit till the date of death. Preparation of deceased partner's capital account, executor's account and preparation of balance sheet. • **Dissolution of partnership firm**: types of dissolution of firm. Settlement of accounts - preparation of realization account, and other related accounts, capital accounts of partners and cash/bank account (excluding piecemeal distribution, sale to a company and insolvency of partner(s)). **Note:** (i) The realised value of each asset must be given at the time of dissolution. (ii) In case, the realisation expenses are borne by a partner, clear indication should be given regarding the payment thereof.	After going through this Unit, the students will be able to : • state the meaning of partnership, partnership firm and partnership deed. • describe the characteristic features of partnership and the contents of partnership deed. explain the significance of provision of Partnership Act in the absence of partnership deed. Differentiate between fixed and fluctuating capital, outline the process and develop the understanding of preparation of Profit and Loss Appropriation Account. • develop the understanding of making past adjustments. • state the meaning, nature and factors affecting goodwill. • develop the understanding of valuation of goodwill using different methods of valuation of goodwill. • describe the meaning of sacrificing ratio, gaining ratio and the change in profit sharing ratio among existing partners. • develop the understanding of accounting treatment of assets and re-assessment of liabilities and treatment of reserves and accumulated profits by preparing revaluation account and balance sheet. • explain the effect of change in profit sharing ratio on admission of a new partner. • develop the understanding of treatment of goodwill as per AS-26, treatment of revaluation of assets and re-assessment of liabilities, treatment of reserves and accumulated profits, adjustment of capital accounts and preparation of balance sheet of the new firm. • explain the effect of retirement / death of a partner on change in profit sharing ratio. • state the meaning of sacrificing ratio. • develop the understanding of accounting treatment of goodwill, revaluation of assets and re-assessment of liabilities and adjustment of accumulated profits and reserves on retirement / death of a partner and capital adjustment. • develop the skill of calculation of deceased partner's share till the time of his death and prepare deceased partner's executor's account. • discuss the preparation of the capital accounts of the remaining partners and the balance sheet of the firm after retirement / death of a partner. • understand the situations under which a partnership firm can be dissolved. • develop the understanding of preparation of realisation account and other related accounts.

Unit 2: Accounting for Companies

60 Periods

Units / Topics	Learning Outcomes
Accounting for Share Capital • Share and share capital: nature and types. • **Accounting for share capital:** issue and allotment of equity shares, private placement of shares, Employee Stock Option Plan (ESOP), Public subscription of shares - over subscription and under subscription of shares; issue at par and at premium, calls in advance and arrears (excluding interest), issue of shares for consideration other than cash. • Accounting treatment of forfeiture and re-issue of shares. • Disclosure of share capital in company's Balance Sheet. **Accounting for Debentures** • **Debentures**: Issue of debentures at par, at a premium and at discount. Issue of debentures for consideration other than cash; Issue of debentures with terms of redemption; debentures as collateral security-concept, interest on debentures. • **Redemption of debentures**: Lump sum, draw of lots and purchase in the open market (excluding ex-interest and cum-interest). **Note :** *Related sections of the Indian Companies Act, 2013 will apply.*	**After going through this Unit, the students will be able to:** • state the meaning of share and share capital and differentiate between equity shares and preference shares and different types of share capital. • understand the meaning of private placement of shares. • explain the accounting treatment of share capital transactions regarding issue of shares. • develop the understanding of accounting treatment of forfeiture and re-issue of forfeited shares. • describe the presentation of share capital in the balance sheet of the company as per schedule III part I of the Companies Act 2013. • explain the accounting treatment of different categories of transactions related to issue of debentures. • develop the skill of calculating interest on debentures and its accounting treatment. • state the meaning of redemption of debentures. • develop the understanding of accounting treatment of transactions related to redemption of debentures.

Part B : Financial Statement Analysis

20 Marks

Unit 3: Analysis of Financial Statements

30 Periods

Units / Topics	Learning Outcomes
• **Financial statements of a company**: Statement of Profit and Loss and Balance Sheet in the prescribed form with major headings and sub headings (as per Schedule III to the Companies Act, 2013). **Scope**: Exceptional Items, Extraordinary Items and Profit (loss) from Discontinued Operations are excluded. • **Financial Statement Analysis**: Objectives, Importance and Limitations. • **Tools for Financial Statement Analysis**: Comparative statements, common size statements, cash flow analysis, ratio analysis. • **Accounting Ratios**: Objectives, classification and computation.	**After going through this Unit, the students will be able to:** • develop the understanding of major headings and sub-headings (as per Schedule III to the Companies Act, 2013) of balance sheet as per the prescribed forms / formats. • state the meaning, objectives and limitations of financial statement analysis. • describe the meaning of different tools of 'financial statements analysis'. • develop the understanding of preparation of comparative and common size financial statements. • know the meaning, objectives and significance of different types of ratios.

Units / Topics	Learning Outcomes
Liquidity Ratios: Current ratio and Quick ratio. **Solvency Ratios**: Debt to Equity Ratio, Total Asset to Debt Ratio, Proprietary Ratio and Interest Coverage Ratio. **Activity Ratios**: Inventory Turnover Ratio, Trade Receivables Turnover Ratio, Trade Payable Turnover Ratio and Working Capital Turnover Ratio. **Profitability Ratios**: Gross Profit Ratio, Operating Ratio, Operating Profit Ratio, Net Profit Ratio and Return on Investment.	• develop the understanding of computation of current ratio and quick ratio. • develop the skill of computation of debt equity ratio, total asset to debt ratio, proprietary ratio and interest coverage ratio. • develop the skill of computation of inventory turnover ratio, trade receivables and trade payables ratio and capital turnover ratio. • develop the skill of computation of gross profit ratio, operating ratio, operating profit ratio, net profit ratio and return on investment.

Unit 4: Cash Flow Statement

20 Periods

Units / Topics	Learning Outcomes
• Meaning, objectives and preparation (as per AS 3 (Revised) (Indirect Method only) **Scope**: (i) Adjustments relating to depreciation and amortisation, profit or loss on sale of assets including investments, dividend (both final and interim) and tax. (ii) Bank overdraft and cash credit to be treated as Short-term borrowing. (iii) Current Investments to be taken as Marketable Securities unless otherwise specified.	**After going through this Unit, the students will be able to:** • state the meaning and objectives of cash flow statement. • develop the understanding of preparation of Cash Flow Statement using indirect method as per AS 3 with given adjustments.

PROJECT WORK

20 Marks 60 Periods

Note : Kindly refer to the Guidelines published by the CBSE.

Suggested Question Paper Design
Accountancy (Code 055)
Class XII (2015-16)
March 2016 Examination

One Paper

Theory : 80 Marks
Duration : 3 Hrs.

Sl. No.	Typology of Questions	Very Short Answer 1 Mark	Short Answer I 3 Marks	Short Answer II 4 Marks	Long Answer I 6 Marks	Long Answer II 8 Marks	Marks	%
1.	**Remembering** - (Knowledge based Simple recall questions, to know specific facts, terms, concepts, principles or theories; Identify, define or recite, information)	3	1	1	1	-	16	20
2.	**Understanding** - (Comprehension - to be familiar with meaning and to understand conceptually, interpret, compare, contrast, explain, paraphrase or interpret information)	2	-	2	1	1	24	30
3.	**Application** - (Use abstract information in concrete situation, to apply knowledge to new situations; Use given content to interpret a situation, provide an example, or solve a problem)	-	2	2	1	-	20	25
4.	**High Order Thinking Skills (Analysis & Synthesis** - Classify, compare, contrast, or differentiate between different pieces of information; Organise and/or integrate unique pieces of information)	2	-	-	1	1	16	20
5.	**Evaluation** - (Appraise, judge and/or justify the value or worth of a decision or outcome, or to predict outcomes based on values)	1	1	-	-	-	04	05
	TOTAL	8x1=8	4x3=12	5x4=20	4x6=24	2x8=16	80 (23) + 20 Projects	100

Scheme of options : All questions carrying 8 marks will have an internal choice.

Note : The Board has introduced Learning Outcomes in the syllabus to motivate students to constantly explore all levels of learning. However, these are only indicative. these do not in any way restrict the scope of questions asked in the examinations. The examination questions will be strictly based on the precribed question paper design and syllabus.

4

Accounting for Share Capital

Syllabus

- **Share and Share Capital** : Nature and Types.
- **Accounting for Share Capital** : Issue and Allotment of Equity Shares; Private Placement of Shares, Employee Stock Option Plan (ESOP). Public Subscription of Shares – Over Subscription and Under Subscription of Shares, Issue at Par and Premium, Calls-in-advance and Arrears (excluding interest), Issue of shares for consideration other than Cash.
- **Accounting Treatment of Forfeiture and Re-issue of Shares**
- **Disclosure of Share Capital in Company's Balance Sheet**

Meaning of A Company

A company is an association of persons for a business purpose. It is incorporated under the Companies Act. Its capital is subscribed by the shareholders. It is a corporate enterprise that has a legal identity separate from that of its members. A company operates as one single unit, in the success of which all the members participate.

As per the provision of Section 2(20) of the Companies Act, 2013 'company' means a company incorporated under this Act or under any previous company law. It is worth mentioning that there were number of Companies Acts / Laws before the enactment of the Companies Act, 2013 such as:

(i) The Companies Act, 1956 (ii) The Companies Act, 1913
(iii) The Companies Act, 1882 (iv) The Companies Act, 1866

It is to be noted that the above definition of company is not comprehensive. To understand the meaning of company, the following definitions given by different authors are very important. Some of the definitions are given below :

Prof. Haney defines a company as "the company is an artificial person created by law, having separate entity, with a perpetual succession and common seal."

Lord Justice Lindley defines a Company as follows :

"By a Company is meant an association of many persons who contribute money or money's worth to a common stock and employ it for a common purpose. The common stock so contributed is denoted in money and is the capital of the Company. The persons who contribute it or to whom it belongs are members. The proportion of capital to which each member is entitled is his share".

Characteristics of a Company

The following are the main characteristics of a Company :

1. ***Incorporation*** : A Company comes into existence only after incorporation under the Companies Act.

2. **Legal Status** : A Company is a legal entity separate and distinct from its members. It can enter into a contract. It can sue and be sued in its own name.

3. ***Capacity of Shareholders*** : A shareholder of a company, in its individual capacity, cannot bind the Company in any way.

4. ***Capital Contribution*** : The equity capital of a company is typically subscribed by shareholders who receive return in the form of dividend.

5. ***Transferability*** : The shareholder of a company can transfer its share and ordinarily the transferee becomes a member of the company.

6. ***Limited Liabilities*** : The liabilities of shareholder of a company are usually limited.

7. ***Management*** : A Company is managed by the Board of Directors, whole time Directors, Managing Director or Manager. These persons are selected according to the provision of the Companies Act and Articles of Association of the Company.

8. ***Perpetual Succession*** : The Company has perpetual succession. The insolvency or death of a shareholder will not affect its existence.

9. ***Registered Office*** : A Company must have a registered office.

10. ***Common Seal*** : A Company must have a common seal.

Types of Companies

The Companies Act, 2013 allows to form a company for economic as well as non-economic purposes. A company may be either :

(i) a company limited by shares; or

(ii) a company limited by guarantee; or

(iii) an unlimited company

(i) 'Company limited by shares' means a company having the liability of its members limited by the memoprandum to the amount, if any, unpaid on the shares respectively held by them [Section 2(22)];

(ii) 'Company limited by guarantee' means a company having the liability of its members limited by the memorandum to such amount as the members may respectively undertake to contribute to the assets of the company in the event of its being wound up [Section 2(21)].

(iii) 'Unlimited company' means a company not having any limit on the liability of its members [Section 2(92)].

The most common types of companies are :

1. Private Companies; and
2. Public Companies

Private Companies

As per the provision of Section 2(68) of the Companies Act, 2013 'private company' means a company having a minimum paid-up share capital of ***one lakh rupees*** or such higher paid-up capital as may be prescribed and which by its articles —

(i) restricts the right to transfer its share;
(ii) except in case of one person company, limits the number of its members to ***two hundred***;
(iii) prohibits any invitation to the public to subscribe for any securities of the company.

Private companies can be re-classified as :

(i) One Person Company (OPC)
(ii) Small Companies

One Person Company (OPC)

The concept of one person company has been introduced for the first time in the Companies Act, 2013. As per the provision of Section 2(62) of the Companies Act, 2013 '***one person company' means a company which has only one person as member***'.

Characteristics of One Person Company

1. It is a one member company.
2. It is a private company.
3. It may be registered as 'limited by shares' or 'limited by guarantee'.
4. The phrase 'one person company' shall be mentioned within a bracket below the name of the company.
5. In the memorandum, it should indicate the name of the 'other person; who shall become member of the company in case of death or incapability of the promoter. Prior written consent in the prescribed form should be taken from such person.
6. It may not have to prepare 'Cash Flow Statement' as part of Financial Statements.
7. There is no need of holding Annual General Meeting.
8. The Financial Statements can be submitted within 6 months from the date of closing of the books of accounts.

Small Company

The concept of small company has been introduced in the Companies Act, 2013. As per the provision of Section 2(85) 'small company' means a company other than a public company—

(i) paid-up share capital of which does not exceed ***fifty lakh rupees*** or such higher amount as may be prescribed which shall not be more than ***five crore rupees***; or
(ii) turnover of which as per last Profit and Loss Account does not exceed two crore rupees, or such higher amount as may be prescribed which shall not be more than twenty crore rupees.

However, this clause shall not apply to

(a) a holding or a subsidiary company;
(b) a company registered under Section 8 (Non-profit association for charitable purposes);
(c) a company or body corporate governed by any special Act.

Public Company

As per the provision of Section 2(71) of the Companies Act, 2013 'public company' means a company which—

(i) is not a private company;
(ii) has a minimum paid-up share capital of ***five lakh rupees*** or such higher paid-up capital as may be prescribed.

However, a company which is a subsidiary of a company, not being a private company, shall be deemed to be public company for the purposes of this Act even where such subsidiary company continues to be a private company in its articles.

Distinction between a Public Company and a Private Company

Sl. No.	Basis of Distinction	Public Company	Private company
1.	**Formation**	Minimum 7 persons are required to form a public company.	Minimum 2 persons are required to form a private company. However, 'one person company' can be formed as per the provision of Section 3 of the Companies Act, 2013 with a single person.
2.	**Maximum Number of Members**	In a public company there may be any number of members.	In a private company (except one person company) maximum number of members cannot ***exceed 200***.
3.	**Restriction on Transfer of Shares**	In a public company the shares are freely transferrable.	In a private company the right to transfer shares is restricted by the Articles of Association.
4.	**Number of Directors**	A public company must have at least 3 directors.	A private company must have least 2 directors or bonds.
5.	**Independent** Director	In case of a ***listed*** public company at least $^{1}/_{3}$rd should be independent directors.	Question of independent director does not arise.
6.	**Invitation to Public**	There is no restriction for a public company to invite the public to purchase its shares or debentures or bonds.	A private company cannot invite the public to purchase its shares or debentures.
7.	**Prospectus**	A public company must file a prospectus or a statement in line of prospectus before public issue.	A private company need not file a prospectus or a statement in line of prospectus.
8.	**Small Company**	In case of a public company there is no concept of 'small company'.	In case of a private company there is a concept of 'small company'. A private company will be treated as a small company when its paid-up capital does not exceed fifty lakh rupees and turnover does not exceed two crore rupees.
9.	**Minimum Paid-up Capital**	In case of a public company minimum paid-up capital is ***five lakh rupees***.	In case of a private company minimum capital is ***one lakh rupees***.
10.	**Special Privilege**	A public company enjoys no special privileges.	A private company enjoys some special privileges.
11.	**Retirement of Directors**	The directors of a public company retires by rotation.	All directors of a private company can be non-rotational directors.

12.	**Managerial Remuneration**	In case of a public company the managerial remuneration is restricted to 11% of the net profit of the company.	In case of a private company there is no restriction on managerial remuneration.
13.	**Acceptance of Public Deposits**	Subject to the provision of Section 76, a public company can accept deposits from public.	A private company cannot accept deposits from the public.
14.	**Name**	The word 'Limited' is used with the name of the company. ***For example***, 'Reliance Industries Limited', 'Tata Motors Limited', etc.	The phrase 'Private Limited' is used with the name of the company. ***For example***, 'McGraw Hill Education (India) Private Limited'.

Sources of Capital of a Company — Shares

A joint stock company (private or public) raises its capital by issuing shares. A private limited company, however, issues shares informally, by personal contact between the directors and investors. It cannot invite the public to buy its shares. On the contrary a public limited company is free to invite the public to buy its shares. It issues a prospectus and takes the help of underwriters in order to sell its shares.

Shares

According to Section 2(84) of the Companies Act, 2013, a share represents a 'unit' into which the capital of a company is divided. ***For example***, the share capital of a company is ₹ 6,00,000. It is divided into 1,20,000 units of ₹ 5 each. Each 'unit of ₹ 5' will be called a ***share of the company***.

Each share in a company is distinguished by its appropriate number. Shares are classified as movable property, transferable in the manner specified by the Articles. A certificate under the common seal of the company is issued to the shareholders to provide them with prima facie evidence of their title to the shares specified therein and is known as a ***Share Certificate***.

The Nature and Kinds of Shares

Every company is financed mainly by the issue of shares. To suit the taste and temperament of different types of investors, company issue different kinds of shares. Section 93 of the Companies Act, 2013 provides that the share capital of a company limited by shares shall be of ***two*** kinds, namely,

(a) Equity Share Capital —
   (i) with voting rights; or
   (ii) with differential rights as to dividend, voting or otherwise in accordance with such rules as may be prescribed.

(b) Preference Share Capital

Equity Share / Equity Share Capital

Equity Share Capital means all share capital which is not 'preference share' capital (to be explained shortly). The holder of an equity share with ***voting rights*** is entitled to vote, proportionately, in general meeting of the company. This gives the equity shareholder the power to appoint directors of the company. The equity shareholders are also entitled to a share of the company's annual profit in the form of dividend. The rate of dividend may vary from year to year depending upon the profit and dividend policy of the company. However, the equity shareholders run two risks. ***First,*** when the company fails to earn profit, the equity shareholders may not get any dividend at all. ***Second,*** when the company is liquidated, the equity shareholders get back their capital at last after satisfying creditors, lenders and preference shareholders.

Normally, the company does not repay its equity shareholders before liquidation. Some companies may buy-back some of the equity shares. If a equity shareholder wants to sell his share, he will have to find out the buyer (applicable to unlisted / private companies). However, equity shareholder of a ***listed*** company can sell its share easily at any stock exchange.

It is to be noted here that the Companies Act, 2013 allows the issue of equity shares without voting rights. However, these shares are to be issued as per Rule 4 of the Companies (Share Capital and Debentures) Rules, 2014.

Features of an Equity Share

(1) It is a part of the capital of the company.
(2) It can be purchased or sold in a stock exchange in case of listed company.
(3) It has no cumulative rights to dividends.
(4) It can vote in the election of directors.
(5) It can take part in the making of certain important company decisions.
(6) It can participate in the profits of the company.
(7) It can purchase a proportionate part of future share issues (i.e., rights issue).
(8) It has the right to share in assets upon liquidation.

Preference Share Capital / Preference Shares

Preference Share Capital means that part of the issued share capital of the company which carries or would carry a preferential right with respect to—

(a) payment of dividend, either as a fixed amount or an amount calculated at a fixed rate, which may either be free of or subject to income-tax; and
(b) repayment, in the case of a winding-up or repayment of capital, of the amount of the share capital paid-up or deemed to have been paid-up, whether or not, there is a preferential right to the payment of any fixed premium or premium on any fixed scale, specified in the memorandum or articles of the company.

Unlike equity shares, preference shares carry no voting rights. The preference shareholders are entitled to a fixed rate or fixed amount of dividend.

For example, 10% Preference Shares of ₹ 100 each means that the preference shareholder will get ₹ 10 per share as dividend. According to the situation and market conditions, a company may issue preference shares at different rate of dividend at different points of time.

Features of a Preference Share

(1) It has preferential rights to dividends at a fixed rate or fixed amount as the case may be.
(2) It has cumulative rights to dividends.
(3) It has preferential rights to assets of the company in the case of liquidation.
(4) It is redeemable before the expiry of a period of ***twenty*** years from the date of its issue.
(5) It can be purchased or sold in a stock exchange at a price above or below its face value.

(6) It has no voting power in general.
(7) It may or may not be converted into equity share(s).

Advantages

From the Company's Point of View

1. Since the rate of dividend / amount of dividend is fixed, the company knows in advance the amount of dividend to be paid to the preference shareholders.
2. It is one of the permanent source of long-term capital which does not have to be repaid immediately (not before 20 years in many cases it is to be repaid within 30 years).

From the Shareholders' Point of View :

1. The rate / amount of dividend is fixed. It is an assured income not depending upon the amount of profit made by the company.
2. No tax is to be paid by the shareholders on dividend received.It is paid by the company.

Disadvantages

From the Company's Point of View :

1. Dividend is not allowable as deduction for calculating taxable income. It is relevant to mention here that interest on debentures or long-term debts are allowable as deduction for calculation of taxable income.
2. The company is liable to pay corporate dividend tax on the dividend paid.

> ***Tutorial Note : Because of the above reasons, it is very unpopular to issue preference shares. Now-a-days, majority of the companies prefer to take long-term loans from bank or other financial institutions, in place of issuing preference shares.***

From Shareholders' Point of View :

1. They can not take part in the election of directors.
2. When the company is earning good profits and paying equity dividend at a higher rate, the preference shareholders only get a fixed percentage of dividend which is very low in many cases.
3. True return on investment is low when the inflation is high.

Sub-division of Preference Shares

Preference Shares can be sub-divided into different classes, such as :

(a) Cumulative and non-cumulative preference shares;
(b) Participating and non-participating preference shares; and
(c) Redeemable and non-redeemable preference shares.

(i) Cumulative and Non-cumulative Preference Shares

A fixed rate / amount of dividend is paid to preference shareholders before payment of dividend paid to the equity shareholders. It may so happen that the company's current year profit is not enough or the company has incurred losses and it cannot pay the dividend to the preference shareholders. In the case of cumulative preference shares, the deficiency accumulates and it is to be paid out of the profits of the subsequent years.

In case of non-cumulative preference shares, dividend is only payable out of net profit of each year and shares do not have the privilege of accumulation of the unpaid dividends. It should be noted that if nothing is specified in the Articles, it will be treated as ***cumulative preference shares***.

(ii) Participating and Non-participating Preference Shares

Participating preference shares are those preference shares which are entitled to a fixed rate of preferencial dividend and in addition, enjoy a right to participate in the surplus profits (along with equity shareholders) after paying dividend to equity shareholders at a certain rate. Further, in the event of winding up, if there is any surplus left after paying preference shareholders and equity shareholders, then participating preference shareholders are entitled to get a portion of the surplus of assets of the company.

If the articles or the terms of issue of preference shares do not specifically allow participation in surplus, then preference shareholders get only the fixed preferencial dividend and return of capital at the time of winding up of the company, after meeting external liabilities and these preference shares are called non-participating preference shares.

(iii) Redeemable and Non-redeemable Preference Shares

Redeemable preference shares are those which are redeemed by the company after certain years (as per the terms and conditions of the issue). Irredeemable preference shares are those which cannot be redeemed before liquidation.

In this respect, the provision of ***Section 55 of the Companies Act, 2013*** is very important. which states that:

(1) No company limited by shares shall, after the commencement of this Act, issue any preference shares which are irredeemable.

(2) A company limited by shares may, if so authorised by its articles, issue preference shares which are liable to be redeemed within a period not exceeding ***twenty years*** from the date of their issue subject to such conditions as may be prescribed.

Distinction Between Equity Share and Preference Share

	Equity Share		Preference Share
1.	It is the risk capital of a company.	1.	It is not the risk capital of a company.
2.	A company must have equity shares.	2.	A company may not have any preference share.
3.	It has higher expected rate of dividend than preference shares.	3.	It has the right to get dividend at a fixed rate / fixed amount.
4.	It has no preferential right to dividend.	4.	It has preferential rights to dividends.
5.	It has no cumulative right to dividend.	5.	It has cumulative right to dividend.
6.	It has voting power.	6.	It has no voting power.
7.	Equity shareholders can take part in the meeting of certain important company decisions.	7.	Preference shareholders have no such right.
8.	It is not redeemable.	8.	It is redeemable before the expiry of twenty years from the date of issue.
9.	It cannot be converted into preference shares.	9.	It may be converted into equity shares.
10.	At the time of liquidation, equity shareholders are paid off last.	10.	At the time of liquidation, preference shareholders are paid off before the equity shareholders.
11.	Equity shareholders can purchase a proportion- ate part of future share issues i.e. rights share.	11.	Preference shareholders have no such right.

Stock

As per the provision of Section 62(1)(c) of the Companies Act, 2013 a limited company having a share capital may, if so authorised by its articles, convert all or any of its fully paid-up shares into stock, and reconvert that stock into fully paid-up shares of any denomination. Stock is the aggregate of fully paid-up shares legally consolidated and portion of which aggregate may be transferred or split up into fractions of any amount without regard to the original nominal amount of shares.

Distinction between Shares and Stock

(1) Shares are in units but stock is in lump holding.
(2) Shares can be issued directly but stock cannot be issued directly.
(3) Shares need not be fully paid but stock must be fully paid.
(4) Shares must be numbered but stock is never numbered.
(5) Shares cannot be transferred in fractional amount but stock can be transferred in fractional amount.

Sub-division of Share Capital of a Company

(i) Authorised Capital or Nominal Capital

It means such capital as is authorised by the memorandum of a company to be the maximum amount of share capital of the company. [Section 2(8)]

For example, Authorised Capital of Reliance Industries Limited is ₹ 6,000 crore (500 crore equity shares of ₹ 10 each + 100 crore preference shares of ₹ 10 each).

(ii) Issued Capital

It means such capital as the company issues from time to time for subscription [Section 2(50)].

For example, Issued Capital of Reliance Industries Limited upto 31st March, 2014 is ₹ 3,232 crore (3,23,19,01,858 equity shares of ₹ 10 each).

(iii) Subscribed Capital

It means such part of the capital which is for the time being subscribed by the members of a company (Section 2(86)].

For example, Subscribed Capital of Reliance Industries Limited as on 31st March, 2014 is ₹ 3,232 crore (3,23,19,01,858 equity shares of ₹ 10 each).

(iv) Paid-up Share Capital or Share Capital Paid-up

It means such aggregate amount of money credited as paid-up as is equivalent to the amount received as paid-up in respect of shares issued and also includes any amount credited as paid-up in respect of shares of the company, but does not include any other amount received in respect of such shares, by whatever name called [Section 2(64)].

For example, money received against share warrants or application money pending allotment will not be treated as paid-up capital.

(v) Uncalled Capital

It is that part of the subscribed capital which has not been called-up by the Board of Directors.

(vi) Reserve Capital

A limited company may, by special resolution, determine that any portion of its share capital which has not been already called-up shall not be capable of being called-up, except in the event and for the purposes of the company being wound up. This uncalled portion of the share capital is called ***Reserve Capital***.

Check Your Progress

Answers : Page 4.***

Tick the write answer :

1. *Which of the following is not a characteristic of a public limited company ?*
   - A *its shares are freely transferable*
   - B *the number of directors should be at least 3*
   - C *in a public company, there may be any number of members*
   - D *a public company can be a small company*
2. *The capital with which a company is registered is called*
   - A *issued capital*
   - B *paid-up capital*
   - C *authorized capital*
   - D *subscribed capital*
3. *Subscribed capital can be*
   - A *more than called-up capital*
   - B *more than issued capital*
   - C *more than authorized capital*
   - D *equal to reserve capital*
4. *Issued capital is the part of*
   - A *subscribed capital*
   - B *authorized capital*
   - C *called-up capital*
   - D *paid-up capital*
5. *'Reserve capital' can be called up*
   - A *in an emergency only*
   - B *any time by passing an ordinary resolution*
   - C *in the event and for the purposes of the company being wound-up*
   - D *if all directors agree*
6. *Which of the following is not a characteristic of a company ?*
   - A *a company is a legal entity separate and distinct from its members.*
   - B *a shareholder of a company, in its individual capacity, can bind the company.*
   - C *the shareholders of a company can enter into a contract with the company.*
   - D *a company must have a registered office.*

The disclosures in respect of Share Capital are to be made in the '***Notes to Accounts***'. The following aspects are to be disclosed for each class of share capital (different classes of preference shares are to be treated separately) :

(a) the number and amount of shares authorized;

(b) the number of shares issued, subscribed and fully paid, and subscribed but not fully paid;

(c) par value per share;

(d) a reconciliation of the number of shares outstanding at the beginning and at the end of the reporting period;

(e) the rights, preferences and restrictions attaching to each class of shares including restrictions on the distribution of dividends and the repayment of capital;

(f) shares in respect of each class in the company held by its holding company or its ultimate holding company including shares held by subsidiaries or associates of the holding company or the ultimate holding company in aggregate;

(g) shares in the company held by each shareholder holding more than 5 percent shares specifying the number of shares held;

(h) shares reserved for issue under options and contracts/commitments for the sale of shares/dis-investment, including the terms and amounts;

(i) for the period of five years immediately preceding the date as at which the Balance Sheet is prepared:

- Aggregate number and class of shares allotted as fully paid up pursuant to contract(s) without payment being received in cash.
- Aggregate number and class of shares allotted as fully paid up by way of bonus shares.
- Aggregate number and class of shares bought back.

(j) terms of any securities convertible into equity/preference shares issued along with the earliest date of conversion in descending order starting from the farthest such date.

(k) calls unpaid (showing aggregate value of calls unpaid by directors and officers)

(l) forfeited shares (amount originally paid up)

Details of Share Capital of a Company are disclosed in the Notes to Accounts as follows :

Particulars	(₹)	(₹)
SHARE CAPITAL		
Authorised Capital :		
... Equity Shares of ₹ ... each	***	***
... Preference Shares of ₹ ... each	***	***
Issued Capital :		
... Equity Shares of ₹ ... each	***	***
... Preference Shares of ₹ ... each	***	***
Subscribed Capital :		
Subscribed and Fully Paid		
... Equity Shares of ₹ ... each	***	***
... Preference Shares of ₹ ... each	***	***
Subscribed but not Fully Paid		
... Equity Shares of ₹ ... each	***	***
... Preference Shares of ₹ ... each	***	***
	***	
Less: Calls-in-Arrear (if any)	***	
	***	
Add: Forfeited Shares (if any)	***	***
TOTAL		***

Explanation of Different Items

(i) ***Authorised Capital*** :Authorised capital means the amount of share capital which a company is authorised to issue by its Memorandum of Association. It is also called 'Nominal Capital' or 'Registered Capital'.

A company cannot issue more than the amount of capital specified in the Memorandum of Association. However, a company can increase its authorised capital after ***observing the procedures*** stated in the Companies Act.

(ii) ***Issued Capital*** : Issued capital is that part of the authorised capital which is issued for subscription to the public and other investors, including the shares allotted to promoters and vendors.

The difference between authorised capital and issued capital is called '***Unissued capital***'. The company can issue those shares in future.

Example : X Ltd. has been incorporated with authorised capital as follows :

10,00,000 equity shares of ₹ 10 each

1,00,000 preference shares of ₹ 50 each.

The company offered to the public 7,50,000 equity shares of ₹ 10 each.

The above matter is to be shown in the ***Notes to Accounts*** as follows :

Particulars	(₹)	(₹)
SHARE CAPITAL		
Authorised Capital :		
10,00,000 Equity Shares of ₹ 10 each	1,00,00,000	
1,00,000 Preference Shares of ₹ 50 each	50,00,000	1,50,00,000
Issued Capital :		
7,50,000 Equity Shares of ₹ 10 each		75,00,000

(iii) ***Subscribed Capital*** : Subscribed capital is that part of the issued capital which has been actually subscribed by the public and taken up by the promoters, other investors and vendors. As per 'Schedule III' subscribed capital is to be disclosed in the ***Notes to Accounts*** as follows :

(a) Subscribed and fully Paid; and

(b) Subscribed but not Fully Paid.

(a) ***Subscribed and Fully Paid*** : The shares which have been subscribed and fully called up and the entire amount has been received by the company will be shown under this heading.

For example, on 1st January, 2015 X Ltd. had issued 7,50,000 equity shares of ₹ 10 each. The issue was fully subscribed by the public. The entire amount was called up and it was received in full before 31st March, 2015.

On 31st March, 2015 it is to be shown in the Notes to Accounts as follows :

Subscribed Capital :

(a) *Subscribed and Fully Paid* :

7,50,000 Equity Shares of ₹ 10 each ₹ 75,00,000

(b) ***Subscribed but not Fully Paid*** : The shares which have been subscribed and fully called up but some of the shareholders could not pay the call money within the stipulated time. The amount not yet received will be treated as calls-in-arrear. In the ***Notes to Account***, the calls-in-arrear will be shown as a deduction from subscribed capital.

For example, on 1st January, 2015, X Ltd. had issued 7,50,000 equity shares of ₹ 10 each. The issue was fully subscribed and called up. Mr. Ramen, holding 5,000 equity shares could not pay the final call of ₹ 2 each by 25th March, 2015, the last date for payment of final call.

On 31st March, 2015, it is to be shown in the Notes to Accounts as follows :

Subscribed Capital :

(b) *Subscribed but not fully paid* :

	₹
7,50,000 equity shares of ₹ 10 each	75,00,000
Less: Calls-in-arrear	10,000
	74,90,000

In this respect, it may be noted that when the company has not yet called up the entire amount of the face value of shares subscribed, the amount received will also be shown under 'Subscribed but not fully paid'.

For example, on 1st January, 2015, X Ltd. had issued 7,50,000 equity shares of ₹ 10 each. The issue was fully subscribed. Till 31st March, 2015, the company called up ₹ 8 per share. The entire amount was received in time.

On 31st March, 2015 it is to be shown in the Notes to Accounts as follows :

Subscribed Capital :

Subscribed but not fully paid

7,50,000 equity shares of ₹ 10 each, ₹ 8 paid up ₹ 60,00,000

Illustration 1

The authorised capital of XYZ Ltd. is ₹ 20,00,000 divided into 2,00,000 equity shares of ₹ 10 each. Out of these, company issued 1,00,000 equity shares of ₹ 10 each. The amount is payable as follows:

On application ₹ 2; On allotment ₹ 5; and On final call ₹ 3.

The public applied for 90,000 equity shares and all the money was duly received.

You are required to :

(a) Show Share Capital in the Balance Sheet of the company as at 31st March, 2015; and

(b) Prepare Notes to Accounts for the same. *[CBSE (Revised Guidelines) — Adapted]*

Solution

XYZ Ltd.
Balance Sheet as at 31st March, 2015

EQUITY AND LIABILITIES	Notes	31.3.2015 ₹	31.3.2014 ₹
1. Shareholders' Funds (a) Share Capital	(1)	9,00,000	?
Total		9,00,000	?

Notes to Accounts :

(1) Share Capital

Particulars	31.3.2015 ₹
Authorised Capital : 2,00,000 Equity Shares of ₹ 10 each	20,00,000
Issued Capital : 1,00,000 Equity Shares of ₹ 10 each	10,00,000
Subscribed Capital : *(1) Subscribed and fully paid* 90,000 Equity Shares of ₹ 10 each	9,00,000

Illustration 2

On 1st April, 2014 Ashok Ltd. was formed with an authorised capital of ₹ 1,00,00,000 divided into 2,00,000 equity shares of ₹ 50 each. The company issued prospectus inviting applications for 1,50,000 shares. The issue price was payable as under :

On application ₹ 15; On allotment ₹ 20; and On call Balance.

The issue was fully subscribed and the company allotted shares to all the applicants.

The company did not make the call during the year.

The company also issued 5,000 shares of ₹ 50 each fully paid-up to the vendor for purchase of office premises.

Show the

(a) Share Capital in the Balance Sheet of the Company as per Schedule III.

(b) Also prepare 'Notes to Accounts'. *[CBSE (Revised Guidelines) — Adapted]*

Solution

Ashok Ltd.
Balance Sheet as at 31st March, 2015

EQUITY AND LIABILITIES	Notes	31.3.2015 ₹	31.3.2014 ₹
1. Shareholders' Funds			
(a) Share Capital	(1)	5,500	***
Total		5,500	***

Notes to Accounts :

(1) Share Capital

Particulars	31.3.2015 (₹ '000)
Authorised Capital :	
2,00,000 Equity Shares of ₹ 50 each	10,00,000
Issued Capital :	
1,50,000 Equity Shares of ₹ 50 each issued to public	7,500
5,000 Equity Shares of ₹ 50 each issued to vendor	250
	7,750
Subscribed Capital :	
(i) *Subscribed and fully paid*	
5,000 Equity Shares of ₹ 50 each(issued to vendor for consideration other than cash)	250
(ii) *Subscribed but not fully paid*	
1,50,000 Equity Shares of ₹ 50 each issued to public, ₹ 35 each called up and paid-up	5,250
Total	5,500

Points to be Noted

(1) Calls unpaid are required to be disclosed, stating separately the aggregate value of calls unpaid by directors and officers of the Company.

(2) The amount of 'Calls paid in advance' does not form part of the paid-up capital. Under Schedule III, calls in advance should be disclosed under 'other current liabilities'. The amount of interest, if any, on such advance should also be shown under 'other current liabilities.

Notes to Accounts related to Share Capital has been shown below taking from the Annual Report of Reliance Industries Ltd. for the year 2013-14. It will help the students to understand the above discussed matter in respect of Share Capital.

Real Life Focus

Reliance Industries Ltd.
Notes on Financial Statements for the Year ended 31st March, 2014

The previous year figures have been regrouped / reclassified wherever necessary to conform to the current year presentation.

(₹ in crore)

1. SHARE CAPITAL		As at 31st March, 2014		As at 31st March, 2013
Authorised Share Capital :				
500,00,00,000 (500,00,00,000) Equity Shares of ₹ 10 each		5,000		5,000
100,00,00,000 (100,00,00,000) Preference Shares of ₹ 10 each		1,000		1,000
		6,000		6,000
Issued, Subscribed and Paid up :				
323,19,01,858 (322,86,63,382) Equity Shares of ₹ 10 each fully paid up	3,232		3,229	
Less : Calls in arrears - by others [₹ 3,113 (Previous year ₹ 3,653)]	-	3,232	-	3,229
TOTAL		3,232		3,229

The Issue of Shares

As per the provision of Section 23(1) of the Companies Act, 2013 a ***public company*** may issue securities :

(a) to public through prospectus (herein referred to as "public offer"). Public offer includes initial public offer, further public offer and offer for sale.
(b) through private placement;
(c) through a rights issue or a bonus issue.

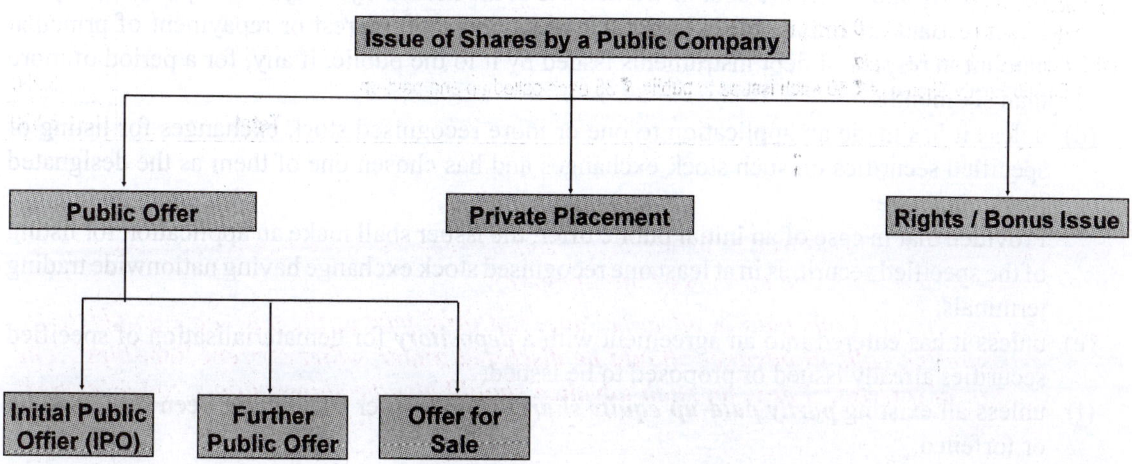

As per the provision of Section 23(2) of the Companies Act, 2013, a ***privtae company*** may issue securities—

(a) by way of rights issue or bonus issue
(b) through private placement

Issue of Shares by a Private Company

- Rights / Bonus Issue
- Private Placement

Public Offer / Public Issue of Shares

Public issue of shares means selling of shares to the public by ***issue of a prospectus***. A number of methods may be used to issue shares to the public, e.g., IPO, FPO and offer for sale. Issue of shares to the public are complex matters. The Government rules and regulations are very strict since the money is collected from the public. Therefore, great care should be taken before an offer is made to the public by the company.

Initial Public Offer (IPO)

Initial public offer means an offer of specified securities by an ***unlisted*** issuer to the public for subscription and includes an 'offer of sale' of specified securities to the public by an existing holder of such securities in an unlisted issuer.

It is to be noted that public offer is governed by the SEBI (Issue of Capital and Disclosure Requirements) Regulation, 2009. Some of the important regulations are given below ;

No issuer shall make a public issue or rights issue of specified securities ;

(a) if the issuer, any of its promoters, promoter group or directors or persons in control of the issuer are ***debarred*** from accessing the capital market by the Board;
(b) if any of the promoters, directors or persons in control of the issuer was or also is a promoter, director or person in control of any other company which is ***debarred*** from accessing the capital market under any order or directions made by the Board;
(c) if the issuer of convertible debt instruments is in the list of ***wilful defaulters*** published by the Reserve Bank of India or it is in default of payment of interest or repayment of principal amount in respect of debt instruments issued by it to the public, if any, for a period of more than six months;
(d) unless it has made an application to one or more recognised stock exchanges for listing of specified securities on such stock exchanges and has chosen one of them as the designated stock exchange:
Provided that in case of an initial public offer, the issuer shall make an application for listing of the specified securities in at least one recognised stock exchange having nationwide trading terminals;
(e) unless it has entered into an agreement with a ***depository*** for dematerialisation of specified securities already issued or proposed to be issued;
(f) unless all existing ***partly paid-up equity shares*** of the issuer have either been fully paid up or forfeited;

(g) unless firm arrangements of finance through verifiable means towards seventy five per cent. of the stated means of finance, excluding the amount to be raised through the proposed public issue or rights issue or through existing identifiable internal accruals, have been made.

Further Public Offer (FPO)

Further public offer means an offer of specified securities by a ***listed issuer*** to the public for subscription and includes an offer for sale of specified securities to the public by an existing holder of such securities in a listed issuer. ***Regulation 27*** of SEBI (ICDR) Regulations, 2009 states that:

An 'issuer' may make a further public offer (FPO) if it satisfies the following conditions :

(1) the aggregate of the proposed issue and all previous issues made in the same financial year in terms of issue size does not exceed 5 times of its pre-issue ***net worth*** as per the audited Balance Sheet of the preceding financial year;

(2) if it has changed its name within ***last one year***, at least 50% of the revenue for the preceding one full year has been earned by it from the activity indicated by the new name.

Private Placement

As per the provision of ***Section 23 of Companies Act, 2013***, both ***public*** company and ***private*** company can issue shares through private placement. Private placement means any offer of securities or invitation to subscribe securities to a select group of persons by a company through issue of a private placement ***offer letter***.

Section 42 of the Companies Act, 2013 has specified certain conditions for 'private placement' of shares. Some of the important conditions are given below :

(1) The offer of securities or invitation to subscribe securities, shall be made to such number of persons ***not exceeding fifty*** or such higher number as may be prescribed, excluding qualified institutional buyers and employees of the company being offered securities under a scheme of employees stock option.

(2) No fresh offer or invitation under this section shall be made unless the allotments with respect to any offer or invitation made earlier have been completed or that offer or invitation has been withdrawn or abandoned by the company.

(3) Any offer or invitation not in compliance with the provisions of this section shall be ***treated as a public offer*** and all provisions of this Act, and the Securities Contracts (Regulation) Act, 1956 and the Securities and Exchange Board of India Act, 1992 shall be required to be complied with.

(4) All monies payable towards subscription of securities under this section shall be paid through cheque or demand draft or other banking channels but not by cash.

Employees Stock Option Scheme / Plan (ESOS)

According to Section 2(37) of the Companies Act, 2013, "employees' stock option" means the option given to the directors, officers or employees of a company or of its holding company or subsidiary company or companies, if any, which gives such directors, officers or employees, the benefit or right to purchase, or to subscribe for, the shares of the company at a future date at a pre-determined price.

Nowadays, under this scheme many companies (particularly software companies and construction engineering companies) are offering equity shares to their employees at a concessional price. The main aim of this scheme is to retain good employees in the organisation and involve them in the affairs of the company.

Under an ESOS (Employee Stock Option Scheme) the employee's gain is the difference between market price of the shares and exercise price. ***For example,*** the market price of share of X Ltd. is ₹ 1,000 but under ESOS an employee can get it at ₹ 600 (the exercise price). The gain per option is ₹ 400 (₹ 1,000 – ₹ 600).

It should be pointed out that the enterprise will lose ₹ 400 for each option. Let us assume that the nyumber of employees are 1,000. Therefore, the total loss will be ₹ 400 × 1,000 = ₹ 4,00,000.

If the vesting period is one year, the entire ₹ 4,00,000 will be recognised as expenses in that year. If the vesting period is 2 years, the amount to be recognised in each year is ₹ 2,00,000 (₹ 4,00,000 ÷ 2) assuming that no employee left the enterprise during these two years.

Face Value of Equity Shares

An issuer making an initial public offer may determine the face value of the equity shares in the following manner :

(a) if the issue price per equity share is ₹ 500 or more, the issuer shall have the option to determine the face at less than ₹ 10 per equity share. However, the face value shall not be less than one rupee per equity share.

(b) if the issue price per equity share is less than ₹ 500, the face value of the equity shares shall be ₹ 10 per equity share.

The disclosure about the face value of equity shares (including statement about issue price being 'X' times of the face value) shall be made in the advertisements, offer documents and application forms in identical front size as that of issue price or price band.

For example, the issue price is ₹ 400. The face value is ₹ 10. It should be stated in the advertisements, offer documents and application form that the issue is 40 times of the face value.

Pricing in Public Issue

Pricing

(1) An issuer may determine the price of specified securities in consultation with the lead merchant banker or through the book building process.

(2) An issuer may determine the coupon rate and conversion price of convertible debt instruments in consultation with the lead merchant banker or through the book building process.

(3) The issuer shall undertake the book building process in a manner specified in Schedule XI of the Companies Act, 2013

New Share Issue Procedures

Equity offerings by companies are offered to the investors in two forms :

(i) Fixed Price Offer Method

(ii) Book-building Method

Fixed Price Offer Method

In this case, the company fixes the issue price and then advertises the number of shares to be issued. If the price is very high, the investors will apply for fewer number of shares. On the other hand, if issue is under-priced, the investors will apply for more number of shares and will lead to huge oversubscription.

The ***main steps*** involved in issue of shares under '***Fixed Price Offer Method***' are the following:

(i) Selection of Merchant Banker;

(ii) Issue of a prospectus;

(iii) Receipt by the company of applications for shares;

(iv) Allotment of shares to applicants; and

(v) Issue of share certificates.

Selection of Merchant Banker : As per the provision of SEBI (Issue of Capital and Disclosure Requirements) Regulations, 2009 — (a) the issuer shall appoint one or more merchant bankers, at least one of whom shall be a lead merchant banker and shall also appoint other intermediaries, in consultation with the lead merchant banker, to carry out the obligations relating to the issue; (b) the issuer shall, in consultation with the lead merchant banker, appoint only those intermediaries which are registered with the Board; (c) where the issue is managed by more than one merchant banker, the rights, obligations and responsibilities, relating inter alia to disclosures, allotment, refund and underwriting obligations, if any, of each merchant banker shall be predetermined and disclosed in the offer document

The merchant bankers will do all the needful in respect of issue of shares on behalf of the company. An agreed amount is paid by the company for the service of the merchant bankers as a commission.

Issue of a Prospectus : In a 'public offer' prospectus is issued as a statutory requirement. As per the provision of ***Section 2(70)*** of the Companies Act, 2013 'prospectus' means any document described or issued as a prospectus and includes a red herring prospectus referred to in Section 32 or shelf prospectus referred to in Section 31 or any notice, circular, advertisement or other document inviting offers from the public for the subscription or purchase of any securities of a body corporate.

Rule 3 of the Companies (Prospectus and Allotment of Securities) Rules, 2014 states that :

The Prospectus to be issued shall contain—

(a) the names, addresses and contact details of the corporate office of the issuer company, compliance officer of the issuer company, merchant bankers and co-managers to the issue, registrar to the issue, bankers to the issue, stock brokers to the issue, credit rating agency for the issue, arrangers, if any, of the instrument, names and addresses of such other persons as may be specified by the Securities and Exchange Board in its regulations;

(b) the dates relating to opening and closing of the issue;

(c) a declaration which shall be made by the Board or the Committee authorised by the Board in the prospectus that the allotment letters shall be issued or application money shall be refunded within fifteen days from the closure of the issue or such lesser time as may be specified by Securities and Exchange Board or else the application money shall be refunded to the applicants forthwith, failing which interest shall be due to be paid to the applicants at the rate of fifteen per cent per annum for the delayed period.

(d) a statement given by the Board that all monies received out of the issue shall be transferred to a separate bank account maintained with a Scheduled Bank;

(e) the details of all utilized and unutilised monies out of the monies collected in the previous issue made by way of public offer shall be disclosed and continued to be disclosed in the balance sheet till the time any part of the proceeds of such previous issue remains unutilized indicating the purpose for which such monies have been utilized, and the securities or other forms of financial assets in which such unutilized monies have been invested;

(f) the names, addresses, telephone numbers, fax numbers and e-mail addresses of the under-writers and the amount underwritten by them;

(g) the consent of trustees, solicitors or advocates, merchant bankers to the issue, registrar to the issue, lenders and experts;

Application for Shares : Application is an offer by an investor to subscribe for a specified number of shares in a company. After the publication of a prospectus, a person who wants to purchase the shares of the company has to fill in the prescribed application form. Each prospectus contains a printed application form and it states the amount per share payable on application, on allotment and on subsequent call(s). Properly filled-in application forms must be forwarded to the bankers to the issue with a cheque (A/c payee) for the amount payable on application.

An applicant may apply for shares on-line through his demat account. The amount payable on application is done through bank transfer.

Allotment of Shares to Applicants : Allotment is the allocation of shares to the successful applicants by the directors of a company. After the closing date, the bankers forward all applications to the company. The Board of Directors then proceed to allot all the shares. The successful applicants are sent ***letters of allotment,*** making them members of the company from the date of posting; unsuccessful applicants receive ***letters of regret,*** together with refunds of their application monies.

As per the provision of ***Section 39 of the Companies Act, 2013*** no allotment of any securities of a company offered to the public for subscription shall be made unless the amount stated in the prospectus as the minimum amount has been subscribed and the sums payable on application for the amount so stated have been paid to and received by the company by cheque or other instrument.

In this respect, it is to be noted that the 'minimum subscription' in an issue shall not be less than 90% of the offer through offer document. However, this is not applicable to offer for sale of specified securities.

The amount payable on application on every security shall not be less than five per cent. of the nominal amount of the security or such other percentage or amount, as may be specified by the Securities and Exchange Board by making regulations in this behalf.

As per SEBI (ICDR) Regulations, 2009, the application money must not be less than 25% of the issue price.

Rule 11 of the Companies (Prospectus and Allotment Securities) Rules, 2014 states that :

(1) If the stated minimum amount has not been subscribed and the sum payable on application is not received within the period specified therein, then the application money shall be repaid within a period of ***fifteen days*** from the closure of the issue and if any such money is not so repaid within such period, the directors of the company who are officers in default shall jointly and severally be liable to repay that money with interest at the rate of ***fifteen percent*** per annum.

(2) The application money to be refunded shall be credited only to the bank account from which the subscription was remitted.

Share Certificate : It is a document that provides evidence of ownership of shares in a limited company. It will bear the name of the shareholder and the number and class of shares owned by the shareholder. It also states the serial number of the shares. It is stamped by the common seal of the company. It is generally signed by at least one director and the company secretary.Every certificate of share or shares shall be in ***Form No. SH-1***. When shares are held in depository form, no share certificate in physical form is issued. The shares are transferred to demat account of the shareholders.

The different steps in connections with the issue of shares is shown in the diagram below :

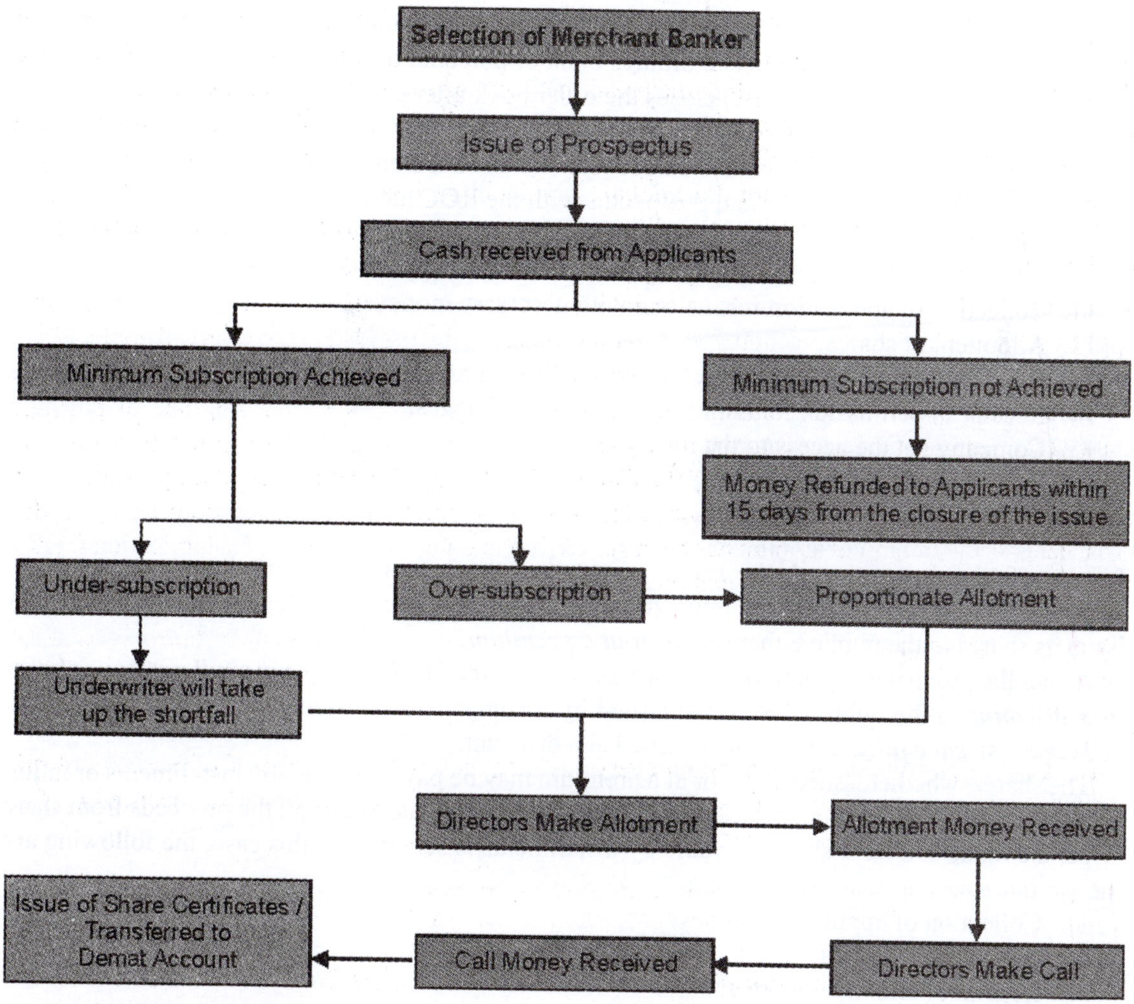

Book-building Method

Under this method, the company does not come out with a ***pre-determined price***. Instead, it offers the investors the opportunity to bid collectively. It then uses the bids to arrive at a ***consensus price***.

As per SEBI (ICDR) Regulations, 'book building' means a process undertaken to elicit demand and to assess the price for determination of the quantum or value of specified securities or Indian Depository Receipts, as the case may be, in accordance with these regulations.

All the applications received are arranged and a final offer price, known as '***Cut-off Price***' is arrived at. The cut-off price is at the bid price with highest demand, subject to all categories bidding at that price. At present, the book-building system is very popular in India. Presently, most IPOs in India use book-building method.

The ***main steps*** involved in the Book-building process are the following :

1. Company appoints Lead Manager (book runner) who is a category-I Merchant Banker registered with SEBI.
2. Submission of draft prospectus with SEBI.
3. Formation of syndicate of Buyers.
4. Roadshow arranged to market the issue to potential investors.
5. Lead Manager (book runner) buildings book of potential demand.
6. Lead Manager (book runner) closes the order book after consulting the issuer company.
7. Price is determined jointly by the Lead manager (book runner) and the issuer company.
8. Procurement agreement is entered between the issuer company and syndicate members.
9. Issuer company files the final prospectus with the ROC along with procurement agreement.
10. Opening of two separate bank accounts (one for private placement and another for the public subscription) by the issuer company for collection of application money.
11. Collection of application form along with necessary money.
12. Allotment of shares.
13. Receipt of approval for allotment from the Stock Exchange.
14. Receipt of permission for listing from Stock Exchanges.
15. Company get the access to the fund.

Shares Payable by Instalments

In case of 'fixed price issue', the issuer may collect the issue price in instalments or at a time. However, in case of book building issue, the entire issue price is collected at a time. The issuer may issue its shares to the public either ***at par*** or ***at a premium***.

As per the provision of Section 53 of the Companies Act, 2013 ***a company shall not issue shares at a discount*** to the public. Any share issued by a company at a discounted price shall be void. However, ***'sweat equity share'*** can be issued at a discount.

The shares, whether issued at par or at a premium may be payable either by installments or in full on application. Where a company does not require the immediate use of all the proceeds from share issue, the request to have shares payable by installments is sensible. In this case, the following are the various stages in share accounting:

1. Collection of application money.
2. Allotment of shares.
3. Receipt of allotment money.
4. Share call.
5. Receipt of share call money.

Issue of Share at Par

Accounting Entries

1. On receipt of application money

*Bank Account	Dr.
To Share Application Account	

Where the share capital of the company consists of shares of different classes, a separate Share Application Account will be opened for each class of share, e.g., Equity Share Application Account or Preference Share Application Account etc.

2. On allotment of shares

(a) Share Application Account Dr.
  To Share Capital Account

> ***It should be noted that the application money received will remain in Share Application Account unless the Board of Directors approve the allotment of shares. Only after approval, it will be treated as a part of the share capital.***

Once allotment is made, the applicants will be treated as shareholders and they are legally liable to pay all monies due on shares allotted to them. ***Dues on account of share allotment are accounted for on an accrual basis***. The entry is:

(b) Share Allotment Account Dr.
  To Share Capital Account

3. When shares are oversubscribed, some applications may be rejected by the Board of Directors and application money will be refunded to the applicants along with a letter of regret.

Share Application Account Dr.
  To Bank Account

4. When shares are oversubscribed, in some cases, the Board of Directors may prefer to allot less number of shares than applied for, the excess application money is adjusted against allotment money.

Share Application Account	Dr.	
To Share Allotment Account		(Adjustment against allotment)
To Calls-in-Advance Account		(Surplus after above adjustment)
To Bank Account		(Surplus refunded)

> ***It should be noted that any surplus money, after adjusting against allotment, should be transferred to Calls-in-Advance Account, and will be adjusted when call is made. Generally, the prospectus contains a clause to this effect. If the prospectus is silent on this point, the surplus should be refunded.***

5. On receipts of allotment money

* Bank Account Dr.
  To Share Allotment Account

6. If some shareholders fail to pay allotment money, Allotment Account will show a debit balance. In practice, the unpaid balance is transferred to "Calls-in-Arrear" Account.

The entry is :

Calls-in-Arrear Account Dr.
  To Share Allotment Account

7. Making calls

Share call denotes a stage subsequent to allotment. Call is a demand by a company to the partly paid-up shareholders to pay a further instalment towards the purchase price of shares. There may be more than one call at intervals. The dates on which calls are due are usually specified in the prospectus. Where no dates are specified, Table A regulates subsequent calls. Whenever a call is made, details connected thereto are recorded in a " Share Call Book". Different calls are distinguished from each other by serial numbers, e.g., First call, Second call, and so on. ***Dues on account of share call are also accounted for on an accrual basis.***

Share Call Account Dr.
To Share Capital Account

8. On receipt of call money

*Bank Account Dr.
To Share Call Account

9. Non-payment of call money

Calls-in-Arrear Account Dr.
To Share Call Account

10. On adjustment of "calls-in-advance", if any

Calls-in-Advance Account Dr.
To Share Call Account

* ***All monies received shall be kept in a separate Bank Account maintained with a scheduled bank.***

In practice , all Cash transactions are directly recorded in the Cash Book in the following manner:

Dr. **Cash Book (with narration)** **Cr.**

To Share Application A/c (Being application money received on ... shares @ ₹ ... each)	****	By Share Application A/c (Refund) (Being the money refunded on ... shares @ ₹ ... each as per Board's Resolution No. ... dated ...)	****
To Share Allotment A/c (Being allotment money received on ... shares @ ₹ ... each)	****		
To Share First Call A/c (Being first call money received on ... shares @ ₹ ... each)	****		
To Share Final Call A/c (Being the final call money received on ... shares @ ₹ ... each)	****		

Application and Allotment Account and Call Accounts — are in fact total or control accounts on share issues. The detailed entries will be made in the Memorandum Accounts of individual shareholder and total amounts only entered in the above mentioned accounts.

Check Your Progress

Answers : Page 4.152

Tick the write answer :

7. *Public issue of shares means selling of shares*
   - A to public by offer letter
   - B to public by issue of prospectus
   - C to a group of investors only
   - D to the central government
8. *Issue of shares to public can be done under*
   - A book building method only
   - B fixed price method only
   - C book building or fixed price method
   - D public auction
9. *Issue of shares to public requires*
   - A prior approval from the controller of capital issue
   - B price approved from the Ministry of Corporate Affairs (MCA)
   - C prior approval for SEBI (Securities and Exchange Board of India)
10. *The provisions of 'minimum subscription' will*
    - A apply where shares are issued through private negotiation
    - B apply where shares are issued to public
    - C not apply if the issue size is less than ₹ 100 crores
    - D not pply if the issue side is more than ₹ 100 crores
11. *Shares may be issued for*
    - A cash only
    - B consideration other than cash only
    - C both for cash and consideration other than cash
    - D credit to promoters only
12. *The minimum subscription clause is applicable*
    - A only to first issue of issuers to public
    - B only to first issue and 2nd issue to public
    - C not only to the first issue but also the shares offered to the public at any time
    - D private placement
13. *The denomination of equity shares should be limited to*
    - A ₹ 10
    - B not exceed ₹ 100
    - C be anything other than in fraction of a rupee
    - D not exceed ₹ 50
14. *Physical share certificate*
    - A is a negotiable instrument
    - B is not a movable property
    - C is not a negotiable instrument

Illustration 3

The Alpha Co. Ltd. Issued 10,000 equity shares of ₹ 10 each at par. The share money was payable as : on application ₹ 3; on allotment ₹ 2; on call ₹ 5. The applications for all the shares were duly received and the shares were properly allotted. The amounts payable were timely received.

Journalise the transactions and show the Equity Share Capital Account in the books of the Company.

Solution

In the books of Alpha Co. Ltd.

Journal

Date	Particulars	L.F.	Dr. ₹	Cr. ₹
	Bank A/c Dr. To Equity Share Application A/c (Being application money received for 10,000 equity shares @ ₹ 3 each)		30,000	30,000
	Equity Share Application A/c Dr. To Equity Share Capital A/c (Being application money on 10,000 equity shares @ ₹ 3 each transferred to Equity Share Capital Account as per Board's Resolution No . . . dated)		30,000	30,000
	Equity Share Allotment A/c Dr. To Equity Share Capital A/c (Being allotment money due on 10,000 equity shares @ ₹ 2 each as per Board's Resolution No . . . Dated . . .)		20,000	20,000
	Bank A/c Dr. To Equity Share Allotment A/c (Being allotment money received on 10,000 equity shares @ ₹ 2 each)		20,000	20,000
	Equity Share Call A/c Dr. To Equity Share Capital A/c (Being call money due on 10,000 equity shares @ ₹ 5 each as per Board's Resolution No . . . Dated . .)		50,000	50,000
	Bank A/c Dr. To Equity Share Call A/c (Being call money received for 10,000 equity shares @ ₹ 5 each)		50,000	50,000
	Total		2,00,000	2,00,000

Dr. **Equity Share Capital Account** **Cr.**

Date	Particulars	₹	Date	Particulars	₹
	To Balance c/d	1,00,000		By Equity Share Application A/c	30,000
				By Equity Share Allotment A/c	20,000
				By Equity Share Call A/c	50,000
		1,00,000			1,00,000

Tutorial Notes :

(1) Where the share capital of the company consists of shares of different classes, a separate Share Application Account will be opened for each class of share. For example, Equity Share Application Account or Preference Share Application Account, etc. Similarly, separate Allotment Account and Call Account are also opened for each class of share.

Illustration 4

Bharat Limited issued at par 10,000 equity shares of ₹ 10 each payable as follows :

on application ₹ 2; on allotment ₹ 3; on final call ₹ 5.

The public applied for 9,000 shares, which were allotted. All the moneys due on shares were received in full.

Pass necessary journal entries including cash.

Solution

In the books of Bharat Limited

Journal

Date	Particulars		L.F.	Dr. ₹	Cr. ₹
	Bank A/c	Dr.		18,000	
	To Equity Share Application A/c				18,000
	(Being application money received for 9,000 equity shares @ ₹ 2 each)				
	Equity Share Application A/c	Dr.		18,000	
	To Equity Share Capital A/c				18,000
	(Being application money on 9,000 equity shares transferred to Equity Share Capital Account as per Board's Resolution No . . . Dated . .)				
	Equity Share Allotment A/c	Dr.		27,000	
	To Equity Share Capital A/c				27,000
	(Being allotment money due on 9,000 equity shares @ ₹ 3 each as per Board's Resolution No . . . Dated . .)				
	Bank A/c	Dr.		27,000	
	To Equity Share Allotment A/c				27,000
	(Being allotment money received on 9,000 equity shares @ ₹ 3 each)				
	Equity Share Final Call A/c	Dr.		45,000	
	To Equity Share Capital A/c				45,000
	(Being final call money due on 9,000 equity shares @ ₹ 5 each as per Board's Resolution No . . . Dated . .)				
	Bank A/c	Dr.		45,000	
	To Equity Share Final Call A/c				45,000
	(Being final call money received on 9,000 equity shares @ ₹ 5 each)				
		Total		1,80,000	1,80,000

Tutorial Note : Company invited application for 10,000 shares but the public applied for only 9,000 shares. Therefore, all entries are to be passed for 9,000 shares only.

Illustration 5

Janata Transport Co. Ltd., was registered with an authorised capital of ₹ 10,00,000 divided into 1,00,000 equity shares of ₹ 10 each.

The company offered for public subscription 80,000 shares at par. The amount was payable as follows :

on application ₹ 2; on allotment ₹ 3; on first call ₹ 3; on final call ₹ 2.

The Company received applications for 90,000 shares. Application money on 10,000 shares were refunded immediately and shares were allotted to the remaining applicants. All moneys due were received in time.

You are required to pass necessary journal entries to record the above transactions in the books of the Company.

Solution

In the books of Janata Transport Co. Ltd.

Journal

Date	Particulars		L.F.	Dr. ₹	Cr. ₹
	Bank A/c	Dr.		1,80,000	
	To Equity Share Application A/c				1,80,000
	(Being application money received for 90,000 equity shares @ ₹ 2 each)				
	Equity Share Application A/c	Dr.		1,60,000	
	To Equity Share Capital A/c				1,60,000
	(Being application money on 80,000 equity shares @ ₹ 2 each transferred to Equity Share Capital Account as per Board's Resolution No . . . Dated . .)				

Particulars	L.F.	Dr. ₹	Cr. ₹
Equity Share Application A/c Dr. To Bank A/c (Being excess application money on 10,000 equity shares @ ₹ 2 each refunded as per Board's Resolution No . . . Dated . .)		20,000	20,000
Equity Share Allotment A/c Dr. To Equity Share Capital A/c (Being allotment money due on 80,000 equity shares @ ₹ 3 each as per Board's Resolution No . . . Dated . .)		2,40,000	2,40,000
Bank A/c Dr. To Equity Share Allotment A/c (Being allotment money received for 80,000 equity shares @ ₹ 3 each)		2,40,000	2,40,000
Equity Share First Call A/c Dr. To Equity Share Capital A/c (Being first call money due on 80,000 equity shares @ ₹ 3 each as per Board's Resolution No . . . Dated . .)		2,40,000	2,40,000
Bank A/c Dr. To Equity Share First Call A/c (Being first call money received for 80,000 equity shares @ ₹ 3 each)		2,40,000	2,40,000
Equity Share Final Call A/c Dr. To Equity Share Capital A/c (Being final call money due on 80,000 equity shares @ ₹ 2 each as per Board's Resolution No . . . Dated . .)		1,60,000	1,60,000
Bank A/c Dr. To Equity Share Final Call A/c (Being final call money received on 80,000 equity shares @ ₹ 2 each)		1,60,000	1,60,000
Total		16,40,000	16,40,000

Illustration 6

Avery Limited issued 10,000, 12% Preference Shares of ₹ 100 each at par. The share money was payable as : on application ₹ 20; on allotment ₹ 30; on first and final call ₹ 50.

Applications were received for 12,000 shares. Excess application money was refunded immediately. Shares were duly allotted. All monies due on allotment and call were received in full.

You are required to pass necessary journal entries in the books of the Company. Show 12% Preference Share Capital Account also.

Solution

In the books of Avery Limited

Journal

Date	Particulars	L.F.	Dr. ₹	Cr. ₹
	Bank A/c Dr. To Preference Share Application A/c (Being application money received on 12,000 preference shares @ ₹ 20 each)		2,40,000	2,40,000
	Preference Share Application A/c Dr. To 12% Preference Share Capital A/c (Being application money on 10,000 preference shares @ ₹ 20 each trans. to 12% Preference Share Capital A/c as per Board's Resolution No . . . Dated . .)		2,00,000	2,00,000
	Preference Share Application A/c Dr. To Bank A/c (Being excess application money on 2,000 preference shares @ ₹ 20 each refunded as per Board's Resolution No . . . Dated . .)		40,000	40,000

Particulars		Dr.	Cr.
Preference Share Allotment A/c Dr. To 12% Preference Share Capital A/c (Being allotment money due on 10,000 preference shares @ ₹ 30 each as per Board's Resolution No . . . Dated . . .)		3,00,000	3,00,000
Bank A/c Dr. To Preference Share Allotment A/c (Being allotment money received on 10,000 preference shares @ ₹ 30 each)		3,00,000	3,00,000
Preference Share First and Final Call A/c Dr. To 12% Preference Share Capital A/c (Being first and final call money due on 10,000 preference shares @ ₹ 50 each as per Board's Resolution No . . . Dated . . .)		5,00,000	5,00,000
Bank A/c Dr. To Preference Share First and Final Call A/c (Being first and final call money received on 10,000 preference shares @ ₹ 50 each.		5,00,000	5,00,000
Total		20,80,000	20,80,000

12% Preference Share Capital Account

Dr. Cr.

Date	Particulars	₹	Date	Particulars	₹
	To Balance c/d	10,00,000		By Preference Share Application A/c	2,00,000
				By Preference Share Allotment A/c	3,00,000
				By Preference Share First & Final Call A/c	5,00,000
		10,00,000			10,00,000

Tutorial Note :

(1) Where the share capital of the company consists of shares of different classes, a separate Share Application Account will be opened for each class of share. For example, Equity Share Application Account or Preference Share Application Account, etc. Similarly, separate Allotment Account and Call Account are also opened for each class of share.

(2) Dividend is paid on preference shares at a fixed rate per annum. 12% Preference Share Capital indicates 12% rate of dividend on the face value of preference shares.

Illustration 7

X Co. Ltd. was registered with a capital of ₹ 10,00,000 divided into 1,00,000 equity shares of ₹ 10 each. The company invited application for 60,000 shares. Amount payable was as follows : on application ₹ 2; on allotment ₹ 2; on first call ₹ 3; on final call ₹ 3.

All the shares were subscribed and allotted. All monies due on allotment and calls were received in full.

Pass necessary journal entries and show Cash Book entries relating to the issue in the books of the company.

Solution

In the books of X Co. Ltd.

Cash Book (Bank column only)

Dr. Cr.

Date	Particulars	₹	Date	Particulars	₹
	To Equity Share Application A/c (Being application money received on 60,000 equity shares @ ₹ 2 each)	1,20,000		By Balance c/d	6,00,000

	To Equity Share Allotment A/c (Being allotment money received on 60,000 equity shares @ ₹ 2 each)	1,20,000			
	To Equity Share First Call A/c (Being first call money received on 60,000 equity shares @ ₹ 3 each)	1,80,000			
	To Equity Share Final Call A/c (Being final call money received on 60,000 equity shares @ ₹ 3 each)	1,80,000			
		6,00,000			6,00,000

Journal

Date	Particulars		L.F.	Dr. ₹	Cr. ₹
	Equity Share Application A/c	Dr.		1,20,000	
	To Equity Share Capital A/c				1,20,000
	(Being application money on 60,000 equity shares @ ₹ 2 each transferred to Equity Share Capital Account as per Board's Resolution No . . . Dated . . .)				
	Equity Share Allotment A/c	Dr.		1,20,000	
	To Equity Share Capital A/c				1,20,000
	(Being allotment money due on 60,000 equity shares @ ₹ 2 each as per Board's Resolution No . . . Dated . . .)				
	Equity Share First Call A/c	Dr.		1,80,000	
	To Equity Share Capital A/c				1,80,000
	(Being first call money due on 60,000 equity shares @ ₹ 3 each as per Board's Resolution No . . . Dated . . .)				
	Equity Share Final Call A/c	Dr.		1,80,000	
	To Equity Share Capital A/c				1,80,000
	(Being final call money due on 60,000 equity shares @ ₹ 3 each as per Board's Resolution No . . . Dated . . .)				
		Total		6,00,000	6,00,000

Tutorial Note : **When it is asked to prepare the Cash Book, then all cash transactions are recorded in the cash book. In the journal non-cash transactions are recorded. It is important to note that if any transaction is recorded in the cash book once, it is not recorded again in the journal because both cash book and journal are books of primary entry.**

Illustration 8

X, Y and Co. Ltd. registered with an authorised capital of ₹ 5,00,000 divided into 50,000 equity shares of ₹ 10 each.

The Company issued all the shares. The amount was payable as follows :

On application	₹ 2 per share
On allotment	₹ 3 per share
On first call	₹ 3 per share
On final call	₹ 2 per share

The whole issue was subscribed and duly paid up. Show the journal entries, cash book and ledger accounts in the books of the company in connection with the issue of such shares.

Solution

In the books of X, Y and Co. Ltd
Journal

Date	Particulars		L.F.	Dr. ₹	Cr. ₹
	Equity Share Application A/c	Dr.		1,00,000	
	To Equity Share Capital A/c				1,00,000
	(Being application money on 50,000 equity shares @ ₹ 2 each transferred to Equity Share Capital Account as per Board's Resolution No . . . Dated . . .)				
	Equity Share Allotment A/c	Dr.		1,50,000	
	To Equity Share Capital A/c				1,50,000
	(Being allotment money due on 50,000 equity shares @ ₹ 3 each as per Board's Resolution No . . . Dated . . .)				
	Equity Share First Call A/c	Dr.		1,50,000	
	To Equity Share Capital A/c				1,50,000
	(Being first call money due on 50,000 equity shares @ ₹ 3 each as per Board's Resolution No . . . Dated . . .)				
	Equity Share Final Call A/c	Dr.		1,00,000	
	To Equity Share Capital A/c				1,00,000
	(Being final call money due on 50,000 equity shares @ ₹ 2 each as per Board's Resolution No . . . Dated . . .)				
		Total		5,00,000	5,00,000

Dr. **Cash Book (Bank column only)** **Cr.**

Date	Particulars	₹	Date	Particulars	₹
	To Equity Share Application A/c (Being application money received on 50,000 equity shares @ ₹ 2 each)	1,00,000		By Balance c/d	5,00,000
	To Equity Share Allotment A/c (Being allotment money received on 50,000 equity shares @ ₹ 3 each)	1,50,000			
	To Equity Share First Call A/c (Being first call money received on 50,000 equity shares @ ₹ 3 each)	1,50,000			
	To Equity Share Final Call A/c (Being final call money received on 50,000 equity shares @ ₹ 2 each)	1,00,000			
		5,00,000			5,00,000

Ledger Accounts

Dr. **Equity Share Capital Account** **Cr.**

Date	Particulars	₹	Date	Particulars	₹
	To Balance c/d	5,00,000		By Equity Share Application A/c	1,00,000
				By Equity Share Allotment A/c	1,50,000
				By Equity Share First Call A/c	1,50,000
				By Equity Share Final Call A/c	1,00,000
		5,00,000			5,00,000

Dr. **Equity Share Application Account** **Cr.**

Date	Particulars	₹	Date	Particulars	₹
	To Equity Share Capital A/c	1,00,000		By Bank A/c	1,00,000

Dr. Equity Share Allotment Account Cr.

Date	Particulars	₹	Date	Particulars	₹
	To Equity Share Capital A/c	1,50,000		By Bank A/c	1,50,000

Dr. Equity Share First Call Account Cr.

Date	Particulars	₹	Date	Particulars	₹
	To Equity Share Capital A/c	1,50,000		By Bank A/c	1,50,000

Dr. Equity Share Final Call Account Cr.

Date	Particulars	₹	Date	Particulars	₹
	To Equity Share Capital A/c	1,00,000		By Bank A/c	1,00,000

Illustration 9

The authorised capital of Suhas Ltd. is ₹ 50,00,000 divided into 25,000 shares of ₹ 200 each. Out of these the company issued 12,000 shares of ₹ 200 each at a premium of 10%. The amount was payable as follows :

₹ 60 per share on application; ₹ 60 per share on allotment (including premium), ₹ 30 per share on first call and balance on final call. Public applied for 11,000 shares. All the money was duly received.

Prepare an extract of Balance Sheet of Suhas Ltd. as per Schedule III Part I of the Companies Act, 2013 disclosing the above information. Also prepare notes to accounts for the same.

[CBSE (Outside Delhi) — Adapted]

Suhas Ltd

Balance Sheet as at .... [Extract] **(Figures in ₹)**

Particulars	Note No.	Figures as at the end of current reporting period
1	2	3
I. EQUITY AND LIABILITIES		
(1) **Shareholders' Funds**		
(a) Share capital	(1)	22,00,000
(b) Reserves and surplus	(2)	2,20,000
(c) Money received against share warrants		—
TOTAL		24,20,000
II. ASSETS		
(2) **Current Assets**		
(d) Cash and cash equivalents	(3)	24,20,000
TOTAL		24,20,000

Notes to Accounts :

	₹	₹
(1) Share Capital		
***Authorised Capital*:** 25,000 Equity Shares of ₹ 200 each		50,00,000
***Issued Capital*:** 12,000 Equity Shares of ₹ 200 each		24,00,000
***Subscribed Capital*:** *Subscribed and Fully Paid:* 11,000 Equity Shares of ₹ 200 each		22,00,000
(2) Reserve and Surplus Securities Premium Reserve 11,000 Shares @ ₹ 20 each		2,20,000
(3) Cash and Cash Equivalents Cash at bank		24,20,000

Illustration 10

X Limited whose authorised share capital is ₹ 45,00,000 divided into 4,50,000 equity shares of ₹ 10 each, issued to the public 3,60,000 shares on the following terms : on application ₹ 5; on allotment ₹ 5. Applications were received for 3,75,000 shares on 25th September, 2014 and allotment was made on 15th October, 2014. On this date, the excess application money was returned to the unsuccessful applicants. The allotment money was duly received on 30th November, 2014.

Show Bank Account, Share Application Account, Share Allotment Account and Equity Shares Capital Account for the year. Show also how the Equity Share Capital of the Company will appear on its Balance Sheet as on 31st December, 2014.

Solution

In the books of X Limited

Bank Account

Dr. | Cr.

Date	Particulars	J.F.	₹	Date	Particulars	J.F.	₹
2014				2014			
Sept.25	To Share Application A/c		18,75,000	Oct. 15	By Share Application A/c		75,000
Nov 30	To Share Allotment A/c		18,00,000	Dec.31	By Balance c/d		36,00,000
			36,75,000				36,75,000

Share Application Account

Dr. | Cr.

Date	Particulars	J.F.	₹	Date	Particulars	J.F.	₹
2014				2014			
Oct. 15	To Equity Share Capital A/c		18,00,000	Sep. 25	By Bank A/c		18,75,000
Oct. 15	To Bank A/c		75,000				
			18,75,000				18,75,000

Share Allotment Account

Dr. | Cr.

Date	Particulars	J.F.	₹	Date	Particulars	J.F.	₹
2014				2014			
Oct. 15	To Equity Share Capital A/c		18,00,000	Nov. 30	By Bank A/c		18,00,000

Equity Share Capital Account

Dr. | Cr.

Date	Particulars	J.F.	₹	Date	Particulars	J.F.	₹
2014				2014			
Dec. 31	To Balance c/d		36,00,000	Oct. 15	By Share Application A/c		18,00,000
				Oct. 15	By Share Allotment A/c		18,00,000
			36,00,000				36,00,000

X Ltd

Balance Sheet as at 31st December, 2014 **(Figures in ₹)**

Particulars	Note No.	Figures as at the end of current reporting period
1	2	3
I. EQUITY AND LIABILITIES		
(1) Shareholders' Funds		
(a) Share capital	(1)	36,00,000
(b) Reserves and surplus		—
(c) Money received against share warrants		—
TOTAL		36,00,000

Notes to Accounts :

(1) Share Capital	₹	₹
Authorised Capital : 4,50,000 Equity Shares of ₹ 10 each		45,00,000
Issued Capital : 3,60,000 Equity Shares of ₹ 10 each		36,00,000
Subscribed Capital : *Subscribed and Fully Paid* 3,60,000 Equity Shares of ₹ 10 each		36,00,000

Calls-in-Arrear

Calls-in-arrear refer to that portion of the capital, which has been called up but not yet paid by the shareholders. When a shareholder(s) fails to pay the amount due on allotment and/or calls, the Allotment Account and/or Calls Account will show debit balance(s) equal to the total unpaid amounts of each installment. Generally, such amount is transferred to a special account called '***Calls-in-Arrear Account***'. For example, a company has not received allotment money @ ₹ 3 per share on 100 shares and first call money @ ₹ 2 per share on 200 shares. These amounts of ₹ 300 (₹ 3 x 100) and ₹ 400 (₹ 2 x 200) due on allotment and first call respectively are called Calls-in-Arrear. The main purpose of opening a Calls-in-Arrear Account is to close allotment or any other Calls Account with the amounts not yet received. ***The entry will be***:

Calls-in-Arrear Account Dr.
To Share Allotment Account
To Share Call Account

When money is collected from such defaulting shareholders, the following entry is passed:

Bank Account Dr.
To Calls-in-Arrear Account

The balance of 'Calls-in-Arrear Account', at the year end, is shown in the Balance Sheet as a deduction from respective Share Capital Account. It is shown in the Balance Sheet until the shares on which money unpaid are forfeited. At the time of forfeiture of shares, the entry will be :

Share Capital Account Dr.
To Calls-in-Arrear Account

Interest on calls-in-arrear :

[***It is outside the scope of the Syllabus***.]

Calls-in-Advance

Calls in advance generally arises when there is an over subscription of shares. Here, the excess application money received is adjusted against the amount due on allotment or calls. The excess application money after adjustment for allotment should be transferred to a special account called ***'Calls-in-Advance Account'***, if the articles of association so provides. Sometimes, to avoid the botheration of paying calls from time to time, some shareholders may prefer to pay the entire amount at the time of allotment. In such a situation, the advance money in respect of future call(s) should also be transferred to ***Calls-in-Advance Account*** and it is adjusted when calls are made.

Accounting Entries

(a) For transferring excess application money

Share Application Account Dr. [Adjustment for excess]
To Calls-in -Advance Account

(b) For money received in advance against call

Bank Account Dr.

To Calls-in-Advance Account

(c) For adjusting with call(s)

Calls-in-Advance Account Dr.

To Call(s) Account

Interest on Calls-in-Advance

[***It is outside the scope of the Syllabus.***]

Illustration 11

A Ltd. was registered with an authorised capital of ₹ 5,00,000 divided into 50,000 equity shares of ₹ 10 each. The company issued 30,000 shares to the public payable as follows :on application ₹ 2 per share; on allotment ₹ 3 per share and the balance in two equal calls. The company received application for 20,000 shares and received all the money except the final call on 200 shares held by Raju. Pass Journal entries and show how the figures will appear in the Balance Sheet of the company.

Solution

In the books of A Ltd.

Journal

Date	Particulars	L.F.	Dr. ₹	Cr. ₹
?	Bank A/c Dr. To Equity Share Application A/c (Being application money received on 20,000 equity shares @ ₹ 2 each)		40,000	40,000
	Equity Share Application A/c Dr. To Equity Share Capital A/c (Being application money on 20,000 equity shares @ ₹ 2 each transferred to Equity Share Capital Account as per Board's Resolution No . . . Dated . . .)		40,000	40,000
	Equity Share Allotment A/c Dr. To Equity Share Capital A/c (Being allotment money due on 20,000 equity shares @ ₹ 3 each as per Board's Resolution No . . . Dated . . .)		60,000	60,000
	Bank A/c Dr. To Equity Share Allotment A/c (Being allotment money received on 20,000 equity shares @ ₹ 3 each)		60,000	60,000
	Equity Share First Call A/c Dr. To Equity Share Capital A/c (Being first call money due on 20,000 equity shares @ ₹ 2.50 each as per Board's Resolution No . . . Dated . . .)		50,000	50,000
	Bank A/c Dr. To Equity Share First Call A/c (Being first call money received on 20,000 equity shares @ ₹ 2.50 each)		50,000	50,000
	Equity Share Final Call A/c Dr. To Equity Share Capital A/c (Being final call money due on 20,000 equity shares @ ₹ 2.50 each as per Board's Resolution No . . . Dated . . .)		50,000	50,000
	Bank A/c Dr. Calls-in-Arrear A/c Dr. To Equity Share Final Call A/c (Being final call money received on 19,800 equity shares @ ₹ 2.50 each. Final call money not received on 200 equity shares @ ₹ 2.50 each transferred to Calls-in-Arrear Account)		49,500 500	50,000
	Total		4,00,000	4,00,000

A Ltd

Balance Sheet as at .... [Extract] **(Figures in ₹)**

Particulars	Note No.	Figures as at the end of current reporting period
1	2	3
I. EQUITY AND LIABILITIES		
(1) **Shareholders' Funds**		
(a) Share capital	(1)	1,99,500
(b) Reserves and surplus		
(c) Money received against share warrants		
TOTAL		1,99,500
II. ASSETS		
(2) **Current Assets**		
(d) Cash and cash equivalents	(2)	1,99,500
TOTAL		1,99,500

Notes to Accounts :

(1) Share Capital	₹	₹
Authorised Capital :		
50,000 Equity Shares of ₹ 10 each		5,00,000
Issued Capital :		
30,000 Equity Shares of ₹ 10 each		3,00,000
Subscribed Capital :		
Subscribed But Not Fully Paid :		
20,000 Equity Shares of ₹ 10 each	2,00,000	
Less: Calls-in-Arrear	500	1,99,500
(2) Cash at Bank		1,99,500

Illustration 12

Fortunate Limited issued 10,000 equity shares of ₹ 10 each. The amount was payable as under :
on application ₹ 2.00; on allotment ₹ 3.00; on first call ₹ 2.50; on final call ₹ 2.50.

The company received applications for 10,000 equity shares. The company allotted the shares. The directors made both the calls. X, holding 100 shares, did not pay both the calls whereas Y, holding 40 shares, did not pay the final call. Record the transactions in the journal of the company. Also show the relevant items as they would appear in the Balance Sheet of the company.

Solution

In the books of Fortunate Limited

Journal

Date	Particulars	L.F.	Dr. ₹	Cr. ₹
?	Bank A/c Dr.		20,000	
	To Equity Share Application A/c			20,000
	(Being application money received on 10,000 equity shares @ ₹ 2 each)			
	Equity Share Application A/c Dr.		20,000	
	To Equity Share Capital A/c			20,000
	(Being application money on 10,000 equity shares @ ₹ 2 each transferred to Equity Share Capital Account as per Board's Resolution No . . . Dated . . .)			
	Equity Share Allotment A/c Dr.		30,000	
	To Equity Share Capital A/c			30,000
	(Being allotment money due on 10,000 equity shares @ ₹ 3 each as per Board's Resolution No . . . Dated . . .)			

Particulars		Dr. (₹)	Cr. (₹)
Bank A/c Dr. To Equity Share Allotment A/c (Being allotment money received on 10,000 equity shares @ ₹ 3 each)		30,000	30,000
Equity Share First Call A/c Dr. To Equity Share Capital A/c (Being first call money due on 10,000 equity shares @ ₹ 2.50 each as per Board's Resolution No . . . Dated . . .)		25,000	25,000
Bank A/c Dr. Calls-in-Arrear A/c Dr. To Equity Share First Call A/c (Being first call money received on 9,900 equity shares @ ₹ 2.50 each. First call money not received on 100 equity shares @ 2.50 each transferred to Calls-in-Arrear Account)		24,750 250	25,000
Equity Share Final Call A/c Dr. To Equity Share Capital A/c (Being final call money due on 10,000 equity shares @ ₹ 2.50 each as per Board's Resolution No . . . Dated . . .)		25,000	25,000
Bank A/c Dr. Calls-in-Arrear A/c (Note 1) Dr. To Equity Share Final Call A/c (Being final call money received on 9,860 equity shares @ ₹ 2.50 each. Final call money not received on 140 equity shares @ ₹ 2.50 each transferred to Calls-in-Arrear Account)		24,650 350	25,000
Total		2,00,000	2,00,000

Working Note : (1) Final call money has not been received on total 140 shares (100 shares of X and 40 shares of Y). Therefore, ₹ 350 has not been received in respect of final call.

Fortunate Ltd

Balance Sheet as at .... [Extract] **(Figures in ₹)**

Particulars	Note No.	Figures as at the end of current reporting period
1	2	3
I. EQUITY AND LIABILITIES		
(1) **Shareholders' Funds**		
(a) Share capital	(1)	99,400
(b) Reserves and surplus		
(c) Money received against share warrants		
TOTAL		99,400
II. ASSETS		
(2) **Current Assets**		
(d) Cash and cash equivalents	(2)	99,400
TOTAL		99,400

Notes to Accounts :

(1) Share Capital	₹	₹
Authorised Capital : ....Equity Shares of ₹ 10 each		?
Issued Capital : 10,000 Equity Shares of ₹ 10 each		1,00,000
Subscribed Capital : *Subscribed But Not fully Paid* : 10,000 Equity Shares of ₹ 10 each	1,00,000	
Less: Calls-in-Arrear	600	99,400
(2) Cash at Bank		99,400

Illustration 13

Assam Traders Limited was registered with an authorised capital of ₹ 50,000 divided into 5,000 equity shares of ₹ 10 each. Applications were invited for 4,000 shares payable as follows :

on application ₹ 2.00; on allotment ₹ 3.00; on first call ₹ 2.50; on final call ₹ 2.50.

All the shares were applied for and were fully allotted. Holder of 200 shares paid all monies payable on those shares at the time of allotment. The company made first call and all monies due were received except on 300 shares. Give journal entries in the books of the company and also prepare Cash Book.

Solution

In the books of Assam Traders Limited

Cash Book (Bank column only)

Dr. **Cr.**

Date	Particulars	₹	Date	Particulars	₹
	To Equity Share Application A/c (Being application money received on 4,000 equity shares @ ₹ 2 each)	8,000		By Balance c/d	29,750
	To Equity Share Allotment A/c (Being allotment money received on 4,000 equity shares @ ₹ 3 each)	12,000			
	To Calls-in-Advance A/c (Note 1) (Being first call on 200 shares @ ₹ 2.50 each and final call on equal shares @ ₹ 2.50 each received in advance)	1,000			
	To Equity Share First Call A/c (Note 2) (Being first call money received on 3,500 equity shares @ ₹ 2.50)	8,750			
		29,750			29,750

In the books of the Assam Traders Ltd.

Journal

Date	Particulars	L.F.	Dr. ₹	Cr. ₹
	Equity Share Application A/c Dr. To Equity Share Capital A/c (Being application money on 4,000 equity shares @ ₹ 2 each transferred to Equity Share Capital Account as per Board's Resolution No . . . Dated . . .)		8,000	8,000
	Equity Share Allotment A/c Dr. To Equity Share Capital A/c (Being allotment money due on 4,000 equity shares @ ₹ 3 each as per Board's Resolution No . . . Dated . . .)		12,000	12,000
	Equity Share First Call A/c Dr. To Equity Share Capital A/c (Being first call money due on 4,000 equity shares @ ₹ 2.50 each as per Board's Resolution No . . . Dated . . .)		10,000	10,000
	Calls-in -Advance A/c Dr. To Equity Share First Call A/c (Being the adjustment of first call money on 200 shares @ ₹ 2.50 each)		500	500
	Calls-in-Arrear A/c Dr. To Equity Share First Call A/c (Being first call money on 300 equity shares @ ₹ 2.50 not paid transferred to Calls-in-Arrear Account)		750	750
	Total		31,250	31,250

Working Notes :

(1) One shareholder holding 200 shares paid first call money @ ₹ 2.50 and final call money also @ ₹ 2.50 along with the allotment money. Total amount = (₹ 2.50 **x** 200) + (₹ 2.50 **x** 200) = ₹ 1,000 will be credited to Calls-in-Advance Account and debited to Bank Account. For adjustment of call money in future, Calls-in-Advance Account will be debited and respective Call Account will be credited.

(2) Total amount payable on first call is ₹ 10,000. One shareholder holding 200 shares paid first call money along with allotment. Another shareholder holding 300 shares could not pay the first call money. Therefore, actual amount received on first call = ₹ 10,000 – (₹ 2.50 **x** 200) – (₹ 2.50 **x** 300) = ₹ 10,000 – ₹ 500 – ₹ 750 = ₹ 8,750.

Illustration 14

X Ltd wanted to issue 10,000 shares of ₹ 10 each of which ₹ 2 per share was payable on Application, ₹ 3 per share on Allotment, ₹ 3 per share on First Call and ₹ 2 per share on Final Call. The company received application money for 12,000 shares, out of which those for 1,200 shares were refunded. Excess application was adjusted towards allotment money due. A shareholder, Ritam, who was allotted 600 shares failed to pay first call money. Except this, the company received all the money due on allotment, first and final call.

Show all the Journal Entries relating to issue of shares in the books of the company.

Solution

In the books of X Ltd.

Journal

Date	Particulars		L.F.	Dr. ₹	Cr. ₹
	Bank A/c	Dr.		24,000	
	To Equity Share Application A/c				24,000
	(Being application money received on 12,000 equity shares @ ₹ 2 each)				
	Equity Share Application A/c	Dr.		2,400	
	To Bank A/c				2,400
	(Being excess application money on 1,200 equity shares @ ₹ 2 each refunded as per Board's Resolution No . . . Dated . . .)				
	Equity Share Application A/c	Dr.		21,600	
	To Equity Share Capital A/c				20,000
	To Equity Share Allotment A/c				1,600
	(Being the application money on 10,000 equity shares @ ₹ 2 each transferred to Equity Share Capital Account and application money on 800 shares @ ₹ 2 each adjusted against allotment as per Board's Resolution No . . . Dated . . .)				
	Equity Share Allotment A/c	Dr.		30,000	
	To Equity Share Capital A/c				30,000
	(Being allotment money due on 10,000 equity shares @ ₹ 3 each as per Board's Resolution No . . . Dated . . .)				
	Bank A/c	Dr.		28,400	
	To Equity Share Allotment A/c				28,400
	(Being allotment money received after adjusting excess application money against allotment)				
	Equity Share First Call A/c	Dr.		30,000	
	To Equity Share Capital A/c				30,000
	(Being first call money due on 10,000 equity shares @ ₹ 3 each as per Board's Resolution No . . . Dated . . .)				

Particulars			Dr.	Cr.
Bank A/c Dr. Calls-in-Arrear A/c Dr. To Equity Share First Call A/c (Being equity share first call money received, except for 600 shares)			28,200 1,800	 30,000
Equity Share Final Call A/c Dr. To Equity Share Capital A/c (Being final call money due on 10,000 equity shares @ ₹ 2 each as per Board's Resolution No . . . Dated . . .)			20,000	 20,000
Bank A/c Dr. Calls-in- Arrear A/c Dr. To Equity Share Final Call A/c (Being equity share final call money received, except for 600 shares)			18,800 1,200	 20,000
Total			2,06,400	2,06,400

Illustration 15

Hopeless Ltd. with an authorised capital of ₹ 5,00,000 in equity shares of ₹ 10 each, issued 10,000 shares payable as ₹ 4 on application, ₹ 2 on allotment, ₹ 2 on first call and the balance on final call. All monies payable up to final call were duly received by the company except that one shareholder holding 500 shares failed to pay the first call and final call money.

Show Journal Entries in the books of the Company and prepare the Balance Sheet of the Company.

Solution

In the books of Hopeless Ltd.

Journal

Date	Particulars	L.F.	Dr. ₹	Cr. ₹
	Bank A/c Dr. To Equity Share Application A/c (Being application money received on 10,000 equity shares @ ₹ 4 each)		40,000	 40,000
	Equity Share Application A/c Dr. To Equity Share Capital A/c (Being application money on 10,000 equity shares @ ₹ 4 each transferred to Equity Share Capital Account as per Board's Resolution No . . . Dated . . .)		40,000	 40,000
	Equity Share Allotment A/c Dr. To Equity Share Capital A/c (Being allotment money due on 10,000 equity shares @ ₹ 2 each as per Board's Resolution No . . . Dated . . .)		20,000	 20,000
	Bank A/c Dr. To Equity Share Allotment A/c (Being allotment money received on 10,000 equity shares @ ₹ 2 each)		20,000	 20,000
	Equity Share First Call A/c Dr. To Equity Share Capital A/c (Being first call money due on 10,000 equity shares @ ₹ 2 each as per Board's Resolution No . . . Dated . . .)		20,000	 20,000
	Bank A/c Dr. Calls-in-Arrear A/c Dr. To Equity Share First Call A/c (Being first call money received on 9,500 equity shares @ ₹ 2 each. First call money not received on 500 equity shares @ ₹ 2 each has been transferred to Calls-in-Arrear Account)		19,000 1,000	 20,000

Particulars		L.F.	Dr.	Cr.
Equity Share Final Call A/c Dr. To Equity Share Capital A/c (Being final call money due on 10,000 equity shares @ ₹ 2 each as per Board's Resolution No . . . Dated . . .)			20,000	20,000
Bank A/c Dr. Calls-in- Arrear A/c Dr. To Equity Share Final Call A/c (Being final call money received on 9,500 equity shares @ ₹ 2 each. Final call money not received on 500 equity shares @ ₹ 2 each has been transferred to Calls-in-Arrear Account)			19,000 1,000	20,000
	Total		2,00,000	2,00,000

Hopeless Ltd

Balance Sheet as at .... [Extract]

(Figures in ₹)

Particulars	Note No.	Figures as at the end of current reporting period
1	2	3
I. EQUITY AND LIABILITIES		
(1) **Shareholders' Funds**		
(a) Share capital	(1)	98,000
(b) Reserves and surplus		
(c) Money received against share warrants		
TOTAL		98,000
II. ASSETS		
(2) **Current Assets**		
(d) Cash and cash equivalents	(2)	98,000
TOTAL		98,000

Notes to Accounts :

(1) Share Capital	₹	₹
Authorised Capital :		
50,000 Equity Shares of ₹ 10 each		5,00,000
Issued Capital :		
10,000 Equity Shares of ₹ 10 each		1,00,000
Subscribed Capital :		
Subscribed But Not Fully Paid :		
10,000 Equity Shares of ₹ 10 each	1,00,000	
Less: Calls-in-Arrear (1,000 + 1,000)	2,000	98,000
(2) Cash at Bank		98,000

Illustration 16

X Company Limited issued 20,000 Equity Shares of ₹ 10 each, payable as follows :

On application	₹ 2.00
On allotment	₹ 3.00
On first call	₹ 2.50
On final call	₹ 2.50

All the shares were subscribed and allotted. Calls were made in due course, but first call money on 1,000 shares and final call money on 1,500 shares were not yet received.

Show Journal Entries (including cash) and show the Equity Share Capital Account.

Solution

In the books of X Company Limited

Journal

Date	Particulars		L.F.	Dr. ₹	Cr. ₹
	Bank A/c	Dr.		40,000	
	To Equity Share Application A/c				40,000
	(Being application money received on 20,000 equity shares @ ₹ 2 each)				
	Equity Share Application A/c.	Dr.		40,000	
	To Equity Share Capital A/c				40,000
	(Being Application money on 20,000 equity shares @ ₹ 2 each transferred to Equity Share Capital Account as per Board's Resolution No . . . Dated . . .)				
	Equity Share Allotment A/c	Dr.		60,000	
	To Equity Share Capital A/c				60,000
	(Being allotment money due on 20,000 equity shares @ ₹ 3 each as per Board's Resolution No . . . Dated . . .)				
	Bank A/c	Dr.		60,000	
	To Equity Share Allotment A/c				60,000
	(Being allotment money received on 20,000 equity shares @ ₹ 3 each)				
	Equity Share First Call A/c	Dr.		50,000	
	To Equity Share Capital A/c				50,000
	(Being first call money due on 20,000 equity shares @ ₹ 2.50 each as per Board's Resolution No . . . Dated . . .)				
	Bank A/c	Dr.		47,500	
	Calls-in -Arrear A/c	Dr.		2,500	
	To Equity Share First Call A/c				50,000
	(Being first call money received on 19,000 equity shares @ ₹ 2.50 each. First call money not received on 1,000 equity shares @ ₹ 2.50 has been transferred to Calls-in-Arrear Account)				
	Equity Share Final Call A/c	Dr.		50,000	
	To Equity Share Capital A/c				50,000
	(Being final call money due on 20,000 equity shares @ ₹ 2.50 each as per Board's Resolution No . . . Dated . . .)				
	Bank A/c	Dr.		46,250	
	Calls-in-Arrear A/c	Dr.		3,750	
	To Equity Share Final Call A/c				50,000
	(Being final call money received on 18,500 equity shares @ ₹ 2.50 each. Final call money not received on 1,500 equity shares @ ₹ 2.50 has been transferred to Calls-in-Arrear Account)				
	Total			4,00,000	4,00,000

Tutorial Note : It is assumed that 1,500 shares on which final call has not been paid include 1,000 shares on which first call also has not been paid.

Dr. **Equity Share Capital Account** **Cr.**

Date	Particulars	J.F.	₹	Date	Particulars	J.F.	₹
?	To Balance c/d		2,00,000	?	By Equity Share Application A/c		40,000
					By Equity Share Allotment A/c		60,000
					By Equity Share First Call A/c		50,000
					By Equity Share Final Call A/c		50,000
			2,00,000				2,00,000

Illustration 17

ABB Limited had an authorised share capital of ₹ 1,25,000 (shares of ₹ 10 each divided into 12,500 equity shares). The company issued 10,000 equity shares payable as ₹ 2 on application, ₹ 3 on allotment, ₹ 3 on first call, ₹ 2 on final call. All the shares were subscribed by the public. The directors made allotments and the money was duly received except for the final call on 500 shares.

Pass the Journal Entries, prepare the Equity Share Capital Account only and show how the share capital will appear in the Balance Sheet.

Solution

In the books of ABB Limited

Journal

Date	Particulars		L.F.	Dr. ₹	Cr. ₹
	Bank A/c	Dr.		20,000	
	To Equity Share Application A/c				20,000
	(Being application money received on 10,000 equity shares @ ₹ 2 each as per Board's Resolution No . . . Dated . . .)				
	Equity Share Application A/c	Dr.		20,000	
	To Equity Share Capital A/c				20,000
	(Being application money on 10,000 equity shares @ ₹ 2 each transferred to Equity Share Capital Account as per Board's Resolution No . . . Dated . . .)				
	Equity Share Allotment A/c	Dr.		30,000	
	To Equity Share Capital A/c				30,000
	(Being allotment money due on 10,000 equity shares @ ₹ 3 each as per Board's Resolution No . . . Dated . . .)				
	Bank A/c	Dr.		30,000	
	To Equity Share Allotment A/c				30,000
	(Being allotment money received on 10,000 equity shares @ ₹ 3 each)				
	Equity Share First Call A/c	Dr.		30,000	
	To Equity Share Capital A/c				30,000
	(Being first call money due on 10,000 equity shares @ ₹ 3 each as per Board's Resolution No . . . Dated . . .)				
	Bank A/c	Dr.		30,000	
	To Equity Share First Call A/c				30,000
	(Being first call money received on 10,000 equity shares @ ₹ 3 each)				
	Equity Share Final Call A/c	Dr.		20,000	
	To Equity Share Capital A/c				20,000
	(Being final call money due on 10,000 equity shares @ ₹ 2 each as per Board's Resolution No . . . Dated . . .)				
	Bank A/c	Dr.		19,000	
	Calls-in-Arrear A/c	Dr.		1,000	
	To Equity Share Final Call A/c				20,000
	(Being final call money received on 9,500 equity shares @ ₹ 2 each .Final call money not received on 500 equity share @ ₹ 2 each has been transferred to Calls-in-Arrear Account)				
		Total		2,00,000	2,00,000

Dr. Equity Share Capital Account Cr.

Date	Particulars	J.F.	₹	Date	Particulars	J.F.	₹
	To Balance c/d		1,00,000		By Equity Share Application A/c		20,000
					By Equity Share Allotment A/c		30,000
					By Equity Share First Call A/c		30,000
					By Equity Share Final Call A/c		20,000
			1,00,000				1,00,000

ABB Limited

Balance Sheet as at .... [Extract] **(Figures in ₹)**

Particulars	Note No.	Figures as at the end of current reporting period
1	2	3
I. EQUITY AND LIABILITIES		
(1) **Shareholders' Funds**		
(a) Share capital	(1)	99,000
(b) Reserves and surplus		
(c) Money received against share warrants		
TOTAL		99,000

Notes to Accounts :

(1) Share Capital	₹	₹
Authorised Capital :		
12,500 Equity Shares of ₹ 10 each		1,25,000
Issued Capital :		
10,000 Equity Shares of ₹ 10 each		1,00,000
Subscribed Capital :		
Subscribed But Not Fully Paid :		
10,000 Equity Shares of ₹ 10 each	1,00,000	
Less: Calls-in-Arrear	1,000	99,000

Illustration 18

X Ltd. was registered with a capital of ₹ 5,00,000 divided into 20,000 equity shares of ₹ 25 each. The company invited applications for 10,000 shares. Amount payable are as under :

On application	₹ 10
On allotment	₹ 5
On first call	₹ 5
On final call	₹ 5

Applications were received for 12,000 shares. Application money on 2,000 shares were returned. All the applicants paid their dues in full with the exception of one applicant holding 500 shares, who did not pay any call money. Give Journal Entries and the Balance Sheet of the company.

Solution

In the books of X Limited

Journal

Date	Particulars	L.F.	Dr. ₹	Cr. ₹
	Bank A/c Dr.		1,20,000	
	To Equity Share Application A/c			1,20,000
	(Being application money received on 12,000 equity shares @ ₹ 10 each)			
	Equity Share Application A/c Dr.		20,000	
	To Bank A/c			20,000
	(Being excess application money on 2,000 equity shares @ ₹ 10 each refunded as per Board's Resolution No . . . Dated . . .)			
	Equity Share Application A/c Dr.		1,00,000	
	To Equity Share Capital A/c			1,00,000
	(Being application money on 10,000 equity shares @ ₹ 10 each transferred to Equity Share Capital Account as per Board's Resolution No . . . Dated . . .)			

Particulars		Dr. (₹)	Cr. (₹)
Equity Share Allotment A/c Dr. To Equity Share Capital A/c (Being allotment money due on 10,000 equity shares @ ₹ 5 each as per Board's Resolution No . . . Dated . . .)		50,000	50,000
Bank A/c Dr. To Equity Share Allotment A/c (Being allotment money received on 10,000 equity shares @ ₹ 5 each)		50,000	50,000
Equity Share First Call A/c Dr. To Equity Share Capital A/c (Being first call money due on 10,000 equity shares @ ₹ 5 each as per Board's Resolution No . . . Dated . . .)		50,000	50,000
Bank A/c Dr. Calls-in-Arrear A/c Dr. To Equity Share First Call A/c (Being first call money received on 9,500 equity shares @ ₹ 5 each. First call money not received on 500 equity shares @ ₹ 5 each transferred to Calls-in-Arrear Account)		47,500 2,500	50,000
Equity Share Final Call A/c Dr. To Equity Share Capital A/c (Being final call money due on 10,000 equity shares @ ₹ 5 each as per Board's Resolution No . . . Dated . . .)		50,000	50,000
Bank A/c Dr. Calls-in-Arrear A/c Dr. To Equity Share Final Call A/c (Being final call money received on 9,500 equity shares @ ₹ 5 each. Final call money not received on 500 equity shares @ ₹ 5 each transferred to Calls-in-Arrear Account)		47,500 2,500	50,000
Total		5,40,000	5,40,000

X Ltd.

Balance Sheet as at .... [Extract] **(Figures in ₹)**

Particulars	Note No.	Figures as at the end of current reporting period
1	2	3
I. EQUITY AND LIABILITIES		
(1) **Shareholders' Funds**		
(a) Share capital	(1)	2,45,000
(b) Reserves and surplus		
(c) Money received against share warrants		
TOTAL		2,45,000
II. ASSETS		
(2) **Current Assets**		
(d) Cash and cash equivalents	(2)	2,45,000
TOTAL		2,45,000

Notes to Accounts :

(1) Share Capital	₹	₹
***Authorised Capital*:**		
20,000 Equity Shares of ₹ 25 each		5,00,000
***Issued Capital*:**		
10,000 Equity Shares of ₹ 25 each		2,50,000

***Subscribed Capital*:** *Subscribed But Not fully Paid* : 10,000 Equity Shares of ₹ 25 each Less: Calls-in-Arrear	2,50,000 5,000	2,45,000
(2) Cash at Bank		2,45,000

Illustration 19

Development Consultant Limited with an authorised capital of ₹ 2,00,000 in equity shares of ₹ 10 each, issued 8,000 equity shares payable as follows :

	₹
On application	2.50
On allotment	2.50
On first call	2.00
On final call	3.00

All monies payable up to final call were duly received by the company, except that one shareholder holding 1,000 shares failed to pay the allotment and call monies.

Show Journal Entries in the books of the company and prepare the Balance Sheet of the Company.

Solution **In the books of Development Consultant Limited**

Journal

Date	Particulars	L.F.	Dr. ₹	Cr. ₹
	Bank A/c Dr. To Equity Share Application A/c (Being application money received on 8,000 equity shares @ 2.50 each)		20,000	20,000
	Equity Share Application A/c Dr. To Equity Share Capital A/c (Being application money on 8,000 equity shares @ ₹ 2.50 each transferred to Equity Share Capital Account as per Board's Resolution No . . . Dated . . .)		20,000	20,000
	Equity Share Allotment A/c Dr. To Equity Share Capital A/c (Being allotment money due on 8,000 equity shares @ ₹ 2.50 each as per Board's Resolution No . . . Dated . . .)		20,000	20,000
	Bank A/c Dr. Calls-in-Arrear A/c Dr. To Equity Share Allotment A/c (Being allotment money received on 7,000 equity shares @ ₹ 2.50 each. Allotment money not received on 1,000 equity shares @ ₹ 2.50 each transferred to calls-in-Arrear Account)		17,500 2,500	20,000
	Equity Share First Call A/c Dr. To Equity Share Capital A/c (Being first call money due on 8,000 equity shares @ ₹ 2 each, as per Board's Resolution No . . . Dated . . .)		16,000	16,000
	Bank A/c Dr. Calls-in-Arrear A/c Dr. To Equity Share First Call A/c (Being first call money received on 7,000 equity shares @ ₹ 2 each. First call money not received on 1,000 equity shares @ ₹ 2 each transferred to Calls-in-Arrear Account)		14,000 2,000	16,000
	Equity Share Final Call A/c Dr. To Equity Share Capital A/c (Being final call money due on 8,000 equity shares @ ₹ 3 each as per Board's Resolution No . . . Dated . . .)		24,000	24,000

Bank A/c Dr. Calls-in-Arrear A/c Dr. To Equity Share Final Call A/c (Being final call money received on 7,000 equity shares @ ₹ 3 each. Final Call money not received on 1,000 equity shares @ ₹ 3 each transferred to Calls-in-Arrear Account)		21,000 3,000	 24,000
Total		1,60,000	1,60,000

Development Consultant Limited
Balance Sheet as at .... [Extract]

Figures in ₹)

Particulars	Note No.	Figures as at the end of current reporting period
1	2	3
I. EQUITY AND LIABILITIES		
(1) **Shareholders' Funds**		
(a) Share capital	(1)	72,500
(b) Reserves and surplus		
(c) Money received against share warrants		
TOTAL		72,500
II. ASSETS		
(2) **Current Assets**		
(d) Cash and cash equivalents	(2)	72,500
TOTAL		72,500

Notes to Accounts :

(1) Share Capital	₹	₹
Authorised Capital : 20,000 Equity Shares of ₹ 10 each		2,00,000
Issued Capital : 8,000 Equity Shares of ₹ 10 each		80,000
Subscribed Capital : *Subscribed But Not Fully Paid* : 8,000 Equity Shares of ₹ 10 each Less: Calls-in-Arrear	 80,000 7,500	 72,500
(2) Cash at Bank		72,500

Issue of Securities at a Premium

The term 'premium' has not been defined in the Companies Act. Price received over the face value of the shares is treated as premium. A company, if a market exists, can issue shares at a premium. Very recently shares of ₹ 10 have been issued by INOX India Limited at a premium of ₹ 300 per share.

Section 52 of the Companies Act, 2013 states that :

(1) Where a company issues shares at a premium, whether for cash or otherwise, a sum equal to the aggregate amount of the premium received on those shares shall be transferred to a "securities premium account" and the provisions of this Act relating to reduction of share capital of a company shall, except as provided in this section, apply as if the securities premium account were the paid-up share capital of the company.

(2) Notwithstanding anything contained in sub-section (1), the securities premium account may be applied by the company—

(a) towards the issue of unissued shares of the company to the members of the company as fully paid bonus shares;
(b) in writing off the preliminary expenses of the company;
(c) in writing off the expenses of, or the commission paid or discount allowed on, any issue of shares or debentures of the company;
(d) in providing for the premium payable on the redemption of any redeemable preference shares or of any debentures of the company; or
(e) for the purchase of its own shares or other securities under section 68 (Buy-back of shares).

(3) The securities premium account may, notwithstanding anything contained in sub-sections (1) and (2), be applied by such class of companies, as may be prescribed and whose financial statement comply ***with the accounting standards*** prescribed for such class of companies under section 133,—
(a) in paying up unissued equity shares of the company to be issued to members of the company as fully paid bonus shares; or
(b) in writing off the expenses of or the commission paid or discount allowed on any issue of equity shares of the company; or
(c) for the purchase of its own shares or other securities under section 68 (Buy-back of shares).

In connection with the issue of securities at a premium, students should note the following :

1. ***Securities premium amount cannot be distributed as dividend in cash.***
2. ***The annual Balance Sheet must disclose the amount of securities premium as a separate item under 'Reserve and Surplus'.***
3. ***Money in Securities Premium Account cannot be treated as free reserves, as they are in the nature of capital reserves.***

Accounting Entries

Premium may be collected with application money or on allotment or along with a subsequent call. Generally, premium is collected along with allotment money.

(i) When premium is collected along with application money

(a) Bank Account Dr. [Total amount received on application]
  To Share Application Account
(b) Share Application Account Dr.
  To Share Capital Account
  To Securities Premium Account

[All other entries in respect of allotment and calls are same as shares issued at par]

(ii) When premium is collected along with allotment money

(a) Bank Account Dr.
  To Share Application Account
(b) Share Application Account Dr.
  To Share Capital Account
(c) Share Allotment Account Dr.
  To Share Capital Account
  To Securities Premium Account

[All other entries in respect of calls are the same as shares issued at par]

Illustration 20

Better Prospects Limited issued 30,000 equity shares of ₹ 10 each at a premium of ₹ 2 per share, payable as follows : On application ₹ 2; On allotment (including premium) ₹ 5; On first and final call ₹ 5.

All shares were applied for and allotted. All monies were received with the exception of first and final call on 500 shares.

Give the journal entries in the books of the company in respect of the above transactions and show the Balance Sheet.

Solution

In the books of Better Prospects Limited

Journal

Date	Particulars	L.F.	Dr. ₹	Cr. ₹
	Bank A/c Dr. To Equity Share Application A/c (Being application money received on 30,000 equity shares @ ₹ 2 each)		60,000	60,000
	Equity Share Application A/c Dr. To Equity Share Capital A/c (Being application money on 30,000 equity shares @ ₹ 2 each transferred to Equity Share Capital Account as per Board's Resolution No . . . Dated . . .)		60,000	60,000
	Equity Share Allotment A/c Dr. To Equity Share Capital A/c To Securities Premium A/c (Being allotment money due on 30,000 equity shares @ ₹ 5 each including a premium of ₹ 2 each as per Board's Resolution No . . . Dated . . .)		1,50,000	90,000 60,000
	Bank A/c Dr. To Equity Share Allotment A/c (Being allotment money received on 30,000 equity shares @ ₹ 5 each)		1,50,000	1,50,000
	Equity Share First and Final Call A/c Dr. To Equity Share Capital A/c (Being first and final call money due on 30,000 equity shares @ ₹ 5 each as per Board's Resolution No . . . Dated . . .)		1,50,000	1,50,000
	Bank A/c Dr. Calls-in-Arrear A/c Dr. To Equity Share First and Final Call A/c (Being first and final call money received on 29,500 equity shares @ ₹ 5 each . First and final call money not received on 500 shares @ ₹ 5 each transferred to Calls-in- Arrear Account)		1,47,500 2,500	1,50,000
	Total		7,20,000	7,20,000

Better Prospect Limited

Balance Sheet as at .... [Extract] **(Figures in ₹)**

Particulars	Note No.	Figures as at the end of current reporting period
1	2	3
I. EQUITY AND LIABILITIES		
(1) Shareholders' Funds		
(a) Share capital	(1)	2,97,500
(b) Reserves and surplus	(2)	60,000
(c) Money received against share warrants		
TOTAL		3,57,500

II. ASSETS		
(2) **Current Assets**		
(d) Cash and cash equivalents	(3)	3,57,500
TOTAL		3,57,500

Notes to Accounts :

(1) Share Capital	₹	₹
Authorised Capital :		
? Equity Shares of ₹ ... each		?
Issued Capital :		
30,000 Equity Shares of ₹ 10 each		3,00,000
Subscribed Capital :		
Subscribed But Not Fully Paid :		
30,000 Equity Shares of ₹ 10 each	3,00,000	
Less: Calls-in-Arrear	2,500	2,97,500
(2) Reserve and Surplus		
Securities Premium		60,000
(3) Cash at Bank		3,57,500

Working Notes :

(1) When premium is payable with the allotment money, Share Allotment Account is debited and Securities Premium Account is credited along with Share Capital Account. This entry is passed on due basis. When cash is received, Bank Account is debited and Share Allotment Account is credited.

(2) Securities premium is shown in the Balance Sheet of the company under the heading "Reserve and Surplus".

Illustration 21

Jindal Limited issued a prospectus inviting applications for 90,000 equity shares of ₹ 10 each at a premium of ₹ 2 per share, payable as follows :

On application (including premium) ₹ 4.50; On allotment ₹ 4.50; On final call ₹ 3.00

All shares were applied for and allotted. The entire money payable by shareholders was received except from Mr X who had taken 1,000 shares, but failed to pay the final call.

You are required to pass necessary journal entries in the books of the company to record the above transactions.

Solution

In the books of Jindal Limited

Journal

Date	Particulars	L.F.	Dr. ₹	Cr. ₹
	Bank A/c Dr. To Equity Share Application A/c (Being application money received on 90,000 equity shares @ ₹ 4.50 each including a premium of ₹ 2 per share)		4,05,000	4,05,000
	Equity Share Application A/c Dr. To Equity Share Capital A/c To Securities Premium A/c (Being application money on 90,000 equity shares @ ₹ 2.50 each transferred to Equity Share Capital Account and @ ₹ 2 each transferred to Securities Premium Account)		4,05,000	2,25,000 1,80,000
	Equity Share Allotment A/c Dr. To Equity Share Capital A/c (Being allotment money due on 90,000 equity shares @ ₹ 4.50 each as per Board's Resolution No . . . Dated . . .)		4,05,000	4,05,000

Date	Particulars	L.F.	Dr. ₹	Cr. ₹
	Bank A/c Dr. To Equity Share Allotment A/c (Being allotment money received on 90,000 equity shares @ ₹ 4.50 each)		4,05,000	4,05,000
	Equity Share Final Call A/c Dr. To Equity Share Capital A/c (Being final call money due on 90,000 equity shares @ ₹ 3 each as per Board's Resolution No . . . Dated . . .)		2,70,000	2,70,000
	Bank A/c Dr. Calls-in-Arrear A/c Dr. To Equity Share Final Call A/c (Being final call money received on 89,000 equity shares @ ₹ 3 each. Final call money not received on 1,000 equity shares @ ₹ 3 each has been transferred to Calls-in-Arrear Account)		2,67,000 3,000	2,70,000
	Total		21,60,000	21,60,000

Tutorial Note : When securities premium is payable with application money, the entire money received is credited to Share Application Account. At the time of allotment, premium is transferred to Securities Premium Account.

Illustration 22

X and Company Limited, with an authorised capital of ₹ 2,00,000 divided into 20,000 equity shares of ₹ 10 each, issued the entire shares payable as follows :

	₹
On application (including ₹ 2 as premium)	5
On allotment	4
On final call	3

All share money is received in full with the exception of the allotment money on 200 shares and final call money on 500 shares (including 200 shares on which allotment money had not been paid).

Make the necessary Journal Entries.

Solution

In the books of X and Company Ltd.

Journal

Date	Particulars	L.F.	Dr. ₹	Cr. ₹
	Bank A/c Dr. To Equity Share Application A/c (Being application money received on 20,000 equity shares @ ₹ 5 each including a premium of ₹ 2 per share)		1,00,000	1,00,000
	Equity Share Application A/c Dr. To Equity Share Capital A/c To Securities Premium A/c (Being application money on 20,000 equity shares @ ₹ 3 each transferred to Equity Share Capital Account and @ ₹ 2 each transferred to Securities Premium Account as per Board's Resolution No . . . Dated . . .)		1,00,000	60,000 40,000
	Equity Share Allotment A/c Dr. To Equity Share Capital A/c (Being allotment money due on 20,000 equity shares @ ₹ 4 each as per Board's Resolution No . . . Dated . . .)		80,000	80,000
	Bank A/c Dr. Calls-in-Arrear A/c Dr. To Equity Share Allotment A/c (Being allotment money received on 19,800 equity shares @ ₹ 4 each. Allotment money not received on 200 equity shares @ ₹ 4 each has been transferred to Calls-in-Arrear Account)		79,200 800	80,000

Date	Particulars	L.F.	Dr. ₹	Cr. ₹
	Equity Share Final Call A/c Dr. To Equity Share Capital A/c (Being final call money due on 20,000 equity shares @ ₹ 3 each as per Board's Resolution No . . . Dated . . .)		60,000	60,000
	Bank A/c Dr. Calls-in-Arrear A/c Dr. To Equity Share Final Call A/c (Being final call money received on 19,500 equity shares @ ₹ 3 each. Final call money not received on 500 equity shares @ ₹ 3 each has been transferred to Calls-in-Arrear Account)		58,500 1,500	60,000
	Total		4,80,000	4,80,000

Illustration 23

ABC Ltd. was registered with a nominal capital of ₹ 10,00,000 divided into 1,00,000 equity shares of ₹ 10 each.

The company offered for public subscription 60,000 shares at a premium of ₹ 5 per share.

The money of the shares were payable as follows :

	₹
On application	3 per share
On allotment (including premium)	7 per share
On first call	3 per share
On final call	the balance amount

Applications were received for 70,000 shares and 60,000 shares were duly allotted. Monies received on excess applications were refunded. All monies due on shares were received in full.

Show Journal Entries (including cash) to record the above transactions in the books of the Company.

Solution

In the books of ABC Ltd.
Journal

Date	Particulars	L.F.	Dr. ₹	Cr. ₹
	Bank A/c Dr. To Equity Share Application A/c (Being application money received on 70,000 equity shares @ ₹ 3 each)		2,10,000	2,10,000
	Equity Share Application A/c Dr. To Equity Share Capital A/c. (Being application money on 60,000 equity shares @ ₹ 3 each transferred to Equity Share Capital Account as per Board's Resolution No . . . Dated . . .)		1,80,000	1,80,000
	Equity Share Application A/c Dr. To Bank A/c (Being excess application money on 10,000 equity shares @ ₹ 3 each refunded as per Board's Resolution No . . . Dated . . .)		30,000	30,000
	Equity Share Allotment A/c Dr. To Equity Share Capital A/c To Securities Premium A/c (Being allotment money due on 60,000 equity shares @ ₹ 7 each including a premium of ₹ 5 per share as per Board's Resolution No . . . Dated . . .)		4,20,000	1,20,000 3,00,000
	Bank A/c Dr. To Equity Share Allotment A/c (Being allotment money received on 60,000 equity shares @ ₹ 7 each)		4,20,000	4,20,000

Particulars		Dr.	Cr.
Equity Share First Call A/c Dr. To Equity Share Capital A/c (Being first call money due on 60,000 equity shares @ ₹ 3 each as per Board's Resolution No . . . Dated . . .)		1,80,000	1,80,000
Bank A/c Dr. To Equity Share First Call A/c (Being first call money received on 60,000 equity shares @ ₹ 3 each)		1,80,000	1,80,000
Equity Share Final Call A/c Dr. To Equity Share Capital A/c (Being final call money due on 60,000 equity shares @ ₹ 2 each as per Board's Resolution No . . . Dated . . .)		1,20,000	1,20,000
Bank A/c Dr. To Equity Share Final Call A/c (Being final call money received on 60,000 equity shares @ ₹ 2 each)		1,20,000	1,20,000
Total		18,60,000	18,60,000

Illustration 24

The authorised capital of Ajanta Company Limited was ₹ 2,00,000 divided into shares of ₹ 1,000 each. The Board of Directors arranged for distribution of 60% of such shares to the public payable as follows :

On application	₹ 200
On allotment (including premium ₹ 50)	₹ 250
On first call, and the second and final call	the balance amount equally

All the shares were subscribed for and all the monies were called for. Karim, a holder of 5 shares failed to pay the first call money. The rest money was received in full.

Show the Journal Entries and give the opening Balance Sheet.

Solution

In the books of Ajanta Company Ltd.

Journal

Date	Particulars	L.F.	Dr. ₹	Cr. ₹
	Bank A/c Dr. To Share Application A/c (Being application money received for 120 shares @ ₹ 200 each)		24,000	24,000
	Share Application A/c Dr. To Share Capital A/c (Note 1) (Being application money on 120 shares @ ₹ 200 each transferred to Share Capital Account as per Board's Resolution No . . . Dated . . .)		24,000	24,000
	Share Allotment A/c Dr. To Share Capital A/c To Securities Premium A/c (Being allotment money due on 120 shares @ ₹ 250 each including a premium of ₹ 50 per Share as per Board's Resolution No . . . Dated . . .)		30,000	24,000 6,000
	Bank A/c Dr. To Share Allotment A/c (Being allotment money received on 120 shares @ ₹ 250 each)		30,000	30,000
	Share First Call A/c Dr. To Share Capital A/c (Being first call money due on 120 shares @ ₹ 300 each as per Board's Resolution No . . . Dated . . .)		36,000	36,000

Particulars			Dr. ₹	Cr. ₹
Bank A/c Dr. Calls-in-Arrear A/c Dr. To Share First Call A/c (Being first call money received on 115 shares @ ₹ 300 each. First call money not received on 5 shares has been transferred to Calls-in-Arrear Account)			34,500 1,500	36,000
Share Final Call A/c Dr. To Share Capital A/c (Being final call money due on 120 shares @ ₹ 300 each as per Board's Resolution No . . . Dated . . .)			36,000	36,000
Bank A/c (Note 2) Dr. Calls-in-Arrear A/c Dr. To Share Final Call A/c (Being final call money received on 115 shares @ ₹ 300 each. Final call money not received on 5 shares has been transferred to Calls-in- Arrear Account)			34,500 1,500	36,000
Total			2,52,000	2,52,000

Ajanta Company Limited

Balance Sheet as at .... [Extract] **(Figures in ₹)**

Particulars	Note No.	Figures as at the end of current reporting period
1	2	3
I. EQUITY AND LIABILITIES		
(1) **Shareholders' Funds**		
(a) Share capital	(1)	1,17,000
(b) Reserves and surplus	(2)	6,000
(c) Money received against share warrants		
TOTAL		1,23,000
II. ASSETS		
(2) **Current Assets**		
(d) Cash and cash equivalents	(3)	1,23,000
TOTAL		1,23,000

Notes to Accounts :

	₹	₹
(1) Share Capital		
Authorised Capital : 200 Equity Shares of ₹ 1,000 each		2,00,000
Issued Capital : 120 Equity Shares of ₹ 1,000 each		1,20,000
Subscribed Capital : *Subscribed But Not Fully Paid* : 120 Equity Shares of ₹ 1,000 each Less: Calls-in-Arrear	1,20,000 3,000	1,17,000
(2) Reserve and Surplus Securities Premium		6,000
(3) Cash at Bank		1,23,000

Working Notes :

(1) It has not been mentioned in the question whether equity shares or preference shares have been issued by the company. Therefore, in the solution it has been ignored.

(2) Karim could not pay the first call money on 5 shares @ ₹ 300 each. Logically, he has also not paid the final call. Therefore, final call money was received for 115 shares only and total amount received was ₹ 34,500 (₹ 300 **x** 115).

Illustration 25

The authorised capital of D.C.M. Limited is 1,00,000 equity shares of ₹ 10 each. 50,000 equity shares are issued for subscription at a premium of ₹ 2 per share. The share money is payable as follows :

On application	₹ 4 (including premium of ₹ 1)
On allotment	₹ 4 (including premium of ₹ 1)
On final call	₹ 4

The shares are fully subscribed — the application and allotment money (including the premium) are received in full. The final call money is received on all shares except on 250 shares.

You are required to pass necessary Journal Entries (including cash) in the books of the Company.

Solution

In the books of D.C.M. Ltd.
Journal

Date	Particulars		L.F.	Dr. ₹	Cr. ₹
	Bank A/c	Dr.		2,00,000	
	To Equity Share Application A/c				2,00,000
	(Being application money received on 50,000 equity shares @ ₹ 4 each including the premium of ₹ 1 per share)				
	Equity Share Application A/c	Dr.		2,00,000	
	To Equity Share Capital A/c				1,50,000
	To Securities Premium A/c				50,000
	(Being application money on 50,000 equity shares @ ₹ 3 each transferred to Equity Share Capital Account and @ ₹ 1 per share transferred to Securities Premium Account as per Board's Resolution No . . . Dated . . .)				
	Equity Share Allotment A/c	Dr.		2,00,000	
	To Equity Share Capital A/c				1,50,000
	To Securities Premium A/c				50,000
	(Being the allotment money due on 50,000 equity shares @ ₹ 4 each including a Premium of ₹ 1 per share as per Board's Resolution No . . . Dated . . .)				
	Bank A/c	Dr.		2,00,000	
	To Equity Share Allotment A/c				2,00,000
	(Being allotment money received on 50,000 equity shares @ ₹ 4 each)				
	Equity Share Final Call A/c	Dr.		2,00,000	
	To Equity Share Capital A/c				2,00,000
	(Being final call money due on 50,000 equity shares @ ₹ 4 each as per Board's Resolution No . . . Dated . . .)				
	Bank A/c	Dr.		1,99,000	
	Calls-in-Arrear A/c	Dr.		1,000	
	To Equity Share Final Call A/c				2,00,000
	(Being final call money received on 49,750 equity shares @ ₹ 4 each. Amount not received on 250 shares @ ₹ 4 each transferred to Calls-in-Arrear Account)				
	Total			12,00,000	12,00,000

Illustration 26

Haldia Petrochemicals Limited issued 10,000 equity shares of ₹ 10 each, payable as ₹ 2.50 on application, ₹ 3.50 on allotment (including ₹ 1 for premium) and the balance in final call. Applications came for 12,000 shares, 2,000 of which were refunded. The shares were fully called up. All monies, excepting the final call money on 2,000 shares were received.

You are required to show : (i) Bank Account; (ii) Equity Share Application Account; (iii) Equity Share Allotment Account; (iv) Equity Share Final Call Account; (v) Securities Premium Account; (vi) Equity Share Capital Account; and (vii) Calls-in-Arrear Account.

Solution

Ledger of Haldia Petrochemical Limited

Bank Account

Dr. Cr.

Date	Particulars	₹	Date	Particulars	₹
	To Equity Share Application A/c	30,000		By Equity Share Application A/c	5,000
	To Equity Share Allotment A/c	35,000		By Balance c/d	1,00,000
	To Equity Share Final Call A/c	40,000			
		1,05,000			1,05,000

Equity Share Application Account

Dr. Cr.

Date	Particulars	₹	Date	Particulars	₹
	To Bank A/c	5,000		By Bank A/c	30,000
	To Equity Share Capital A/c	25,000			
		30,000			30,000

Equity Share Allotment Account

Dr. Cr.

Date	Particulars	₹	Date	Particulars	₹
	To Equity Share Capital A/c	25,000		By Bank A/c	35,000
	To Securities Premium A/c	10,000			
		35,000			35,000

Equity Share Final Call Account

Dr. Cr.

Date	Particulars	₹	Date	Particulars	₹
	To Equity Share Capital A/c	50,000		By Bank A/c	40,000
				By Calls-in-Arrear A/c	10,000
		50,000			50,000

Securities Premium Account

Dr. Cr.

Date	Particulars	₹	Date	Particulars	₹
	To Balance c/d	10,000		By Equity Share Allotment A/c	10,000

Equity Share Capital Account

Dr. Cr.

Date	Particulars	₹	Date	Particulars	₹
	To Balance c/d	1,00,000		By Equity Share Application A/c	25,000
				By Equity Share Allotment A/c	25,000
				By Equity Share Final Call A/c	50,000
		1,00,000			1,00,000

Calls-in-Arrear Account

Dr. Cr.

Date	Particulars	₹	Date	Particulars	₹
	To Equity Share Final Call A/c	10,000		By Balance c/d	10,000

Issue of Shares for "Consideration other than Cash"

Public limited companies, generally, issue their shares for cash and use such cash to buy the various types of assets needed in the business. Sometimes, however, a company may issue shares in a direct exchange for land, buildings or other assets. Shares may also be issued in payment for services rendered by promoters, lawyers in the formation of the company. In the Balance Sheet, these shares should be shown separately.

Within one month of allotment, the company must produce before the Registrar a written contract of sale of service in respect of which shares have been allotted.

Accounting Entries for Purchase of Assets

(a) When assets are purchased in exchange of shares

Assets Account Dr.
  To Vendor's Account

(b) When shares are issued to vendor at par

Vendor Account Dr.
  To Share Capital Account

(c) When shares are issued to vendor at a premium

Vendor Account Dr.
  To Share Capital Account
  To Securities Premium Account

Accounting Entries for Issue of Shares to Promoters, Lawyers at Free of Cost

Goodwill Account Dr.
  To Share Capital Account

Illustration 27

X Co. Ltd was incorporated with an authorised share capital of 1,00,000 equity shares of ₹ 10 each. The directors decided to allot 10,000 shares credited as fully paid to the promoters for their services.

The company also purchased land and buildings from Y Co. Ltd for ₹ 4,00,000 payable in fully paid-up shares of the company. The balance of the shares were issued to the public, which were fully subscribed and paid for.

You are required to pass journal entries and to prepare the Balance Sheet.

Solution

In the books of X Co. Ltd.

Journal

Date	Particulars	L.F.	Dr. ₹	Cr. ₹
	Goodwill A/c Dr.		1,00,000	
	To Equity Share Capital A/c			1,00,000
	(Being the issue of 10,000 shares of ₹ 10 each fully paid to the promoters for their services as per Board's Resolution No. ... dated ...)			
	Land and Buildings A/c Dr.		4,00,000	
	To Y Co. Ltd A/c			4,00,000
	(Being the Land and Buildings purchased from Y Co. Ltd as per agreement dtd ...)			
	Y Co. Ltd A/c Dr.		4,00,000	
	To Equity Share Capital A/c			4,00,000
	(Being the issue of 40,000 shares of ₹ 10 each to Y Co. Ltd against purchase of land and buildings as per Board's Resolution No. ... dated ...)			
	Bank A/c Dr.		5,00,000	
	To Equity Share Capital A/c			5,00,000
	(Being issue of 50,000 shares of ₹ 10 each as per Board's Resolution No. ... dtd ...)			
	Total		14,00,000	14,00,000

X & Co. Ltd

Balance Sheet as at .... **(Figures in ₹)**

Particulars	Note No.	Figures as at the end of current reporting period
1	2	3
I. EQUITY AND LIABILITIES		
(1) **Shareholders' Funds**		
(a) Share capital	(1)	10,00,000
(b) Reserves and surplus		
(c) Money received against share warrants		
TOTAL		10,00,000
II. ASSETS		
(1) **Non-current Assets**		
(a) Fixed assets		
(i) Tangible assets	(2)	4,00,000
(ii) Intangible assets	(3)	1,00,000
(2) **Current Assets**		
(d) Cash and cash equivalents	(4)	5,00,000
TOTAL		10,00,000

Notes to Accounts :

(1) Share Capital	₹	₹
Authorised Capital :		
1,00,000 Equity Shares of ₹ 10 each		10,00,000
Issued Capital :		
1,00,000 Equity Shares of ₹ 10 each		10,00,000
Subscribed Capital :		
Subscribed and Fully Paid :		
1,00,000 Equity Shares of ₹ 10 each		
(Of the above 50,000 shares have been allotted for consideration other than cash)		10,00,000
(2) Tangible Assets		
Land and Building		4,00,000
(3) Intangible Assets		
Goodwill		1,00,000
(4) Cash at Bank		5,00,000

Illustration 28

A limited company purchased machine worth ₹ 1,15,000 from Indian Traders. Payment was made as to ₹ 10,000 by a crossed cheque and remaining amount by issue of equity shares of the face value of ₹ 10 each fully paid at an issue price of ₹ 10.50 each. Make entries in the company's journal.

Solution **In the books of the Company**

Journal

Date	Particulars		L.F.	Dr. ₹	Cr. ₹
	Machinery A/c	Dr.		1,15,000	
	To Indian Traders A/c				1,15,000
	(Being the purchase value of machinery)				
	Indian Traders A/c	Dr.		10,000	
	To Bank A/c				10,000
	(Being paid by cheque)				

Indian Traders A/c Dr. To Equity Share Capital A/c To Securities Premium A/c (Being the issue of 10,000 shares of ₹ 10 each at a premium of ₹ 0.50 per share as per Board's Resolution No. ... dated ...)		1,05,000	1,00,000 5,000
Total		2,30,000	2,30,000

Forfeiture of Shares

The term 'forfeit' actually means 'penalty for a breach of contract or neglect; a fine', here 'forfeiture' means cancellation. It is very common that one or more shareholders fail to pay their allotment and/or calls on the due dates. Failure to pay any money results in forfeiture of shares. Forfeiture of shares is the action taken by a Company to cancel the shares as a final action against the defaulting shareholder(s). The directors are usually empowered by the Articles of Association for forfeiture of those shares by serving proper notice (usually fourteen days) to the defaulting shareholder(s). When shares are forfeited, the title of such shareholder(s) is extinguished. However, the amount paid to date is not refunded to him (them).

Accounting Entries

At the time of passing entry for forfeiture of shares, students must be careful about the following matters :

(1) Amount called up in respect of forfeited shares.
(2) Amount already received in respect of those shares.
(3) Amount due but has not been received in respect of those shares.

We know that the shares can be issued at par or at a discount or at a premium. Accounting entry for forfeiture will vary according to situations.

Situation 1 : Forfeiture of Shares which were Issued at Par

In this case, Share Capital Account will be debited with the called-up value of shares forfeited. Allotment or Calls Account will be credited with the amount due but not paid by the shareholder(s). (Alternatively, Calls-in-Arrear Account can be credited for all amount due, if it was transferred to Calls-in- Arrear Account). Forfeited Shares Account will be credited with the amount already received in respect of those shares.

Share Capital Account	Dr.	[No. of shares x Amount called-up]
To Share Allotment Account		[Amount due, but not paid]
To Share First Call Account		[Amount due, but not paid]
To Share Final Call Account		[Amount due, but not paid]
To Forfeited Shares Account		[Amount received]

Where all amounts due on allotment, first call and final call have been transferred to Calls-in-Arrear Account, the entry will be :

Share Capital Account	Dr.	[No. of Shares × Amount called-up]
To Calls-in-Arrear Account		[Total amount due, but not paid]
To Forfeited Shares Account		[Amount received]

Illustrative Example 1

K Limited forfeited 500 equity shares of ₹ 10 each, fully called up, held by Mr A for non-payment of final call money @ ₹ 3 each. However, he paid application money @ ₹ 2 per share, allotment money @ ₹ 3 per share and first call money @ ₹ 2 per share. These shares were originally issued at par.

Give journal entry for the forfeiture. (i) Assume all money due was transferred to Calls-in-Arrear Account; and (ii) Assume that money due has not been transferred to Calls-in-Arrear Account.

In the books of K Limited

(i) Journal Dr. Cr.

Date	Particulars	L.F.	₹	₹
	Equity Share Capital A/c (500 x ₹ 10) Dr.		5,000	
	To Calls-in-Arrear A/c (500 x ₹ 3)			1,500
	To Forfeited Shares A/c (500 x ₹ 7)			3,500
	(Being the forfeiture of 500 equity shares of ₹ 10 each fully called up for non-payment of final call money @ ₹ 3 each as per Board's Resolution No . . . Dated . . .)			

(ii) Journal Dr. Cr.

Date	Particulars	L.F.	₹	₹
	Equity Share Capital A/c (500 x ₹ 10) Dr.		5,000	
	To Equity Shares Final Call A/c (500 x ₹ 3)			1,500
	To Forfeited Share A/c (500 x ₹ 7)			3,500
	(Being the forfeiture of 500 equity shares of ₹ 10 each fully called up for non- payment of final call money @ ₹ 3 each as per Board's Resolution No ... Dtd ...)			

Illustrative Example 2

H. Limited forfeited 300 equity shares of ₹ 10 each, ₹ 8 called up for non-payment of first call money @ ₹ 2 each. Application money @ ₹ 2 per share and allotment money @ ₹ 4 per share have already been received by the Company. Give journal entries for the forfeiture.

In the books of H Limited

Journal Dr. Cr.

Date	Particulars	L.F.	₹	₹
	Equity Share Capital A/c (300 x ₹ 8) Dr.		2,400	
	To Equity Share First Call A/c (300 x ₹ 2)			600
	To Forfeited Shares A/c (300 x ₹ 6)			1,800
	(Being the forfeiture of 300 equity shares of ₹ 10 each, ₹ 8 being called-up for non-payment of first call money @ ₹ 2 each as per Board's Resolution No . . . Dated . . .)			

Tutorial Note: Share Capital Account will be debited with the called up value of forfeited shares only.

Illustration 29

Hero Limited has an authorised capital of ₹ 10,00,000 divided into 1,00,000 equity shares of ₹ 10 each. The company issued 80,000 equity shares. The share money is payable as follows :

on application ₹ 3 per share; on allotment ₹ 3 per share; on final call ₹ 4 per share

The shares are fully subscribed. The Company received all money except final call money on 1,000 shares. The Company decided to forfeit those shares.

Pass necessary journal entries (including cash) in the books of the company.

Solution

In the books of Hero Limited
Journal

Date	Particulars	L.F.	Dr. ₹	Cr. ₹
	Bank A/c Dr. To Equity Share Application A/c (Being application money received on 80,000 equity shares @ ₹ 3 each)		2,40,000	 2,40,000
	Equity Share Application A/c Dr. To Equity Share Capital A/c (Being application money on 80,000 equity shares @ ₹ 3 each transferred to Equity Share Capital Account as per Board's Resolution No . . . Dated . .)		2,40,000	 2,40,000
	Equity Share Allotment A/c Dr. To Equity Share Capital A/c (Being allotment money due on 80,000 equity shares @ ₹ 3 each as per Board's Resolution No . . . Dated . . .)		2,40,000	 2,40,000
	Bank A/c Dr. To Equity Share Allotment A/c (Being allotment money received on 80,000 equity shares @ ₹ 3 each)		2,40,000	 2,40,000
	Equity Share Final Call A/c Dr. To Equity Share Capital A/c (Being final call money due on 80,000 equity shares @ ₹ 4 each as per Board's Resolution No , . . Dated . . .)		3,20,000	 3,20,000
	Bank A/c Dr. To Equity Share Final Call A/c (Being final call money received on 79,000 equity shares @ ₹ 4 each)		3,16,000	 3,16,000
	Equity Share Capital A/c (1,000 x ₹ 10) Dr. To Equity Share Final Call A/c (1,000 x ₹ 4) To Forfeited Shares A/c (1,000 x ₹ 6) (Being the forfeiture of 1,000 equity shares of ₹ 10 each fully called up for non-payment of final call money @ ₹ 4 each as per Board's Resolution No ... Dtd . . .)		10,000	 4,000 6,000
	Total		16,10,000	16,10,000

Illustration 30

X Limited made an issue of 10,000 equity shares of ₹ 10 each payable as follows :

On application	₹ 2 per share
On allotment	₹ 4 per share
On final call	₹ 4 per share

All these shares were subscribed. Money due on all shares were received excepting Ram holding 100 shares failed to pay the final call. These shares were forfeited after giving due notice to the shareholder.

You are required to pass necessary Journal Entries (including cash transactions) in the books of the company and also show the Balance Sheet of the company.

Solution

In the books of X Limited
Journal

Date	Particulars	L.F.	Dr. ₹	Cr. ₹
	Bank A/c Dr. To Equity Share Application A/c (Being application money received for 10,000 equity shares @ ₹ 2 each)		20,000	 20,000
	Equity Share Application A/c Dr. To Equity Share Capital A/c (Being application money on 10,000 equity shares @ ₹ 2 each transferred to Equity Share Capital Account as per Board's Resolution No . . . Dated . . .)		20,000	 20,000

Particulars		Dr. (₹)	Cr. (₹)
Equity Share Allotment A/c Dr. To Equity Share Capital A/c (Being allotment money due on 10,000 equity shares @ ₹ 4 each as per Board's Resolution No . . . Dated . . .)		40,000	40,000
Bank A/c Dr. To Equity Share Allotment A/c (Being allotment money received on 10,000 equity shares @ ₹ 4 each)		40,000	40,000
Equity Share Final Call A/c Dr. To Equity Share Capital A/c (Being final call money due on 10,000 equity shares @ ₹ 4 each as per Board's Resolution No . . . Dated . . .)		40,000	40,000
Bank A/c Dr. Calls-in-Arrear A/c Dr. To Equity Share Final Call A/c (Being final call money received on 9,900 equity shares @ ₹ 4 each. Amount not received on 100 equity shares @ ₹ 4 each has been transferred to Calls-in-Arrear Account)		39,600 400	40,000
Equity Share Capital A/c (100 x ₹ 10) Dr. To Calls-in-Arrear A/c To Forfeited Shares A/c (Being the forfeiture of 100 equity shares of ₹ 10 each fully called up for non-payment of final call money @ ₹ 4 each as per Board's Resolution No . . . Dated . . .)		1,000	400 600
Total		2,01,000	2,01,000

X Limited

Balance Sheet as at .... [Extract] **(Figures in ₹)**

Particulars	Note No.	Figures as at the end of current reporting period
1	2	3
I. EQUITY AND LIABILITIES		
(1) **Shareholders' Funds**		
(a) Share capital	(1)	99,600
(b) Reserves and surplus		
(c) Money received against share warrants		
TOTAL		99,600
II. ASSETS		
(2) **Current Assets**		
(d) Cash and cash equivalents	(2)	99,600
TOTAL		99,600

Notes to Accounts :

(1) Share Capital	₹	₹
Authorised Capital :		
... Equity Shares of ₹ ... each		?
Issued Capital :		
10,000 Equity Shares of ₹ 10 each		1,00,000
Subscribed Capital :		
Subscribed and Fully Paid :		
9,900 Equity Shares of ₹ 10 each	99,000	
Add: Forfeited Shares	600	99,600
(2) Cash at Bank		99,600

Tutorial Note: Till the forfeited shares are re-issued, balance of Forfeited Shares Account will be shown in the Balance Sheet as a part of the paid-up capital.

Illustration 31

The authorised capital of Assam Trading Co. Ltd. was ₹ 10,00,000 divided into equity shares of ₹ 20 each. The company invited application for 10,000 such shares payable as follows :

On application — 35%; On allotment — 40%; On first and final call — 25%.

The company received applications for 12,500 shares. They allotted 10,000 shares and refunded the excess application money. Mr Gupta, holder of 35 shares, failed to pay the allotment money. All the balance monies (including the call money) were duly received. These 35 shares were forfeited. Show the necessary Journal Entries and prepare the opening Balance Sheet of the company.

Solution

In the books of Assam Trading Co. Ltd.

Journal

Date	Particulars	L.F.	Dr. ₹	Cr. ₹
	Bank A/c Dr. To Equity Share Application A/c (Being application money received on 12,500 shares @ ₹ 7 each)		87,500	87,500
	Equity Share Application A/c Dr. To Equity Share Capital A/c (Being application money on 10,000 equity shares @ ₹ 7 each transferred to Equity Share Capital Account as per Board's Resolution No . . . Dated . . .)		70,000	70,000
	Equity Share Application A/c Dr. To Bank A/c (Being excess application money on 2,500 equity shares @ ₹ 7 each refunded as per Board's Resolution No . . . Dated . . .)		17,500	17,500
	Equity Share Allotment A/c Dr. To Equity Share Capital A/c (Being allotment money due on 10,000 equity shares @ ₹ 8 each as per Board's Resolution No . . . Dated . . .)		80,000	80,000
	Bank A/c Dr. Calls-in-Arrear A/c Dr. To Equity Share Allotment A/c (Being allotment money received on 9,965 equity shares @ ₹ 8 each. Amount not received on 35 shares @ ₹ 8 each has been transferred to Calls-in-Arrear Account)		79,720 280	80,000
	Equity Share First and Final Call A/c Dr. To Equity Share Capital A/c (Being first and final call money due on 10,000 equity shares @ ₹ 5 each as per Board's Resolution No . . . Dated . . .)		50,000	50,000
	Bank A/c Dr. Calls-in-Arrear A/c Dr. To Equity Share First and Final Call A/c (Being first and final call money received on 9,965 equity shares @ ₹ 5 each. Amount not received on 35 shares @ ₹ 5 each has been transferred to Calls-in-Arrear Account)		49,825 175	50,000
	Equity Share Capital A/c (35 x ₹ 20) Dr. To Calls-in-Arrear A/c (₹ 280 + ₹ 175) To Forfeited Shares A/c (35 x ₹ 7) (Being the forfeiture of 35 equity shares of ₹ 20 each for non-payment of allotment money @ ₹ 8 each and first and final call money @ ₹ 5 each as per Board's Resolution No . . . Dated . . .)		700	455 245
	Total		4,35,700	4,35,700

Assam Trading Co. Limited

Balance Sheet as at ....[Extract] **(Figures in ₹)**

Particulars	Note No.	Figures as at the end of current reporting period
1	2	3
I. EQUITY AND LIABILITIES		
(1) **Shareholders' Funds**		
(a) Share capital	(1)	1,99,545
(b) Reserves and surplus		
(c) Money received against share warrants		
TOTAL		1,99,545
II. ASSETS		
(2) **Current Assets**		
(d) Cash and cash equivalents	(2)	1,99,545
TOTAL		1,99,545

Notes to Accounts :

(1) Share Capital	₹	₹
Authorised Capital : 50,000 Equity Shares of ₹ 20 each		10,00,000
Issued Capital : 10,000 Equity Shares of ₹ 20 each		2,00,000
Subscribed Capital :		
Subscribed and Fully Paid :		
9,965 Equity Shares of ₹ 20 each	1,99,300	
Add: Forfeited Shares	245	1,99,545
(2) Cash at Bank		1,99,545

Illustration 32

Sugandha Exports Limited invited applications for 10,000 Equity Shares of ₹ 10 each for public subscription. The amount payable on shares is as under :

on application ₹ 1; on allotment ₹ 2; on first call ₹ 3 ; on final call ₹ 4.

All moneys payable on application, allotment and calls have been duly received with the following exceptions :

'A' who holds 100 shares, failed to pay the money on allotment and calls.

'B' to whom 50 shares have been allotted failed to pay the money on first and final calls.

'C' who holds 30 shares, has not paid the amount due on final call.

The shares of A, B and C were forfeited.

Pass the journal entries in the books of Sugandha Exports Limited including bank transactions.

Solution

In the books of Sugandha Exports Limited

Journal

Date	Particulars	L.F.	Dr. ₹	Cr. ₹
	Bank A/c Dr.		10,000	
	To Equity Share Application A/c			10,000
	(Being application money received on 10,000 equity shares @ ₹ 1 each)			
	Equity Share Application A/c Dr.		10,000	
	To Equity Share Capital A/c			10,000
	(Being application money on 10,000 equity shares @ ₹ 1 each transferred to Equity Share Capital Account as per Board's Resolution No . . . Dated . .)			

Particulars		Dr. (₹)	Cr. (₹)
Equity Share Allotment A/c Dr. To Equity Share Capital A/c (Being allotment money due on 10,000 equity shares @ ₹ 2 each as per Board's Resolution No . . . Dated . . .)		20,000	20,000
Bank A/c (Note 1) Dr. To Equity Share Allotment A/c (Being allotment money received on 9,900 equity shares @ ₹ 2 each)		19,800	19,800
Equity Share First Call A/c Dr. To Equity Share Capital A/c (Being first call money due on 10,000 equity shares @ ₹ 3 each as per Board's Resolution No . . . Dated . . .)		30,000	30,000
Bank A/c (Note 2) Dr. To Equity Share First Call A/c (Being first call money received on 9,850 equity shares @ ₹ 3 each)		29,550	29,550
Equity Share Final Call A/c Dr. To Equity Share Capital A/c (Being final call money due on 10,000 equity shares @ ₹ 4 each as per Board's Resolution No . . . Dated . . .)		40,000	40,000
Bank A/c (Note 3) Dr. To Equity Share Final Call A/c (Being final call money received on 9,820 equity shares @ ₹ 4 each)		39,280	39,280
Equity Share Capital A/c (180 x ₹ 10) Dr. To Equity Share Allotment A/c (100 x ₹ 2) To Equity Share First Call A/c (150 x ₹ 3) To Equity Share Final Call A/c (180 x ₹ 4) To Forfeited Shares A/c (Note 4) (Being the forfeiture of 180 equity shares for non-payment of allotment money on 100 shares, first call money on 150 shares and final call money on 180 shares as per Board's Resolution No . . . Dated . . .)		1,800	 200 450 720 430
Total		2,00,430	2,00,430

Working Notes :

(1) A has not paid allotment money on 100 shares. Therefore, allotment money was received on 9,900 shares (10,000 – 100) @ ₹ 2 each, i.e., ₹ 19,800.

(2) First call money has not been paid by A for 100 shares and B for 50 shares. Therefore, first call money was received on 9,850 shares (10,000 – 100 – 50) @ ₹ 3 each, i.e., ₹ 29,550.

(3) Final call money has not been paid by A for 100 shares, B for 50 shares and C for 30 shares. Therefore, final call money was received on 9,820 shares (10,000 – 100 – 50 – 30) @ ₹ 4 each, i.e., ₹ 39,280.

(4) Amount forfeited :

	₹
A [100 × Application money @ ₹ 1 each]	100
B [50 × Application money @ ₹ 1 each plus Allotment money @ ₹ 2 each]	150
C [30 × Application money @ ₹ 1 plus Allotment money @ ₹ 2 each plus First Call money @ ₹ 3 each]	180
	430

Illustration 33

Paliwal Exports Ltd., with a share capital of ₹ 1,00,000 divided into 2,000 shares of ₹ 50 each, offers the shares to the public as under :

₹ 10 per share payable on application; ₹ 10 per share payable on allotment.

₹ 15 per share payable on first call; and ₹ 15 per share payable on second call.

Shareholder 'A' who holds 30 shares, has paid only the application money.

Shareholder 'B' who holds 20 shares, has paid application money on 20 shares and allotment money only on 10 shares.

Shareholder 'C' who holds 28 shares, has paid only the application and allotment money.

Shareholder 'D' who holds 5 shares has paid application, allotment and first call money.

Shareholder 'E' who holds 3 shares, has paid application, allotment and first call money in full and second call money on only 2 shares.

The company forfeits the shares of the above shareholders who have not paid the arrears.

Journalise the transactions including entries relating to bank in the books of Paliwal Exports Ltd.

[CBSE — Adapted]

Solution

In the books of Paliwal Exports Ltd

Journal

Date	Particulars		L.F.	Dr. ₹	Cr. ₹
	Bank A/c	Dr.		20,000	
	To Equity Share Application A/c				20,000
	(Being application money received on 2,000 equity shares @ ₹ 10 each)				
	Equity Share Application A/c	Dr.		20,000	
	To Equity Share Capital A/c				20,000
	(Being application money on 2,000 equity shares @ ₹ 10 each transferred to Equity Share Capital Account as per Board's Resolution No . . . Dated . .)				
	Equity Share Allotment A/c	Dr.		20,000	
	To Equity Share Capital A/c				20,000
	(Being allotment money due on 2,000 equity shares @ ₹ 10 each as per Board's Resolution No . . . Dated . . .)				
	Bank A/c (Note 1)	Dr.		19,600	
	To Equity Share Allotment A/c				19,600
	(Being allotment money received on 1,960 equity shares @ ₹ 10 each)				
	Equity Share First Call A/c	Dr.		30,000	
	To Equity Share Capital A/c				30,000
	(Being first call money due on 2,000 equity shares @ ₹ 15 each as per Board's Resolution No . . . Dated . . .)				
	Bank A/c (Note 2)	Dr.		28,980	
	To Equity Share First Call A/c				28,980
	(Being first call money received on 1,932 equity shares @ ₹ 15 each)				
	Equity Share Second Call A/c	Dr.		30,000	
	To Equity Share Capital A/c				30,000
	(Being second call money due on 2,000 equity shares @ ₹ 15 each as per Board's Resolution No . . . Dated . . .)				
	Bank A/c (Note 3)	Dr.		28,890	
	To Equity Share Second Call A/c				28,890
	(Being the second call money received on 1,926 equity shares @ ₹ 15 each)				
	Equity Share Capital A/c (74 x ₹ 50)	Dr.		3,700	
	To Equity Share Allotment A/c (40 x ₹ 10)				400
	To Equity Share First Call A/c (68 x ₹ 15)				1,020
	To Equity Share Final Call A/c (74 x ₹ 15)				1,110
	To Forfeited Shares A/c (Note 4)				1,170
	(Being the forfeiture of 74 equity shares for non-payment of allotment money on 40 shares, first call money on 68 shares and second call money on 74 shares as per Board's Resolution No . . . Dated . . .)				
	Total			2,01,170	2,01,170

Working Notes :

(1) A has not paid allotment money on 30 shares and B has not paid allotment money on 10 shares. Therefore, allotment money has not been received in total on 40 shares. Allotment money received on 1,960 shares (2,000 – 30 – 10) @ ₹ 10 each, i.e., ₹ 19,600.

(2) First call money has not been paid by A for 30 shares, by B for 10 and by C for 28 shares. Therefore, first call money has not been received in total on 68 shares. First call money received on 1,932 shares (2,000 – 30 – 10 – 28) @ ₹ 15 each, i.e., ₹ 28,980.

(3) Second call money has not been paid by A for 30 shares, by B for 10 shares, by C for 28 shares, by D for 5 shares and by E for 1 share. Therefore, second call money has not been received in total on 74 shares. Second call money received on 1,926 shares (2,000 – 30 – 10 – 28 – 5 – 1) @ ₹ 15 each, i.e., ₹ 28,890.

(4) Amount Forfeited :

	₹
A [30 × ₹ 10]	300
B [10 × ₹ 10]	100
C [(28 × ₹ 10) + (28 × ₹ 10)]	560
D [(5 × ₹ 10) + (5 × ₹ 10) + (5 × ₹ 15)]	175
E [(1 × ₹ 10) + (1 × ₹ 10) + (1 × ₹ 15)]	35
	1,170

Illustration 34

A Ltd has an authorised capital of ₹ 2,00,000 divided into shares of ₹ 10 each. Of these 6,000 shares were issued as fully paid in payment of building purchased from B Ltd. 8,000 shares were subscribed for by the public and during the first year ₹ 5 per share was called up payable as ₹ 2 on application, ₹ 1 on allotment, ₹ 1 on first call and ₹ 1 on second call. The amounts received in respect of these shares were as : on 6,000 shares Full amounts called; on 1,250 shares ₹ 4; on 500 shares ₹ 3; on 250 shares ₹ 2. The directors forfeited the 750 shares, on which less than ₹ 4 per share were paid. Show journal entries to record the above transactions.

Solution

In the books of A Limited

Journal

Date	Particulars	L.F.	Dr. ₹	Cr. ₹
	Buildings A/c Dr. To B Ltd A/c (Being the purchase of building from B Ltd as per agreement dated . . .)		60,000	60,000
	B Ltd A/c Dr. To Equity Share Capital A/c (Being the issue of 6,000 shares of ₹ 10 each against purchase of building as per Board's Resolution No. . . . dated . . .)		60,000	60,000
	Bank A/c Dr. To Equity Share Application A/c (Being application money received on 8,000 shares @ ₹ 2 each)		16,000	16,000
	Equity Share Application A/c Dr. To Equity Share Capital A/c (Being application money on 8,000 shares @ ₹ 2 each transferred to Equity Share Capital Account as per Board's Resolution No. . . . dated . . .)		16,000	16,000
	Equity Share Allotment A/c Dr. To Equity Share Capital A/c (Being allotment money due on 8,000 shares @ ₹ 1 each as per Board's Resolution No. . . . dated . . .)		8,000	8,000

Particulars			Dr. (₹)	Cr. (₹)
Bank A/c (Note 1) To Equity Share Allotment A/c (Being the allotment money received except for 250 shares)	Dr.		7,750	7,750
Equity Share First Call A/c To Equity Share Capital A/c (Being first call money due on 8,000 shares @ ₹ 1 each)	Dr.		8,000	8,000
Bank A/c (Note 2) To Equity Share First Call A/c (Being first call money received except for 750 shares)	Dr.		7,250	7,250
Equity Share Second Call A/c To Equity Share Capital A/c (Being second call money due on 8,000 shares @ ₹ 1 each)	Dr.		8,000	8,000
Bank A/c (Note 3) To Equity Share Second Call A/c (Being second call money received except for 2,000 shares)	Dr.		6,000	6,000
Equity Share Capital A/c (750 x ₹ 5) To Equity Share Allotment A/c (250 x ₹ 1) To Equity Share First Call A/c (750 x ₹ 1) To Equity Share Second Call A/c (750 x ₹ 1) To Forfeited Shares A/c (Note 4) (Being the forfeiture of 750 shares for non-payment of allotment money on 250 shares, first and second call money on 750 shares as per Board's Resolution No. . . . dated . . .)	Dr.		3,750	 250 750 750 2,000
	Total		2,00,750	2,00,750

Working Notes :

(1) Holder of 250 shares paid only application money. He has not paid allotment money and call money. Therefore, allotment money has been received on 7,750 shares (8,000 – 250) @ ₹ 1 each, i.e., ₹ 7,750.

(2) First call money has not been paid by the holder of 250 shares and the holder of 500 shares. In total, first call money has not been received on 750 shares.
Therefore, first call money has been received on 7,250 shares (8,000 – 750) @ ₹ 1, i.e., 7,250.

(3) Second call money has not been paid by the holder of 250 shares, holder of 500 shares and holder of 1,250 shares. In total, second call money has not been received on 2,000 shares. Therefore, second call money has been received on 6,000 shares (8,000 – 2,000) @ ₹ 1.

(4) Amount Forfeited

	₹
(i) For 250 shares, application money @ ₹ 2 per share	500
(ii) For 500 shares, application money @ ₹ 2 per share and allotment money @ ₹ 1 per share	1,500
	2,000

Situation 2 : Forfeiture of Shares which were Issued at a Premium

In this case, Share Capital Account will be debited with the called-up value of shares forfeited. If the premium on such shares has not been paid by the shareholder, the Securities Premium Account will be debited to cancel it (if it was credited earlier). Allotment, Calls and Forfeited Accounts will be credited in the usual manner.

Students should note that if the premium has already been received by the company, it cannot be cancelled even if the shares are forfeited in the future.

Illustrative Example 3

X Ltd forfeited 500 equity shares of ₹ 10 each fully called-up which were issued at a premium of 20%. Amount payable on shares were : on application ₹ 2; on allotment ₹ 5 (including premium) on first and final call ₹ 5. Only application money was paid by the shareholders in respect of these shares. Pass Journal Entries for the forfeiture.

Solution

In the books of X Ltd

Journal

Date	Particulars		L.F.	Dr. ₹	Cr. ₹
	Equity Share Capital A/c (500 x ₹ 10)	Dr.		5,000	
	Securities Premium A/c (See Note)	Dr.		1,000	
	To Equity Share Allotment A/c (500 x ₹ 5)				2,500
	To Equity Share First and Final Call A/c (500 x ₹ 5)				2,500
	To Forfeited Shares A/c (500 x ₹ 2)				1,000
	(Being the forfeiture of 500 equity shares of ₹ 10 each fully called-up, issued at a premium of 20%, for non-payment of allotment and call money as per Board's Resolution No. . . dated . .)				

Tutorial Note : Securities premium @ ₹ 2 on 500 shares has not been received by the company. Therefore, at the time of forfeiture, Securities Premium Account will be debited to cancel it (because Securities Premium Account was credited at the time of allotment).

Illustration 35

B Ltd issued 20,000 equity shares of ₹ 10 each at a premium of ₹ 2 per share payable as follows : on application ₹ 5; on allotment ₹ 5 (including premium); on final call ₹ 2. Applications were received for 24,000 shares. Letters of regret were issued to applicants for 4,000 shares and shares were allotted to all the other applicants. Mr.A, the holder of 150 shares, failed to pay the allotment money. On his subsequent failure to pay the call money, the shares were forfeited.

Show the journal entries and Cash Book in the books of B. Ltd.

Solution

In the books of B Ltd

Dr. Cash Book (Bank column only) Cr.

Date	Particulars	₹	Date	Particulars	₹
	To Equity Share Application A/c (Being application money received on 24,000 shares @ ₹ 5 each)	1,20,000		By Equity Share Application A/c (Being excess money refunded on 4,000 shares @ ₹ 5 each as per Board's Resolution No... dated ...)	20,000
	To Equity Share Allotment A/c (Being allotment money received on 19,850 shares @ ₹ 5 each)	99,250		By Balance c/d	2,38,950
	To Equity Share Final Call A/c (Being final call money received on 19,850 shares @ ₹ 2 each)	39,700			
		2,58,950			2,58,950

Journal

Date	Particulars		L.F.	Dr. ₹	Cr. ₹
	Equity Share Application A/c	Dr.		1,00,000	
	To Equity Share Capital A/c				1,00,000
	(Being application money on 20,000 shares @ ₹ 5 each transferred to Equity Share Capital Account as per Board's Resolution No. ... dated ...)				

Date	Particulars	L.F.	Dr. ₹	Cr. ₹
	Equity Share Allotment A/c Dr. To Equity Share Capital A/c To Securities Premium A/c (Being allotment money due on 20,000 shares @ ₹ 5 each including premium as per Board's Resolution No. ... dated ...)		1,00,000	 60,000 40,000
	Equity Share Final Call A/c Dr. To Equity Share Capital A/c (Being final call money due on 20,000 shares @ ₹ 2 each as per Board's Resolution No. ... dated ...)		40,000	 40,000
	Equity Share Capital A/c (150 x ₹ 10) Dr. Securities Premium A/c (150 x ₹ 2) Dr. To Equity Share Allotment A/c To Equity Share Final Call A/c To Forfeited Shares A/c (Being forfeiture of 150 shares for non-payment of allotment money and final call money as per Board's Resolution No. ... dated ...)		1,500 300	 750 300 750
	Total		2,41,800	21,41,800

Illustration 36

Hind Limited issued 20,000 equity shares of ₹ 10 each at a premium of ₹ 2 per share. Amount payable on shares were :

	₹
On application	5 per share
On allotment	5 per share (including premium)
On final call	2 per share

Applications were received for 24,000 shares. Excess application money on 4,000 shares were refunded. Mr A holder of 100 shares failed to pay the allotment money. On his subsequent failure to pay the call money, his shares were forfeited. All other monies were received in time.

You are required to pass necessary Journal Entries in the books of the company.

Solution

In the books of Hind Limited

Journal

Date	Particulars	L.F.	Dr. ₹	Cr. ₹
	Bank A/c Dr. To Equity Share Application A/c (Being the application money received on 24,000 equity shares @ 5 each)		1,20,000	 1,20,000
	Equity Share Application A/c Dr. To Bank A/c (Being the excess application money on 4,000 equity shares @ ₹ 5 each refunded as per Board's Resolution No . . . Dated . . .)		20,000	 20,000
	Equity Share Application A/c Dr. To Equity Share Capital A/c (Being application money on 20,000 equity shares @ ₹ 5 each transferred to Equity Share Capital Account as per Board's Resolution No . . . Dated . . .)		1,00,000	 1,00,000
	Equity Share Allotment A/c Dr. To Equity Share Capital A/c To Securities Premium A/c (Being allotment money due on 20,000 equity shares @ ₹ 5 each including premium of ₹ 2 per share as per Board's Resolution No . . . Dated . . .)		1,00,000	 60,000 40,000

	Particulars		Dr. (₹)	Cr. (₹)
	Bank A/c Dr. Calls-in-Arrear A/c Dr. To Equity Share Allotment A/c (Being allotment money received on 19,900 equity shares @ ₹ 5 each. Amount not received on 100 equity shares @ ₹ 5 each has been transferred to Calls-in-Arrear Account)		99,500 500	 1,00,000
	Equity Share Final Call A/c Dr. To Equity Share Capital A/c (Being final call money due on 20,000 equity shares @ ₹ 2 each as per Board's Resolution No . . . Dated . . .)		40,000	 40,000
	Bank A/c Dr. Calls-in-Arrear A/c Dr. To Equity Share Final Call A/c (Being final call money received on 19,900 equity shares @ ₹ 2 each. Amount not received on 100 equity shares @ ₹ 2 each transferred to Calls-in-Arrear Account)		39,800 200	 40,000
	Equity Share Capital A/c (100 x ₹ 10) Dr. Securities Premium A/c (100 x ₹ 2) Dr. To Calls-in-Arrear A/c (₹ 500 + ₹ 200) To Forfeited Shares A/c (100 x ₹ 5) (Being the forfeiture of 100 equity shares of ₹ 10 each fully called-up for non-payment of allotment money and call money @ ₹ 5 each and ₹ 2 each respectively as per Board's Resolution No . . . Dated . . .)		1,000 200	 700 500
	Total		5,21,200	5,21,200

Forfeiture of Fully Paid-up Shares

Forfeiture for non-payment of calls, premium, or the unpaid portion of the face value of the shares is one of the many causes for which a share may be forfeited. But fully paid-up shares may be forfeited for realisation of debts of the shareholder if the Articles specifically provide it. ***[Sri Gopal Jalan & Co. vs. Calcutta Stock Exchange Association Ltd; Naresh Chandra Sanyal vs. Calcutta Stock Exchange Association Ltd]***

Re-issue of Forfeited Shares

A forfeited share is merely a share available to the company for sale and remains vested in the company for that purpose only. Re-issue of forfeited shares is not allotment of shares but only a sale. When shares are re-issued, return of the forfeited shares need not be filed under Section 75(1) of the Companies Act, 1956.

The share, after forfeiture, in the hands of the company is subject to an obligation to dispose it of. In practice, forfeited shares are disposed of by auction. These shares can be re-issued at any price so long as the total amount received (from the original allottee and the second purchaser) for those shares is not less than the amount in arrear on those shares.

Accounting Entries

(a) Bank Account Dr. [Actual amount received]
Forfeited Shares Account Dr. [Loss on re-issue]
To Share Capital Account
(Being the re-issue of . . . shares @ ₹ . . . each as per Board's Resolution No. . . . Dated . . .)

(b) Forfeited Shares Account Dr.
To Capital Reserve Account
(Being the profit on re-issue transferred to capital reserve)

In connection with re-issue, the following points are important :

1. *Loss on re-issue should not exceed the forfeited amount.*
2. *If the loss on re-issue is less than the amount forfeited, the surplus should be transferred to Capital Reserve.*
3. *The forfeited amount on shares not yet reissued should be shown in the Balance Sheet as an addition to the share capital.*
4. *When only a portion of the forfeited shares are re-issued, then the profit made on reissue of such shares must be transferred to Capital Reserve.*
5. *When the shares are re-issued at a loss, such loss is to be debited to "Forfeited Shares Account".*
6. *If the shares are re-issued at a price which is more than the face value of the shares, the excess amount will be credited to Securities Premium Reserve Account.*
7. *If the re-issued amount and forfeited amount (taken together) exceeds the face value of the shares re-issued, it is not necessary to transfer such amount to Securities Premium Reserve Account.*

Re-Issue of Forfeited Shares Originally Issued at Par

Illustration 37

A limited company forfeited 100 Equity Shares of the face value of ₹ 10 each, ₹ 6 per share called up, for non payment of first call of ₹ 2 per share. The forfeited shares were subsequently re-issued as fully paid @ ₹ 7 each.

Give entries in company's journal. *[CBSE — Adapted]*

Solution

In the books of the Company
Journal

Date	Particulars	L.F.	Dr. ₹	Cr. ₹
	Equity Share Capital A/c (100 x ₹ 6) Dr.		600	
	To Equity Share First Call A/c (100 x ₹ 2)			200
	To Forfeited Shares A/c			400
	(Being the forfeiture of 100 equity shares of ₹ 10 each, ₹ 6 per share called-up for non-payment of first call of ₹ 2 per share as per Board's Resolution No... dtd ...)			
	Bank A/c (100 x ₹ 7) Dr.		700	
	Forfeited Shares A/c Dr.		300	
	To Equity Share Capital A/c			1,000
	(Being the re-issue of 100 equity shares of ₹ 10 each as fully paid up at ₹ 7 per share as per Board's Resolution No. . . . dated . . .)			
	Forfeited Shares A/c (Note 1) Dr.		100	
	To Capital Reserve A/c			100
	(Being the profit on re-issue transferred to capital reserve)			
	Total		1,700	1,700

Working Note :

(1) Calculation of Amount Transferred to Capital Reserve

	₹
Amount forfeited (100 × ₹ 4)	400
Less : Loss on re-issue [(₹ 10 – 7) × 100]	300
	100

Illustration 38

Alok Ltd forfeited 300 Equity Shares of ₹ 10 each, fully called up, held by Ram for non-payment of allotment money of ₹ 3 per share and final call money of ₹ 4 per share. Out of these shares, 250 were re-issued to Shyam for a total payment of ₹ 2,000.

Give journal entries for forfeiture and re-issue. *[CBSE — Adapted]*

Solution

In the books of Alok Ltd
Journal

Date	Particulars		L.F.	Dr. ₹	Cr. ₹
	Equity Share Capital A/c (300 x ₹ 10)	Dr.		3,000	
	To Equity Share Allotment A/c (300 x ₹ 3)				900
	To Equity Share Final Call A/c (300 x ₹ 4)				1,200
	To Forfeited Shares A/c				900
	(Being the forfeiture of 300 equity shares of ₹ 10 each,fully called up, for non-payment of allotment and final call money @ ₹ 3 and ₹ 4 respectively, as per Board's Resolution No. . . . dated . . .)				
	Bank A/c	Dr.		2,000	
	Forfeited Shares A/c	Dr.		500	
	To Equity Share Capital A/c				2,500
	(Being the re-issue of 250 equity shares of ₹ 8 each as fully paid up as per Board's Resolution No. . . . dated . . .)				
	Forfeited Shares A/c (Note 1)	Dr.		250	
	To Capital Reserve A/c				250
	(Being the profit on re-issue transferred to capital reserve)				
	Total			5,750	5,750

Working Note :

(1) Calculation of Amount Transferred to Capital Reserve

	₹
Amount forfeited (250 × ₹ 3*)	750
Less : Loss on re-issue (250 × ₹ 2**)	500
	250

* Face value of share is ₹ 10. Amount payable on allotment ₹ 3 and on final call ₹ 4. Therefore, ₹ 3 was paid with application.

** Amount received on re-issue ₹ 2,000 for 250 shares. Amount received per share = ₹ 8 (₹ 2,000 / 250).

Loss on re-issue per share = (₹ 10 – ₹ 8) = ₹ 2.

Illustration 39

A company forfeited 100 Equity Shares of ₹ 100 each issued at a premium of 50% (to be paid at the time of allotment) on which first call money of ₹ 30 per share was not received; final call of ₹ 20 is yet to be made. These shares were subsequently re- issued at ₹ 70 per share as ₹ 80 paid up.

Give necessary journal entries regarding forfeiture and re-issue of shares.

[CBSE — Adapted]

Solution

In the books of the Company

Journal

Date	Particulars		L.F.	Dr. ₹	Cr. ₹
	Equity Share Capital A/c (100 x ₹ 80)	Dr.		8,000	
	To Equity Share First Call A/c (100 x ₹ 30)				3,000
	To Forfeited Shares A/c				5,000
	(Being the forfeiture of 100 equity shares of ₹ 100 each, ₹ 80 per share called-up for non-payment of first call money of ₹ 30 per share as per Board's Resolution No. . . . dated . .)				
	Bank A/c (100 x ₹ 70)	Dr.		7,000	
	Forfeited Shares A/c (100 x ₹ 10)	Dr.		1,000	
	To Equity Share Capital A/c				8,000
	(Being the re-issue of 100 equity shares of ₹ 70 per share as ₹ 80 paid-up as per Board's Resolution No. . . . dated . . .)				
	Forfeited Shares A/c	Dr.		4,000	
	To Capital Reserve A/c				4,000
	(Being the profit on re-issue transferred to capital reserve)				
		Total		20,000	20,000

Working Note :

(1) Calculation of Amount Transferred to Capital Reserve

	₹
Amount forfeited (100 × ₹ 50)	5,000
Less : Loss on re-issue (100 × ₹ 10)	1,000
	4,000

Illustration 40

Indian Express Ltd. has forfeited the following shares of ₹ 100 for non-payment of allotment and call money.

(a) 100 shares held by X who has paid only the application money @ ₹ 10 each.

(b) 200 shares held by Y who has paid only the application and allotment money @ ₹ 10 and ₹ 20 each respectively.

(c) 300 shares held by Z who has paid only the application, allotment and the first call money @ ₹ 10, ₹ 20 and ₹ 30 respectively.

Shares have been fully called up. All the shares are forfeited and are re-issued at 10% discount. Give Journal Entries.

Solution

In the books of the Indian Express Ltd.

Journal

Date	Particulars		L.F.	Dr. ₹	Cr. ₹
	Share Capital A/c [600 x ₹ 100]	Dr.		60,000	
	To Share Allotment A/c [100 x 20]				2,000
	To Share First Call A/c [300 x 30]				9,000
	To Share Final Call A/c [600 x 40]				24,000
	To Forfeited Shares A/c (Note 2)				25,000
	(Being the forfeiture of 600 shares for non-payment of allotment money on 100 shares, first call money on 300 shares and final call money on 600 shares as per Board's Resolution No. ... dated ...)				

Particulars		L.F.	Dr.	Cr.
Alternatively,				
Share Capital A/c	Dr.		60,000	
To Calls-in-Arrear A/c (Note 1)				35,000
To Forfeited Shares A/c (Note 2)				25,000
(Being the forfeiture of 600 shares of ₹ 10 each for non-payment of allotment money on 100 shares, first call money on 300 shares and final call money on 600 shares as per Board's Resolution No. ... dated ...)				
Bank A/c [600 x ₹ 90]	Dr.		54,000	
Forfeited Shares A/c	Dr.		6,000	
To Share Capital A/c				60,000
(Being the re-issue of 600 shares @ ₹ 90 each as per Board's Resolution No. ... dtd ...)				
Forfeitured Shares A/c	Dr.		19,000	
To Capital Reserve A/c				19,000
(Being the profit on forfeiture transferred to Capital Reserve)				
	Total		1,99,000	1,99,000

Working Notes :

(1) Calculation of Calls-in-Arrear

X has paid only application money @ ₹ 10 each. He has not paid allotment, first call and final call monies @ ₹ 20, 30 and 40 respectively.

Y has paid only application and allotment money but has not paid first call and final call monies.

Z has not paid only final call money. Therefore, total calls-in-arrear :

	₹
X : 100 × [20 + 30 + 40]	9,000
Y : 200 × [30 + 40]	14,000
Z : 300 × 40	12,000
Total	35,000

(2) Amount Forfeited

X : 100 × 10	1,000
Y : 200 × [10 + 20]	6,000
Z : 300 × [10 + 20 + 30]	18,000
Total	25,000

(3) Amount transferred to Capital Reserve

Amount forfeited	25,000
Less: Loss on re-issue	6,000
Total	19,000

Illustration 41

Sony Ltd. issued 10,000 equity shares of ₹ 100 each, payable at ₹ 30 on application, ₹ 50 on allotment and ₹ 20 on first and final call.

The shares were fully subscribed, called up and paid up except the following :

(a) Rajeev holding 500 shares failed to pay allotment and call money; and

(b) Sanjeev holding 800 shares failed to pay the call money.

All these shares were forfeited and subsequently re-issued as fully paid at a discount of ₹ 20 per share. Expenses on re-issue was ₹ 500.

Give Journal Entries in the books of the Company.

Solution

In the books of Sony Ltd.

Journal

Date	Particulars	L.F.	Dr. ₹	Cr. ₹
	Bank A/c Dr. To Equity Share Application A/c (Being application money received on 10,000 equity shares @ ₹ 30 each)		3,00,000	3,00,000
	Equity Share Application A/c Dr. To Equity Share Capital A/c (Being the application money on 10,000 equity shares @ ₹ 30 each transferred to Equity Share Capital Account as per Board's Resolution No. ... dated ...)		3,00,000	3,00,000
	Equity Share Allotment A/c Dr. To Equity Share Capital A/c (Being allotment money due on 10,000 equity shares @ ₹ 50 each as per Board's Resolution No. ... dated ...)		5,00,000	5,00,000
	Bank A/c [9,500 × 50] Dr. Calls-in-Arrear A/c Dr. To Equity Share Allotment A/c (Being the allotment money received on 9,500 equity shares @ ₹ 50 each. Allotment money not paid on 500 equity shares has been transferred to Calls-in-Arrear Account)		4,75,000 25,000	5,00,000
	Equity Shares First and Final Call A/c Dr. To Equity Shares Capital A/c (Being the first and final call money due on 10,000 equity shares @ ₹ 20 each as per Board's Resolution No. ... dated ...)		2,00,000	2,00,000
	Bank A/c [8,700 × 20] Dr. Calls-in-Arrear A/c [1,300 x 20] Dr. To Equity Share First and Final Call A/c (Being first and final call money received on 8,700 shares @ ₹ 20 each)		1,74,000 26,000	2,00,000
	Equity Share Capital A/c [1,300 x ₹ 100] Dr. To Calls-in-Arrear A/c To Forfeited Shares A/c (Note 1) (Being the forfeiture of 1,300 shares for non-payment of allotment money on 500 shares and first and final call monies on 1,300 shares as per Board's Resolution No. ... dated ...)		1,30,000	51,000 79,000
	Bank A/c [1,300 x ₹ 80] Dr. Forfeited Shares A/c [1,300 x ₹ 20] Dr. To Equity Share Capital A/c (Being the re-issue of 1,300 shares @ ₹ 80 each as per Board's Resolution No. ... dated...)		1,04,000 26,000	1,30,000
	Expenses on Re-issue A/c Dr. To Bank A/c (Being the expenses on re-issue paid)		500	500
	Forfeited Shares A/c Dr. To Expenses on Re-issue A/c To Capital Reserve A/c (Being profit on re-issue transferred to Capital Reserve)		53,000	500 52,500

Working Notes :

(1) Calculation of Amount Forfeited :

	₹
Rajeev paid : [500 × ₹ 30]	15,000
Sanjeev paid : [800 × (30 + 50)]	64,000
	79,000

(2) Amount transferred to Capital Reserve

Amount forfeited		79,000
Less: Loss on re-issue (₹ 20 × 1,300)	26,000	
Less: Expenses on re-issue	500	26,500
		52,500

Illustration 42

Famous Company Ltd. issued 6,000 equity shares of ₹ 10 each at a premium of ₹ 2 per share payable as follows :

On application ₹ 3 per share;
On allotment ₹ 5 per share including premium
On first and final call ₹ 4 per share

Subscriptions were received for 10,000 shares. The excess money was refunded and the allotment money was received in full. In due course, the first and final call was made and the amount due was received with the exception of 200 shares.

These 200 shares were forfeited and 50 of the forfeited shares were subsequently re-issued as fully paid for a consideration of ₹ 6 per share.

Prepare the Cash Book and pass necessary Journal Entries in the books of the company recording the above tramnsactions.

Also show the Equity Share Capital Account.

Solution

In the books of Famous Company Ltd.
Cash Book (Bank column only)

Dr. Cr.

Date	Particulars	₹	Date	Particulars	₹
	To Equity Share Application A/c (Being application money received on 10,000 shares @ ₹ 3 each)	30,000		By Equity Share Application A/c (Being excess application money refunded on 4,000 shares @ ₹ 3 each as per Board's Resolution No... dated ...)	12,000
	To Equity Share Allotment A/c (Being allotment money received on 6,000 shares @ ₹ 5 each)	30,000		By Balance c/d	71,500
	To Equity Share First and Final Call A/c (Being first and final call money received on 5,800 shares @ ₹ 4 each)	23,200			
	To Equity Share Capital A/c (Being re-issue of 50 shares @ ₹ 6 each)	300			
		83,500			83,500

Solution

In the books of Famous Company Ltd
Journal

Date	Particulars		L.F.	Dr. ₹	Cr. ₹
	Equity Share Application A/c	Dr.		18,000	
	To Equity Share Capital A/c				18,000
	(Being application money on 6,000 shares @ ₹ 3 each transferred to Equity Share Capital Account as per Board's Resolution No. ... dated ...)				
	Equity Share Allotment A/c	Dr.		30,000	
	To Equity Share Capital A/c				18,000
	To Securities Premium A/c				12,000
	(Being allotment money due on 6,000 shares @ ₹ 5 including premium of ₹ 2 per share as per Board's Resolution No. ... dated ...)				

Particulars		Dr. (₹)	Cr. (₹)
Equity Share First and Final Call A/c Dr. To Equity Share Capital A/c (Being first and final call money due on 6,000 shares @ ₹ 4 per share as per Board's Resolution No. ... dated ...)		24,000	24,000
Calls-in-Arrear A/c Dr. To Equity Share First and Final Call A/c (Being the amount not paid on 200 shares @ ₹ 4 each, transferred to Calls-in-Arrear Account)		800	800
Equity Share Capital A/c Dr. To Calls-in-Arrear A/c To Forfeited Shares A/c (Note 1) (Being the forfeiture of 200 equity shares of ₹ 10 each for non-payment of first and final call money @ ₹ 4 per share, as per Board's Resolution No. ... dated ...)		2,000	800 1,200
Forfeited Shares A/c Dr. To Equity Share Capital A/c (Being the re-issue of 50 shares at a discount of ₹ 4 per share, as per Board's Resolution No. ... dated ...)		200	200
Forfeited Shares A/c Dr. To Capital Reserve A/c (Being the profit on re-issue of 50 shares transferred to Capital Reserve)		100	100

Dr. Equity Share Capital Account Cr.

Particulars	₹	Particulars	₹
To Calls-in-Arrear A/c	800	By Equity Share Application A/c	18,000
To Forfeited Shares A/c	1,200	By Equity Share Allotment A/c	18,000
To Balance c/d	58,500	By Equity Share First and Final Call A/c	24,000
		By Bank A/c	300
		By Forfeited Shares A/c	200
	60,500		60,500

Tutorial Notes :

(1) Profit on re-issue of 50 shares (50 × ₹ 2) ₹ 100 is to be transferred to Capital Reserve.

(2) The balance of forfeited amount ₹ 900 (1,200 – 200 – 100) will be shown in the Balance Sheet as a part of the paid-up capital.

Working Notes :

(1) Calculation of Amount Forfeited

200 × [₹ 3 on application + ₹ 3 on allotment excluding premium] = ₹ 1,200

(2) Amount transferred to Capital Reserve = 50 × [₹ 6 – ₹ 4] = ₹ 100.

Illustration 43

C Ltd invited applications for 20,000 Equity Shares of ₹ 10 each payable as under :

on application ₹ 2; on allotment ₹ 2; on first call ₹ 3; on final call ₹ 3.

The entire issue was subscribed for and paid with the following exceptions :

(i) P, who was allotted 200 shares, failed to pay the money due on allotment and calls.

(ii) Q, who held 150 shares, did not pay the first call and final call.

(iii) R, who held 50 shares, did not pay the amount on final call.

The Board of Directors passed a resolution forfeiting all the shares of P, Q and R. These shares were subsequently re-issued as fully paid at a discount of 20%.

Give journal entries to record transactions in the books of C Ltd. *[CBSE — Adapted]*

Solution

In the books of the C Ltd
Journal

Date	Particulars	L.F.	Dr. ₹	Cr. ₹
	Bank A/c Dr. To Equity Share Application A/c (Being application money received on 20,000 shares @ ₹ 2 each)		40,000	40,000
	Equity Share Application A/c Dr. To Equity Share Capital A/c (Being the application money on 20,000 equity shares @ ₹ 2 each transferred to Equity Share Capital Account as per Board's Resolution No. . . . dated . . .)		40,000	40,000
	Equity Share Allotment A/c Dr. To Equity Share Capital A/c (Being allotment money due on 20,000 equity shares @ ₹ 2 each as per Board's Resolution No. . . . dated . . .)		40,000	40,000
	Bank A/c Dr. To Equity Share Allotment A/c (Being the allotment money received on 19,800 shares @ ₹ 2 each)		39,600	39,600
	Equity Share First Call A/c Dr. To Equity Share Capital A/c (Being first call money due on 20,000 shares @ ₹ 3 each as per Board's Resolution No. . . . dated . . .)		60,000	60,000
	Bank A/c (Note 1) Dr. To Equity Share First Call A/c (Being the first call money received on 19,650 shares @ ₹ 3 each)		58,950	58,950
	Equity Share Final Call A/c Dr. To Equity Share Capital A/c (Being final call money due on 20,000 shares @ ₹ 3 each as per Board's Resolution No. . . . dated . . .)		60,000	60,000
	Bank A/c (Note 2) Dr. To Equity Share Final Call A/c (Being the final call money received on 19,400 shares @ ₹ 3 each)		58,800	58,800
	Equity Share Capital A/c (400 x ₹ 10) Dr. To Equity Share Allotment A/c (200 x ₹ 2) To Equity Share First Call A/c (350 x ₹ 3) To Equity Share final Call A/c (400 x ₹ 3) To Forfeited Shares A/c (Being the forfeiture of 400 shares for non-payment of allotment money on 200 shares, first call money on 150 shares and final call money on 50 shares as per Board's Resolution No. . . . dated . . .)		4,000	 400 1,050 1,200 1,350
	Bank A/c (400 x ₹ 8) Dr. Forfeited Shares A/c (400 x ₹ 2) Dr. To Equity Share Capital A/c (Being the re-issue of 400 shares of ₹ 10 each as fully paid at a discount of 20% as per Board's Resolution No. . . . dated . . .)		3,200 800	 4,000
	Forfeited Shares A/c (Note 4) Dr. To Capital Reserve A/c (Being the profit on re-issue transferred to Capital Reserve)		550	550
	Total		4,05,900	4,05,900

Working Notes :

(1) P has not paid allotment money on 200 shares. It means he has not paid first call money as well as final call money on those shares. Q has not paid first call money on 150 shares. He

has also not paid final call money on those shares. Therefore, first call money has not been received on 200 shares of P + 150 shares of Q, i.e., on 350 shares.
First call money received on (20,000 – 350) = 19,650 shares @ ₹ 3 each, i.e., ₹ 58,950.

(2) R has not paid final call money on 50 shares. In addition to R, P and Q has not paid final call money on 200 shares and 150 shares respectively. Therefore, final call money has not been received on 200 shares of P + 150 shares of Q + 50 shares of R, i.e., on 400 shares. Final call money received on (20,000 – 400) = 19,600 shares @ ₹ 3 each, i.e., ₹ 58,800.

(3) Amount Forfeited

	₹
P [200 × ₹ 2]	400
Q [150 (₹ 2 + ₹ 2)]	600
R [50 (₹ 2 + ₹ 2 + ₹ 3)]	350
	1,350

(4) Amount forfeited ₹ 1,350. Loss on re-issue ₹ 800. Amount transferred to Capital Reserve Account = (₹ 1,350 – ₹ 800) = ₹ 550.

Illustration 44

Record the journal entries for forfeiture and reissue of shares in the following cases :

(a) X Ltd. forfeited 20 shares of ₹ 10 each, ₹ 7 called up on which the shareholder had paid application and allotment money of ₹ 5 per share. Out of these, 15 shares were re-issued to Naresh as ₹ 7 per share paid up for ₹ 8 per share.

(b) Y Ltd. forfeited 90 shares of ₹ 10 each, ₹ 8 called up issued at a premium of ₹ 2 per share to 'R' for non-payment of allotment money of ₹ 5 per share (including premium). Out of those, 80 shares were re-issued to Sanjay as ₹ 8 called up for ₹ 10 per share.

[CBSE (Delhi) — 2013]

Solution

(a)

In the books of X Ltd

Journal

Date	Particulars		L.F.	Dr. ₹	Cr. ₹
	Share Capital A/c (20 x ₹ 7)	Dr.		140	
	To Calls-in-Arrear A/c (20 x ₹ 2)				40
	To Forfeited Shares A/c (20 x ₹ 5)				100
	(Being the forfeiture of 20 shares of ₹ 10, for non-payment of call money @ ₹ 2 per share, ₹ 7 called-up per share as per Board's Resolution No. ... dated ...)				
	Bank A/c (15 x ₹ 8)	Dr.		120	
	To Share Capital A/c (15 x ₹ 7)				105
	To Securities Premium A/c)15 x ₹ 1)				15
	(Being the re-issue of 15 shares @ ₹ 8, ₹ 7 per share paid-up as per Board's Resolution No. ... dated ...)				
	Forfeited Shares A/c (15 x 5)	Dr.		75	
	To Capital Reserve A/c				75
	(Being the transfer of profit on re-issue to Capital Reserve)				

Tutorial Note : Amount forfeited per share = 100/20 = ₹ 5. Number of shares re-issued = 15. Therefore, amount to be transferred to Capital Reserve = ₹ 5 × 15 = ₹ 75.

Re-issue of Forfeited Shares Originally Issue at a Premium

Illustration 45

The Direcotrs of a company forfeited 600 equity shares of ₹ 10 each issued at a premium of ₹ 3 per share, for the non-payment of the first call money of ₹ 3 per share. The final call of ₹ 2 per share has not been made. Half of the forfeited shares were reissued at ₹ 3,000 fully paid.

Record the journal entries for the forfeiture and reissue of shares. *[CBSE (Outside Delhi) — 2009]*

Solution

Amount called up = ₹ 8 per share.
Number of shares to be forfeited = 600,
Money due on 1st call = ₹ 3 per share.
Money paid on application and allotment = ₹ 5.
Premium paid per share = ₹ 3.

Journal

Date	Particulars	L.F.	Dr. ₹	Cr. ₹
	Equity Share Capital A/c (600 x ₹ 8) Dr.		4,800	
	To Equity Share First Call A/c (600 x ₹ 3)			1,800
	To Forfeited Shares A/c (600 x ₹ 5)			3,000
	(Being the forfeiture of 600 equity shares for non-payment of first call money @ ₹ 3 per share as per Board's Resolution No. . . . dated . . .)			
	Bank A/c (300 x ₹ 10)		3,000	
	To Equity Share Capital A/c			3,000
	(Being the re-issue of 300 equity shares for ₹ 3,000 as per Board's Resolution No. . . . dated . . .)			
	Forfeited Shares A/c (Note 3) Dr.		1,500	
	To Capital Reserve A/c			1,500
	(Being the profit on re-issue of 300 shares transferred to Capital Reserve)			

Tutorial Note : Premium has already been received, so it should be retained in the Securities Premium Account. At the time of forfeiture of shares, it should not be cancelled.

Illustration 46

National Heavy Chemicals Ltd issued 5,000 shares of ₹ 10 each at a premium at ₹ 2 per share for public subscriptions payable as ₹ 5 on application and ₹ 7 on allotment (including premium). Rajesh, who was allotted 200 shares by the company, failed to pay the allotment amount and his shares were forfeited by the company. 100 out of these forfeited shares were allotted to Brijesh as fully paid up for ₹ 8 per share.

Record these transactions relating to forfeiture and re-issue of shares.

[CBSE — Adapted]

Solution

In the books of National Heavy Chemicals Ltd

Journal

Date	Particulars	L.F.	Dr. ₹	Cr. ₹
	Equity Share Capital A/c (200 x ₹ 10) Dr.		2,000	
	Equity Securities Premium A/c (200 x ₹ 2) Dr.		400	
	To Equity Share Allotment A/c (200 x ₹ 7)			1,400
	To Forfeited Shares A/c (200 x ₹ 5)			1,000
	(Being the forfeiture of 200 equity shares of ₹ 10 each for non-payment of allotment money @ ₹ 7 each including premium of ₹ 2 per share as per Board's Resolution No. . . . dated . . .)			

Particulars		L.F.	Dr. ₹	Cr. ₹
Bank A/c (100 x ₹ 8) Dr. Forfeited Shares A/c Dr. To Equity Share Capital A/c (Being the re-issue of 100 equity shares of ₹ 10 each, at ₹ 8 per share as fully paid-up as per Board's Resolution No. . . . dated . . .)			800 200	 1,000
Forfeited Shares A/c (Note 2) Dr. To Capital Reserve A/c (Being the profit on re-issue transferred to capital reserve)			300	 300
Total			3,700	3,700

Working Notes :

(1) When the shares are issued at a premium and the premium on such shares has not been paid by the shareholder, the Securities Premium Account will be debited to cancel it.

(2) Calculation of Amount Transferred to Capital Reserve

	₹
Amount forfeited on re-issued shares (100 × ₹ 5)	500
Less : Loss on re-issue (100 × ₹ 2)	200
	300

Illustration 47

Kailash Ltd was formed for the purpose of purchasing Ramesh Ltd. with a nominal capital of ₹ 20,00,000 divided into 20,000 shares of ₹ 100 each. 10,000 shares were issued to the vendors against their assets. The balance 10,000 shares were offered to public at a premium of ₹ 5 per share. Amounts payable were :

Application ₹ 10; Allotment (including premium) ₹ 25; First call ₹ 40; Final call ₹ 30.

Applications were received for 9,000 shares. All money was received except first call money on 1,000 shares. These shares were forfeited. These shares were re-issued at ₹ 60 per share — ₹ 70 paid-up. Final call was not made.

Give journal entries to record the above transactions. *[CBSE — Adapted]*

Solution

In the books of Kailash Ltd

Journal

Date	Particulars	L.F.	Dr. ₹	Cr. ₹
	Sundry Assets A/c Dr. To Ramesh Ltd A/c (Being sundry assets purchased from Ramesh Ltd as per agreement dated . . .)		10,00,000	 10,00,000
	Ramesh Ltd A/c Dr. To Equity Share Capital A/c (Note 3) (Being the issue of 10,000 shares of ₹ 10 each against purchase of sundry assets as per Board's Resolution No. . . . dated . . .)		10,00,000	 10,00,000
	Bank A/c Dr. To Equity Share Application A/c (Being application money received on 9,000 shares @ ₹ 10 each)		90,000	 90,000
	Equity Share Application A/c Dr. To Equity Share Capital A/c (Being the application money on 9,000 equity shares @ ₹ 10 each transferred to Equity Share Capital Account as per Board's Resolution No. . . . dated . . .)		90,000	 90,000
	Equity Share Allotment A/c Dr. To Equity Share Capital A/c To Equity Securities Premium A/c (Being allotment money due on 9,000 equity shares @ ₹ 25 each including a premium @ ₹ 5 per share, as per Board's Resolution No. . . . dated . . .)		2,25,000	 1,80,000 45,000

Particulars		Dr.	Cr.
Bank A/c Dr. To Equity Share Allotment A/c (Being the allotment money received on 9,000 shares @ ₹ 25 each)		2,25,000	2,25,000
Equity Share First Call A/c Dr. To Equity Share Capital A/c (Being first call money due on 9,000 shares @ ₹ 40 each as per Board's Resolution No. . . . dated . . .)		3,60,000	3,60,000
Bank A/c Dr. To Equity Share First Call A/c (Being the first call money received on 8,000 shares @ ₹ 40 each)		3,20,000	3,20,000
Equity Share Capital A/c (1,000 x ₹ 70) Dr. To Equity Share First Call A/c (1,000 x ₹ 40) To Forfeited Shares A/c (1,000 x ₹ 30) (Being the forfeiture of 1,000 shares for non-payment of first call money @ ₹ 40 each, as per Board's Resolution No. . . . dated . . .)		70,000	40,000 30,000
Bank A/c (1,000 x ₹ 60) Dr. Forfeited Shares A/c Dr. To Equity Share Capital A/c (1,000 x ₹ 70) (Being the re-issue of 1,000 shares of ₹ 60 per share, ₹ 70 paid-up as per Board's Resolution No. . . . dated . . .)		60,000 10,000	70,000
Forfeited Shares A/c (Note 1) Dr. To Capital Reserve A/c (Being the profit on re-issue transferred to Capital Reserve)		20,000	20,000
Total		34,70,000	34,70,000

Working Note :

(1) Calculation of Amount Transferred to Capital Reserve

	₹
Amount forfeited (1,000 × ₹ 30)	30,000
Less : Loss on re-issue (1,000 × ₹ 10)	10,000
	20,000

(2) Securities premium has been received in full. Therefore, at the time of forfeiture, Securities Premium Account will not be debited.

(3) It is assumed that shares issued to Ramesh Ltd was at par.

Illustration 48

A limited company issues 20,000 Equity Shares of ₹ 10 each at a premium of ₹ 5 per share, payable as to ₹ 7 (including premium) on application, ₹ 5 on allotment and the balance after three months of allotment. A shareholder, to whom 200 shares were allotted, failed to pay the allotment and call money, and his shares were forfeited, 160 of the forfeited shares were re-issued for ₹ 1,600.

Give necessary entries in Company's journal and the Balance Sheet. *[CBSE — Adapted]*

Solution

In the books of the Company

Journal

Date	Particulars	L.F.	Dr. ₹	Cr. ₹
	Bank A/c Dr. To Equity Share Application A/c (Being application money received on 20,000 shares @ ₹ 7 each)		1,40,000	1,40,000
	Equity Share Application A/c Dr. To Equity Share Capital A/c To Securities Premium A/c (Being the application money on 20,000 equity shares @ ₹ 2 each transferred to Equity Share Capital Account and @ ₹ 5 each transferred to Equity Securities Premium Account as per Board's Resolution No. . . . dated . . .)		1,40,000	40,000 1,00,000

Particulars		Dr. (₹)	Cr. (₹)
Equity Share Allotment A/c Dr. To Equity Share Capital A/c (Being allotment money due on 20,000 equity shares @ ₹ 5 each, as per Board's Resolution No. . . . dated . . .)		1,00,000	1,00,000
Bank A/c Dr. To Equity Share Allotment A/c (Being the allotment money received on 19,800 shares @ ₹ 5 each)		99,000	99,000
Equity Share Final Call A/c Dr. To Equity Share Capital A/c (Being the final call money due on 20,000 shares @ ₹ 3 each as per Board's Resolution No. . . . dated . . .)		60,000	60,000
Bank A/c Dr. To Equity Share Final Call A/c (Being the final call money received on 19,800 shares @ 3 each)		59,400	59,400
Equity Share Capital A/c (200 x ₹ 10) Dr. To Equity Share Allotment A/c (200 x ₹ 5) To Equity Share Final Call A/c (200 x ₹ 3) To Forfeited Shares A/c (200 x ₹ 2) (Being the forfeiture of 200 shares of ₹ 10 each fully paid-up for non-payment of allotment money and final call money @ ₹ 5 and ₹ 3 each respectively, as per Board's Resolution No. . . . dated . . .)		2,000	1,000 600 400
Bank A/c Dr. To Equity Share Capital A/c (Being the re-issue of 160 shares of ₹ 10 each, as fully paid-up as per Board's Resolution No. . . . dated . . .)		1,600	1,600
Forfeited Shares A/c (Note 2) Dr. To Capital Reserve A/c (Being the profit on re-issue transferred to Capital Reserve)		320	320
Total		6,02,320	6,02,320

Balance Sheet as at ... [Extract] (Figures in ₹)

Particulars	Note No.	Figures as at the end of current reporting period
1	2	3
I. EQUITY AND LIABILITIES		
(1) **Shareholders' Funds**		
(a) Share capital	(1)	1,99,680
(b) Reserves and surplus	(2)	1,00,320
(c) Money received against share warrants		—
TOTAL		3,00,000
II. ASSETS		
(2) **Current Assets**		
(d) Cash and cash equivalents	(3)	3,00,000
TOTAL		3,00,000

Notes to Accounts :

(1) Share Capital	₹	₹
Authorised Capital :		
... Equity Shares of ₹ ... each		***
Issued Capital :		
20,000 Equity Shares of ₹ 10 each		2,00,000
Subscribed Capital :		
Subscribed and Fully Paid :		
19,960 Equity Shares of ₹ 10 each		1,99,600
Add: Forfeited Shares (40 x ₹ 2)		80
		1,99,680

(2) Reserve and Surplus		
Securities Premium Reserve		1,00,000
Capital Reserve		320
		1,00,320
(3) Cah and Cash Equivalents		
Cash at Bank		3,00,000

Working Notes :

(1) Securities premium has been received in full. Therefore, at the time of forfeiture of shares, Securities Premium Account will not be debited.

(2) Amount forfeited per share is ₹ 2. There is no loss on re-issue. Therefore (160 × ₹ 2) = ₹ 320 will be transferred to Capital Reserve Account. It should be noted that forfeited amount of share not yet re-issued will be shown in the Balance Sheet as a part of capital.

Illustration 49

P Ltd issued 10,000 equity shares of ₹ 10 each at a premium of ₹ 2 per share payable as ₹ 3 per share on application; ₹ 5 per share on allotment including premium of ₹ 4 per share on final call.

All the shares were subscribed, money due on all shares was fully received excepting Anil, holding 100 shares failed to pay allotment and final call money and Sunil holding 200 shares, failed to pay the final call money. All these 300 shares were forfeited. Of the shares forfeited, 150 shares (including all of Anil) were subsequently reissued to Amar @ ₹ 8 per share as fully paid-up.

Pass necessary journal entries in the books of the company (including cash) to record the forfeiture and re-issue only.

Also show the presentation in the Balance Sheet ***before and after forfeiture*** and ***after re-issue.***

Solution

In the books of P Ltd

Journal

Date	Particulars		L.F.	Dr. ₹	Cr. ₹
	Equity Share Capital A/c (300 x ₹ 10)	Dr.		3,000	
	Securities Premium A/c (100 x ₹ 2)	Dr.		200	
	To Calls-in-Arrear A/c (Note 1)				1,700
	To Forfeited Shares A/c				1,500
	(Being the forfeiture of 300 equity shares of ₹ 10 each fully called-up for non-payment of allotment and final call money on 100 shares and final call money on 200 shares as per Board's Resolution No. . . dated . . .)				
	Bank A/c (150 x ₹ 8)	Dr.		1,200	
	Forfeited Shares A/c (150 x ₹ 2)	Dr.		300	
	To Equity Share Capital A/c				1,500
	(Being the re-issue of 150 forfeited shares @ ₹ 8 each as fully paid-up as per Board's Resolution No. . . . dated . . .)				
	Forfeited Shares A/c	Dr.		300	
	To Capital Reserve A/c				300
	(Being the profit on re-issue transferred to Capital Reserve)				
		Total		5,000	5,000

P Ltd

Balance Sheet ... [Extract] [Before Forfeiture] **(Figures in ₹)**

Particulars	Note No.	Figures as at the end of current reporting period
1	2	3
I. EQUITY AND LIABILITIES		
(1) **Shareholders' Funds**		
(a) Share capital	(1)	98,500
(b) Reserves and surplus	(2)	19,800
(c) Money received against share warrants		—
TOTAL		??

Notes to Accounts :

(1) Share Capital	₹	₹
Authorised Capital :		
... Equity Shares of ₹ ... each		***
Issued Capital :		
10,000 Equity Shares of ₹ 10 each		1,00,000
Subscribed Capital :		
Subscribed But Not Fully Paid :		
10,000 Equity Shares of ₹ 10 each	1,00,000	
Less: Calls-in-Arrear	1,500	98,500
(2) Reserve and Surplus		
Securities Premium Reserve	20,000	
Less: Calls-in-Arrear (100 x ₹ 2)	200	19,800

P Ltd

Balance Sheet ... [Extract] [After Forfeiture] **(Figures in ₹)**

Particulars	Note No.	Figures as at the end of current reporting period
1	2	3
I. EQUITY AND LIABILITIES		
(1) **Shareholders' Funds**		
(a) Share capital	(1)	98,500
(b) Reserves and surplus	(2)	19,800
(c) Money received against share warrants		—
TOTAL		??

Notes to Accounts :

(1) Share Capital	₹	₹
Authorised Capital :		
... Equity Shares of ₹ ... each		***
Issued Capital :		
10,000 Equity Shares of ₹ 10 each		1,00,000
Subscribed Capital :		
Subscribed and Fully Paid :		
9,700 Equity Shares of ₹ 10 each fully paid	97,000	
Add: Forfeited Shares	1,500	98,500
(2) Reserve and Surplus		
Securities Premium Reserve		19,800

P Ltd
Balance Sheet..... [Extract] [After Re-issue] **(Figures in ₹)**

Particulars	Note No.	Figures as at the end of current reporting period
1	2	3
I. EQUITY AND LIABILITIES		
(1) **Shareholders' Funds**		
(a) Share capital	(1)	98,400
(b) Reserves and surplus	(2)	20,100
(c) Money received against share warrants		—
TOTAL		??

Notes to Accounts :

(1) Share Capital	₹	₹
Authorised Capital :		
... Equity Shares of ₹ ... each		***
Issued Capital :		
10,000 Equity Shares of ₹ 10 each		1,00,000
Subscribed Capital :		
Subscribed and Fully Paid :		
9,850 Equity Shares of ₹ 10 each fully paid-up	98,500	
Add: Forfeited Shares	900	99,400
(2) Reserve and Surplus		
Capital Reserve (Note 3)	300	
Securities Premium Reserve	19,800	20,100

Working Notes :

(1) Calculation of Calls-in-Arrear

	₹
Anil : Allotment money not paid (100 x ₹ 5)	500
Final call money not paid (100 x ₹ 4)	400
Sunil : Final call money not paid (200 x ₹ 4)	800
	1,700

(2) Forfeited Shares

	₹
Anil : Application money paid (100 x ₹ 3)	300
Sunil : Application money paid (200 x ₹ 3)	600
Allotment money paid excluding premium (200 x ₹ 3)	600
	1,500

(3) Profit on Re-issue :

On Anil's Share :

	₹
Amount paid	3
Less : Loss on re-issue	2
Profit	1

Total profit on re-issue of Anil's share = 100 × ₹ 1 = ₹ 100.

On Sunil's share :

Amount paid	6
Less : Loss on re-issue	2
Profit on re-issue	4

Total profit on re-issue of Sunil's share = 50 × ₹ 4 = ₹ 200.

Amount transferred to Capital Reserve = (₹ 100 + ₹ 200) = ₹ 300.

Oversubscription and Pro-rata Allotment

In case of oversubscription, the application for shares exceeds the number of shares offered to the public by the Company.

It usually occurs in case of good issues and depends upon many factors like pricing of the issue, general economic conditions, boom in the share market, investors' confidence on the promoter of the company.

When the shares are oversubscribed, the company cannot satisfy all the applicants. The Board of Directors of the company may:

(a) accept an application in full; or

(b) reject it completely; or

(c) allote shares on pro-rata basis.

Pro-rata allotment means allotment in proportion of shares applied for. ***For example***, a company offers to the public 1,00,000 shares for subscription. The company receives application for 2,00,000 shares. If the shares are to be allotted on pro-rata basis, applicants for 2,00,000 shares are to be allotted 1,00,000 shares, i.e., in the ratio of 2,00,000 : 1,00,000 or 2 : 1. Any applicant who has applied for 2 shares will get 1 share.

In case of pro-rata allotment, the excess application money received is adjusted against the amount due on allotment or calls. Surplus money, if any, after making adjustment against future calls is refunded to the applicants.

Accounting Entries

(a) For rejected application:

Share Application Account Dr.
To Bank Account

(b) For pro-rata allotment

Share Application Account Dr.
To Share Allotment Account

Under pro-rata allotment also same journal entry is passed for forfeiture of shares.

But it requires to calculate the net amount due on allotment or any other call, and also the total amount forfeited. When there is a pro-rata allotment, the total application money paid by an applicant is more than the exact amount due on application. The excess amount is treated as an advance against allotment or any other future calls. The net amount due on allotment or any other calls is the difference between the amount due on allotment or any other calls and the excess amount received in application.

Illustration 57

Meena Ltd. issued 30,000 shares of ₹ 10 each at a premium of ₹ 2 per share payable as ₹ 3 on application, ₹ 5 (including premium) on allotment and the balance on first and final call. Applications were received for 62,000 shares. The Directors resolved to allot as follows :

A. Applicants of 20,000 shares — 10,000 shares
B. Applicants of 40,000 shares — 30,000 shares
C. Applicants of 2,000 shares — Nil

Balu who had applied for 1,500 shares in Category A and Ganesh who was allotted 600 shares in Category B failed to pay the allotment money.

Calculate the amount received on allotment. ***[CBSE (Outside Delhi) — 2009]***

Solution

Calculation of Money Received on Allotment

		₹
Total amount due on allotment (30,000 x 5)		1,50,000
Less: Excess application money adjusted on allotment (30,000 x 3)		90,000
		60,000
Less: Money not paid on allotment :		
Balu (Note 1)	1,500	
Ganesh (Note 2)	1,200	2,700
Money Received on Allotment		57,300

Working Notes :

(1) Money Due from Balu in Respect of Allotment	₹
Money received on application (1,500 x 3)	4,500
Less: Amount adjusted on application [10,00/20,000 x 1,500=750] (750 x 3)	2,250
Excess Application Money	2,250
Money due on allotment (750 x 5)	3,750
Less: Excess application money	2,250
Money not paid on allotment	1,500
(2) Money Due from Ganesh in Respect of Allotment	
Money received on application $[(\frac{40,000}{20,000} \times 600) \times 3]$	3,600
Less: Amount adjusted on application (600 x 3)	1,800
Excess Application Money	1,800
Amount due on allotment (600 x 5)	3,000
Less: Excess application money	1,800
Money not paid on allotment	1,200

Illustration 52

A Co. Ltd. issued to the public for subscription 40,000 equity shares of ₹ 10 each at par, payable as ₹ 2 each on application, allotment and first call and ₹ 4 on the final call. Applicants were received for 60,000 shares and allotment was made pro-rata to 80% of applicants. R to whom 1,600 shares were allotted paid only the application money, and S who had applied for 2,400 shares paid the entire call money due along with the allotment.

Pass the necessary Journal entries to record the above transactions.

[CBSE (Delhi) — Adapted]

Solution

(i)

In the books of A Co. Ltd
Journal

Date	Particulars	L.F.	Dr. ₹	Cr. ₹
	Bank A/c (60,000 x ₹ 2) Dr.		1,20,000	
	To Equity Share Application A/c			1,20,000
	(Being application money received for 60,000 shares @ ₹ 2 each)			
	Equity Share Application A/c Dr.		1,20,000	
	To Equity Share Capital A/c (40,000 x 2)			80,000
	To Bank A/c (12,000 x 2)			24,000
	To Equity Share Allotment A/c (8,000 x 2)			16,000
	(Being application money on 40,000 equity shares @ ₹ 2 transferred to Equity Share Capital Account, application money on 12,000 equity shares @ ₹ 2 refunded and application money on 8,000 equity shares transferred to Equity Shares Allotment Account as per Board's Resolution No. ... dated ...)			

Particulars		L.F.	Dr. (₹)	Cr. (₹)
Equity Share Allotment A/c (40,000 x 2) To Equity Shares Capital A/c (Being allotment money due on 40,000 shares @ ₹ 3 per share as per Board's Resolution No. ... dated ...)	Dr.		80,000	 80,000
Bank A/c (Note 4) Calls-in-Arrear A/c (Note 1) To Equity Shares Allotment A/c To Calls-in-Advance A/c (Note 3) (Being allotment money received except on 1,600 shares held by R. S paid ₹ 10,000 as calls-in-advance)	Dr. Dr.		73,440 2,560	 64,000 12,000
Equity Share First Call A/c (40,000 x ₹ 2) To Equity Shares Capital A/c (Being first call money due on 40,000 shares @ ₹ 2 each as per Board's Res. dt ...)	Dr.		80,000	 80,000
Bank A/c Calls-in-Advance A/c (2,000 x ₹ 2) Calls-in-Arrear A/c (1,600 x ₹ 2) To Equity Shares First Call A/c (Being first call money received except on 1,600 shares and adjustment of calls-in-advance on 2,000 shares))	Dr. Dr. Dr.		72,800 4,000 3,200	 80,000
Equity Shares Final Call A/c To Equity Shares Capital A/c (Being final call money due on 40,000 equity shares @ ₹ 4 each as per Board's Resolution No. ... dated ...)	Dr.		1,60,000	 1,60,000
Bank A/c To Calls-in-Advance A/c (2,000 x 4) To Calls-in-Arrear A/c (1,600 x 4) To Equity Shares Final Call A/c (Being final call money received except on 1,600 shares and adjustment of calls-in-advance on 2,000 shares)	Dr.		1,45,600 8,000 6,400	 1,60,000

Working Notes :

(1) Calculation of Calls-in-Arrear

40,000 equity shares were allotted to 48,000 applicants (80% of 60,000).

1 share was allotted to the applicants for 48,000 / 40,000

1,600 shares were allotted to the applicants for $\frac{48,000}{40,000} \times 1,600 = 1,920$ shares

R paid application money = 1,920 × ₹ 2 = ₹ **3,840.**

Money Due from R on Allotment

Application money paid	3,840
Less: Application money adjusted (1,600 x ₹ 2)	3,200
Excess application money to be adjusted in allotment	640
Allotment money due (1,600 × ₹2)	3,200
Less: Excess application money	640
Allotment money not paid by R	2,560

(2) Money Received on Allotment

Money due on allotment (40,000 × ₹ 2)	80,000
Less: Excess application money (8,000 × ₹ 2)	16,000
	64,000
Less: Amount not paid by R	2,560
Money reeived in respect of allotment	61,440

(3) Calculation of Calls-in-Advance

S applied for 2,400 shares. He was allotted 40,000/48,000 × 2,400 = **2,000 shares.**

S paid 1st call money ₹ 2 and final call money ₹ 3 at the time of allotment. Therefore, calls-in-advance = 2,000 × (2 + 4) = ₹ 12,000.

(4) Total Money Received on Allotment

As allotment money	61,440
As calls-in-advance	12,000
	73,440

Illustration 53

Petromax Ltd. issued 50,000 equity shares of ₹ 10 each at a premium of ₹ 2 per share payable as ₹ 3 on application, ₹ 5 including premium on allotment and the balance in equal instalments over two calls. Applications were received for 92,000 shares and the allotment was done as under:

A. Applicants of 40,000 shares	30,000 shares
B. Applicants of 40,000 shares	20,000 shares
C. Applicants of 12,000 shares	Nil

Suresh, who had applied for 2,000 shares in Category A did not pay any money other than application money.

Chander, who was allotted 800 shares in Category B paid the call money due alongwith allotment money.

All other allottes were paid their dues as per schedule.

Pass the necessary journal entries in the books of Petromax Ltd. to record the above.

[CBSE (Delhi) — 2009]

Solution

(i)

In the books of Petromax Ltd

Journal

Date	Particulars		L.F.	Dr. ₹	Cr. ₹
	Bank A/c (92,000 x ₹ 3)	Dr.		2,76,000	
	To Equity Share Application A/c				2,76,000
	(Being application money received for 92,000 shares @ ₹ 3 each)				
	Equity Share Application A/c	Dr.		2,76,000	
	To Equity Share Capital A/c (50,000 x 3)				1,50,000
	To Equity Share Allotment A/c (30,000 x 3)				90,000
	To Bank A/c (12,000 x 3)				36,000
	(Being application money on 50,000 equity shares transferred to Equity Share Capital Account. Money on 12,000 equity shares refunded and money on 30,000 equity shares adjusted in allotment as per Board's Resolution No. ... dated ...)				
	Equity Share Allotment A/c	Dr.		2,50,000	
	To Equity Shares Capital A/c				1,50,000
	To Securities Premium A/c				1,00,000
	(Being allotment due on 50,000 shares @ ₹ 5 including premium of ₹ 2 per share as per Board's Resolution No. ... dated ...)				
	Bank A/c (Note 4)	Dr.		**1,57,200**	
	Calls-in-Arrear A/c (Note 1)	Dr.		**6,000**	
	To Equity Shares Allotment A/c				**1,60,000**
	To Calls-in-Advance A/c (Note 3)				**3,200**
	(Being allotment money received except on 1,500 of Suresh. Call money ₹ 3,200 received in advance in respect of 800 shares held by Chander)				

Particulars		L.F.	Dr. (₹)	Cr. (₹)
Equity Share First Call A/c	Dr.		1,00,000	
To Equity Shares Capital A/c				1,00,000
(Being first call money due on 50,000 shares @ ₹ 2 as per Board's Resolution No. ... dated ...)				
Bank A/c	Dr.		95,400	
Calls-in-Advance A/c (800 x 2)	Dr.		1,600	
Calls-in-Arrear A/c (1,500 x 2)			3,000	
To Equity Shares First Call A/c				1,00,000
(Being first call money received except for 1,500 shares and calls-in-advance adjusted for 800 shares held by Chander)				
Equity Shares Final Call A/c	Dr.		1,00,000	
To Equity Shares Capital A/c				1,00,000
(Being final call money due on 50,000 equity shares @ ₹ 2 each as per Board's Resolution No. ... dated ...)				
Bank A/c	Dr.		95,400	
Calls-in-Advance A/c			1,600	
Calls-in-Arrear A/c			3,000	
To Equity Shares Final Call A/c				1,00,000
(Being final call money received except on 1,500 shares and calls-in-advance adjusted for 800 shares held by Chander)				

Working Notes :

(1) Calculation of Calls-in-Arrear

Suresh applied for 2,000 shares in 'A' category. He was allotted =

$$\frac{30,000}{40,000} \times 2,000 = 1,500 \text{ shares}$$

Suresh paid application money for 2,000 shares, i.e., 2,000 × 3 = ₹ **6,000.**

Money Due from Suresh on Allotment

Application money paid	6,000
Less: Application money adjusted (1,500 x ₹ 2)	4,500
Excess application money to be adjusted in allotment	1,500
Allotment money due (1,500 × ₹ 5)	7,500
Less: Excess application money	1,500
Allotment money not paid by Suresh	6,000

(2) Money Received on Allotment

Money due on allotment	2,50,000
Less: Excess application money	90,000
	1,60,000
Less: Amount not paid by Suresh	6,000
Money reeived in respect of allotment	1,54,000

(3) Calculation of Calls-in-Advance

Chander was allotted 800 shares. He paid in advance 800 × ₹ 4 = ₹ **3,200.**

(4) Total Money Received on Allotment

As allotment money	1,54,000
As calls-in-advance	3,200
	1,57,200

Illustration 54

Shubham Ltd. invited applications for the allotment of 80,000 equity shares of ₹ 10 each at par. The amount was payable as follows :

On application	₹ 2 per share
On allotment	₹ 4 per share
On first and final call	Balance

Applications for 1,10,000 shares were received. Applications for 10,000 shares were rejected. Shares were allotted on pro-rata basis to the remaining applicants. Excess application money received on application was adjusted towards sums due on allotment. All calls were made and were duly received. Manoj who had applied for 2,000 shares failed to pay the allotment and first and final call. His shares were forfeited. The forfeited shares were re-issued for ₹ 24,000 fully paid-up.

Pass necessary journal entries in the books of the company for the above transactions.

[CBSE (Outside Delhi) — Adapted]

Solution

(i)

In the books of Shubham Ltd

Journal

Date	Particulars		L.F.	Dr. ₹	Cr. ₹
	Bank A/c	Dr.		2,20,000	
	To Equity Share Application A/c				2,20,000
	(Being application money received for 1,10,000 shares @ ₹ 2 each)				
	Equity Share Application A/c	Dr.		2,20,000	
	To Equity Share Capital A/c (80,000 x 2)				1,60,000
	To Bank A/c (10,000 x 2)				20,000
	To Equity Share Allotment A/c (20,000 x 2)				40,000
	(Being application money on 80,000 equity shares @ ₹ 2 transferred to Equity Share Capital Account. Application money on 10,000 shares refunded and application money on 20,000 shares adjusted in allotment as per Board's Resolution No. ... dated ...)				
	Equity Share Allotment A/c	Dr.		3,20,000	
	To Equity Shares Capital A/c				3,20,000
	(Being allotment due on 80,000 shares @ ₹ 4 per share as per Board's Resolution No. ... dated ...)				
	Bank A/c (Note 2)	Dr.		2,74,400	
	Calls-in-Arrear A/c (Note 1)	Dr.		5,600	
	To Equity Shares Allotment A/c				2,80,000
	(Being allotment money received except on 1,600 shares held by Manoj)				
	Equity Shares First and Final Call A/c	Dr.		3,20,000	
	To Equity Shares Capital A/c				3,20,000
	(Being first and final call money due on 80,000 equity shares @ ₹ 4 each as per Board's Resolution No. ... dated ...)				
	Bank A/c	Dr.		3,13,600	
	Calls-in-Arrear A/c			6,400	
	To Equity Shares First and Final Call A/c				3,20,000
	(Being first and final call money received on all shares except of on 1,600 shares held by Manoj)				
	Equity Share Capital A/c (1,600 x 10)	Dr.		16,000	
	To Calls-in-Arrear A/c (₹ 5,600 + ₹ 6,400)				12,000
	To Forfeited Shares A/c				4,000
	(Being the forfeiture of 1,600 equity shares of ₹ 10 each for non-payment of allotment money and first and final call money as per Board's Resolution No. ... dated ...)				

Bank A/c Dr. To Equity Shares Capital A/c To Securities Premium A/c (Being the re-issue of 1,600 equity shares of ₹ 10 each fully paid for ₹ 24,000 as per Board's Resolution No. ... dated ...)		24,000	 16,000 8,000
Forfeited Shares A/c To Capital Reserve A/c (Being the profit on re-issue of 1,600 shares transferred to Capital Reserve Account)		4,000	 4,000

Working Notes :

(1) Calculation of Calls-in-Arrear

No. of shares allotted to Manoj $\frac{80,000}{1,00,000} \times 2,000 = 1,600$ shares.

Money Due from Manoj on Allotment	₹
Money paid on application (2,000 × 2)	4,000
Less: Application money adjusted (1,600 × 2)	3,200
Excess application money to be adjusted in allotment	800
Allotment money due (1,600 × ₹ 4)	6,400
Less: Excess application money	800
Allotment money not paid by Manoj to be transferred to Calls-in-Arrear Account	5,600

(2) Money Received on Allotment

Money due on allotment (80,000 × 4)	3,20,000
Less: Excess application money	40,000
	2,80,000
Less: Amount not paid by Manoj	5,600
Money reeived in respect of allotment	2,74,400

Illustration 55

Janata Ltd. invited applications for issuing 70,000 equity shares of ₹ 10 each at a premium of ₹ 2 per share. The amount was payable as follows :

On application	₹ 4 per share (including premium)
On allotment	₹ 3 per share
On first and final call	Balance

Applications for 1,00,000 shares were received. Applications for 10,000 shares were rejected. Shares were allotted to the remaining applicants on pro-rata basis.

Excess money received with applications were adjusted towards sums due on allotment. All calls were made and were duly received except first and final call on 700 shares allotted to Kanwar. His shares were forfeited. The forfeited shares were re-issued for ₹ 77,000 fully paid-up.

Pass necessary journal entries in the books of the company for the above transactions.

[CBSE (Outside Delhi) — 2008]

Solution (i)

In the books of Janata Ltd
Journal

Date	Particulars	L.F.	Dr. ₹	Cr. ₹
	Bank A/c Dr. To Equity Share Application A/c (Being application money received for 1,00,000 equity shares @ ₹ 4 each including premium of ₹ 2 per share)		4,00,000	4,00,000
	Equity Share Application A/c Dr. To Equity Share Capital A/c To Securities Premium A/c To Bank A/c (10,000 x 4) To Equity Share Allotment A/c (Note 1) (Being application money on 70,000 equity shares t@ ₹ 2 each ransferred to Equity Share Capital Account. ₹ 1,40,000 transferred to Security Premium Account and ₹ 40,000 refunded. The balance of ₹ 80,000 adjusted in allotment as per Board's Resolution No. ... dated ...)		4,00,000	1,40,000 1,40,000 40,000 80,000
	Equity Share Allotment A/c Dr. To Equity Shares Capital A/c Being allotment money due on 70,000 shares @ ₹ 3 each as per Board's Resolution No. ... dated ...)		2,10,000	2,10,000
	Bank A/c Dr. To Equity Shares Allotment A/c (Being allotment money received on 70,000 shares @ ₹ 3 each after adjusting excess application money)		1,30,000	1,30,000
	Equity Share First and Final Call A/c Dr. To Equity Shares Capital A/c (Being first and final call money due on 70,000 shares @ ₹ 5 each as per Board's Resolution No. ... dated ...)		3,50,000	3,50,000
	Bank A/c Dr. Calls-in-Arrear A/c To Equity Shares and Final First Call A/c (Being first and final call money received on 69,300 shares @ ₹ 5 each. Amount not paid on 700 shares transferred to Calls-in-Arrear Account)		3,46,500 3,500	3,50,000
	Equity Share Capital A/c (700 x 10) Dr. To Calls-in-Arrear A/c To Forfeited Shares A/c (Being the forfeiture of 700 equity shares of ₹ 10 each fully paid up as per Board's Resolution No. ... dated ...)		7,000	3,500 3,500
	Bank A/c Dr. To Equity Shares Capital A/c To Securities Premium A/c (Being re-issue of 700 equity shares of ₹ 10 each for ₹ 77,000 as per Board's Resolution No. ... dated ...)		77,000	7,000 70,000
	Forfeitured Shares A/c Dr. To Capital Reserve A/c (Being profit on re-issue of 700 shares transferred to Capital Reserve Account)		3,500	3,500

Working Notes :

(1) Calculation of Money Adjusted on Allotment

Application money received	4,00,000
Less: Application money transferred to Share Capital (70,000 × 2)	(1,40,000)
Less: Application money transferred to Securities Premium (70,000 × 2)	(1,40,000)
	1,20,000
Less: Amount refunded (10,000 × 4)	40,000
Adjusted in Allotment Account	80,000

Illustration 56

Eastern Traders Ltd. offered for public subscription 20,000 equity shares of ₹ 100 each at a premium of ₹ 10 per share. The payment was to be made as follows :

On application ₹ 20

On allotment ₹ 40 (including premium)

On first and final call ₹ 50

Applications received were for 35,000 shares. Application for 10,000 shares were rejected and money was returned and those totalling for 15,000 shares were allotted 10,000 shares on prorata and the remaining application were allotted in full.

The directors made the final call and one shareholder holding 500 shares, failed to pay the call money and as a consequence his shares were forfeited. 200 of these shares were re-issued as fully paid at ₹ 80 per share and the amount was received.

Give Journal Entries in the books of the company.

Solution

(i)

In the books of Eastern Traders Ltd.

Journal

Date	Particulars	L.F.	Dr. ₹	Cr. ₹
	Bank A/c Dr. To Equity Share Application A/c (Being application money received on 35,000 shares @ ₹ 20 each)		7,00,000	7,00,000
	Equity Share Application A/c Dr. To Equity Share Capital A/c (Being application money on 20,000 shares @ ₹ 20 each transferred to Equity Share Capital Account as per Board's Resolution No. ... dated ...)		4,00,000	4,00,000
	Equity Share Application A/c Dr. To Bank A/c (Being application money on 10,000 shares @ ₹ 20 each refunded as per Board's Resolution No. ... dated ...)		2,00,000	2,00,000
	Equity Share Application A/c Dr. To Equity Share Allotment A/c (Being excess application money for 5,000 shares @ ₹ 20 each transferred to Equity Share Allotment Account)		1,00,000	1,00,000
	Equity Share Allotment A/c Dr. To Equity Share Capital A/c To Securities Premium A/c (Being the allotment money due on 20,000 shares @ ₹ 40 per share as per Board's Resolution No. ... dated ...)		8,00,000	6,00,000 2,00,000
	Bank A/c Dr. To Equity Share Allotment A/c (Being the balance allotment money received)		7,00,000	7,00,000
	Equity Share First and Final Call A/c Dr. To Equity Share Capital A/c (Being first and final call money due on 20,000 shares @ ₹ 50 each as per Board's Resolution No. ... dated ...)		10,00,000	10,00,000
	Bank A/c Dr. Calls-in-Arrear A/c Dr. To Equity Share First and Final Call A/c (Being first and final call money received on 19,500 shares @ ₹ 50 per share. Money not received on 500 shares has been transferred to Calls-in-Arrear Account)		9,75,000 25,000	10,00,000

Date	Particulars	L.F.	Dr. ₹	Cr. ₹
	Equity Share Capital A/c [500 x 100] Dr. To Calls-in-Arrear A/c To Forfeited Shares A/c [50 x ₹ 50] (Being the forfeiture of 500 equity shares for non-payment of first and final call @ ₹ 50 each as per Board's Resolution No. ... dated ...)		50,000	 25,000 25.000
	Bank A/c [200 x ₹ 80] Dr. Forfeited Shares A/c [200 x ₹ 20] Dr. To Equity Share Capital A/c (Being the re-issue of 200 equity shares of ₹ 100 each @ ₹ 80 as fully paid up as per Board's Resolution No. ... dated ...)		16,000 4,000	 20,000
	Forfeited Shares A/c (Note 1) Dr. To Capital Reserve A/c (Being the profit on re-issue of 200 shares transferred to Capital Reserve Account)		6,000	 6,000

Working Notes :

(1) Amount transferred to Capital Reserve = 200 [₹ 50 – 20] = ₹ 6,000.

(2) Forfeited amount on 300 shares @ ₹ 50 (total ₹ 15,000) will be shown in the Balance Sheet as a part of the paid-up capital.

Illustration 57

Amrit Ltd issued a prospectus, inviting applications for 20,000 shares at a premium of ₹ 2 per share payable as follows :

on application ₹ 5 (including premium); on allotment ₹ 4; on call ₹ 3

Applications were received for 30,000 shares and ***pro-rata*** allotment was made on application for 24,000 shares. Excess money paid on application for these shares was utilised towards allotment money. Atul, who applied for 600 shares, failed to pay the allotment money and on his subsequent failure to pay the call, his shares were forfeited.

Pass the necessary entries in the books of Amrit Limited.

Solution

In the books of Amrit Ltd

Journal

Date	Particulars	L.F.	Dr. ₹	Cr. ₹
	Bank A/c Dr. To Equity Share Application A/c (Being application money received on 30,000 shares @ ₹ 5 each)		1,50,000	 1,50,000
	Equity Share Application A/c Dr. To Bank A/c (Being application money on 6,000 shares were refunded as per Board's Resolution No. . . . dated . . .)		30,000	 30,000
	Equity Share Application A/c Dr. To Equity Share Capital A/c To Equity Securities Premium A/c (Being the application money on 20,000 equity shares @ ₹ 3 each transferred to Equity Share Capital Account @ ₹ 2 each transferred to Equity Securities Premium Account as per Board's Resolution No. . . . dated . . .)		1,00,000	 60,000 40,000
	Equity Share Application A/c Dr. To Equity Share Allotment A/c (Being the excess application money on 4,000 shares @ ₹ 5 each transferred to Equity Share Allotment Account as per Board's Resolution No. . . . dated . . .)		20,000	 20,000

Particulars		L.F.	Dr. ₹	Cr. ₹
Equity Share Allotment A/c To Equity Share Capital A/c (Being allotment money due on 20,000 shares @ ₹ 4 each as per Board's Resolution No. . . . dated . . .)	Dr.		80,000	80,000
Bank A/c (Note 2) To Equity Share Allotment A/c (Being the allotment money received on 19,500 shares @ ₹ 3 each)	Dr.		58,500	58,500
Equity Share Call A/c To Equity Share Capital A/c (Being the call money due on 20,000 shares @ ₹ 3 each as per Board's Resolution No. . . . dated . . .)	Dr.		60,000	60,000
Bank A/c To Equity Share Call A/c (Being the call money received on 19,500 shares @ ₹ 3 each)	Dr.		58,500	58,500
Equity Share Capital A/c (500 x ₹ 10) To Equity Share Allotment A/c (Note 1) To Equity Share Call A/c To Forfeited Shares A/c (Note 3) (Being the forfeiture of 500 shares for non-payment of allotment money and call money as per Board's Resolution No. . . . dated . . .)	Dr.		5,000	 1,500 1,500 2,000
	Total		5,62,000	5,62,000

Working Notes :

(1) Money Due from Atul on Allotment

	₹
Money paid on application (600 x ₹ 5)	3,000
Less: Amount adjusted on application (500 x ₹ 5)	2,500
Excess application money	500
Money due on allotment (500 x ₹ 4)	2,000
Less: Excess application money	500
Money due from Atul	1,500

(2) Money Received on Allotment

	₹
Total amount due on allotment	80,000
Less: Excess application money adjusted	20,000
	60,000
Less: Money not paid by Atul (Note 1)	1,500
	58,500

(3) Actual amount received from Atul is ₹ 3,000. Out of which ₹ 1,000 (500 × ₹ 2) is to be transferred to Securities Premium Account. The balance amount is to be transferred to Forfeited Shares Account.

Illustration 58

On 1st February, 2014, the directors of X Ltd issued 50,000 equity shares of ₹ 10 each at ₹ 12 per share, payable as to ₹ 5 on application including the premium, ₹ 4 on allotment and the balance on 1st May, 2014.

The lists were closed on 10th February, 2014, by which date applications for 70,000 shares had been received. Of the cash received, ₹ 40,000 was returned and ₹ 60,000 was applied to the amount due on allotment — the balance of which was paid on 16th February, 2014. All shareholders paid the call due on 1st May, 2014, with the exception of one allottee of 500 shares. These shares were forfeited on 29th September, 2014.

Show the journal entries and the Cash Book of the company and also give the Balance Sheet of the company.

[CBSE — Adapted]

Solution

In the books of X Ltd.

Dr. Cash Book (Bank column only) Cr.

Date	Particulars	₹	Date	Particulars	₹
2014 Feb 10	To Equity Share Application A/c (Being application money reced on 70,000 equity shares @ ₹ 5 each)	3,50,000	2014 Feb 10	By Equity Share Application A/c (Being excess application money refunded on 8,000 shares @ ₹ 5 each as per Board's ₹s. No... dt ...)	40,000
Feb 16	To Equity Share Allotment A/c (Being allotment money received on 50,000 equity shares @ ₹ 4 each after adjustment of excess application money)	1,40,000		By Balance c/d	5,98,500
May 1	To Equity Share Call A/c (Being the call money received on 49,500 equity shares @ ₹ 3 each)	1,48,500			
		6,38,500			6,38,500

Journal

Date	Particulars		L.F.	Dr. ₹	Cr. ₹
2014 Feb 10	Equity Share Application A/c	Dr.		60,000	
	To Equity Share Allotment A/c				60,000
	(Being excess application money transferred to Equity Share Allotment Account as per Board's Resolution No. . . . dated . . .)				
	Equity Share Application A/c	Dr.		2,50,000	
	To Equity Share Capital A/c				1,50,000
	To Securities Premium A/c				1,00,000
	(Being the application money on 50,000 equity shares @ ₹ 3 each transferred to Equity Share Capital Account and ₹ 2 each transferred to Securities Premium Account as per Board's Resolution No. . . . dated . . .)				
	Equity Share Allotment A/c	Dr.		2,00,000	
	To Equity Share Capital A/c				2,00,000
	(Being allotment money due on 50,000 shares @ ₹ 4 each as per Board's Resolution No. . . . dated . . .)				
May 1	Equity Share Call A/c	Dr.		1,50,000	
	To Equity Share Capital A/c				1,50,000
	(Being the call money due on 50,000 shares @ ₹ 3 each as per Board's Resolution No. . . . dated . . .)				
Sep. 29	Equity Share Capital A/c (500 x ₹ 10)	Dr.		5,000	
	To Equity Share Call A/c (500 x ₹ 3)				1,500
	To Forfeited Shares A/c (500 x ₹ 7)				3,500
	(Being the forfeiture of 500 shares of ₹ 10 each fully paid up for non-payment of call money @ ₹ 3 each as per Board's Resolution No. . . . dated . . .)				
		Total		6,65,000	6,65,000

X Ltd

Balance Sheet as at 29 th September, 2014 **(Figures in ₹)**

Particulars	Note No.	Figures as at the end of current reporting period
1	2	3
I. EQUITY AND LIABILITIES		
(1) **Shareholders' Funds**		
(a) Share capital	(1)	4,98,500
(b) Reserves and surplus	(2)	1,00,000
(c) Money received against share warrants		
TOTAL		5,98,500

II. ASSETS		
(2) **Current Assets**		
(d) Cash and cash equivalents	(2)	5,98,500
TOTAL		5,98,500

Notes to Accounts :

(1) Share Capital	₹	₹
Authorised Capital :		
... Equity Shares of ₹ ... each		?
Issued Capital :		
50,000 Equity Shares of ₹ 10 each		5,00,000
Subscribed Capital :		
Subscribed and Fully Paid :		
49,500 Equity Shares of ₹ 10 each	4,95,000	
Add: Forfeited Shares	3,500	4,98,500
(2) Reserve and Surplus		
Securities Premium Reserve		1,00,000
(3) Cash at Bank		5,98,500

Illustration 59

Gupta & Co Ltd invited applications for 10,000 shares of ₹ 100 each at 10% premium included in the allotment money. Applications were received for 18,000 shares, of which applications for 3,000 shares were rejected and their money was refunded. Rest of the applicants were issued shares on *pro-rata* basis and their excess money was adjusted towards allotment. The money was called as :

on application ₹ 20; on allotment ₹ 40; on first call ₹ 30; on second and final call ₹ 20.

Hari, a holder of 300 shares paid only the application money and Shyam, a holder of 600 shares paid up to the first call money. All the calls were made and the payment received except that in case of Hari and Shyam. Their shares were forfeited after the second and Final Call and re-issued at 15% discount.

Pass necessary journal entries to give effect to the above transactions.

[CBSE — Adapted]

Solution

In the books of Gupta & Co. Ltd.
Journal

Date	Particulars	L.F.	Dr. ₹	Cr. ₹
	Bank A/c Dr. To Equity Share Application A/c (Being application money received on 18,000 shares @ ₹ 20 each)		3,60,000	3,60,000
	Equity Share Application A/c Dr. To Bank A/c (Being application money on 3,000 shares @ ₹ 20 were refunded as per Board's Resolution No. . . . dated . . .)		60,000	60,000
	Equity Share Application A/c Dr. To Equity Share Capital A/c (Being the application money on 10,000 equity shares @ ₹ 20 each transferred to Equity Share Capital Account as per Board's Resolution No. . . . dated . . .)		2,00,000	2,00,000
	Equity Share Application A/c Dr. To Equity Share Allotment A/c (Being the excess application money on 5,000 shares @ ₹ 20 each transferred to Equity Share Allotment Account as per Board's Resolution No. . . . dated . . .)		1,00,000	1,00,000

Particulars		L.F.	Dr. (₹)	Cr. (₹)
Equity Share Allotment A/c	Dr.		4,00,000	
To Equity Share Capital A/c				3,00,000
To Securities Premium A/c				1,00,000
(Being allotment money due on 10,000 shares @ ₹ 40 each including premium of ₹ 10 per share as per Board's Resolution No. . . . dated . . .)				
Bank A/c (Note 2)	Dr.		2,91,000	
To Equity Share Allotment A/c				2,91,000
(Being balance allotment money received except for 300 shares)				
Equity Share First Call A/c	Dr.		3,00,000	
To Equity Share Capital A/c				3,00,000
(Being the first call money due on 10,000 shares @ ₹ 30 each as per Board's Resolution No. . . . dated . . .)				
Bank A/c	Dr.		2,91,000	
To Equity Share First Call A/c				2,91,000
(Being the first call money received on 9,700 shares @ ₹ 30 each)				
Equity Share Second and Final Call A/c	Dr.		2,00,000	
To Equity Share Capital A/c				2,00,000
(Being the second and final call money due on 10,000 shares @ ₹ 20 each as per Board's Resolution No. . . . dated . . .)				
Bank A/c	Dr.		1,82,000	
To Equity Share Second and Final Call A/c				1,82,000
(Being the second and final call money received on 9,100 shares @ ₹ 20 each)				
Equity Share Capital A/c (900 x ₹ 100)	Dr.		90,000	
Securities Premium A/c (Note 5)	Dr.		3,000	
To Equity Share Allotment A/c (Note 1)				9,000
To Equity Share First Call A/c (300 x ₹ 30)				9,000
To Equity Share Second and Final Call A/c (900 x ₹ 20)				18,000
To Forfeited Shares A/c (Note 3)				57,000
(Being the forfeiture of 900 shares for non-payment of allotment and call money on 300 shares and non-payment of final call money on 600 shares as per Board's Resolution No. . . . dated . . .)				
Bank A/c (900 x ₹ 85)	Dr.		76,500	
Forfeited Shares A/c (900 x ₹ 15)	Dr.		13,500	
To Equity Share Capital A/c				90,000
(Being the re-issue of 900 shares @ ₹ 100 each at 15% discount as per Board's Resolution No. . . . dated . . .)				
Forfeited Shares A/c (₹ 57,000 – ₹ 13,500)	Dr.		43,500	
To Capital Reserve A/c				43,500
(Being the profit on re-issue transferred to Capital Reserve)				
Total			26,10,500	26,10,500

Working Notes :

(1) Money Due from Hari on Allotment

	₹
Money paid on application (Note 4)	9,000
Less: Amount adjusted on application (300 x ₹ 20)	6,000
Excess application money	3,000
Money due on allotment (300 x ₹ 40)	12,000
Less: Excess application money	3,000
Money due from Hari	9,000

(2) Money Received on Allotment

	₹
Total amount due on allotment	4,00,000
Less: Excess application money adjusted	1,00,000
	3,00,000
Less: Money not paid by Hari (Note 1)	9,000
	2,91,000

(3) Calculation of Amount Forfeited

	₹
Amount paid by Hari (Note 4)	9,000
Amount paid by Shyam excluding premium (600 x ₹ 80)	48,000
	57,000

(4) 10,000 shares were allotted to the applicants for (18,000 – 3,000) 15,000 shares.
1 share was allotted to the applicants for 15,000 / 10,000 shares.
300 shares were allotted to the applicants for (15,000 / 10,000) × 300 = 450 shares.
Therefore, application money paid by Hari = 450 × ₹ 20 = ₹ 9,000.

(5) Premium on share has not been received from Hari. Therefore, at the time of forfeiture, Securities Premium Account will be debited with ₹ 3,000, i.e., premium not received from Hari on 300 shares @ ₹ 10 each.

Illustration 60

K Limited has been registered with an authorised capital of ₹ 3,00,000 divided into 3,000 shares of ₹ 100 each, of which 1,500 shares were offered for public subscription at a premium of ₹ 5 per share, payable as : on application ₹ 10; on allotment ₹ 25 (including premium); on first call ₹ 40; on final call ₹ 30. Applications were received for 2,000 shares, of which application for 200 shares were rejected, the rest of the applications were allotted 1,500 shares on *pro-rata* basis. Excess application money was transferred to allotment. All the monies were duly received except from Sundar, holder of 300 shares, who failed to pay allotment money and first call money.

His shares were later forfeited, and re-issued to Shyam at ₹ 60 per share — ₹ 70 paid-up. Final call has not been made. Prepare the Cash Book and pass necessary journal entries.

[CBSE — Adapted]

Solution

In the books of K Limited
Cash Book (Bank column only)

Dr. **Cr.**

Date	Particulars	₹	Date	Particulars	₹
	To Equity Share Application A/c (Being application money recd on 2,000 equity shares @ ₹ 10 each)	20,000		By Equity Share Application A/c (Being the excess application money refunded on 200 shares @ ₹ 10 each as per Board's ₹s. No. . . dated ...)	2,000
	To Equity Share Allotment A/c (Note 2) (Being allotment money received on 1,200 equity shares @ ₹ 25 each after adjustment of excess application money)	27,600		By Balance c/d	1,11,600
	To Equity Share First Call A/c (Being the first call money recd on 1,200 equity shares @ ₹ 40 each)	48,000			
	To Share Capital A/c (Being the re-issue of 300 shares at ₹ 60 per share — ₹ 70 paid-up)	18,000			
		1,13,600			1,13,600

In the books of K Limited
Journal

Date	Particulars		L.F.	Dr. ₹	Cr. ₹
	Equity Share Application A/c	Dr.		15,000	
	To Equity Share Capital A/c				15,000
	(Being application money on 1,500 shares @ ₹ 10 each transferred to Equity Share Capital Account as per Board's Resolution No. . . . dated . . .)				
	Equity Share Application A/c	Dr.		3,000	
	To Equity Share Allotment A/c				3,000
	(Being the excess application money on 300 shares @ ₹ 10 each transferred to Equity Share Allotment Account as per Board's Resolution No. . . . dated . . .)				

Particulars			Dr. (₹)	Cr. (₹)
Equity Share Allotment A/c	Dr.		37,500	
To Equity Share Capital A/c				30,000
To Securities Premium A/c				7,500
(Being allotment money due on 1,500 shares @ ₹ 25 each including premium as per Board's Resolution No. . . . dated . . .)				
Equity Share First Call A/c	Dr.		60,000	
To Equity Share Capital A/c				60,000
(Being the first call money due on 1,500 shares @ ₹ 40 each as per Board's Resolution No. ... dated ...)				
Equity Share Capital A/c (300 x ₹ 70)	Dr.		21,000	
Securities Premium A/c (Note 3)	Dr.		1,500	
To Equity Share Allotment A/c (Note 1)				6,900
To Equity Share First Call A/c (300 x ₹ 40)				12,000
To Forfeited Shares A/c (Note 4)				3,600
(Being the forfeiture of 300 shares of ₹ 100 each, ₹ 70 called-up, for non- payment of allotment and first call money as per Board's Resolution No. ... dt ...)				
Forfeited Shares A/c (300 x ₹ 10)	Dr.		3,000	
To Equity Share Capital A/c				3,000
(Being the discount on re-issue adjusted against the credit balance of Forfeited Shares Account)				
Forfeited Shares A/c (₹ 3,600 – ₹ 3,000)	Dr.		600	
To Capital Reserve A/c				600
(Being the profit on re-issue of 300 shares transferred to Capital Reserve)				
	Total		1,41,600	1,41,600

Working Notes :

(1) Money Due from Sundar on Allotment

	₹
Money paid on application (Note 4)	3,600
Less: Amount adjusted on application (300 x ₹ 10)	3,000
Excess application money	600
Money due on allotment (300 x ₹ 25)	7,500
Less: Excess application money	600
Money not paid by Sundar	6,900

(2) Money Received on Allotment

	₹
Total amount due on allotment	37,500
Less: Excess application money adjusted	3,000
	34,500
Less: Money not paid by Sundar (Note 1)	6,900
	27,600

(3) Premium has not been received on 300 shares @ ₹ 5 each. Therefore, at the time of forfeiture of these shares, Securities Premium Account will be debited with ₹ 1,500.

(4) 1,500 shares were allotted to the applicants from 1,800 shares.
1 share was allotted to the applicants from 1,800 / 1,500 shares.
300 shares were allotted to the applicants from (1,800 / 1,500) × 300 = 360 shares.
Therefore, application money paid by Sunder = 360 × ₹ 10 = ₹ 3,600.

Illustration 61

A company offered 10,000 shares of ₹ 10 each, payable as ₹ 2 on application, ₹ 3 on allotment, ₹ 3 on first call and ₹ 2 on final call. The public applied for 15,000 shares. The shares were allotted on a *pro-rata* basis to the applicants of 12,000 shares. All the shareholders paid the allotment money excepting one shareholder who was allotted 200 shares. These shares were forfeited. The first call was made thereafter. The forfeited shares were re- issued @ ₹ 9 per share, ₹ 8 paid-up. The final call was not yet made.

You are required to prepare the Cash Book and pass journal entries.

Solution

In the books of the Company

Cash Book (Bank column only)

Dr.					Cr.
Date	Particulars	₹	Date	Particulars	₹
	To Equity Share Application A/c (Being application money recd on 15,000 equity shares @ ₹ 2 each)	30,000		By Equity Share Application A/c (Being the excess application money refunded on 3,000 shares @ ₹ 2 each as per Board's Res. No. . . dated ...)	6,000
	To Equity Share Allotment A/c (Note 2) (Being allotment money received on 9,800 equity shares @ ₹ 3 each after adjustment of excess application money.)	25,480		By Balance c/d	80,680
	To Equity Share First Call A/c (Being the first call money received on 9,800 equity shares @ ₹ 3 each)	29,400			
	To Equity Share Capital A/c (Being the re-issue of 200 shares @ ₹ 8 paid-up)	1,600			
	To Securities Premium A/c (Note 5) (Being the premium received on 200 shares @ ₹ 1 each)	200			
		86,680			86,680

Journal

Date	Particulars		L.F.	Dr. ₹	Cr. ₹
	Equity Share Application A/c	Dr.		20,000	
	To Equity Share Capital A/c				20,000
	(Being the application money on 10,000 equity shares transferred to Equity Share Capital Account as per Board's Resolution No. . . . dated . . .)				
	Equity Share Application A/c	Dr.		4,000	
	To Equity Share Allotment A/c				4,000
	(Being the excess application money on 2,000 shares transferred to Equity Share Allotment Account as per Board's Resolution No. . . . dated . . .)				
	Equity Share Allotment A/c	Dr.		30,000	
	To Equity Share Capital A/c				30,000
	(Being allotment money due on 10,000 shares @ ₹ 3 each as per Board's Resolution No. . . . dated . . .)				
	Equity Share Capital A/c (200 x ₹ 5)	Dr.		1,000	
	To Equity Share Allotment A/c (Note 1)				520
	To Forfeited Shares A/c (Note 3)				480
	(Being the forfeiture of 200 shares for non-payment of allotment money @ ₹ 3 per share as per Board's Resolution No. . . . dated . . .)				
	Equity Share First Call A/c	Dr.		29,400	
	To Equity Share Capital A/c				29,400
	(Being the first call money due on 9,800 shares @ ₹ 3 each as per Board's Resolution No. . . . dated . . .)				
	Forfeited Shares A/c (Note 4)	Dr.		480	
	To Capital Reserve A/c				480
	(Being the profit on re-issue of 200 shares transferred to Capital Reserve)				
	Total			84,880	84,880

Working Notes :

(1) Money Not Paid on Allotment	₹	(2) Money Received on Allotment	₹
Money paid on application (Note 3)	480	Total amount due on allotment	30,000
Less: Amount adjusted with application (200 x ₹ 2)	400	Less: Excess application money adjusted	4,000
Excess application money	80		26,000
Money due on allotment (200 x ₹ 3)	600	Less: Money not received on allotment (Note 1)	520
Less: Excess application money	80		25,480
Money not paid on allotment	520		

(3) 10,000 shares were allotted to the applicants from 12,000 shares.
1 share was allotted to the applicants from 12,000 / 10,000 shares.
300 shares were allotted to the applicants from (12,000 / 10,000) × 200 = 240 shares.
Therefore, application money paid by the defaulter shareholder = 240 × ₹ 2 = ₹ 480.

(4) Entire amount forfeited will be transferred to capital reserve because there is no loss on re-issue.

(5) ₹ 9 per share has been received for issue of 200 shares, ₹ 8 called up. Therefore, ₹ 1 (₹ 9 – ₹ 8) per share will be treated as premium. Total premium will be ₹ 200.

Illustration 62

A limited company invites applications for 50,000 equity shares of ₹ 10 each payable as follows : on application ₹ 3; on allotment ₹ 4; on first call ₹ 2; on final call, the balance.

Applications were received for 55,000 shares. Allotments were made on the following basis : (i) To applicants for 35,000 shares — in full; (ii) To applicants for 20,000 shares — 15,000 shares. Excess money paid on application was utilised towards allotment money.

A shareholder, who was allotted 1,500 shares out of the group applying for 20,000 shares, failed to pay allotment money and money due on calls. These shares were forfeited. 1,000 forfeited shares were re-issued as fully paid on receipt of ₹ 8 per share. Show the journal entries in the books of the company. *[CBSE — Adapted]*

Solution **In the books of the Company**

Journal

Date	Particulars	L.F.	Dr. ₹	Cr. ₹
	Bank A/c Dr. To Equity Share Application A/c (Being application money received on 55,000 shares @ ₹ 3 each)		1,65,000	1,65,000
	Equity Share Application A/c Dr. To Equity Share Capital A/c (Being the application money on 50,000 equity shares @ ₹ 3 each transferred to Equity Share Capital Account as per Board's Resolution No. . . . dated . . .)		1,50,000	1,50,000
	Equity Share Application A/c Dr. To Equity Share Allotment A/c (Being the excess application money on 5,000 shares @ ₹ 3 each transferred to Equity Share Allotment Account as per Board's Resolution No. . . . dated . . .)		15,000	15,000
	Equity Share Allotment A/c Dr. To Equity Share Capital A/c (Being allotment money due on 50,000 shares @ ₹ 4 each as per Board's Resolution No. . . . dated . . .)		2,00,000	2,00,000
	Bank A/c (Note 2) Dr. To Equity Share Allotment A/c (Being balance allotment money received except for 1,500 shares)		1,80,500	1,80,500

Particulars		L.F.	Dr. ₹	Cr. ₹
Equity Share First Call A/c	Dr.		1,00,000	
To Equity Share Capital A/c				1,00,000
(Being the first call money due on 50,000 shares @ ₹ 2 each as per Board's Resolution No. . . . dated . . .)				
Bank A/c	Dr.		97,000	
To Equity Share First Call A/c				97,000
(Being the first call money received on 48,500 shares @ ₹ 2 each)				
Equity Share Final Call A/c	Dr.		50,000	
To Equity Share Capital A/c				50,000
(Being the final call money due on 50,000 shares @ ₹ 1 each as per Board's Resolution No. . . . dated . . .)				
Bank A/c	Dr.		48,500	
To Equity Share Final Call A/c				48,500
(Being the final call money received on 48,500 shares @ ₹ 1 each)				
Equity Share Capital A/c (1,500 x ₹ 10)	Dr.		15,000	
To Equity Share Allotment A/c (Note 2)				4,500
To Equity Share First Call A/c (1,500 x ₹ 2)				3,000
To Equity Share Final Call A/c (1,500 x ₹ 1)				1,500
To Forfeited Shares A/c (Note 3)				6,000
(Being the forfeiture of 1,500 shares for non-payment of allotment money and both the calls as per Board's Resolution No. . . . dated . . .)				
Bank A/c (1,000 x ₹ 8)	Dr.		8,000	
Forfeited Shares A/c (1,000 x ₹ 2)	Dr.		2,000	
To Equity Share Capital A/c				10,000
(Being the re-issue of 1,000 shares @ ₹ 8 each as fully paid-up as per Board's Resolution No. . . . dated . . .)				
Forfeited Shares A/c (Note 5)	Dr.		2,000	
To Capital Reserve A/c				2,000
(Being the profit on re-issue transferred to Capital Reserve)				
Total			10,33,000	10,33,000

Working Notes :

(1) Money Due on Allotment

	₹
Money paid on application (Note 4)	6,000
Less: Amount adj. on application (1,500 x ₹ 3)	4,500
Excess application money	1,500
Money due on allotment (1,500 x ₹ 4)	6,000
Less: Excess application money	1,500
Money not paid on allotment	4,500

(2) Money Received on Allotment

	₹
Total amount due on allotment	2,00,000
Less: Excess application money adjusted	15,000
	1,85,000
Less: Money not received on allotment (Note 1)	4,500
	1,80,500

(3) Amount forfeited (₹ 2,000 × 3) = ₹ 6,000.

(4) 15,000 shares were allotted to the applicants for 20,000 shares.
1 share was allotted to the applicants for 20,000 / 15,000 shares.
1,500 shares were allotted to the applicants for (20,000 / 15,000) × 1,500 = 2,000 shares.
Therefore, application money paid by the defaulter shareholder = 2,000 × ₹ 3 = ₹ 6,000.

(5) Amount forfeited per share (6,000 / 1,500) = ₹ 4
Less: Loss on re-issue (₹ 10 – ₹ 8) = ₹ 2
Profit on re-issue of each = ₹ 2
Amount transferred to capital reserve = 1,000 × ₹ 2 = ₹ 2,000.

Illustration 63

A company issued for public subscription 40,000 equity shares of ₹ 10 each at a premium of ₹ 2 per share payable as : on application ₹ 2; on allotment ₹ 5 (including premium); on first call ₹ 2; on final call ₹ 3.

Applications were received for 60,000 shares.

Allotment was made *pro-rata* to the applicants for 48,000 shares, the remaining applications being refused. Money overpaid on application was utilised towards sum due on allotment. Ram, to whom 1,600 shares were allotted, failed to pay the allotment money and the two calls. Shyam, to whom 2,000 shares were allotted, failed to pay the two calls. These shares were subsequently forfeited after the second call was made. All the forfeited shares were sold as fully paid up at ₹ 8 per share.

Give the necessary journal entries for the above transactions. *[CBSE — Adapted]*

Solution

In the books of the Company

Journal

Date	Particulars		L.F.	Dr. ₹	Cr. ₹
	Bank A/c	Dr.		1,20,000	
	To Equity Share Application A/c				1,20,000
	(Being application money received on 60,000 shares @ ₹ 2 each)				
	Equity Share Application A/c	Dr.		24,000	
	To Bank A/c				24,000
	(Being the application money on 12,000 equity shares @ ₹ 2 each were refunded as per Board's Resolution No. . . . dated . . .)				
	Equity Share Application A/c	Dr.		80,000	
	To Equity Share Capital A/c				80,000
	(Being the application money on 40,000 shares @ ₹ 2 each transferred to Equity Share Capital Account as per Board's Resolution No. . . . dated . . .)				
	Equity Share Application A/c	Dr.		16,000	
	To Equity Share Allotment A/c				16,000
	(Being the excess application money on 8,000 shares @ ₹ 2 each transferred to Equity Share Allotment Account as per Board's Resolution No. . . . dated . . .)				
	Equity Share Allotment A/c	Dr.		2,00,000	
	To Equity Share Capital A/c				1,20,000
	To Securities Premium A/c				80,000
	(Being allotment money due on 40,000 shares @ ₹ 5 each including premium of ₹ 2 per share as per Board's Resolution No. . . . dated . . .)				
	Bank A/c (Note 2)	Dr.		1,76,640	
	To Equity Share Allotment A/c				1,76,640
	(Being balance allotment money received except for 1,600 shares)				
	Equity Share First Call A/c	Dr.		80,000	
	To Equity Share Capital A/c				80,000
	(Being the first call money due on 40,000 shares @ ₹ 2 each as per Board's Resolution No. . . . dated . . .)				
	Bank A/c	Dr.		72,800	
	To Equity Share First Call A/c				72,800
	(Being the first call money received on 36,400 shares @ ₹ 2 each)				
	Equity Share Final Call A/c	Dr.		1,20,000	
	To Equity Share Capital A/c				1,20,000
	(Being the final call money due on 40,000 shares @ ₹ 3 each as per Board's Resolution No. . . . dated . . .)				

Particulars		Dr. (₹)	Cr. (₹)
Bank A/c Dr. To Equity Share Final Call A/c (Being the final call money received on 36,400 shares @ ₹ 3 each)		1,09,200	1,09,200
Equity Share Capital A/c (3,600 x ₹ 10) Dr. Securities Premium A/c (1,600 x ₹ 2) Dr. To Equity Share Allotment A/c (Note 1) To Equity Share First Call A/c (3,600 x ₹ 2) To Equity Share Final Call A/c (3,600 x ₹ 3) To Forfeited Shares A/c (Note 3) (Being the forfeiture of 3,600 shares for non-payment of allotment money on 1,600 shares and non-payment of call monies for 3,600 shares as per Board's Resolution No. . . . dated . . .)		36,000 3,200	7,360 7,200 10,800 13,840
Bank A/c (3,600 x ₹ 8) Dr. Forfeited Shares A/c (3,600 x ₹ 2) Dr. To Equity Share Capital A/c (Being the re-issue of 3,600 shares @ ₹ 8 each as fully paid-up as per Board's Resolution No. . . . dated . . .)		28,800 7,200	36,000
Forfeited Shares A/c (₹ 13,840 – 7,200) Dr. To Capital Reserve A/c (Being the profit on re-issue transferred to Capital Reserve)		6,640	6,640
Total		10,80,480	10,80,480

Working Notes :

(1) Money Due from Ram on Allotment

	₹
Money paid on application (Note 4)	3,840
Less: Amount adjusted on application (1,600 x ₹ 2)	3,200
Excess application money	640
Money due on allotment (1,600 x ₹ 5)	8,000
Less: Excess application money	640
Money not paid by Ram	7,360

(2) Money Received on Allotment

	₹
Total amount due on allotment	2,00,000
Less: Excess application money adjusted	16,000
	1,84,000
Less: Money not paid by Ram	7,360
	1,76,640

(3) Calculation of Amount Forfeited

	₹
Amount paid by Ram (Note 4)	3,840
Amount paid by Shyam excluding premium (2,000 × ₹ 5)	10,000
	13,840

(4) 40,000 shares were allotted to the applicants for 48,000 shares.
1 share was allotted to the applicants for 48,000 / 40,000 shares.
1,600 shares were allotted to the applicants for (48,000 / 40,000) × 1,600 = 1,920 shares.
Therefore, application money paid by Ram = 1,920 × ₹ 2 = ₹ 3,840.

Illustration 64

Hindusthan Steel Ltd invited applications for 50,000 equity shares of ₹ 10 each at a premium of ₹ 4 per share. The amount was payable as follows :

on application ₹ 4 (including premium ₹ 2); on allotment ₹ 6 (including premium ₹ 2)
on first and final call the balance.

Applications for 60,000 shares were received. Allotment was made to all applicants on *pro-rata* basis. Excess application money was adjusted towards sums due on allotment. Ram, to whom 400 shares were allotted, failed to pay allotment and the call money. Shyam, to whom 200 shares were allotted, failed to pay the call money. These shares were forfeited. The forfeited shares were re-issued @ ₹ 8 per share fully paid-up.

Pass the necessary journal entries in the books of the company. *[CBSE — Adapted]*

Solution

In the books of the Hindusthan Steel Ltd.

Journal

Date	Particulars		L.F.	Dr. ₹	Cr. ₹
	Bank A/c	Dr.		2,40,000	
	To Equity Share Application A/c				2,40,000
	(Being application money received on 60,000 shares @ ₹ 4 each)				
	Equity Share Application A/c	Dr.		2,00,000	
	To Equity Share Capital A/c				1,00,000
	To Securities Premium A/c				1,00,000
	(Being the application money on 50,000 shares @ ₹ 4 each transferred to Equity Share Capital Account and Equity Securities Premium Account as per Board's Resolution No. . . . dtd . . .)				
	Equity Share Application A/c	Dr.		40,000	
	To Equity Share Allotment A/c				40,000
	(Being the excess application money on 10,000 shares @ ₹ 4 each transferred to Equity Share Allotment Account as per Board's Resolution No. . . . dated . . .)				
	Equity Share Allotment A/c	Dr.		3,00,000	
	To Equity Share Capital A/c				2,00,000
	To Equity Securities Premium A/c				1,00,000
	(Being allotment money due on 50,000 shares @ ₹ 6 each including premium @ ₹ 2 per share as per Board's Resolution No. . . . dated . . .)				
	Bank A/c (Note 2)	Dr.		2,57,920	
	To Equity Share Allotment A/c				2,57,920
	(Being balance allotment money received except for 400 shares)				
	Equity Share First and Final Call A/c	Dr.		2,00,000	
	To Equity Share Capital A/c				2,00,000
	(Being the first and final call money due on 50,000 shares @ ₹ 4 each as per Board's Resolution No. . . . dated . . .)				
	Bank A/c	Dr.		1,97,600	
	To Equity Share First and Final Call A/c				1,97,600
	(Being the first and final call money received on 49,400 shares @ ₹ 4 each)				
	Equity Share Capital A/c (600 x ₹ 10)	Dr.		6,000	
	Securities Premium A/c (400 x ₹ 2)	Dr.		800	
	To Equity Share Allotment A/c (Note 1)				2,080
	To Equity Share First and Final Call A/c (600 x ₹ 4)				2,400
	To Forfeited Shares A/c (Note 3)				2,320
	(Being the forfeiture of 600 shares for non-payment of allotment money on 400 shares and non-payment of first and final call money on 600 shares as per Board's Resolution No. ... dtd...)				
	Bank A/c (600 x ₹ 8)	Dr.		4,800	
	Forfeited Shares A/c (600 x ₹ 2)	Dr.		1,200	
	To Equity Share Capital A/c				6,000
	(Being the re-issue of 600 shares @ ₹ 8 each as fully paid-up as per Board's Resolution No. . . . dated . . .)				
	Forfeited Shares A/c (₹ 2,320 – 1,200)	Dr.		1,120	
	To Capital Reserve A/c				1,120
	(Being the profit on re-issue transferred to Capital Reserve)				
	Total			14,49,440	14,49,440

Working Notes :

(1) Money Due from Ram on Allotment	₹	(2) Money Received on Allotment	₹
Money paid on application (Note 4)	1,920	Total amount due on allotment	3,00,000
Less: Amount adj. on application (400 x ₹ 4)	1,600	Less: Excess application money adjusted	40,000
Excess application money	320		2,60,000
Money due on allotment (400 x ₹ 6)	2,400	Less: Money not paid by Ram (Note 1)	2,080
Less: Excess application money	320		2,57,920
Money not paid by Ram	2,080		

(3) Calculation of amount forfeited

	₹
Amount paid by Ram excluding premium (1,920 – 800)	1,120
Amount paid by Shyam excluding premium (200 × ₹ 6)	1,200
	2,320

(4) 50,000 shares were allotted to the applicants for 60,000 shares
1 share was allotted to the applicants for 60,000 / 50,000 shares.
400 shares were allotted to the applicants for (60,000 / 50,000) × 400 = 480 shares.
Therefore, application money paid by Ram = 480 × ₹ 4 = ₹ 1,920.

Illustration 64

A company issued for public subscription 75,000 equity shares of ₹ 10 each at a premium of ₹ 2 per share payable as under :

on application ₹ 2; on allotment ₹ 5 (including premium); on first call ₹ 2; on final call ₹ 3.

Applications were received for 1,12,500 shares. Shares were allotted to the applicants for 90,000 shares, the remaining applications being rejected. Money overpaid on application was utilised towards sum due on allotment.

A, to whom 3,000 shares were allotted, failed to pay the allotment money and two calls, B to whom 3,750 shares were allotted, failed to pay the two calls. All these shares were forfeited after the final call. 5,000 shares including all shares of A were re-issued as fully paid shares for ₹ 7.50 per share excluding premium.

Give journal entries to record the above transactions in the books of the company.

[CBSE — Adapted]

Solution

In the books of the Company
Journal

Date	Particulars	L.F.	Dr. ₹	Cr. ₹
	Bank A/c Dr. To Equity Share Application A/c (Being application money received on 1,12,500 shares @ ₹ 2 each)		2,25,000	2,25,000
	Equity Share Application A/c Dr. To Bank A/c (Being application money on 22,500 shares were refunded as per Board's Resolution No. . . . dated . . .)		45,000	45,000
	Equity Share Application A/c Dr. To Equity Share Capital A/c (Being the application money on 75,000 shares @ ₹ 2 each transferred to Equity Share Capital Account as per Board's Resolution No. . . . dated . . .)		1,50,000	1,50,000
	Equity Share Application A/c Dr. To Equity Share Allotment A/c (Being the excess application money on 15,000 shares @ ₹ 2 each transferred to Equity Share Allotment Account as per Board's Resolution No. . . . dated . . .)		30,000	30,000

Particulars		Dr. (₹)	Cr. (₹)
Equity Share Allotment A/c	Dr.	3,75,000	
To Equity Share Capital A/c			2,25,000
To Securities Premium A/c			1,50,000
(Being allotment money due on 75,000 shares @ ₹ 5 each including premium @ ₹ 2 per share as per Board's Resolution No. . . . dated . . .)			
Bank A/c (Note 2)	Dr.	3,31,200	
To Equity Share Allotment A/c			3,31,200
(Being balance allotment money received on 72,000 shares)			
Equity Share First Call A/c	Dr.	1,50,000	
To Equity Share Capital A/c			1,50,000
(Being the first call money due on 75,000 shares @ ₹ 2 each as per Board's Resolution No. . . . dated . . .)			
Bank A/c	Dr.	1,36,500	
To Equity Share First Call A/c			1,36,500
(Being the first call money received on 68,250 shares @ ₹ 2 each)			
Equity Share Final Call A/c	Dr.	2,25,000	
To Equity Share Capital A/c			2,25,000
(Being the final call money due on 75,000 shares @ ₹ 3 each as per Board's Resolution No. . . . dated . . .)			
Bank A/c	Dr.	2,04,750	
To Equity Share Final Call A/c			2,04,750
(Being the final call money received on 68,250 shares @ ₹ 3 each)			
Equity Share Capital A/c (6,750 x ₹ 10)	Dr.	67,500	
Securities Premium A/c (3,000 x ₹ 2)	Dr.	6,000	
To Equity Share Allotment A/c (Note 1)			13,800
To Equity Share First Call A/c (6,750 x ₹ 2)			13,500
To Equity Share Final Call A/c (6,750 x ₹ 3)			20,250
To Forfeited Shares A/c (Note 3)			25,950
(Being the forfeiture of 6,750 shares for non-payment of allotment money on 3,000 shares and non-payment of first and final call monies on 6,750 shares as per Board's Resolution No. . . . dated . . .)			
Bank A/c (5,000 x ₹ 7.50)	Dr.	37,500	
Forfeited Shares A/c (5,000 x ₹ 2.50)	Dr.	12,500	
To Equity Share Capital A/c			50,000
(Being the re-issue of 5,000 shares @ ₹ 7.50 each as fully paid-up as per Board's Resolution No. . . . dated . . .)			
Forfeited Shares A/c (Note 5)	Dr.	4,700	
To Capital Reserve A/c			4,700
(Being the profit on re-issue transferred to Capital Reserve)			
Total		20,00,650	20,00,650

Working Notes :

(1) Money Due from A on Allotment

	₹
Money received on application (Note 4)	7,200
Less: Amount adj. on application (3,000 x ₹ 2)	6,000
Excess application money	1,200
Money due on allotment (3,000 x ₹ 5)	15,000
Less: Excess application money	1,200
Money not paid by A	13,800

(2) Money Received on Allotment

	₹
Total amount due on allotment	3,75,000
Less: Excess application money adjusted	30,000
	3,45,000
Less: Money not paid by A (Note 1)	13,800
	3,31,200

(3) Calculation of amount forfeited

	₹
A : (3,600 × ₹ 2)	7,200
B : (3,750 × ₹ 5)	18,750
	25,950

(4) 75,000 shares were allotted to the applicants for 90,000 shares.
1 share was allotted to the applicants for 90,000 / 75,000 shares.
3,000 shares were allotted to the applicants for (90,000 / 75,000) × 3,000 = 3,600 shares.
Therefore, application money paid for A = 3,600 × ₹ 2 = ₹ 7,200.

(5) Amount transferred to capital reserve

(i) Amount forfeited in respect of A's share (Note 4)	7,200	
Less : Loss on re-issue (3,000 × ₹ 2.50)	7,500	(300)
(ii) Amount forfeited per share of B (₹ 18,750 / 3,750)	5.00	
Less : Loss on re-issue per share	2.50	
Profit on re-issue per share	2.50	
Total profit on re-issue (2,000 × ₹ 2.50)		5,000
		4,700

Illustration 66

Nav Lakshmi Ltd issued a prospectus inviting applications for 50,000 shares of ₹ 10 each. These shares were issued at par on the following terms :

on application ₹ 3; on allotment ₹ 4; on first call ₹ 2; on final call the balance.

Applications were received for 60,000 shares. Allotments were made on the following basis :

(i) to applicants for 10,000 shares — in full; (ii) to applicants for 20,000 shares — 15,000 shares; and (iii) to applicants for 30,000 shares — 25,000 shares. All excess amount paid on application is to be adjusted against amount due on allotment.

The shares were fully called and paid up except amounts of allotment, first and final call not paid by those who applied for 2,000 shares out of the group applying for 20,000 shares.

All the shares on which calls were not paid were forfeited by the Board of Directors.

1,000 forfeited shares were re-issued as fully paid up on receipt of ₹ 8 per share.

Show the journal entries in the books of Nav Lakshmi Ltd. *[All India Secondary Board — Adapted]*

Solution

In the books of Nav Lakshmi Ltd.
Journal

Date	Particulars	L.F.	Dr. ₹	Cr. ₹
	Bank A/c Dr.		1,80,000	
	To Equity Share Application A/c			1,80,000
	(Being application money received on 60,000 shares @ ₹ 3 each)			
	Equity Share Application A/c Dr.		1,50,000	
	To Equity Share Capital A/c			1,50,000
	(Being application money on 50,000 shares @ ₹ 3 each transferred to Share Capital Account as per Board's Resolution No. . . . dated . . .)			
	Equity Share Application A/c Dr.		30,000	
	To Equity Share Allotment A/c			30,000
	(Being the excess application money on 10,000 shares @ ₹ 3 each transferred to Equity Share Allotment Account as per Board's Resolution No. . . . dated . . .)			

Particulars		L.F.	Dr. (₹)	Cr. (₹)
Equity Share Allotment A/c To Equity Share Capital A/c (Being allotment money due on 50,000 shares @ ₹ 4 each as per Board's Resolution No. . . . dated . . .)	Dr.		2,00,000	2,00,000
Bank A/c (Note 2) To Equity Share Allotment A/c (Being allotment money received except for 1,500 shares)	Dr.		1,65,500	1,65,500
Equity Share First Call A/c To Equity Share Capital A/c (Being the first call money due on 50,000 shares @ ₹ 2 each as per Board's Resolution No. . . . dated . . .)	Dr.		1,00,000	1,00,000
Bank A/c To Equity Share First Call A/c (Being the firstl call money received on 48,500 shares @ ₹ 2 each)	Dr.		97,000	97,000
Equity Share Final Call A/c To Equity Share Capital A/c (Being the final call money due on 50,000 shares @ ₹ 1 each as per Board's Resolution No. . . . dated . . .)	Dr.		50,000	50,000
Bank A/c To Equity Share Final Call A/c (Being the final call money received on 48,500 shares @ ₹ 1 each)	Dr.		48,500	48,500
Equity Share Capital A/c (1,500 x ₹ 10) To Equity Share Allotment A/c (1,500 x ₹ 3) To Equity Share First Call A/c (1,500 x ₹ 2) To Equity Share Final Call A/c (1,500 x ₹ 1) To Forfeited Shares A/c (2,000 x ₹ 3) (Being the forfeiture of 1,500 shares for non-payment of allotment, first and final call monies as per Board's Resolution No. . . . dated . . .)	Dr.		15,000	 4,500 3,000 1,500 6,000
Bank A/c (1,000 x ₹ 8) Forfeited Shares A/c (1,000 x ₹ 2) To Equity Share Capital A/c (Being the re-issue of 1,000 shares @ ₹ 8 each as fully paid-up as per Board's Resolution No. . . . dated . . .)	Dr. Dr.		8,000 2,000	 10,000
Forfeited Shares A/c (Note 3) To Capital Reserve A/c (Being the profit on re-issue transferred to Capital Reserve)	Dr.		2,000	2,000
	Total		10,48,000	10,48,000

Working Notes :

(1) Money Due on Allotment

	₹
Money received on application (2,000 x ₹ 3)	6,000
Less: Amount adjusted on application (Note 4)	4,500
Excess application money	1,500
Money due on allotment (1,500 x ₹ 4)	6,000
Less: Excess application money	1,500
Money not paid on allotment	4,500

(2) Money Received on Allotment

	₹
Total amount due on allotment	2,00,000
Less: Excess application money adjusted	30,000
	1,70,000
Less: Money not paid on allotment (Note 1)	4,500
	1,65,500

(3) Total amount forfeited = ₹ 6,000 ₹

Amount forfeited per share = ₹ 6,000 / 1,500 4

Less : Loss on re-issue per share 2

Profit on re-issue 2

Amount transferred to capital reserve = 1,000 × ₹ 2 = ₹ 2,000.

(4) Applicant for 20,000 shares were allotted 15,000 shares.

Applicant for 1 share was allotted 15,000 / 20,000 shares.

Applicant for 2,000 shares were allotted (15,000 / 20,000) × 2,000 = 1,500.

Therefore, amount adjusted on application = 1,500 × ₹ 3 = ₹ 4,500.

Illustration 67

XY Ltd invited applications for issuing 50,000 equity shares of ₹ 10 each. The amount was payable as : on application ₹ 3 per share; on allotment ₹ 4 per share; on first and final call ₹ 3 per share.

Applications were received for 75,000 shares and *pro-rata* allotment was made as follows :

Applicants for 40,000 shares were allotted 30,000 shares on *pro- rata* basis. Applicants for 35,000 shares were allotted 20,000 shares on *pro-rata* basis.

Ramu, to whom 1,200 shares were allotted out of the group applying for 40,000 shares, failed to pay the allotment money. His shares were forfeited immediately after allotment.

Shamu, who had applied for 700 shares out of the group applying for 35,000 shares, failed to pay the first and final call. His shares were also forfeited. Out of the forfeited shares, 1,000 shares were re-issued @ ₹ 8 per share fully paid up. The re- issued shares included all the forfeited shares of Shamu. Pass necessary journal entries to record the above transactions. *[CBSE — Adapted]*

Solution

In the books of XY Ltd

Journal

Date	Particulars	L.F.	Dr. ₹	Cr. ₹
	Bank A/c Dr. To Equity Share Application A/c (Being application money received on 75,000 shares @ ₹ 3 each)		2,25,000	2,25,000
	Equity Share Application A/c Dr. To Equity Share Capital A/c (Being application money on 50,000 shares @ ₹ 3 each transferred to Share Capital Account as per Board's Resolution No. . . . dated . . .)		1,50,000	1,50,000
	Equity Share Application A/c Dr. To Equity Share Allotment A/c (Being the excess application money on 25,000 shares @ ₹ 3 each transferred to Equity Share Allotment Account as per Board's Resolution No. . . . dated . . .)		75,000	75,000
	Equity Share Allotment A/c Dr. To Equity Share Capital A/c (Being allotment money due on 50,000 shares @ ₹ 4 each as per Board's Resolution No. . . . dated . . .)		2,00,000	2,00,000
	Bank A/c (Note 2) Dr. To Equity Share Allotment A/c (Being balance allotment money received except on 1,200 shares)		1,21,400	1,21,400
	Equity Share Capital A/c (1,200 x ₹ 7) Dr. To Equity Share Allotment A/c (Note 1) To Forfeited Shares A/c (Note 4) (Being the forfeiture of 1,200 shares for non-payment of allotment money as per Board's Resolution No. . . . dated . . .)		8,400	3,600 4,800

Particulars		L.F.	Dr. ₹	Cr. ₹
Equity Share First and Final Call A/c To Equity Share Capital A/c (Being the first and final call money due on 48,800 shares @ ₹ 3 each as per Board's Resolution No. . . . dated . . .)	Dr.		1,46,400	1,46,400
Bank A/c (Note 5) To Equity Share First and Final Call A/c (Being the first and final call money received on 48,400 shares @ ₹ 3 each)	Dr.		1,45,200	1,45,200
Equity Share Capital A/c (400 x ₹ 10) To Equity Share First and Final Call A/c (400 x ₹ 3) To Forfeited Shares A/c (400 x ₹ 7) (Being the forfeiture of 400 shares for non-payment of first and final call money as per Board's Resolution No. . . . dated . . .)	Dr.		4,000	 1,200 2,800
Bank A/c (1,000 x ₹ 8) Forfeited Shares A/c (1,000 x ₹ 2) To Equity Share Capital A/c (Being the re-issue of 1,000 shares @ ₹ 8 each as fully paid-up as per Board's Resolution No. . . . dated . . .)	Dr. Dr.		8,000 2,000	 10,000
Forfeited Shares A/c (Note 3) To Capital Reserve A/c (Being the profit on re-issue transferred to Capital Reserve)	Dr.		3,200	3,200
	Total		10,88,600	10,88,600

Working Notes :

(1) Money Due from Ramu on Allotment

	₹
Money paid on application (Note 4)	4,800
Less: Amount adj. on application (1,200 x ₹ 3)	3,600
Excess application money	1,200
Money due on allotment (1,200 x ₹ 4)	4,800
Less: Excess application money	1,200
Money not paid by Ramu	3,600

(2) Money Received on Allotment

	₹
Total amount due on allotment	2,00,000
Less: Excess application money adjusted	75,000
	1,25,000
Less: Money not paid by Ramu (Note 1)	3,600
	1,21,400

(3) Total shares forfeited = 1,600 (1,200 of Ramu and 400 of Shamu). Out of these shares only 1,000 shares are re-issued, which includes 400 of Shamu and 600 of Ramu. Amount to be transferred to capital reserve has been calculated as follows :

	₹
Amount forfeited in respect of 400 shares of Shamu	2,800
Amount forfeited in respect of 600 shares of Ramu (1/2 of ₹ 4,800)	2,400
	5,200
Less : Loss on re-issue (1,000 × ₹ 2)	2,000
Amount to be transferred to capital reserve	3,200

(4) 30,000 shares were allotted to the applicants for 40,000 shares.
1 share was allotted to the applicants for 40,000 / 30,000 shares.
1,200 shares were allotted to the applicants for (40,000 / 30,000) × 1,200 = 1,600 shares.
Therefore, application money paid by Ramu = 1,600 × ₹ 3 = ₹ 4,800.

(5) Applicants for 35,000 shares were allotted 20,000 shares.
Applicants for 1 share was allotted 20,000 / 35,000 shares.
Applicants for 700 shares were allotted (20,000/35,000) × 700 = 400 shares.

Illustration 68

Sudershan Ltd invited applications for 1,00,000 equity shares of ₹ 10 each. The shares were issued at a premium of ₹ 5 per share. The amount was payable as follows : On application and allotment ₹ 8 per share (including premium ₹ 3). Balance including premium on the first and final call.

Applications for 1,50,000 shares were received. Applications for 10,000 shares were rejected and *pro-rata* allotment was made to the remaining applicants on the following basis : (i) Applicants for 80,000 shares were allotted 60,000 shares; and (ii) Applicants for 60,000 shares were allotted 40,000 shares. X, who belonged to the first category and was allotted 300 shares, failed to pay the first call money. Y, who belonged to the second category and was allotted 200 shares also failed to pay the first call money. Their shares were forfeited. The forfeited shares were re-issued @ ₹ 12 per share fully paid-up. Prepare the Cash Book and pass necessary journal entries.

[CBSE — Adapted]

Solution

In the books of Sudershan Ltd

Cash Book (Bank column only)

Dr. Cr.

Date	Particulars	₹	Date	Particulars	₹
	To Equity Share Application & Allotment A/c (Being application money recd on 1,50,000 equity shares @ ₹ 8 each)	12,00,000		By Equity Share Application & Allotment A/c (Being the excess application money refunded on 10,000 shares @ ₹ 8 each)	80,000
	To Equity Share First & Final Call A/c (Note 3) (Being the first and final call money received on 9,500 equity shares @ ₹ 7 each after adjustment of excess application & allotment money)	3,78,100		By Balance c/d	15,04,100
	To Equity Share Capital A/c (Being the re-issue of 500 shares at @ ₹ 10 each)	5,000			
	To Securities Premium A/c (Being the premium received on 500 shares @ ₹ 2 each)	1,000			
		15,84,100			15,84,100

In the books of Sudershan Ltd

Journal

Date	Particulars	L.F.	Dr. ₹	Cr. ₹
	Equity Share Application and Allotment A/c Dr.		8,00,000	
	To Equity Share Capital A/c			5,00,000
	To Securities Premium A/c			3,00,000
	(Being the application money on 1,00,000 shares @ ₹ 8 each transferred to Share Capital Account @ ₹ 5 per share and to Securities Premium Account @ ₹ 3 per share as per Board's Resolution No. . . .)			
	Equity Share Application and Allotment A/c Dr.		3,20,000	
	To Equity Share First and Final Call A/c			3,20,000
	(Being the excess application and allotment money on 40,000 shares transferred to Equity Share First and Final Call Account as per Board's Resolution No. . . . dated . . .)			
	Equity Share First and Final Call A/c Dr.		7,00,000	
	To Equity Share Capital A/c			5,00,000
	To Securities Premium A/c			2,00,000
	(Being the first and final call money due on 1,00,000 shares @ ₹ 7 each including premium of ₹ 2 per share as per Board's Resolution No. . . . dated . . .)			

Particulars		Dr. (₹)	Cr. (₹)
Equity Share Capital A/c (500 x ₹ 10) Dr. Securities Premium A/c (500 x ₹ 2) Dr. To Equity Share First and Final Call A/c To Forfeited Shares A/c (Note 6) (Being the forfeiture of 500 shares for non-payment of allotment money @ ₹ 7 per share as per Board's Resolution No. . . . dated . . .)		5,000 1,000	 1,900 4,100
Forfeited Shares A/c (Note 7) Dr. To Capital Reserve A/c (Being the profit on re-issue of 500 shares transferred to Capital Reserve)		4,100	 4,100
Total		18,30,100	18,30,100

Working Notes :

(1) Money Due from X on First and Final Call

Money paid on application (Note 4)	3,200
Less: Amount adjusted on application and allotment (300 x ₹ 8)	2,400
Excess application money	800
Money due on first and final call (300 x ₹ 7)	2,100
Less: Excess application money	800
Money not paid by X	1,300

(2) Money Due from Y on First and Final Call

Money paid on application (Note 5)	2,400
Less: Amount adjusted on application (200 x ₹ 8)	1,600
Excess application money	800
Money due on first and final call (200 x ₹ 7)	1,400
Less : Excess application money	800
Money not paid by Y	600

(3) Amount received on first and final call

	₹
Total amount due on first and final call	7,00,000
Less : Excess application money adjusted	3,20,000
	3,80,000
Less : Money not paid by X (Note 1)	1,300
Less : Money not paid by Y (Note 2)	600
	3,78,100

(4) 60,000 shares were allotted to the applicants for 80,000 shares.
1 share was allotted to the applicants for 80,000 / 60,000 shares.
300 shares were allotted to the applicants for (80,000/60,000) × 300 = 400 shares.
Therefore, application money paid by X = 400 shares × ₹ 8 = ₹ 3,200.

(5) 40,000 shares were allotted to the applicant for 60,000 shares.
1 share was allotted to the applicant for 60,000/40,000 shares.
200 shares were allotted to the applicant (60,000/40,000) × 200 = 300 shares.
Therefore, application money paid by Y = 300 × ₹ 8 = 2,400.

(6) Amount forfeited

	₹
X paid (Note 4)	3,200
Y paid (Note 5)	2,400
	5,600
Less : Premium on 500 shares @ ₹ 3 per share	1,500
	4,100

(7) Entire amount forfeited will be transferred to capital reserve because, there is no loss on re-issue.

Illustration 69

A company offered 1,00,000 shares of ₹ 10 each to the public on the following terms :

₹ 3 on application; ₹ 4 on allotment; and the balance as and when required.

Applications were received for 1,40,000 shares. Allotment was made as : 80,000 applicants were given 80,000 shares; 50,000 applicants were given 20,000 shares; 10,000 applicants were given NIL.

Application money is to applied towards allotment and the balance beyond that is to be returned. A shareholder, who applied for 1,000 shares and was given 1,000 shares, failed to pay the allotment money. His shares were forfeited.

Pass journal entries to record the above transactions. *[CBSE — Adapted]*

Solution

In the books of the Company

Journal

Date	Particulars	L.F.	Dr. ₹	Cr. ₹
	Bank A/c (Note 1 — Column 3) Dr. To Equity Share Application A/c (Being application money received on 1,40,000 shares @ ₹ 3 each)		4,20,000	4,20,000
	Equity Share Application A/c (Note 1 — Column 6) Dr. To Bank A/c (Being application money refunded as per Board's Resolution No. . . . dated . . .)		40,000	40,000
	Equity Share Application A/c (Note 1 — Column 4) Dr. To Equity Share Capital A/c (Being application money on 1,00,000 shares @ ₹ 3 each transferred to Equity Share Capital Account as per Board's Resolution No. . . . dated . . .)		3,00,000	3,00,000
	Equity Share Application A/c (Note 1 — Column 5) Dr. To Equity Share Allotment A/c (Being the excess application money on 20,000 shares @ ₹ 4 each transferred to Equity Share Allotment Account as per Board's Resolution No. . . . dated . . .)		80,000	80,000
	Equity Share Allotment A/c Dr. To Equity Share Capital A/c (Being allotment money due on 1,00,000 shares @ ₹ 4 each as per Board's Resolution No. ... dated ...)		4,00,000	4,00,000
	Bank A/c (Note 2) Dr. To Equity Share Allotment A/c (Being the allotment money received except for 1,000 shares)		3,16,000	3,16,000
	Equity Share Capital A/c (1,000 x ₹ 7) Dr. To Equity Share Allotment A/c 1,000 x ₹ 4) To Forfeited Shares A/c (1,000 x ₹ 3) (Being the forfeiture of 1,000 shares for non-payment of allotment money as per Board's Resolution No. . . . dated . . .)		7,000	4,000 3,000
	Total		15,63,000	15,63,000

Working Notes :

(1) Calculation for Adjustment and Refund

Category	No. of Shares applied for (1)	No. of Shares allotted (2)	Amount received on application (3)	Amount required on application (4)	Amount adjusted on allotment (5)	Refund [3 – (4 + 5)] (6)	Amount due on allotment (7)	Amount receivable on allotment (8)
(i)	80,000	80,000	2,40,000	2,40,000	Nil	Nil	3,20,000	3,20,000
(ii)	50,000	20,000	1,50,000	60,000	80,000	10,000	80,000	Nil
(iii)	10,000	Nil	30,000	Nil	Nil	30,000	Nil	Nil
Total	1,40,000	1,00,000	4,20,000	3,00,000	80,000	40,000	4,00,000	3,20,000

(2) Amount received on allotment

	₹
Amount receivable on allotment (Note 1 — Column 8)	3,20,000
Less : Amount not paid on 1,000 shares @ ₹ 4 each	4,000
	3,16,000

Illustration 70

Moneyplus Company Ltd. issued for public subscription, 75,000 shares of the value of ₹ 10 each at par payable as follows :

₹ 2 per share on application, ₹ 4 per share on allotment and ₹ 4 per share on call.

The company received applications for 1,50,000 shares. The allotment was done as under :

(A) Applicants of 15,000 shares were allotted 5,000 shares.

(B) Applicants of 70,000 shares were allotted 40,000 shares.

(C) Remaining applicants was allotted 30,000 shares.

Money in excess to allotments was returned. Hari, a shareholder who had applied for 3,500 shares out of group B failed to pay allotment and call money. Rohan, a shareholder who was allotted 3,000 shares paid the call money along with the allotment. Rohan also belonged to group B.

Pass necessary journal entries to record the above transactions in the books of the Company. Show your working notes clearly.

[CBSE (Delhi) — Adapted]

Solution

In the books of MoneyPlus Company Ltd

Journal

Date	Particulars		L.F.	Dr. ₹	Cr. ₹
	Bank A/c (1,50,000 x 2)	Dr.		3,00,000	
	To Share Application A/c				3,00,000
	(Being application money received for 1,50,000 shares @ ₹ 2 each)				
	Share Application A/c	Dr.		3,00,000	
	To Share Capital A/c				1,50,000
	To Share Allotment A/c (See Cl. 5)				1,50,000
	(Being application money for 75,000 shares @ ₹ 2 transferred to Share Capital Account. Application money of ₹ 1,50,000 adjusted towards allotment as per Board's Resolution No. ... dated ...)				
	Share Allotment A/c	Dr.		3,00,000	
	To Share Capital A/c				3,00,000
	(Being allotment money due on 75,000 shares @ ₹ 4 each as per Board's Resolution No. ... dated ...)				
	Bank A/c	Dr.		1,45,000	
	Calls-in-Arrear A/c	Dr.		5,000	
	To Share Allotment A/c				1,50,000
	(Being allotment money received on all shares except on 2,000 shares held by Hari)				
	Bank A/c (3,000 x 4)	Dr.		12,000	
	To Calls-in-Advance A/c				12,000
	(Being money received on 3,000 shares @ ₹ 4 as calls-in-advance from Rohan)				
	Share Final Call A/c	Dr.		3,00,000	
	To Share Capital A/c				3,00,000
	(Being final call money due on 75,000 shares @ ₹ 4 each as per Board's Resolution No. ... dated ...)				

Bank A/c	Dr.	2,80,000	
Calls-in-Arrear A/c	Dr.	8,000	
Calls-in-Advance A/c	Dr.	12,000	
To Share Final Call A/c			3,00,000
(Being final call money received on all shares except on 2,000 shares held by Hari)			

Working Notes : **(1) Calculation for Adjustment and Refund**

Category	No. of Shares applied for (1)	No. of Shares allotted (2)	Amount received on application (3)	Amount required on application (4)	Amount adjusted on allotment (5)	Refund [3 – (4 + 5)] (6)	Amount due on allotment (7)	Amount receivable on allotment (8)
A	15,000	5,000	30,000	10,000	25,000	Nil	20,000	Nil
B	70,000	40,000	1,40,000	80,000	60,000	Nil	1,60,000	1,00,000
C	65,000	30,000	1,30,000	60,000	70,000	Nil	1,20,000	50,000
Total	1,50,000	75,000	3,00,000	1,50,000	1,50,000	Nil	3,00,000	1,50,000

(2) Applicants of Category 'B' were allotted 40,000 shares against 70,000 application. Hari applied for 3,500 shares under category 'B'. He was allotted (40,000 / 70,000 × 3,500) = **2,000 shares.**

Amount due from Hari on allotment

Application money received (3,500 × 2)	7,000
Less: Application money used (2,000 × 2)	4,000
Excess application money to be adjusted on allotment	3,000
Allotment money due (2,000 × 4)	8,000
Less: Excess application money	3,000
Money due from Hari	5,000

Amount Received on Allotment

Amount to be received on allotment (See Cl. 8)	1,50,000
Less: Amount not paid by Hari	5,000
Net amount received	1,45,000

Illustration 71

Reliable Investments Limited issued a prospectus inviting applications for 4,000 equity shares of ₹ 20 each at a premium of ₹ 4 per share payable as follows :

on application ₹ 4; on allotment ₹ 10 (including the premium);
on first call ₹ 6; on second call ₹ 4.

Applications were received for 6,000 shares and allotment was made *pro-rata* to the applicants of 4,800 shares, the applications for remaining shares being refused. Money overpaid on application was used on account of sums due on allotment.

Harish, to whom 80 shares were allotted, could not pay the allotment money and on his subsequent failure to pay the first call, his shares were forfeited after the first call.

Mukesh, to whom 120 shares were allotted, failed to pay the two calls and his shares were forfeited after the second call.

Of the shares forfeited, 160 shares were sold to Suresh credited as fully paid at ₹ 18 per share, all of Harish's forfeited shares being included. Pass journal entries in the books of the company to record the above transactions. *[CBSE — Adapted]*

Solution

In the books of Reliable Investments Limited
Journal

Date	Particulars		L.F.	Dr. ₹	Cr. ₹
	Bank A/c	Dr.		24,000	
	To Equity Share Application A/c				24,000
	(Being application money received on 6,000 shares @ ₹ 4 each)				
	Equity Share Application A/c	Dr.		4,800	
	To Bank A/c				4,800
	(Being application money on 1,200 shares were refunded as per Board's Resolution No. . . . dated . . .)				
	Equity Share Application A/c	Dr.		16,000	
	To Equity Share Capital A/c				16,000
	(Being the application money on 4,000 shares @ ₹ 4 each transferred to Equity Share Capital Account as per Board's Resolution No. . . . dated . . .)				
	Equity Share Application A/c	Dr.		3,200	
	To Equity Share Allotment A/c				3,200
	(Being the excess application money on 800 shares @ ₹ 4 each transferred to Equity Share Allotment Account as per Board's Resolution No. . . . dated . . .)				
	Equity Share Allotment A/c	Dr.		40,000	
	To Equity Share Capital A/c				24,000
	To Securities Premium A/c				16,000
	(Being the allotment money due on 4,000 shares @ ₹ 10 each including premium as per Board's Resolution No. . . . dated . . .)				
	Bank A/c (Note 2)	Dr.		36,064	
	To Equity Share Allotment A/c				36,064
	(Being balance allotment money received on 3,920 shares)				
	Equity Share First Call A/c	Dr.		24,000	
	To Equity Share Capital A/c				24,000
	(Being the first call money due on 4,000 shares @ ₹ 6 each as per Board's Resolution No. . . . dated . . .)				
	Bank A/c	Dr.		22,800	
	To Equity Share First Call A/c				22,800
	(Being the first call money received on 3,800 shares @ ₹ 6 each				
	Equity Share Capital A/c (80 x ₹ 16)	Dr.		1,280	
	Securities Premium A/c (80 x ₹ 4)	Dr.		320	
	To Equity Share Allotment A/c (Note 1)				736
	To Equity Share First Call A/c (80 x ₹ 6)				480
	To Forfeited Shares A/c (Note 3)				384
	(Being the forfeiture of 80 shares for non-payment of allotment and first call monies as per Board's Resolution No. . . . dated . . .)				
	Equity Share Second Call A/c	Dr.		15,680	
	To Equity Share Capital A/c				15,680
	(Being the second call money due on 3,920 shares @ ₹ 4 per share as per Board's Resolution No. . . . dated . . .)				
	Bank A/c	Dr.		15,200	
	To Equity Share Second Call A/c				15,200
	(Being the second call money received on 3,800 shares @ ₹ 4 each)				

Particulars		L.F.	Dr. (₹)	Cr. (₹)
Equity Share Capital A/c (120 x ₹ 20)	Dr.		2,400	
To Equity Share First Call A/c (120 x ₹ 6)				720
To Equity Share Second Call A/c (120 x ₹ 4)				480
To Forfeited Shares A/c (Note 3)				1,200
(Being the forfeiture of 120 shares for non-payment of first and second call monies as per Board's Resolution No. . . . dated . . .)				
Bank A/c (160 x ₹ 18)	Dr.		2,880	
Forfeited Shares A/c (160 x ₹ 2)	Dr.		320	
To Equity Share Capital A/c				3,200
(Being the re-issue of 160 shares @ ₹ 18 each as fully paid-up as per Board's Resolution No. . . . dated . . .)				
Forfeited Shares A/c (Note 5)	Dr.		864	
To Capital Reserve A/c				864
(Being the profit on re-issue transferred to Capital Reserve)				
	Total		2,09,808	2,09,808

Working Notes :

(1) Money Due from Harish on Allotment

	₹
Money paid on application (Note 4)	384
Less: Amount adjusted on application (80 x ₹ 4)	320
Excess application money	64
Money due on allotment (80 x ₹ 10)	800
Less: Excess application money	64
Money not paid by Harish	736

(2) Money Received on Allotment

	₹
Total amount due on allotment	40,000
Less: Excess application money adjusted	3,200
	36,800
Less: Money not paid by Harish (Note 1)	736
	36,064

(3) Amount forfeited

	₹
Harish (96 × ₹ 4)	384
Mukesh (120 × ₹ 10)	1,200

(4) 4,000 shares were allotted to the applicants for 4,800 shares.

1 share was allotted to the applicants for 4,800 / 4,000 shares.

80 shares were allotted to the applicants for (4,800 / 4,000) × 80 = 96 shares.

Therefore, application money paid by Harish = 96 × ₹ 4 = ₹ 384.

(5) Amount transferred to capital reserve

	₹	₹
(i) Amount forfeited in respect of Harish's share	384	
Less : Loss on re-issue (80 × ₹ 2)	160	224
(ii) Amount forfeited per share of Mukesh (1,200 / 120)	10	
Less : Loss on re-issue of each share	2	
Profit on re-issue of each share of Mukesh	8	
Total profit on re-issue of 80 shares of Mukesh (80 × ₹ 8)		640
		864

Chapter Summary

- As per the provision of Section 2(20) of the Companies Act, 2013 'company' means a company incorporated under this Act or under any previous company law.
- ***Prof. Haney*** defines a company as "the company is an artificial person created by law, having separate entity, with a perpetual succession and common seal."
- ***Lord Justice Lindley*** defines a company as :
  "By a company is meant an association of many persons who contribute money or money's worth to a common stock and employ it for a common purpose. The common stock so contributed is donated in money and is the capital of the company. The persons who contribute it or to whom it belongs are members. The proportion of capital to which each member is entitled is his share".
- Some of the characteristics of a Company are :
  1. A Company comes into existence only after registration under the Companies Act.
  2. A Company is a legal entity separate and distinct from its members. It can enter into a contract. It can sue and be sued in its own name.
  3. A shareholder of a company, in its individual capacity, cannot bind the Company in any way. The shareholder of a Company can enter into contract with the Company and can be an employee of the Company.
  4. The equity capital of a Company is typically subscribed by shareholders who receive return in the form of dividend.
- As per the provision of Section 2(68) of the Companies Act, 2013 'private company' means a company having a minimum paid-up share capital of ***one lakh rupees*** or such higher paid-up capital as may be prescribed and which by its articles —
  (i) restricts the right to transfer its share;
  (ii) except in case of one person company, limits the number of its members to ***two hundred***;
  (iii) prohibits any invitation to the public to subscribe for any securities of the company.
- As per the provision of Section 2(62) of the Companies Act, 2013 '***one person company' means a company which has only one person as member***'.
- As per the provision of Section 2(85) 'small company' means a company other than a public company—
  (i) paid-up share capital of which does not exceed ***fifty lakh rupees*** or such higher amount as may be prescribed which shall not be more than ***five crore rupees***; or
  (ii) turnover of which as per last Profit and Loss Account does not exceed two crore rupees, or such higher amount as may be prescribed which shall not be more than twenty crore rupees.
- As per the provision of Section 2(71) of the Companies Act, 2013 'public company' means a company which—
  (i) is not a private company;
  (ii) has a minimum paid-up share capital of ***five lakh rupees*** or such higher paid-up capital as may be prescribed.
- Section 93 of the Companies Act, 2013 provides that the share capital of a company limited by shares shall be of ***two*** kinds, namely,
  Equity Share Capital —
  (i) with voting rights; or
  (ii) with differential rights as to dividend, voting or otherwise in accordance with such rules as may be prescribed.

Chapter Summary (contd.)

- Equity Share Capital means all share capital which is not 'preference share' capital (to be explained shortly). The holder of an equity share with ***voting rights*** is entitled to vote, proportionately, in general meeting of the company.
- Preference Share Capital means that part of the issued share capital of the company which carries or would carry a preferential right with respect to—
  - (a) payment of dividend, either as a fixed amount or an amount calculated at a fixed rate, which may either be free of or subject to income-tax; and
  - (b) repayment, in the case of a winding-up or repayment of capital, of the amount of the share capital paid-up or deemed to have been paid-up, whether or not, there is a preferential right to the payment of any fixed premium or premium on any fixed scale, specified in the memorandum or articles of the company.
- Some of the features of equity shares are :
  1. It is the risk capital of the company.
  2. It can be purchased or sold in a stock exchange.
  3. It cannot be redeemed during the lifetime of the company. However, a company may purchase its own shares if certain conditions are satisified u/s 77A.
  4. Equity shareholders can vote in the election of directors.
- Features of a Preference Share
  - (1) It has preferential rights to dividends at a fixed rate or fixed amount as the case may be.
  - (2) It has cumulative rights to dividends.
  - (3) It has preferential rights to assets of the company in the case of liquidation.
  - (4) It is redeemable before the expiry of a period of ***twenty*** years from the date of its issue.
  - (5) It can be purchased or sold in a stock exchange at a price above or below its face value.
- **Reserve Capital** : A limited company may, by special resolution, determine that any portion of its share capital which has not been already called-up shall not be capable of being called up, except in the event and for the purposes of the company being wound-up. This uncalled portion of the share capital is called "Reserve Capital".
- Private placement is the issue of securities of a company direct to one investor or a small group of investors without resulting to underwriting.
- According to Section 2(37) of the Companies Act, 2013, "employees' stock option" means the option given to the directors, officers or employees of a company or of its holding company or subsidiary company or companies, if any, which gives such directors, officers or employees, the benefit or right to purchase, or to subscribe for, the shares of the company at a future date at a pre-determined price.
- Public issue of shares means selling of shares to public by issue of prospectus.
- Procedure of Issuing Shares Consists of the Following Steps
  - (i) Selection of Merchant Banker;
  - (ii) Issue of a prospectus;
  - (iii) Receipt by the company of applications for shares;
  - (iv) Allotment of shares to applicants; and
  - (v) Issue of share certificates.

Chapter Summary (contd.)

- As per SEBI (ICDR) Regulations, 'book building' means a process undertaken to elicit demand and to assess the price for determination of the quantum or value of specified securities or Indian Depository Receipts, as the case may be, in accordance with these regulations.
- A **letter of allotment** is a letter sent by a company to a person to whom the company has made an allotment of shares. The letter informs the applicant of the number of shares allotted to him, the sum and date of payment and the procedure to be followed (if payable in instalments, the respective payment dates, etc.).
- A **letter of regret** is a letter sent by a company to a person who has applied for shares, regretting that no shares have been allotted to him. It arises only when the issue has been oversubscribed.
- Share Certificate is a document that provides evidence of ownership of shares in a limited company. It will bear the name of the shareholder and the number and class of shares owned by the shareholder.
- As per the provision of Section 53 of the Companies Act, 2013 ***a company shall not issue shares at a discount*** to the public. Any share issued by a company at a discounted price shall be void.
- Minimum Subscription (Section 39) : The minimum subscription is the minimum amount which, in the opinion of the director, must be raised in cash by the issue of those shares to provide for :
  (i) the purchase price of any property to be acquired.
  (ii) any preliminary expenses, including commission, payable by the company.
  (iii) the repayment of any money borrowed for the above expenditure;
  (iv) working capital
  (v) any other expenditure stating the nature and purposes thereof and estimated amount in each case.
- When the application money is received for *more number* of shares than the number of shares offered to the public by a company, it is called over-subscription.
- When the application money is received for *less number* of shares than the number of shares offered to the public by a Company, it is called under-subscription.
- Calls-in-arrear refer to that portion of the capital, which has been called up but not yet paid by the shareholders.
- Calls in advance generally arises when there is an over subscription of shares. Here, the excess application money received is adjusted against the amount due on allotment or calls.
- In connection with the issue of **securities at a premium**, students should note the following :
  1. Securities premium amount cannot be distributed as dividend in cash.
  2. The annual Balance Sheet must disclose the amount of securities premium as a separate item.
  3. Money in Securities Premium Account cannot be treated as free reserves, as they are in the nature of capital reserves.
- As per Schedule III, "Discount on Issue of Shares Account" will not be shown on the assets side of the Balance Sheet. It is to be adjusted against profit and loss balance or general reserve. If profit and loss balance or resreve is insufficient, then it is to be shown as negative figure under ***'Reserve and Surplus'***.

THEORETICAL QUESTIONS

A. Multiple Choice

[1 Mark each]

Select the best choice to answer the following questions :

1. Shares can be issued
   A at par only
   B at a discount only
   C at a premium only
   D at par / at a premium
2. At the time of public issue of shares, which of the following steps are observed ?
   A issue of prospectus→select of merchant banker→cash received from applicants
   B issue of prospectus→cash received from applicants→selection of merchant banker
   C selection of merchant banker→cash received from applicants→issue of prospectus
   D selection of merchant banker→issue of prospectus→cash received from applicant
3. Which of the following is not true for stock ?
   A stock is in lump holding
   B stock can be issued directly
   C stock must be fully paid
   D stock is never numbered
4. Calls-in-advance is shown in the Balance Sheet
   A as a part of share capital under Shareholder's Fund
   B under 'Other Current Liabilities' as a separate item
   C as a deduction of cash and bank
   D as a separate item under 'Current Assets, Loans and Advances'
5. In case of a public issue, the underwriting of shares is
   A mandatory
   B optional
   C mandatory if the issue size is more than 100 crores
   D mandatory if the issue size is more than 100 crores but less than 500 crores
6. Shares are issued
   A for cash only
   B on credit only
   C for cash or for consideration other than cash
7. Profit on re-issue of shares is transferred to
   A profit and loss account
   B general reserve
   C capital redemption reserve
   D capital reserve
8. Which of the following statement is true for 'Premium on Issue of Shares' ?
   A it is shown in the Balance Sheet as a liability
   B it is capitalised and shown in the Balance Sheet permanently
   C it is capitalised and shown as an asset
   D it is shown in the 'Reserve and Surplus'

9. When shares are issued at a premium the 'Share Capital Account' is credited with
   A the face value of the shares in full
   B the face value of shares plus premium on issue of shares
   C the face value of shares plus brokerage on issue
   D the face value of the shares in full less brokerage
10. At the time of forfeiture of shares
   A share capital account is credited with the called-up value of shares forfeited
   B share capital account is debited with the face value of shares forfeited
   C share capital account is debited with the called-up value of shares forfeited
   D share capital account is neither debited nor credited
11. Till the forfeited shares are re-issued, balance of Forfeited Shares Account will be shown in Balance Sheet
   A as a separate item
   B as a part of the subscribed capital
   C as an item of reserve and surplus
   D as a part of the paid-up capital
12. Calls-in-arrear account shows
   A only credit balance
   B only debit balance
   C both debit and credit balances
   D none of the above
13. Calls-in-advance shows
   A only credit balance
   B only debit balance
   C both debit and credit balances
   D none of the above
14. Securities premium can be used by the company for
   A adjusting trading loss
   B issuing bonus shares
   C paying dividend
   D none of the above

B. Short Answer Questions : Type I

[1 Mark each]

1. Define company
2. What is authorized capital ?
3. What is issued capital ?
4. What is subscribed capital ?
5. What is paid-up capital ?
6. What do you mean by issue of shares at par ?
7. What do you mean by issue of shares at a premium ?
8. What do you mean by issue of shares for consideration other than cash ?

9. What is calls-in-arrear ?
10. What is calls-in-advance ?
11. What is minimum subscription ?
12. What is under subscription ?
13. What is over subscription ?
14. What do you mean by preference shares ?
15. What is forfeiture of shares ?
16. What do you mean by redeemable preference shares ?
17. What do you mean by cumulative preference shares ?
18. What do you mean by re-issue of shares ?
19. When shares are forfeited ?
20. How do you close Forfeited Shares Account ?
21. How profit on re-issue is treated ?
22. What is private placement ?
23. What do you mean by one man company ?
24. What do you mean by public offer of shares ?
25. What is reserve capital ?
26. What is capital reserve ?
27. What do you mean by allotment of shares ?
28. What is a Private Ltd. Company ?
29. What is uncalled capital ?
30. What do you mean by book-building method of issue of shares ?

C. Short Answer Questions : Type II

[3 Marks each]

1. (a) What are the characteristics of a company ?
   (b) What are the different types of companies ?
   (c) Distinguish between Public Limited Company and Private Limited Company.
2. (a) What are the features of an equity share ?
   (b) What are the features of a preference share ?
3. (a) What are the different ways of issue of shares ?
   (b) State the steps for public issue of shares.
4. Write short notes on:
   (a) Private Placement of Shares;
   (b) Public Subscription;
   (c) Minimum Subscription.
5. (a) What do you mean by pro-rata allotment ?
   (b) What do you mean by calls-in-arrear ?

PRACTICAL QUESTIO

Shares Issued at Par

1. The authorised capital of Suhani Ltd. is ₹ 45,00,000 divided into 30,000 shares of ₹ 150 each. Out of these the company issued 15,000 shares of ₹ 150 each at a premium of ₹ 10 per share. The amount was payable as follows :
   ₹ 50 per share on application; ₹ 40 per share on allotment (including premium), ₹ 30 per share on first call and balance on final call. Public applied for 14,000 shares. All the money was duly received.
   Prepare an extract of Balance Sheet of Suhani Ltd. as per Schedule III Part I of the Companies Act, 2013 disclosing the above information. Also prepare notes to accounts for the same.
   [CBSE (Delhi) — Adapted]
2. ABB Limited had an authorised share capital of ₹ 1,25,000 (shares of ₹ 10 each divided into 12,500 equity shares). The company issued 10,000 equity shares payable as ₹ 2 on application, ₹ 3 on allotment, ₹ 3 on first call, ₹ 2 on final call. All the shares were subscribed by the public. The directors made allotments and the money was duly received except for the final call on 500 shares. Pass the journal entries, prepare the Equity Share Capital Account only and show how the share capital will appear in the Balance Sheet.
3. X Ltd. was registered with a capital of ₹ 5,00,000 divided into 20,000 equity shares of ₹ 25 each. The company invited applications for 10,000 shares. Amount payable are as under ;
   On application ₹ 10; On allotment ₹ 5; On first call ₹ 5; and On final call ₹ 5
   Applications were received for 12,000 shares. Application money on 2,000 shares were returned. All the applicants paid their dues in full with the exception of one applicant holding 500 shares, who did not pay any call money. Give journal entries and the Balance Sheet of the company.
4. Development Consultant Ltd. was registered with an authorised capital of ₹ 2,00,000 in equity shares of ₹ 10 each issued 8,000 equity shares payable as follows :
   On application ₹ 2.50; On allotment ₹ 2.50; On first call ₹ 2.00; and On final call ₹ 3.00
   All monies payable upto final call were duly received by the company, except that one shareholder holding 1,000 shares failed to pay the allotment and call monies.
   Show journal entries in the books of the company and prepare the Balance Sheet of the Company.
5. X Limited whose authorised share capital is ₹ 5,00,000 divided into 50,000 equity shares of ₹ 10 each, issued 20,000 shares to the public on the following terms :
   On application ₹ 5; and On allotment ₹ 5
   Applications were received for 25,000 shares on 17.7.2013 and allotment was made on 3.8.2013 on which date excess application money was refunded to the unsuccessful candidates. The allotment money was duly received by 31.8.2013 excepting for 100 shares.
   Show the Bank Account, Equity Share Application Account, Equity Shares Allotment Account, Calls-in-Arrear Account and Equity Share Capital Account for the year.
   Show also how the relevant items would appear in the Balance Sheet on 31.12.2013.
6. Srijani Limited registered with a nominal capital of ₹ 50,000 consisting of 5,000 equity shares of ₹ 10 each, made a public issue of 4,000 shares payable as under :
   On application ₹ 3.00; On allotment ₹ 3.00; On first call ₹ 2.50; and On final call ₹ 2.50

All the shares were applied for and all cash were received on the due dates except that —

(i) a holder of 200 shares paid the entire amount due along with the allotment and

(ii) another holder of 300 shares paid the amount due on first call with the amount due on final call.

Make the journal entries required to record the issue (including cash transactions) in the Company's books.

7. A company made an issue of 10,000 equity shares of ₹ 10 each, payable as: ₹ 3 on application; ₹ 4 on allotment and the balance on call. 43,825 equity shares were applied for including on application for 300 shares from a person who paid for the full face value of the shares. Owing to over-subscription, allotments were scaled down as follows:

Applicants for 11,825 equity shares (in respect of applications for 500 or less) received 5,750 equity shares (including the application for 300 shares who got 150 equity shares). Applicants for 32,000 shares (in respect of applications for 500 equity shares), received 4,250 equity shares. The amounts received were first applied towards allotment and call money (after satisfying amount due on application) and any balance left was returned. You are required to show the Cash Book (without narration) and Ledger Accounts to record the above transactions.

Shares Issued at a Premium

8. ABC Ltd. was registered with a nominal capital of ₹ 10,00,000 divided into 1,00,000 equity shares of ₹ 10 each.

The company offered for public subscription 60,000 shares at a premium of ₹ 5 per share. The money of the shares were payable as follows :

On application ₹ 3; On allotment (including premium) ₹ 7; On first call ₹ 3; and On final call the balance amount

Applications were received for 70,000 shares and 60,000 shares were duly allotted. Monies received on excess applications were refunded. All monies due on shares were received in full. Show journal entries (including cash) to record the above transactions in the books of the Company.

9. Tezpur Company Limited was registered with a nominal capital of ₹ 10,00,000 divided into 1,00,000 Equity Shares of ₹ 10 each. The company offered for public subscription 40,000 shares payable as follows:

On application ₹ 3; On allotment (including premium of ₹ 5) ₹ 7; and On call the balance

Applications were received for 45,000 shares and 40,000 shares were duly allotted. Monies received on excess applications were refunded. All the monies due on the shares were duly received except call money on 1,000 shares. Show necessary journal entries to record the above transactions in the books of the Company.

10. The authorised capital of Ajanta Company Limited was ₹ 2,00,000 divided into shares of ₹ 1,000 each. The Board of Directors arranged for distribution of 60% of such shares to the public payable as : On application ₹ 200; On allotment (including premium ₹ 50) ₹ 250; On first call, and the second and final call the balance amount equally. All the shares were subscribed for and all the monies were called for. Karim, a holder of 5 shares failed to pay the first call money. The rest money was received in full. Show the journal entries and give the opening Balance Sheet.

11. Hero India Ltd. was registered with an authorised capital of ₹ 5,00,000 divided into 10,000 equity shares of ₹ 50 each. The company issued 6,000 shares, payable ₹ 12 per share on application, ₹ 18 per share (including ₹ 3 for premium) on allotment, ₹ 15 per share on first call and the rest on final call. The company received application money for 7,000 shares out of which that on 600 shares were refunded. Excess application money was adjusted towards allotment money due. A shareholder who was the owner of 150 shares failed to pay first and final call money. Except this, the company received all the money due on allotment, first and final calls. Show all the journal entries relating to issue of shares in the books of the Company and also prepare the Balance Sheet of the Company.

12. National Electronics Ltd. invited applications for 80,000 equity shares of ₹ 10 each issued at a premium of ₹ 5 per share. The amount was payable as follows :
On application ₹ 4 (including ₹ 2 premium); On allotment ₹ 6 (including ₹ 3 premium); Balance on first and final call. Application for 1,00,000 shares were received. Excess application money were refunded at the time of allotment. All money due were received. You are required to pass necessary journal entries in the books of the company.

Miscellaneous

13. X Limited whose authorised capital is ₹ 50,00,000 divided into 5,00,000 equity shares of ₹ 10 each, issued to public 1,00,000 shares at par.
The amount was payable as: On application ₹ 2; On allotment ₹ 8. Application were received for 1,25,000 shares on 20th September, 2014 and allotment was made on 16th October 2014. On this date excess application money were refunded to the unsuccessful applicants. The allotment money was duly received on 4th November, 2014.
You are required to pass the journal entries (including cash transactions) in the books of the company and also show the Balance Sheet after issue of shares.

14. National Textiles Limited invited applications for 10,000 equity shares of ₹ 100 each. The amount was payable as follows:
On application ₹ 30; On allotment ₹ 40; On first and final call ₹ 30. The public applied for 9,000 shares and these were allotted. All money due was collected with the exception of allotment and first and final call on 400 shares.
You are required to pass necessary journal entries in the books of the company and prepare its Balance Sheet.

15. XYZ Co. Ltd. issued 1,00,000 equity shares of ₹ 10 each at a premium of ₹ 2 per share and 1,000, 10% preference shares of ₹ 100 each at par payable as follows :

	Equity Share (₹)	Preference Share (₹)
On application	2	20
On allotment (including premium)	5	35
On first call	3	25
On final call	2	20

All the shares offered were subscribed for by the public and cash duly received.
Pass necessary journal entries to record the above issue of shares.

Calls-in-Arrears / Calls-in-Advance

16. The Decoy Trading Company Limited was registered with a nominal capital of ₹ 1,00,000 in shares of ₹ 10 each, 9,000 of which were issued payable as ₹ 1 on application, ₹ 2 on allotment, ₹ 3 on first call and the balance on final call. All the shares were applied for and allotted and all cash was received on the due dates except that one shareholder holding 100 shares failed to pay the allotment money and another shareholder holding 200 shares paid the first and final call together with allotment money.

    You are required to journalise the above transactions in the books of the company, particularly through Calls-in-Arrear Account and Calls-in-Advance Account as and when necessary.

Shares Issued for Consideration Other than Cash

17. DCM Limited was registered with 20,000 equity shares of ₹ 10 each. The company offered to the public for subscription 8,000 shares payable as follows :

    On application ₹ 4; On allotment ₹ 4; Balance on final call. The issue was fully subscribed. The company also issued 2,000 equity shares as fully paid up against the purchase consideration for a plot of land. Excepting allotment and call money on 200 shares, the company received in full for all other shares.

    You are required to pass necessary journal entries in the books of the company.

18. X Ltd. purchased two computers worth ₹ 1,40,000 from HCL. Payment was made as to ₹ 20,000 by cheque and remaining amount by issue of equity shares of the face value of ₹ 10 each fully paid at an issue price of ₹ 12 each. Pass necessary journal entries in the books of the company.

19. Y Ltd. issued 10,000 equity shares of ₹ 100 each as fully paid up in consideration of the purchase of a plot of land worth ₹ 10,00,000. Pass necessary journal entries in the books of the company.

Forfeiture and Reissue of Shares

20. Janta Ltd. invited applications for issuing 2,00,000 equity shares of ₹ 10 each at par. The amount was payable as follows :

    On application ₹ 2 per share; On allotment ₹ 4 per share;

    On first and final call : balance amount.

    The issue was undersubscribed to the extent of 20,000 shares. Shares were allotted to all the applicants. All calls were made and were duly received. A to whom 1,500 shares were allotted failed to pay allotment and call money and B to whom 1,200 shares were allotted paid the full amount due at the time of allotment. The shares on which allotment and call money was not received were forfeited. The forfeited shares were re-ssied at ₹ 8 per share fully paid-up.

    Pass necessary journal entries in the books of Janta Ltd. for the above transactions.

    [CBSE (Delhi) —Adapted]

21. Shyam Ltd. invited applications for issuing 80,000 equity shares of ₹ 10 each at a premium of ₹ 40 per share. The amount was payable as follows :

    On application ₹ 35 per share (including ₹ 30 premium)

    On allotment ₹ 8 per share (including ₹ 4 premium)

    On first and final call - Balance.

    Applications for 77,000 shares were received. Shares were allotted to all the applicants. Sundram to whom 7,000 shares were allotted failed to pay the allotment money. His shares were forfeited immediately after allotment. Afterwards the first and final call was made. Satyam the holder of

500 shares failed to pay the first and final call. His shares were also forfeited. Out of the forfeited shares 1,000 shares were re-issued at ₹ 50 per share fully paid up. The re-issued shares included all the shares of Satyam.

Pass necessary journal entries for the above transactions in the books of Shyam Ltd.

[CBSE (Delhi) — 2012]

22. X Ltd. issued 80,000 shares of ₹ 10 each at a premium of ₹ 2 per share payable as follows :
₹ 3 on application; ₹ 6 on allotment (including premium); and
₹ 3 on call.
Applications were received for 75,000 shares and a pro-rata allotment was made as follows : To the applicants of 40,000 shares, 30,000 shares were issued and for the rest 20,000 shares were issued. All money due were received except the allotment and call money from Ram who had applied for 1,200 shares (out of the group of 40,000 shares). All his shares were forfeited. The forfewited shares were re-issued for ₹ 8 per share fully paid-up.
Pass necessary journal entries for the above transactions.

[CBSE (Outside Delhi) — 2010]

23. Record the journal entries for forfeiture and reissue of shares in the following cases :
   (a) X Ltd. forfeited 200 shares of ₹ 100 each, ₹ 70 called up on which the shareholder had paid application and allotment money of ₹ 50 per share. Out of these, 15 shares were re-issued to Naresh as ₹ 70 per share paid up for ₹ 80 per share.
   (b) Y Ltd. forfeited 180 shares of ₹ 10 each, ₹ 8 called up issued at a premium of ₹ 2 per share to 'R' for non-payment of allotment money of ₹ 5 per share (including premium). Out of those, 160 shares were re-issued to Sanjay as ₹ 8 called up for ₹ 10 per share.

[CBSE (Outside Delhi) —Adapted]

24. R. K. Ltd. invited applications for issuing 70,000 equity shares of ₹ 10 each at a premium of ₹ 35 per share. The amount was payable as follows :
On application ₹ 15 (including ₹ 12 premium); On allotment ₹ 10 (including ₹ 8 premium)
On first and final call - Balance
Applications for 65,000 shares were received and allotment was made to all the applicants. A shareholder, Ram, who was allotted 2,000 shares, failed to pay the allotment money. His shares were forfeited immediately after allotment. After wards the first and final call was made. Sohan, who had 3,000 shares, failed to pay the first and final call. His shares were also forfeited. Out of the forfeited shares, 4,000 shares were re-issued at ₹ 50 per share fully paid up. The re-issued shares included all the shares of Ram.
Pass necessary journal entries for the above transactions in the books of R.K. Ltd.

[CBSE (Outside Delhi) — 2012]

25. A Ltd. invited applications for 15,000 equity shares of ₹ 10 each payable as follows :
On application ₹ 2; On allotment ₹ 3 ; On first call ₹ 4; and On final call ₹ 1.
All the shares have been subscribed and paid for except the following :
(i) X who held 300 shares, failed to pay the money on allotment and calls.
(ii) Y, to whom 200 shares have been allotted, failed to pay the money due on first and final call.
(iii) Z, to whom 500 shares were allotted, has not paid the amount due on final call.
The shares of X, Y and Z are forfeited by the Board of Directors.
Give necessary Journal Entries to record these transactions in the books of A Ltd.

26. A Limited was registered with an authorised capital of ₹ 2,00,000 divided in ₹ 10 shares. During the first year, 6,000 shares out of the above, were issued to the vendors of building, 8,000 shares were offered to the public and ₹ 5 per share were called up. On application ₹ 2, on allotment ₹ 1, 1st call ₹ 1and ₹ 1 on second call. The amounts received on these shares were as : on 6,000 shares full amount called; on 1,250 shares ₹ 4 per share; on 500 shares ₹ 3 per share; on 250 shares ₹ 2 per share. The directors forfeited 750 shares on which less than ₹ 4 per share were paid. Show journal entries to record the above transactions.
27. A Ltd. invited applications for 15,000 equity shares of ₹ 10 each payable as follows :
    On application ₹ 2; On allotment ₹ 3 ; On first call ₹ 4; and On final call ₹ 1.
    All the shares have been subscribed and paid for except the following :
    (i) X who held 300 shares, failed to pay the money on allotment and calls.
    (ii) Y, to whom 200 shares have been allotted, failed to pay the money due on first and final call.
    (iii) Z, to whom 500 shares were allotted, has not paid the amount due on final call.
    The shares of X, Y and Z are forfeited by the Board of Directors.
    Give necessary journal entries to record these transactions in the books of A Ltd.
28. Give necessary journal entries in the following cases :
    (a) The directors of Devendra Ltd., resolved on 1st January, 2014 that 200 equity shares of ₹ 10 each, ₹ 8 paid, be forfeited for non-payment of final call of ₹ 2. On 1st February, 100 of these shares were re-issued at ₹ 7 per share fully paid up.
    (b) Virendra Limited forfeited 20 shares of ₹ 100 each (₹ 60 called up) issued at par to Mukesh on which he had paid ₹ 40 per share. Out of these, 15 shares were re-issued to Sanjeev as ₹ 60 paid up for ₹ 45 per share.
    (c) A share of ₹ 10, on which ₹ 8 has been called and ₹ 6 has been paid, is forfeited. It is re-issued for ₹ 7 as fully paid.
29. A company makes an issue of 5,00,000 equity shares of ₹ 10 each at 10% discount. The net amount is payable as follows:
    On application and allotment ₹ 4.00; On first call ₹ 2.50; On final call ₹ 3.50. A shareholder holding 200 shares did not pay final call money. His shares were forfeited. Out of these 100 shares were re-issued to Y at ₹ 7 per share to be credited as fully paid. Pass journal entries in respect of forfeiture and re-issue of shares only.
30. Give separate journal entries for the following :
    (a) A Ltd forfeited 100 equity shares of ₹ 10 each held by X on 15th December, 2014 for non-payment of first call of ₹ 2 per share and the final call of ₹ 3 per share. These shares were re-issued to Y on 28th December, 2014 at a discount of ₹ 3.50 per share.
    (b) B Ltd forfeited 100 equity shares of ₹ 10 each, issued at a premium of ₹ 5 per share, held by Romen on 15th December, 2013, for non-payment of the final call of ₹ 3 per share. These shares were re-issued to Ramu on 28th December, 2014 at a discount of ₹ 4 per share.
    (c) C Ltd forfeited 150 equity shares of ₹ 10 each issued at a premium of ₹ 5 per share, held by Robin on 15th December, 2014, for non-payment of allotment money of ₹ 8 per share (including securities premium of ₹ 5 per share), the first call of ₹ 2 per share and the final call of ₹ 3 per share. Out of these 100 equity shares were re-issued to Shri Bhagwan at ₹ 15 per share on 28th December, 2014.

31. Mr X who was the holder of 200 preference shares of ₹ 100 each, on which ₹ 75 per share has been called up could not pay his dues on allotment and first call each at ₹ 25 per share. The directors forfeited the above shares and reissued 150 of such shares to Mr Y at ₹ 65 per share paid-up as ₹ 75 per share.
Give journal entries to record the above forfeiture and re-issue in the books of the company.

32. A Ltd, invited applications for 10,000 shares of ₹ 100 each at a premium of ₹ 10 per share. The amount is payable as follows: On application ₹ 25, on allotment ₹ 35 (including Premium), on first call ₹ 25 and on final call ₹ 25.
The applications were received for 9,000 shares and these were accepted in full. All money due were received except the first and final call money on 200 shares, which were forfeited. Out of these shares, 100 shares were subsequently re- issued @ ₹ 90 per share. You are required to pass journal entries for recording the above transactions including cash.

33. X Limited made an issue of 10,000 Equity Shares of ₹ 15 each payable as follows :
(i) ₹ 4 per share on application;
(ii) ₹ 7 per share (including ₹ 2 per share as premium) on allotment; and
(iii) ₹ 6 per share on first and final call.
Das holding 50 shares failed to pay the allotment and call monies. Pal holding 80 shares failed to pay the call money.All these shares were forfeited and subsequently re-issued to Roy as fully paid-up at a discount of ₹ 3 per share. Pass journal entries (including cash transactions) to record the above issue, forfeiture and re-issue of shares in the books of the company.

34. Beautiful Co. Ltd issued 3,000 equity shares of ₹ 10 each payable as ₹ 3 per share on Application, ₹ 5 per share (including ₹ 2 as premium) on Allotment and ₹ 4 per share on Call. All the shares were subscribed. Money due on all shares was fully received excepting Ram, holding 50 shares, failed to pay the Allotment and Call money and Shyam, holding 100 shares, failed to pay the Call Money. All those 150 shares were forfeited. Of the shares forfeited, 125 shares (including whole of Ram's shares) were subsequently re-issued to Jadu as fully paid up at a discount of ₹ 2 per share.
Pass the necessary entries in the Journal of the company to record the forfeiture and re-issue of the share. Also prepare the Balance Sheet of the company as per provisions of Part 1, Schedule VI of the Companies Act, 1956.

35. A Ltd authorised with ₹ 2,50,000 capital divided into 25,000 shares of ₹ 10 each, issued 20,000 shares payable at ₹ 3 on application, ₹ 5 on allotment (including ₹ 2 as premium) and ₹ 2 on each of two calls. All the 20,000 shares were subscribed. Holders of 1,000 shares failed to pay the allotment money and further on 500 shares there were arrears of first call. All these shares were declared forfeited. Then the second call was made. This was not paid on 200 shares. These shares were also forfeited. All the shares on which only application money was paid and half of the shares on which there was default of first call money were re-issued at ₹ 9 each as fully paid shares. Pass journal entries in respect of the above transactions.

36. P Ltd. invited applications for 10,000 equity shares of ₹ 10 each payable as follows :
On application ₹ 1; On allotment ₹ 4; On first call ₹ 2; On second call ₹ 3 per share
All shares were subscribed for and paid for with the following exceptions :
(i) A who held 300 shares did not pay the allotment money and calls money.

(ii) B who was allotted 600 shares failed to pay the money due on first call and final call.
(iii) C who held 100 shares did not pay the amount due on final call.

The Board of Directors passed a resolution forfeiting all the shares held by A, B and C. These shares were subsequently reissued as fully paid at a discount of 10%. Give necessary journal entries to record these transactions in the books of P Ltd.

37. Dynamic Ltd makes an issue of 5,000 equity shares of ₹ 100 each at a premium of ₹ 12.50 per share payable as follows: (1) ₹ 12.50 on Application. (2) ₹ 25 on Allotment including premium. (3) ₹ 50 on First call. (4) ₹ 15 on Second call, and (5) ₹ 10 on Final call.

The Application and Allotment moneys are duly received and in addition, holders of 2,500 shares pay in full on allotment. Holders of 100 shares fail to pay the First call and after due notice, their shares are forfeited. The amounts payable on the Second call (made after the forfeiture) are paid in full except that a holder of 50 shares fails to pay. 75 of the 100 shares forfeited are re-issued, credited with ₹ 90 paid for ₹ 65 per share. The new holder pays for these shares in full. The balance of ₹ 10 per share being treated as call-in-advance. The final call is met in full including the arrears of the Second Call. Show the necessary journal entries including cash in the Books of Dynamic Ltd.

38. Messrs Accountancy Publications Ltd. issued 50,000 equity shares of ₹ 10 each at a premium of 10% payable as under:

on application ₹ 2; on allotment (including premium ₹ 1) ₹ 5
on first call ₹ 2; on final call ₹ 2

The whole of the issue was called for by the company and all the money was duly received except the allotment and call money on 500 shares. These shares were, therefore, forfeited and later on reissued at ₹ 9 per share as fully paid.

Pass the necessary journal entries to record the above transactions.

Pro-rata Allotment

39. Meena Ltd. issued 60,000 shares of ₹ 10 each at a premium of ₹ 2 per share payable as ₹ 3 on application, ₹ 5 (including premium) on allotment and the balance on first and final call. Applications were received for 1,02,000 shares. The Directors resolved to allot as follows :

A. Applicants of 60,000 shares 30,000 shares
B. Applicants of 40,000 shares 30,000 shares
C. Applicants of 2,000 shares Nil

Nikhil who had applied for 1,000 shares in Category A and Vish who was allotted 600 shares in Category B failed to pay the allotment money.

Calculate the amount received on allotment. *[CBSE (Delhi) — 2009]*

40. DN Ltd. issued 50,000 shares of ₹ 10 each at par payable as ₹ 2 per share on application, ₹ 4 on allotment and ₹ 2 each on first and final calls. Applications were received for 70,000 shares. It was decided that :

(a) refuse allotment to the applicants for 10,000 shares;
(b) allot 20,000 shares to Mohan who had applied for similar number; and
(c) allot the remaining shares on pro-rata basis.

Mohan failed to pay the allotment money and Sohan who belonged to category 'C' was allotted 3,000 shares and paid both the calls with allotment.

Calculate the amount received on allotment.

[CBSE (Delhi) — Adapted]

41. X Ltd. issued 50,000 shares of ₹ 10 each at a premium of ₹ 2 per share payable as follows :

₹ 3 on application;

₹ 6 on allotment (including premium); and

₹ 3 on call.

Applications were received for 75,000 shares and a pro-rata allotment was made as follows : To the applicants of 40,000 shares, 30,000 shares were issued and for the rest 20,000 shares were issued. All money due were received except the allotment and call money from Ram who had applied for 1,200 shares (out of the group of 40,000 shares). All his shares were forfeited. The forfeited shares were re-issued for ₹ 7 per share fully paid-up.

Pass necessary journal entries for the above transactions. *[CBSE (Outside Delhi) — 2010]*

42. Jain Ltd. invited applications for issuing 35,000 equity shares of ₹ 10 each at par. The amount was payable as follows :

On application ₹ 5 per share; On allotment ₹ 3 per share; On first call - Balance

Applications for 50,000 shares were received. Applications for 8,000 shares were rejected and the application money of these applicants was refunded. Shares were allotted on pro-rata basis to the remaining applicants and the excess money received with applications from these applicants were adjusted towards sums due on allotment. Jeevan who had applied for 600 shares failed to pay allotment and the first and final call money. Naveen the holder of 400 shares failed to pay the first and final call money. Shares of Jeevan and Naveen were forfeited. Of the forfeited 800 shares were re-issued at ₹ 15 per share fully paid. The re-issued shares included all the shares of Naveen.

Pass the necessary journal entries for the above transactions in the books of the Jain Ltd.

[CBSE (Delhi) — Adapted]

43. Starplus Company issued for public subscription, 1,50,000 shares of the value of ₹ 100 each at a premium of 10% payable as follows :

₹ 20 per share on application, ₹ 50 per share on allotment (including premium) and ₹ 40 per share on call.

The company received applications for 3,00,000 shares. The allotment was done as under :

(A) Applicants of 30,000 shares were allotted 10,000 shares.

(B) Applicants of 1,40,000 shares were allotted 80,000 shares.

(C) Remaining applicants was allotted 60,000 shares.

After adjusting excess money in allotment, the money was returned. Harit, a shareholder who had applied for 7,000 shares out of group B failed to pay allotment and call money.

Roshan, a shareholder who was allotted 6,000 shares paid the call money along with the allotment. Rohan also belonged to group B.

Pass necessary journal entries to record the above transactions in the books of the Company. Show your working notes clearly. *[CBSE (Outside Delhi) — Adapted]*

44. Y Ltd. invited applications for issuing 10,000 equity shares of ₹ 100 each at par. The amount was payable as follows :
On application ₹ 20 per share.
On allotment ₹ 44 per share and the balance on first and final call.
Applications for 13,000 shares were received. applications for 500 shares were rejected and pro-rata allotment was made to the remaining applicants. Over payments received with applications were adjusted towards sums due on allotment. All calls were made and were duly received except Kanwar who had applied for 250 shares failed to pay allotment and call money. His shares were forfeited. The forfeited shares were re-issued at ₹ 22,000 fully paid-up.
Pass necessary journal entries in the books of the company. *[CBSE (Delhi) — Adapted]*

45. A company invited applications for 50,000 equity shares of ₹ 10 each on the following terms: on application ₹ 3; on allotment ₹ 2; on first and final call ₹ 5
Applications were received for 1,10,000 shares. It was decided (i) to refuse allotment to the applicants for 10,000 shares; (ii) to allot 50% to Mr X who has applied for 20,000 shares; (iii) to allot in full to Mr Y who has applied for 10,000 shares; (iv) to allot balance of the available shares pro-rata among the other applicants; and (v) to utilise excess application money in part payment of allotment and final call. Give journal entries till the stage of allotment assuming that the entire sum due on allotment is received in full.

46. East Coast Ltd made an issue of 30,000 shares of ₹ 10 each payable as ₹ 3 on application; ₹ 5 on allotment; and ₹ 2 on call. 93,200 shares were applied for and owing to this heavy over-subscription, allotments were made as under: (1) Applicants for 21,500 shares (in respect of applications for 2,000 shares or more) received 10,200 shares. (2) Applicants for 50,600 shares (in respect of applications for 1,000 shares or more but less than 2,000 shares) received 12,600 shares. (3) Applicants for 21,100 shares (in respect of applications for less than 1,000 shares) received 7,200 shares. Cash thus received after satisfying the amount due on application was applied towards allotment and call money and any balance was then returned. All monies due on allotment and calls were received. Pass necessary journal entries and show Cash Book and Ledger Accounts relating to this issue in the books of the company.

47. A Ltd. company issued 2,000 shares of ₹ 10 each at a premium of ₹ 2 per share payable as follows: on application ₹ 2; on allotment (including premium) ₹ 5; on first call ₹ 3
on second and final call ₹ 2
Applications were received for 3,000 shares. Applications for 600 shares were altogether rejected and to the applicants of 2,400 shares, allotment was made pro rata. Money overpaid on application was adjusted on allotment.
Manohar, to whom 80 shares were allotted, failed to pay the allotment money and on his subsequent failure, to pay first call, his shares were forfeited. Show the journal entries.

48. Shagoon India Ltd. issued for public subscription 40,000 equity shares of ₹ 10 each, at a premium of ₹ 2 per share payable as under :
On application ₹ 2 per share, on allotment ₹ 5 per share (including premium), on first call ₹ 2 per share, on second call ₹ 3 per share.

Applications were received for 60,000 shares. Allotment was made pro rata to the applicants for 48,000 shares, the remaining applications being refused. Money overpaid on application was applied towards sums due on allotment.

A, to whom 1,600 shares were allotted, failed to pay the allotment money and B, to whom 2,000 shares were allotted, failed to pay the two calls. These were subsequently forfeited after the second call was made.

Pass journal entries in the books of Shagoon India Ltd. to record the above transactions including the bank entries.

49. Rippy Co. Ltd. offered to public for subscription 10,000, 12% preference shares of ₹ 100 each at a premium of ₹ 5 per share. Payment was to be made as follows :
with application ₹ 20; with allotment (including premium) ₹ 55; on first and final call ₹ 30
Applications were received for 34,000 shares.
Applications for 2,000 shares were accepted in full. The remaining 8,000 shares were allotted to the applicants for 32,000 shares on pro rata basis. No money was refunded, the surplus being treated as call-in-advance on which interest was payable @ 6% per annum. The call was made three months after the date of allotment. All monies were duly received. The company promptly paid interest on calls-in-advance to shareholders. Journalise the above-mentioned transactions. Also prepare Calls- in-Advance Account and 12% Preference Share Capital Account.

50. The Fancy Co. Ltd issued 4,000 equity shares of ₹ 10 each at a Premium of ₹ 2 per share payable as follows: On application ₹ 2; On allotment ₹ 6 (including premium); On first call ₹ 2; On final call ₹ 2. 6,000 shares were applied for and allotment was made pro-rata. Excess application moneys were utilized towards dues on allotment. Mr. B who held 120 shares failed to pay first call and final call and these shares were forfeited. Out of these forfeited shares, 100 forfeited shares were re-issued to Mr. K. as fully paid-up for ₹ 9 per share. Show the journal entries and the Cash Book of the company and also draw up the Balance Sheet.

51. Mandal Limited invited applications for 1,00,000 shares of ₹ 10 each at an issue price of ₹ 12, payable as ₹ 5 (including premium) on application, ₹ 4 on allotment, and the balance by way of first and final call.
Applications for 1,20,000 shares were received. The Board of Directors allotted (i) in full to applicants for 70,000 shares and (ii) the balance of the shares pro rata to the remaining applicants. The board also utilised any excess application money towards the amount due on allotment.
Sunil, to whom 2,100 shares were allotted on a ***pro rata*** basis, failed to pay the amounts due from him in respect of allotment and the call. These shares were forfeited and subsequently reissued at ₹ 11 each.
Prepare the following Ledger Accounts in the books of Mandal Limited : (i) Share Capital Account; (ii) Share Application Account; (iii) Share Allotment Account; (iv) Share Call Account; (v) Share Forfeited Account; (vi) Securities Premium Account; and, (vii) Cash Book.

52. Pioneer Construction Company Ltd issued for public subscription 20,000 Equity Shares of ₹ 10 each at par payable ₹ 2 per share on Application, ₹ 3 per share on Allotment and the balance in two calls of equal amount. Applications were received for 30,000 shares. The shares were allotted pro-rata to the applicants for 24,000 shares, the remaining applications being rejected. Money overpaid on application was utilized towards sums due on allotment. All money due were received except that a shareholder named Bimal to whom 1,000 shares were allotted failed to

pay both the calls. These shares were forfeited and subsequently re-issued to Parimal at ₹ 11 per share as fully paid-up. Show the Journal Entires (including cash transactions) in the books of the company and also draw up the Balance Sheet.

53. S. M. Ltd. issued 5,000 equity shares of ₹ 10 each at a premium of ₹ 15 per share payable ₹ 12.50 on application (including premium ₹ 7.50) and the balance on allotment.
Applications were received for 9,000 equity shares, out of which letters of regret were issued to 2,000. Full allotment was made to applicants for 1,000 shares. ***Pro-rata*** allotment was made on the balance. Money overpaid on application was used in allotment. All money due on allotment was received except from a shareholder holding 100 shares to whom pro-rata allotment was made. These shares were forfeited and reissued for ₹ 18 per share as fully paid up.
Give journal entries to record these transactions in the books of the company.

54. Mohan Ltd. has authorised capital of ₹ 5,00,000 divided into 50,000 shares of ₹ 10 each. The company issued a prospectus inviting applications for 30,000 shares of ₹ 10 each at a premium of ₹ 2 per share, payable as follows :
on application ₹ 2; on allotment (including premium) ₹ 5; on first call ₹ 3;
on second and final call ₹ 2
The company received applications for 45,000 shares and pro-rata allotment was made in respect of application of 40,000 shares and the remaining applications were rejected. Money overpaid on applications was employed on account of sum due on allotment. All the calls were made.
B to whom 30 shares were allotted failed to pay the two calls. The company decided to forfeit the shares allotted to B. These shares were subsequently re-issued to C as fully paid for ₹ 9 per share.
Pass the necessary journal entries in the books of the company and prepare the opening Balance Sheet.

55. A company issued for public subscription 50,000 equity shares of ₹ 10 each at a premium of ₹ 2 per share, payable as under :
on application ₹ 2 per share; on allotment (including premium) ₹ 5 per share
on first call ₹ 2 per share; on final call ₹ 3 per share
Applications were received for 75,000 equity shares. The shares were allotted pro-rata to the applicants for 60,000 shares, the remaining applications being rejected. Money over-paid on applications was utilised towards the sum due on allotment.
A, to whom 2,000 shares were allotted, failed to pay allotment and two calls and B, to whom 2,500 shares were allotted, failed to pay the two calls. These shares were subsequently forfeited after the final call was made. All the forfeited shares were sold to X as fully paid up at ₹ 8 per share.
Pass the journal entries required to record the above transactions.

56. Ashish Ltd. invited applications for 80,000 shares of ₹ 10 each at a premium of ₹ 2.50 per share payable as follows:
on application ₹ 3.00; on allotment (including premium) ₹ 4.50
on first call ₹ 2.00; on second call ₹ 3.00
Applications were received for 1,70,000 shares, out of which applications for 10,000 shares were rejected and money refunded to them. The allotment was made pro rata to the remaining applicants. Money overpaid on application was used against allotment money due. Anil to whom

2,000 shares were allotted failed to pay the allotment money, and on his subsequent failure to pay the first call, his shares were forfeited.

Sunil, the holder of 1,200 shares failed to pay the two calls, and his shares were forfeited after the final call. Of the forfeited shares, 2,400 shares were re-issued at the rate of ₹ 8 per share credited as fully paid, including the whole of the Anil's shares forfeited. Show necessary journal entries and prepare the Balance Sheet of the company.

57. Radhika Textiles Ltd invited applications for 75,000 equity shares of ₹ 10 each issued at a premium of ₹ 4 per share. The amount was payable as follows :
on application ₹ 5 (including ₹ 2 premium); on allotment ₹ 5 (including ₹ 2 premium)
Balance on first and final call.
Applications for 1,00,000 shares were received. Allotment was made to all the applicants on pro rata basis.
Puneet to whom 300 shares were allotted failed to pay allotment and call money. Sumeet to whom 150 shares were allotted failed to pay the call money. These shares were forfeited. The forfeited shares were re-issued @ ₹ 8 per share fully paid up.
Pass the necessary journal entries.

58. Bharat Tyres Ltd. invited applications for 1,00,000 equity shares of ₹ 10 each issued at a premium of ₹ 4 per share. The amount was payable as follows :
on application ₹ 6 (including premium ₹ 2); on allotment ₹ 6 (including premium ₹ 2)
Balance on first and final call
Applications for 1,50,000 shares were received. Allotment was made to all the applicants on pro rata basis.
Subodh, to whom 200 shares were allotted, failed to pay allotment and call money. Vikram, to whom 100 shares wer allotted, failed to pay the call money. Their shares were forfeited and afterwards re-issued @ ₹ 8 per share fully paid up. Pass necessary journal entries.

59. K. Limited has been registered with an authorised capital of ₹ 4,00,000 divided into 4,000 shares of ₹100 each, of which 2,000 shares were offered for public subscription at a premium of ₹ 5 per share, payable as under : on application ₹ 10; on allotment (including premium) ₹ 25; on first call ₹ 40; on final call ₹ 30.
Applications were received for 3,600 shares; of which applications for 600 shares were rejected; the rest of the applicants were allotted 2,000 shares on pro rata basis. Excess application money was transferred to allotment.
All the monies were duly received except from Sundar, holder of 200 shares, who failed to pay allotment and first call money.
His shares were later forfeited, and reissued to Shyam at ₹ 60 per share ₹ 70 paid up. Final call has not been made.
Pass necessary Cash Book and journal entries in the books of K Limited.

60. Nav Lakshmi Ltd. issued a prospectus inviting applications for 50,000 shares of ₹ 10 each. These shares were issued at par on the following terms :
On application ₹ 3, on allotment ₹ 4, on first call ₹ 2 and on final call the balance.
Applications were received for 60,000 shares. Allotments were made on the following basis :
(i) To applicants for 10,000 shares in full.
(ii) To applicants for 20,000 shares - 15,000 shares.

(iii) To applicants for 30,000 shares - 25,000 shares.
All excess amount paid on application is to be adjusted against amount due on allotment.
The shares were fully called and paid up except amounts on allotment, first and final call not paid by those who applied for 2,000 shares out of the group applying for 20,000 shares.
All the shares on which calls were not paid were forfeited by the Board of Directors.
1,000 forfeited shares were reissued as fully paid on receipt of ₹ 8 per share.
Show the journal entries in the books of Nav Lakshmi Ltd.

61. A B Ltd. invited applications for issuing 1,00,000 equity shares of ₹ 10 each. The amount was payable as follows :
on application ₹ 2 per share; on allotment ₹ 3 per share; on first and final call ₹ 5 per share
Applications for 1,50,000 shares were received and pro-rata allotment was made to all applicants as follows:
Applicants for 80,000 shares were allotted 60,000 shares on pro- rata basis.
Applicants for 70,000 shares were allotted 40,000 shares on pro- rata basis.
Sudha to whom 600 shares were allotted out of the group applying for 80,000 shares failed to pay the allotment money. Her shares were forfeited immediately after allotment.
Asha who had applied for 1400 shares out of the group applying for 70,000 shares failed to pay the first and final call. Her shares were also forfeited.
Out of the forfeited shares 1000 shares were reissued @ ₹ 8 per share fully paid up. The reissued shares included all the forfeited shares of Sudha.
Pass necessary journal entries to record the above transactions.

62. A Co Ltd. offered to the public 20,000 equity shares of ₹ 100 each at a premium of ₹ 10 per share. The payment was to be as follows :
on application ₹ 20; on allotment ₹ 40 (including premium);
on first call ₹ 25; on second and final call ₹ 25.
Applications were received for 35,000 shares. Applications for 10,000 shares were rejected. Applicants for 15,000 shares were allotted 10,000 shares and remaining applications were accepted in full. The directors made both the calls. One shareholder holding 500 shares failed to pay the two calls and as a consequence his shares were forfeited. 200 of these shares were reissued as fully paid at ₹ 80 per share.
Expenses of issue came to ₹ 10,000.
Prepare Cash Book, the journal and the Balance Sheet on the basis of information given above.

63. X Ltd. invited applications for 20,000 equity shares of ₹ 10 each, payable ₹ 2.50 on application; ₹ 5 on allotment (including premium ₹ 2.50); and ₹ 5 on first and final call.
The company received application for 25,000 shares. It was decided :
(a) to refuse allotment to the applicants for 1,000 shares;
(b) to allot in full to the applicants for 4,000 shares;
(c) to allot balance of the available shares ***pro-rata*** among the other applicants; and
(d) to utilise the excess application money in part payment of allotment money.
All the money due was received except from one applicant to whom shares had been allotted on pro-rata basis. He failed to pay allotment and call money and his 100 shares were forfeited. These shares were reissued at ₹ 9 as fully paid.
Give journal entries to record the above transactions in the books of the company.

64. Applications were invited by the directors of Grobigg Ltd for 15,000 of its equity shares at ₹ 115 per share payable as follows: (a) On application on 1st April, 2014 (including premium of ₹ 15 per share) ₹ 75; (b) On allotment on 30th April, 2014 ₹ 20; and (c) On first & final call on 31st May 2014 ₹ 20. Applications were received for 18,000 shares and it was decided to deal with these as follows:
    1. to refuse allotment on applicants for 800 shares.
    2. to give full allotment to applicants for 2,200 shares.
    3. to allot the remainder of the available shares pro-rata among the other applicants.
    4. to utilize the surplus received on applications in part payment of amounts due on allotment.

    An applicant, to whom 400 shares had been allotted, failed to pay the amount due on the first and final call and his shares were declared forfeited on 31st July 2014. These share were re-issued on 3rd September, 2014, as fully paid at ₹ 90 per share. Pass journal entries including cash items.

65. New Industries Limited issued a prospectus, inviting applications for 1,00,000 shares of ₹ 10 each at a premium of ₹ 5 per share, payable as follows :
    on application ₹ 2.50 per share; on allotment (including premium) ₹ 7.50 per share;
    on first call ₹ 4.00 per share; on final call ₹ 1.00 per share
    Applications were received for 1,50,000 shares and allotment was made pro-rata to the applicants of 1,20,000 shares, the remaining applications being refused. Money received in excess on the application was adjusted towards the amount due on allotment.
    D, to whom 2,000 shares were allotted, failed to pay allotment money and on his failure to pay the first call, his shares were forfeited. M, the holder of 3,000 shares, failed to pay the two calls, and so his shares were also forfeited. All these shares were sold to R, credited as fully paid for ₹ 8 per share. Pass necessary journal entries (including cash transactions) to record the above issue of shares by the company.

66. X Co. Ltd issued 40,000 equity shares of ₹ 10 each at a premium of ₹ 2.50 per share. The amount was payable ₹ 2 on application, ₹ 4.50 on allotment (including premium) and ₹ 6 on call. 96,400 shares were applied for and owing to heavy over-subscription, allotment was made as follows: Applicants for 23,000 shares (in respect of application for 2,000 or more shares) were allotted 10,560 shares. Applicants for 48,000 shares (in respect of application for 1,000 or more shares) were allotted 14,200 shares. Applicants for 25,400 shares were allotted 15,240 shares *pro-rata.* It was decided that the excess amount received on application would be utilised in payment of allotment money and the surplus, if any, would be refunded. P, to whom 300 shares were allotted on pro-rata basis, failed to pay the allotment money. Q, who was allotted 450 shares also on pro-rata basis, failed to pay the call money. Their shares were consequently forfeited after the call was made.
    Pass the necessary journal entries to record the above transactions (including cash transactions).

67. H Limited Company issued a prospectus inviting applications for 2,000 shares of ₹ 10 each at a premium of ₹ 2 per share payable as follows :
    on applications ₹ 2; on allotment (including premium) ₹ 5;
    on first call ₹ 3; on second and final calls ₹ 2.

Applications were received for 3,000 shares and pro-rata allotment was made on the applications for 2,400 shares. Money overpaid on application was employed on account of sum due on allotment.

Ramesh, to whom 40 shares were allotted, failed to pay the allotment money and on his subsequent failure to pay the first call his shares were forfeited. Mohan, the holder of 60 shares, failed to pay the two calls, and his shares were forfeited after the second call. Of the shares forfeited, 80 shares were sold to Krishna credited as fully paid for ₹ 9 per share, the whole of Ramesh's shares being included.

Show journal entries and the Balance Sheet.

68. M/s Blue Chips Ltd issued 5,000 Equity Shares of ₹ 100 each at a premium of ₹ 25 per share. On 1st January, 2014 the company received 12,000 applications of which 2,000 applications were totally rejected and their amount was refunded on 1st February, 2014, when remaining applicants were allotted shares on pro-rata basis. The amount of shares receivable is : On application ₹ 30; on Allotment ₹ 45 (including premium); On 1st Call ₹ 25; on 2nd Call ₹ 25. Allotment money was received in full on 15th February, 2014.

First call was made on 15th May, 2014 and received on 1st June 2013 except on 25 shares hold by Mr Azad. His shares were forfeited on 1st October, 2013 and re-issued on 15th October, 2013, credited at ₹ 75 paid for ₹ 110 per share to Mr. Anand. Final call was made on 1st November, 2014 and received on 15th November, 2014 except on 100 shares held by Mr. Banarasidas. Pass journal entries in the books of Blue chips Ltd (including relating the Cash).

69. Bharat Ltd. invited applications for issuing 2,00,000 equity shares of ₹ 10 each. The amount was payable as follows :

on application ₹ 3 per share; on allotment ₹ 5 per share; on first and final call ₹ 2 per share

Applications for 3,00,000 shares were received and pro-rata allotment was made to all the applicants on the following basis:

Applicants for 2,00,000 shares were allotted 1,50,000 shares on pro-rata basis.

Applicants for 1,00,000 shares were allotted 50,000 shares on pro-rata basis.

Bajaj, who was allotted 3,000 shares out of the group applying for 2,00,000 shares, failed to pay the allotment money. His shares were forfeited immediately after allotment.

Sharma, who had applied for 2,000 shares out of the group applying for 1,00,000 shares failed to pay the first and final call. His shares were also forfeited. Out of the forfeited shares, 3,500 shares were re-issued as fully paid up @ ₹ 8 per share. The re-issued shares included all the forfeited shares of Bajaj.

Pass the necessary journal entries to record the above transactions.

70. Super Star Ltd offered 10,000 equity shares of ₹ 100 each for subscription at a premium of ₹ 20 per share payable as follows: on application ₹ 10; on allotment ₹ 40 (including premium); on 1st call ₹ 20; on 2nd call ₹ 30 and on final call ₹ 20. The company received applications for 12,000 shares and 10,000 shares were allotted pro-rata.

Holder of 400 shares failed to pay the 1st call and after due notice their shares were forfeited. The amount payable on the 2nd call were paid in full, except that a holder of 200 shares failed to pay. 250 of the 400 shares forfeited were re-issued, credited with ₹ 80 paid for ₹ 50 per share. The final call was met in full including the arrears of the second call. Show necessary journal entries including cash in the books of the company.

GUIDE TO ANSWERS

Check Your Progress

1. D **2.** C **3.** A **4.** B **5.** C **6.** B **7.** B **8.** C **9.** C **10.** B **11.** C **12.** C **13.** C **14.** C

Multiple Choice

1. D **2.** D **3.** B **4.** B **5.** B **6.** C **7.** D **8.** D **9.** A **10.** C **11.** D **12.** B **13.** A **14.** B

Practical Questions

1. (i) Share capital ₹ 21,00,000;
   (ii) Reserve and Surplus ₹ 1,40,000;
   (iii) Cash and cash equivalents ₹ 22,40,000.
2. Calls in arrear ₹ 1,000;
   Paid up capital ₹ 99,000.
3. Calls in arrear ₹ 5,000;
   Paid up capital ₹ 2,45,000.
4. Calls in arrear ₹ 7,500;
   Paid up capital ₹ 72,500.
5. Calls in arrear ₹ 500;
   Paid up capital ₹ 1,99,500.
6. Calls in advance ₹ 1,000;
   Money actually received on 1st call ₹ 8,750.
7. Calls in advance ₹ 13,200;
   Money refunded ₹ 55,000;
   Money received on call ₹ 16,800.
8. Money refunded ₹ 30,000;
   Securities premium ₹ 3,00,000.
9. Securities premium ₹ 2,00,000;
   Calls in arrear ₹ 5,000.
10. Calls in arrear ₹ 3,000;
    Paid up capital ₹ 1,17,000;
    Balance Sheet total ₹ 1,23,000.
11. Calls in arrear ₹ 3,450;
    Paid up capital ₹ 2,96,550;
    Securities premium ₹ 18,000;
    Balance Sheet total ₹ 3,14,550.
12. Amount refunded at the time of allotment ₹ 80,000.
13. Money refunded ₹ 50,000;
    Share capital ₹ 10,00,000;
    Cash and cash equivalent ₹ 10,00,000.
14. Calls in arrear ₹ 28,000;
    Balance Sheet total ₹ 8,72,400.
15. Securities premium ₹ 2,00,000.
16. Calls in arrear ₹ 200;
    Calls in advance ₹ 1,400.
17. Calls in arrear ₹ 1,200.

18. Securities premium ₹ 20,000;
    No. of shares to be issued 10,000.
20. (i) Money received on application ₹ 3,60,000.
21. Money received on application ₹ 26,95,000;
    Calls-in-arrear ₹ 56,000 and ₹ 3,500;
    Forfeited amount transferred to Capital Reserve ₹ 7,000 (₹ 4,500 + 2,500).
22. (i) Shares allotted to Ram : 900 shares;
    (ii) Allotment money not paid by Ram : ₹ 4,500;
    (iii) Money received on allotment : ₹ 2,20,500;
    (iv) Amount transferred to Capital Resere ₹ 1,800.
23. (a) Forfeited shares ₹ 10,000; Amount transferred to Capital Reserve ₹ 7,500;
    (b) Forfeited shares ₹ 900; Amount transferred to Capital Reerve ₹ 800.
24. Amount transferred to Capital Reserve ₹ 16,000 (₹ 6,000 + 10,000).
    Allotment money received ₹ 6,30,000.
    Amount forfeited in respect of Ram's shares = ₹ 6,000.
    Amount transferred in respect of Sohan's shares = ₹ 15,000.
25. Amount transferred to capital reserve ₹ 800.
26. Amount forfeited ₹ 2,000.
27. Total amount forfeited ₹ 6,100.
28. (a) Amount forfeited ₹ 800; Amount transferred to capital reserve ₹ 500.
    (b) Amount forfeited ₹ 200; Amount transferred to capital reserve ₹ 375.
    (c) Amount transferred to capital reserve ₹ 3.
29. Amount transferred to capital reserve ₹ 350; Forfeited shares account ₹ 650;
30. (a) Amount forfeited ₹ 500;
    Amount transferred to capital reserve ₹ 150.
    (b) Amount forfeited ₹ 700;
    Amount transferred to capital reserve ₹ 300.
    (c) Amount forfeited ₹ 300;
    Amount transferred to capital reserve ₹ 200.
31. Amount forfeited ₹ 5,000;
    Amount transferred to capital reserve ₹ 2,250.
32. Capital reserve ₹ 4,000,
    ₹ 5,000 should be shown as an addition to share capital.
33. Capital reserve ₹ 530;
    Amount actually received on allotment ₹ 69,650;
    Amount forfeited ₹ 920.
34. Amount transferred to capital reserve ₹ 350;
    Securities premium ₹ 5,900;
    Share capital ₹ 29,900 (including forfeited shares ₹ 150);
    Balance Sheet total ₹ 36,150.
35. Amount transferred to capital reserve ₹ 3,250;
    Amount received on allotment ₹ 95,000.
36. Amount transferred to capital reserve ₹ 3,000.
37. Calls in advance ₹ 1,87,500; Amount forfeited ₹ 2,500.
38. Amount transferred to capital reserve ₹ 500.

39. Amount received on allotment ₹ 1,76,600.
    Amount not paid by Nikhil ₹ 1,000. Amount not paid by Vish ₹ 2,400.
40. Amount received on allotment ₹ 1,12,000 (₹ 1,00,000 + ₹ 12,000).
41. Amount not paid by Ram ₹ 4,500.
    Amount transferred to Capital Reserve ₹ 1,800.
    Money received on allotment ₹ 2,20,500.
42. Allotment money not paid by Jeevan ₹ 1,000;
    Allotment money received ₹ 69,000.
    Amount transferred to Capital Reserve ₹ 5,600.
43. (i) Money adjusted in allotment ₹ 30,00,000;
    (ii) Allotment money not paid by Hari ₹ 1,40,000.
    (iii) Money received on allotment ₹ 43,60,000.
44. Number of shares allotted to Kanwar = 200 shares.
    Allotment money not paid by Kanwar ₹ 7,800.
    Amount received on allotment ₹ 3,82,200.
    Amount transferred to Capital Reserve ₹ 5,000.
45. Calls in advance ₹ 70,000;
    Money adjusted with allotment ₹ 80,000.
46. Amount adjusted against allotment ₹ 1,32,900;
    Amount refunded ₹ 25,800;
    Calls in advance ₹ 30,900.
47. Amount adjusted with allotment ₹ 800;
    Money refunded ₹ 1,200; Amount forfeited ₹ 192;
    Money received on allotment ₹ 8,832.
48. Money not paid on allotment ₹ 7,300;
    Actual amount received on allotment ₹ 1,76,640;
    Amount forfeited ₹ 13,840.
49. Calls-in-advance ₹ 4,40,000;
    Interest on calls in advance ₹ 600.
50. Amount transferred to capital reserve ₹ 500;
    Securities premium ₹ 8,000;
    Paid up capital ₹ 39,920;
    Balance Sheet total ₹ 48,420.
51. Allotment money received ₹ 2,98,600;
    Amount transferred to Forfeited Account ₹ 13,300.
52. Amount transferred to capital reserve ₹ 5,000;
    Securities premium ₹ 1,000;
    Balance Sheet total ₹ 2,06,000.
53. Amount transferred to capital reserve ₹ 1,125.
54. Amount forfeited ₹150;
    Amount transferred to capital reserve ₹ 120;
    Balance Sheet total ₹ 3,60,120.
55. Amount transferred to capital reserve ₹ 8,300;
    Money actually received on allotment ₹ 2,20,800.

56. Amount transferred to capital reserve ₹ 9,200;
    Securities premium ₹ 1,95,000;
    Share capital ₹ 7,96,000 (including balance of forfeited shares ₹ 4,000).
57. Amount transferred to capital reserve ₹ 1,400.
58. Amount transferred to capital reserve ₹ 1,600;
    Allotment money not paid by Subodh ₹ 600.
59. Amount transferred to capital reserve ₹ 500;
    Allotment money actually received ₹ 18,000;
    Money not paid by Sundar ₹ 2,000.
60. Money received on allotment ₹ 1,65,500;
    Amount forfeited ₹ 4,500;
    Amount transferred to capital reserve ₹ 2,000.
61. Amount trasnferred to capital reserve ₹ 1,600;
    Amount forfeited on : Sudha's shares ₹ 1,600; Asha's shares ₹ 4,000.
62. Money received on first call ₹ 4,87,500;
    Amount forfeited ₹ 25,000;
    Amount transferred to capital reserve ₹ 6,000; Balance Sheet total ₹ 21,91,000;
    Expenses of issue ₹ 10,000 will be treated as preliminary expenses.
63. Amount transferred to capital reserve ₹ 212.50.
64. Amount transferred to capital reserve ₹ 28,000;
    Money adjusted with allotment ₹ 1,65,000;
    Ratio of pro-rata allotment 75 : 64.
65. Amount transferred to capital reserve ₹ 11,000;
    Money received on allotment ₹ 6,86,000.
66. Money not paid by P ₹ 950;
    Amount received on allotment ₹ 69,950; Refund ₹ 3,700;
    Amount forfeited ₹ 2,800.
67. Amount transferred to capital reserve ₹ 216;
    Money not paid by Romesh ₹ 184;
    Money received on allotment ₹ 9,016; Securities premium ₹ 3,920;
    Balance Sheet total ₹ 24,036.
68. Amount forfeited ₹ 1,250.
69. Amount transferred to capital reserve ₹ 9,000;
    Amount forfeited on Bajaj's shares ₹ 12,000;
    Amount forfeited on Sharma's shares ₹ 16,000.
70. Amount forfeited ₹ 12,000;
    Amount transferred to capital reserve Nil;
    ₹ 4,500 will be shown in the Balance Sheet as an addition to capital.

5

Accounting for Debentures

Syllabus

- **Debentures** : Issue of debentures at par, at premium and at discount, Issue of Debentures for consideration other than cash, Issue of debentures with terms of redemption, debentures as collateral security-concept; Interest on debentures.
- Redemption of debentures : Lump sum, draw of lots and purchase in the open market (excluding ex-interest and cum-interest); Creation of Debenture Redemption Reserve.

Section A : Issue of Debentures

Meaning of Debentures

Debenture is a certificate issued by the company, stamped with official seal, which contains the details of an interest-bearing loan made by the company on long term basis.

According to Section 2(30) of the Companies Act, 2013, debenture includes debenture stock, bonds and any other instruments of the company evidencing a debt, whether constituting a charge on the assets of the company or not.

Features of a Debenture

The following are the features of a Debenture :

1. It is a document which evidences a loan made by a company.
2. It is a fixed interest-bearing security where interest falls due on specific dates.
3. Interest is payable at a predetermined fixed rate, regardless of the level of profit.
4. It is repaid at a specified future date or it is converted into shares or other debentures.
5. It creates a charge on the assets of a company as security.
6. It can generally be bought or sold through the stock exchange at a price above or below its face value.
7. It is a movable property (Section 44 of the Companies Act, 2013).

Factors to be Considered for the Issue of Debentures

Whether a company will be able to raise further capital by the issue of debentures depends on the following factors:

From the viewpoint of the investors —

1. Past performance of the company and the quality of its management.
2. Future potential of the company, both in sales value and efficiency in controlling costs.
3. The availability of collateral security, either in fixed assets or current assets.
4. The borrowing capacity of the company as indicated by its debt/equity ratio.
5. The ability of the company to pay interest on time.

From the viewpoint of the company —

1. The required profits and cash available to pay debenture interest and to redeem debentures at some point in the future.
2. Borrowing power clauses in the Articles of Association.
3. The company's attitude towards capital gearing.
4. The availability of debenture finance.
5. The cost of debentures and the ability of the company to provide satisfactory return on equity share capital.

Distinction between Debentures and Shares

Sl.No.	Debentures	Sl.No.	Shares
1.	Debenture represents a loan capital.	1.	Share represents own capital.
2.	There are different kinds of debentures, such as secured/ unsecured; redeemable/ irredeemable; registered/ bearers; convertible/ non-convertible.	2.	There are only two kinds of shares — Equity Shares and Preference Shares.
3.	Debentures are shown in the company Balance Sheet under "***Non-current Liabilities***".	3.	Shares are shown in the company Balance Sheet under "***Shareholders' Funds***".
4.	As per the terms of issue, debentures can be converted into shares.	4.	Shares cannot be converted into debentures in any circumstances.
5.	Debenture interest is paid at a pre-determined fixed rate. It is payable, whether there is any profit or not. Debentures rank ahead of all types of shares for payment of the interest due on them.	5.	Dividend on equity shares is paid at a ***variable rate*** which is vastly affected by the profits of the company (however, dividend on preference shares is paid at a ***fixed rate***).
6.	Interests on debentures are the charges against profits and they are deductible as an expense in determining taxable profit of the company.	6.	Dividends are appropriation of profits and these are not deductible in determining taxable profit of the company.
7.	Debentures cannot be forfeited for non-payment of calls money as per the provision of Section 122 of the Companies Act, 1956.	7.	Shares can be forfeited for non-payment of allotment and call monies.

Distinction between Debentureholders and Shareholders

Sl.No.	Debentureholders	Sl.No.	Shareholders
1.	Debentureholders are the creditors of the company.	1.	Shareholders are the owners of the company.
2.	Debentureholders have no voting rights and consequently do not pose any threat to the existing control of the company.	2.	Shareholders have voting rights and consequently control the total affairs of the company.
3.	At maturity, debentureholders get back their money as per the terms and conditions of redemption.	3.	Equity shareholders cannot get back their money before the liquidation of the company.
4.	At the time of liquidation, debentureholders are paid-off before the shareholders.	4.	At the time of liquidation shareholders are paid at last, after paying debentureholders, creditors, etc.

Nature of Debenture Capital (Loan Capital)

The capital structure of a company consists of share capital as well as loan capital. Debenture is the most common form of loan capital. Large and financially sound companies may obtain some long-term loans from financial institutions, for example, Industrial Development Bank of India; Life Insurance Corporation of India and so on. But for financing large project, such as laying of gas pipe line or building a steel plant, a company may need more loan capital than what any single lender can provide. To arrange huge amounts of loan capital perhaps ₹ 1,000 to ₹ 1,200 crores — a company issue debentures, thus splitting a large loan into a great many units.

A pre-determined fixed rate of interest is payable on debentures (whether the company has earned any profit or not). Rate of interest is used as a prefix of the debenture, e.g., 14% Debenture.

Types of Debentures

The following are the types of debentures issued by a company. They can be classified on the basis of : (1) Security; (2) Convertibility; (3) Permanence; (4) Negotiability; and (5) Priority.

1. Security

(a) Secured Debentures : These debentures are secured by a charge upon some or all assets of the company. There are two types of charges: (i) Fixed charge; and (ii) Floating charge. A fixed charge is a mortgage on specific assets. These assets cannot be sold without the consent of the debentureholders. The sale proceeds of these assets are utilised first for repaying debentureholders. A floating charge generally covers all the assets of the company including future one.

(b) Unsecured or "naked" Debentures : These debentures are not secured by any charge upon any assets. A company merely promises to pay interest on due dates and to repay the amount due on maturity date. These types of debentures are very risky from the view point of investors.

It is very important to note that '***unsecured debentures***' will be treated as '***deposit***' and the Companies (Acceptance of Deposits) Rules, 2014 will be applicable.

2. Convertibility

(a) Convertible Debentures : These are debentures which will be converted into equity shares (either at par or premium or discount) after a certain period of time from the date of its issue. These

debentures may be fully or partly convertible. In future, these debentureholders get a chance to become the shareholders of the company.

(b) Non-Convertible Debentures : These are debentures which cannot be converted into shares in future. As per the terms of issue, these debentures are repaid.

3. Permanence

(a) Redeemable Debentures : These debentures are repayable as per the terms of issue, for example, after 10 years from the date of issue.

(b) Irredeemable Debentures : These debentures are not repayable during the life time of the company. These are also called ***perpetual debentures***. These are repaid only at the time of liquidation.

In the Companies Act, 2013, there is no provision for issuing irredeemable debentures. As per Rule 18 of the Companies (Share Capital and Debentures) Rules, 2014 a company can issue only secured and redeemable debentures.

4. Negotiability

(a) Registered Debentures : These debentures are payable to a registered holder whose name, address and particulars of holding recorded in the Register of Debentureholders. Debenture interest is paid either to the order of registered holder as expressed in the warrant issued by the company or the bearer of the interest coupons.

(b) Bearer Debentures : These debentures are transferable by delivery. These are negotiable instruments payable to the bearer. No kind of record is kept by the company in respect of the holders of such debentures.

5. Priority

(a) First Mortgage Debentures : These debentures are payable first out of the property charged.

(b) Second Mortgage Debentures : These debentures are payable after satisfying the first mortgage debentures.

Authorisation of a Debenture Issue

The memorandum of association must contain the provision for borrowing by the company. As per the provision of Section 179(3)(c),the Board of Directors of a company has the power to issue debentures on behalf of the company. However, a resolution of the Board of Directors is to be passed in this respect. After the Board of Directors has decided upon the details of debenture issue, the debenture certificates are printed and deed of trust is drawn. The trust deed contains the full details of the property to be mortgaged. The trustees are appointed to safeguard the interest of the debentureholders.

It is convenient to the company to make trustees parties to the deed instead of all the debentureholders. On the other hand, the debentureholders who are ignorant of law, can protect their rights and can bring an action against the company through trustees.

Issue of Debentures Under the Companies Act, 2013

A company ***may issue debentures*** after complying with the provisions of the Companies Act, 2013 and the Companies (Share Capital and Debentures) Rules 2014 and SEBI Regulations.

Section 71 of the Companies Act, 2013 states that :

(1) A company may issue debentures with an option to convert such debentures into shares, either wholly or partly at the time of redemption:

Provided that the issue of debentures with an option to convert such debentures into shares, wholly or partly, shall be approved by ***a special resolution*** passed at a general meeting.

(2) No company shall issue any debentures carrying any voting rights.

(3) Secured debentures may be issued by a company subject to such terms and conditions as may be prescribed.

(4) Where debentures are issued by a company under this section, the company shall create a debenture redemption reserve account out of the profits of the company available for payment of dividend and the amount credited to such account shall not be utilised by the company except for the redemption of debentures.

(5) No company shall issue a prospectus or make an offer or invitation to the public or to its members exceeding ***five hundred*** for the subscription of its debentures, unless the company has, before such issue or offer, appointed one or more debenture trustees and the conditions governing the appointment of such trustees shall be such as may be prescribed.

(6) A debenture trustee shall take steps to protect the interests of the debentureholders and redress their grievances in accordance with such rules as may be prescribed.

(7) Any provision contained in a trust deed for securing the issue of debentures, or in any contract with the debenture-holders secured by a trust deed, shall be void in so far as it would have the effect of exempting a trustee thereof from, or indemnifying him against, any liability for breach of trust, where he fails to show the degree of care and due diligence required of him as a trustee, having regard to the provisions of the trust deed conferring on him any power, authority or discretion:

Provided that the liability of the debenture trustee shall be subject to such exemptions as may be agreed upon by a majority of debenture-holders holding not less than threefourths in value of the total debentures at a meeting held for the purpose.

(8) A company shall pay interest and redeem the debentures in accordance with the terms and conditions of their issue.

(9) Where at any time the debenture trustee comes to a conclusion that the assets of the company are insufficient or are likely to become insufficient to discharge the principal amount as and when it becomes due, the debenture trustee may file a petition before the Tribunal and the Tribunal may, after hearing the company and any other person interested in the matter, by order, impose such restrictions on the incurring of any further liabilities by the company as the Tribunal may consider necessary in the interests of the debenture-holders.

(10) Where a company fails to redeem the debentures on the date of their maturity or fails to pay interest on the debentures when it is due, the Tribunal may, on the application of any or all of the debenture-holders, or debenture trustee and, after hearing the parties concerned, direct, by order, the company to redeem the debentures forthwith on payment of principal and interest due thereon.

(11) If any default is made in complying with the order of the Tribunal under this section, every officer of the company who is in default shall be punishable with imprisonment for a term which may extend to three years or with fine which shall not be less than two lakh rupees but which may extend to five lakh rupees, or with both.

(12) A contract with the company to take up and pay for any debentures of the company may be enforced by a decree for specific performance.

(13) The Central Government may prescribe the procedure, for securing the issue of debentures, the form of debenture trust deed, the procedure for the debenture-holders to inspect the trust deed and to obtain copies thereof, quantum of debenture redemption reserve required to be created and such other matters.

The Companies (Share Capital and Debentures) Rules, 2014

Rule 18 of the companies (Share Capital and Debentures) Rules, 2014 states that :
A company ***shall not issue secured debentures***, unless it complies with the following conditions, namely:-

(a) An issue of secured debentures may be made, provided the date of its redemption shall not exceed ***ten years*** from the date of issue.
Provided that a company engaged in the setting up of infrastructure projects may issue secured debentures for a period exceeding ten years but not ***exceeding thirty years***;

(b) such an issue of debentures shall be secured by the creation of a charge, on the properties or assets of the company, having a value which is sufficient for the due repayment of the amount of debentures and interest thereon;

(c) the company shall appoint a debenture trustee before the issue of prospectus or letter of offer for subscription of its debentures and not later than sixty days after the allotment of the debentures, execute a debenture trust deed to protect the interest of the debenture holders ; and

(d) the security for the debentures by way of a charge or mortgage shall be created in favour of the debenture trustee on-
(i) any specific movable property of the company (not being in the nature of pledge); or
(ii) any specific immovable property wherever situate, or any interest therein.

Presentation of Debentures in the Balance Sheet

As per 'Schedule III' the debentures are shown under main heading — '***Non-Current Liabilities***' and sub-heading '***Long-term Borrowings***'. The details of debentures are shown in the 'Notes to Accounts', e.g., (i) debentures shall further be sub-classified as secured and unsecured; (ii) nature of security shall be specified separately in each case; (iii) debentures (along with the rate of interest and particulars of redemption or conversion as the case may be) shall be stated in descending order of maturity or conversion, starting from farthest redemption or conversion date, as the case may be. Where debentures are redeemable by installments, the date of maturity for this purpose must be reckoned as the date on which the first installment becomes due.

Example

X Ltd. issued 10,000, 12% Debentures of ₹ 100 each at a discount of 10% payable in full on application by 31st May, 2015. Applications were received for 12,000 debentures. Debentures were allotted on 9th June, 2015. Excess monies were refunded on the same date. Show relevant items in the Balance Sheet. All debentures are secured.

The ***relevant items*** will appear in the Balance sheet as follows :

Balance Sheet of X Ltd. as at 9th June, 2015 [Extract],

Particulars	Note No.	Amount (₹)
(1)	(2)	(3)
I. EQUITY AND LIABILITIES		
(1) Shareholders' Funds :		
(a) Share Capital		?
(b) Reserves and Surplus	(1)	(1,00,000)
(c) Money Received against Share Warrants		?
(2) Share Application Money Pending Allotment :		
(3) Non-current Liabilities :		
(a) Long-term Borrowings	(2)	10,00,000
(b) Deferred Tax Liabilities (Net)		?
(c) Other Long-term Liabilities		?
(d) Long-term Provisions		?
(4) Current Liabilities :		?
(a) Short-term Borrowings		?
(b) Trade Payables		?
(c) Other Current Liabilities		?
(d) Short-term Provisions		?
TOTAL		
II. ASSETS		
(1) Non-current Assets :		
(a) Fixed Assets		
(i) Tangible Assets		?
(ii) Intangible Assets		?
(iii) Capital Work-in-progress		?
(iv) Intangible Assets under Development		?
(b) Non-current Investments		?
(c) Deferred Tax Assets (Net)		?
(d) Long-term Loans and Advances		?
(e) Other Non-current Assets		?
(2) Current Assets :		
(a) Current Investments		?
(b) Inventories		?
(c) Trade Receivables		?
(d) Cash and Cash Equivalents		9,00,000
(e) Short-term Loans and Advances		?
(f) Other Current Assets		?
TOTAL		

Notes to Accounts :

(1) Reserve and Surplus

Particulars	₹
Discount on Issue of Debentures	(1,00,000)

(2) Long-term Borrowings (Secured)

Particulars	₹
10,000, 12% Debentures of ₹ 100 each	10,00,000

Tutorial Note : As per 'Schedule III', no 'Miscellaneous Expenditure' is to be shown on the assets section of the Balance Sheet. If there is any item, e.g., discount on issue of debentures, loss on issue of debentures or commission on isue of shares or debentures, it should be shown under 'Reserve and Surplus' on the 'Equity and Liability' section of the Balance Sheet. If there is no balance of Reserve and Surplus, it is to be shown as a negative balance. These are written-off over the life of the debentures.

Check Your Progress

Answers : Page 5.59

Tick the correct answer :

1. ***Debenture represents***
   - *A own capital*
   - *B loan capital*
   - *C government grant*
   - *D none of the above*
2. ***Debentures are shown in the Schedule III under***
   - *A current liabilities*
   - *B shareholders' funds*
   - *C non-current liabilities*
   - *D none of the above*
3. ***Debentures***
   - *A can be forfeited for non-payment of calls money*
   - *B can be forfeited under certain circumstances*
   - *C can not be forfeited for non-payment of calls money*
   - *D can be forfeited by passing special resolution only*
4. ***Debentures***
   - *A can be converted into shares as per the terms of issue*
   - *B can not be converted into shares under any circumstances*
   - *C can be converted into shares only after the approval of the High Court*
   - *D must be converted into shares after one year*
5. ***Debentureholders have***
   - *A voting rights like equity shareholders*
   - *B no voting rights like equity shareholders*
   - *C voting rights at the time of passing special resolution only*
   - *D voting rights in the general meeting only*
6. ***Debenture***
   - *A is a non-movable property*
   - *B is a movable property*
   - *C is a short-term borrowing*
   - *D is an item of shareholders' funds*
7. ***As per the provision of the Companies Act, 2013 a company can issue***
   - *A secured but irredeemable debentures only*
   - *B unsecured but redeemable debentures only*
   - *C secured and redeemable debentures only*
   - *D none of the above*

Recording the Issue of Debentures

Accounting entries for issue of debentures are similar to that of shares. Money payable on debentures may be paid in full with application or may be paid in instalments. For example, on application 20%, on allotment 40% and balance on final call. Accounting entries will differ to some extent in either case.

Money Payable in Full on Application

In this case, entire money is payable with application. A separate Debenture Application Account is opened for each class of debentures, for example — 12% Debentures Application Account or 10% Debentures Application Account.

These accounts are used to record the moneys received from the applicants of debentures. In case of oversubscription, these accounts are used to record the refund of moneys to the unsuccessful applicants.

When debentures are allotted, the amount in Debenture Application Account is transferred to the respective Debentures Account.

Just like shares, debentures are issued at par, at a premium, or at a discount.

Debentures Issued at Par

The debentures which are issued at par are issued at the same price as their nominal value; that is, if a debenture with a nominal value of ₹ 100 is issued at par, the company receives ₹ 100.

The accounting entries would be as follows :

(a) When cash is received

Bank Account Dr.

To Debentures Application Account

(Being money received on ... debentures @ ₹ ... each)

(b) When excess money is refunded

Debentures Application Account Dr.

To Bank Account

(Being excess money on ... debentures refunded as per Board's Resolution No. ... dated ...)

(c) When the debentures are allotted

Debentures Application Account Dr.

To Debentures Account

(Being the allotment of ... debentures of ₹ ... each as per Board's Resolution No... dated ...)

Illustration 1

X Limited issued 20,000, 10% Debentures of ₹ 100 each at par payable in full on application by 1st January, 2015.

Applications were received for 24,000 debentures.

Debentures were allotted on 5th January, 2015.

Excess application money were refunded on the same date.

You are required to pass necessary journal entries (including cash transactions) in the books of the company.

Solution

In the books of X Limited
Journal

Date	Particulars	L.F.	Dr. ₹	Cr. ₹
2015 Jan. 1	Bank A/c Dr. To 10% Debentures Application A/c (Being money received on 24,000 debentures @ ₹ 100 each)		24,00,000	24,00,000
5	10% Debentures Application A/c Dr. To 10% Debentures A/c (Being the allotment of 20,000, 10% debentures of ₹ 100 each at par, as per Board's Resolution No. . . . dated . . .)		20,00,000	20,00,000
	10% Debentures Application A/c Dr. To Bank A/c (Being excess money on 4,000 debentures @ ₹ 100 each refunded as per Board's Resolution No. . . . dated . . .)		4,00,000	4,00,000

Debentures Issued at a Premium

Debentures are rarely issued at a premium. A company issues debentures at a premium when the market rate of interest is lower than the debenture interest rate. The debentures, which are issued at a premium, are issued at a higher price than their nominal value; that is, if a debenture with a nominal value of ₹ 100 is issued at 10% premium, the company receives ₹ 110 where the investor gets slightly less interest than stated in the debenture. For example, 12% Debentures of ₹ 100 issued at a premium of 10%. The investor will get ₹ 12 p.a. for his investment of 110. Therefore, the effective rate of interest on investment is (12/110 x 100) = 10.91%.

The accounting entries would be as follows:

(a) When cash is received

Bank Account Dr. [Nominal value plus premium]
To Debentures Application Account
(Being money received on ... debentures @ ₹ .... each including premium of ₹ ... each)

(b) When excess money is refunded

Debentures Application Account Dr.
To Bank Account
(Being refund of money on ... debentures @ ₹ ... each, as per Board's Resolution No ... dated ...)

(c) When the debentures are allotted

Debentures Application Account Dr.
To Debentures Account
To Securities Premium Account
(Being the allotment of ... debentures, premium transferred to Securities Premium Account, as per Board's Resolution No ... dated ...)

Illustration 2

Y Limited issued 10,000, 10% Debentures of ₹ 100 each at a premium of 10% payable in full on application by 1st March, 2015. The issue was fully subscribed and debentures were allotted on 10th March, 2015.

Pass necessary journal entries (including cash transactions).

Solution

In the books of Y Limited

Journal

Date	Particulars	L.F.	Dr. ₹	Cr. ₹
2015 March 1	Bank A/c Dr. To 10% Debentures Application A/c (Being money received on 10,000 debentures @ ₹ 110 each including premium of ₹ 10 each)		11,00,000	11,00,000
10	10% Debentures Application A/c Dr. To 10% Debentures A/c To Securities Premium A/c (Being the allotment of 10,000 debentures of ₹ 100 each, premium @ ₹ 10 each transferred to Securities Premium Account as per Board's Resolution No. . . . dated . . .)		11,00,000	10,00,000 1,00,000

Illustration 3

Narain Laxmi Ltd. invited applications for issuing 7,500, 12% Debentures of ₹ 100 each at a premium of ₹ 35 per Debenture. The full amount was payable on application. Applications were received for 10,000 Debentures. Applications for 2,500 Debentures were rejected and the application money was refunded. Debentures were allotted to the remaining applicants.

Pass necessary journal entries for the above transactions in the books of Narain Laxmi Ltd.

[CBSE (Delhi) — 2012]

Solution

In the books of Narain Laxmi

Journal

Date	Particulars	L.F.	Dr. ₹	Cr. ₹
	Bank A/c Dr. To 10% Debentures Application A/c (Being application money received on 10,000 debentures @ ₹ 135 each)		13,50,000	13,50,000
	10% Debentures Application A/c Dr. To 12% Debentures A/c To Securities Premium A/c To Bank A/c (Being the allotment of 7,500, 12% debentures at a premium 35%. Excess application money on 2,500 debentures refunded as per Board's Resolution No. . . . dated . . .)		13,50,000	7,50,000 2,62,500 3,37,500

Debentures Issued at a Discount

The Companies Act does not impose any restriction on the price at which debentures can be issued. Unlike shares, there is no maximum limit for discount on issue of debenture. This is why it is very common that debentures are issued at a discount.

The debentures which are issued at a discount are issued at a lower price than nominal value, that is, if a debenture with a nominal value of ₹ 100 is issued at 10% discount, the company receives ₹ 90 only. The issue of debentures at a discount slightly increases the true rate of interest payable.

For example, 12% Debentures of ₹ 100 issued at a discount of 10%. The Company will have to pay ₹ 12 for a loan of ₹ 90. Therefore, the true rate of interest is (12/90 × 100) = 13.33%.

A company issues debentures at a discount when the market rate of interest is ***higher*** than the debenture interest rate. Like shares, Debentures Account is credited with the nominal value. The difference between the nominal value of debentures and cash received is transferred to "***Discount on Issue of Debentures Account.***"

5.12 Issue of Debentures

In the Balance Sheet, "Discount on Issue of Debentures" is shown as a negative figure under 'Reserve and Surplus'. It is generally adjusted against securities premium or surplus if it is there in the Balance Sheet at the time of issue of debentures.

In many cases, companies are writing off discount on issue of debentures on equitable basis over different years. In this case, only balance amount is carried forward to next year and shown under 'Reserve and Surplus' as a negative figure.

The accounting entries would be as follows :

(a) When cash is received

Bank Account Dr. [Actual cash received]
To Debentures Application Account
(Being money received on ... debentures @ ₹ ... each)

(b) When excess money is refunded

Debentures Application Account Dr.
To Bank Account
(Being excess money on ... debentures refunded as per Board's Resolution No ,.. dated .,.,)

(c) When the debentures are allotted

Debentures Application Account Dr. [Actual cash received]
Discount on Issue of Debentues Account Dr. [Discount on debentures]
To Debentures Account [Nominal value of debentures]
(Being the allotment of ... debentures of ₹ ... each @ ₹ ... each as per Board's Resolution No ... dated ...)

Illustration 4

Z Ltd issued 15,000, 10% Debentures of ₹ 100 each at a discount of 10% payable in full on application by 1st April, 2014.

Applications were received for 18,000 debentures.

Debentures were allotted on 15th April, 2014. Excess monies were refunded on the same date.

Pass necessary journal entries (including cash transactions).

Also show Ledger Accounts and Balance Sheet after issue.

Solution

In the books of Z Ltd

Journal

Date	Particulars		L.F.	Dr. ₹	Cr. ₹
2014 April 1	Bank A/c	Dr.		16,20,000	
	To 10% Debentures Application A/c				16,20,000
	(Being money received for 18,000 debentures @ ₹ 90 each)				
15	10% Debentures Application A/c	Dr.		2,70,000	
	To Bank A/c				2,70,000
	(Being excess money on 3,000 debentures @ ₹ 90 each refunded as per Board's Resolution No. . . . dated . . .)				
	10% Debentures Application A/c	Dr.		13,50,000	
	Discount on Issue of Debentures A/c	Dr.		1,50,000	
	To 10% Debentures A/c				15,00,000
	(Being the allotment of 15,000 debentures of ₹ 100 each at a discount of ₹ 10 each as per Board's Resolution No. . . . dated . . .)				

Dr. Bank Account Cr.

Date	Particulars	₹	Date	Particulars	₹
2014			2014		
April 1	To 10% Debentures Application A/c	16,20,000	April 15	By 10% Debentures Application A/c	2,70,000
			"	By Balance c/d	13,50,000
		16,20,000			16,20,000

Dr. 10% Debentures Account Cr.

Date	Particulars	₹	Date	Particulars	₹
2014			2014		
April 15	To Balance c/d	15,00,000	April 15	By 10% Debentures Application A/c	13,50,000
				By Disc. on Issue of Debentures A/c	1,50,000
		15,00,000			15,00,000

Dr. 10% Debentures Application Account Cr.

Date	Particulars	₹	Date	Particulars	₹
2014			2014		
April 15	To Bank A/c	2,70,000	April 15	By Bank A/c	16,20,000
"	To 10% Debentures A/c	13,50,000			
		16,20,000			16,20,000

Dr. Discount on Issue of Debentures Account Cr.

Date	Particulars	₹	Date	Particulars	₹
2014			2014		
April 15	To 10% Debentures A/c	1,50,000	April 15	By Balance c/d	1,50,000

Balance Sheet of Z Ltd. as at 15th April, 2014 [Extract],

Particulars	Note No.	Amount (₹)
(1)	(2)	(3)
I. EQUITY AND LIABILITIES		
(1) Shareholders' Funds :		
(a) Share Capital		?
(b) Reserves and Surplus	(1)	(1,50,000)
(c) Money Received against Share Warrants		?
(2) Share Application Money Pending Allotment :		
(3) Non-current Liabilities :		
(a) Long-term Borrowings	(2)	15,00,000
(b) Deferred Tax Liabilities (Net)		?
(c) Other Long-term Liabilities		?
(d) Long-term Provisions		?
(4) Current Liabilities :		?
(a) Short-term Borrowings		?
(b) Trade Payables		?
(c) Other Current Liabilities		?
(d) Short-term Provisions		?
TOTAL		

II. ASSETS		
(1) Non-current Assets :		
(a) Fixed Assets		
(i) Tangible Assets		?
(ii) Intangible Assets		?
(iii) Capital Work-in-progress		?
(iv) Intangible Assets under Development		?
(b) Non-current Investments		?
(c) Deferred Tax Assets (Net)		?
(d) Long-term Loans and Advances		?
(e) Other Non-current Assets		?
(2) Current Assets :		
(a) Current Investments		?
(b) Inventories		?
(c) Trade Receivables		?
(d) Cash and Cash Equivalents		13,50,000
(e) Short-term Loans and Advances		?
(f) Other Current Assets		?
TOTAL		

Notes to Accounts :

(1) Reserve and Surplus

Particulars	₹
Discount on Issue of Debentures	(1,50,000)

(3) Cash and Cash Equivalents

Particulars	₹
Cash at Bank	13,50,000

(2) Long-term Borrowings (Secured)

Particulars	₹
15,000, 10% Debentures of ₹ 100 each	15,00,000

Treatment of Discount on Issue of Debentures

Discount on issue of debentures is written off over a period of time by debiting Statement of Profit and Loss and crediting Discount on Issue of Debenture Account. Amount to be written-off every year will depend upon the terms of redemption.

(a) If the debentures are redeemable after a certain period of time, say at the end of 5 or 10 years, the total amount of discount should be written-off ***equally*** throughout the life of the debentures. The main advantage of this method is that it spreads the burden of discount equally over the years.

(b) If the debentures are redeemable at ***different dates***, the total amount of discount should be written-off in the ***ratio of benefit derived*** from debenture loan in any particular year (applying the sum of the years digit method). This method is suitable when debentures are redeemed by unequal instalments. The amount of discount to be written-off each year should be in proportion to the amount outstanding against debentures. Generally, the amount to be written-off per year is based on the number of months that the debentures are outstanding.

(c) If the debentures are irredeemable, the discount should be written-off gradually over a ***long period. The accounting entries would be as follows***:

Statement of Profit and Loss Dr.

To Discount on Issue of Debentures Account

Illustration 5

A Limited Company has issued ₹ 1,00,000, 9% Debentures at a discount of 6%. These debentures are to be redeemed equally, spread over 5 annual instalments. Show the Discount on Issue of Debentures Account for 5 years.

Solution

Workings :

Total amount of discount on issue of debentures comes to ₹ 6,000 (6% on ₹ 1,00,000). The debentures are to be redeemed equally, spread over 5 annual instalments, i.e., ₹ 20,000 every year. At the end of the firs t year, the company redeemed ₹ 20,000. The company enjoyed benefit in the first year ₹ 1,00,000 and in the second year ₹ 80,000 and so on. The calculation of amount of discount to be written off is as under :

Calculation of amount of discount to be written-off

At the end of	Debentures Outstanding (₹)	Ratio of Benefits Derived	Amount of Discount to be written-off
1st year	1,00,000	5	5/15 of ₹ 6,000 = ₹ 2,000
2nd year	80,000	4	4/15 of ₹ 6,000 = ₹ 1,600
3rd year	60,000	3	3/15 of ₹ 6,000 = ₹ 1,200
4h year	40,000	2	2/15 of ₹ 6,000 = ₹ 800
5th year	20,000	1	1/15 of ₹ 6,000 = ₹ 400
Total		15	₹ 6,000

In the books of the Company

Dr. Discount on Issue of Debentures Account Cr.

Date	Particulars	₹	Date	Particulars	₹
1st year	To 9% Debentures A/c	6,000	1st year End	By Statement of Profit and Loss By Balance c/d	2,000 4,000
		6,000			6,000
2nd year	To Balance b/d	4,000	2nd year End	By Statement of Profit and Loss By Balance c/d	1,600 2,400
		4,000			4,000
3rd year	To Balance b/d	2,400	3rd year End	By Statement of Profit and Loss By Balance c/d	1,200 1,200
		2,400			2,400
4th year	To Balance b/d	1,200	4th year End	By Statement of Profit and Loss By Balance c/d	800 400
		1,200			1,200
5th year	To Balance b/d	400	5th year	By Statement of Profit and Loss	400
		400			400

Illustration 6

X Limited issued 12% Debentures of ₹ 20,00,000 at 8% discount redeemable at par. Assume that the debentures are redeemable by drawings method in the following manner :

Year end	Face value (₹)
2	2,00,000
3	4,00,000
4	6,00,000
5	8,00,000

Prepare Discount on Issue of Debentures Account.

Solution

Total amount of discount on issue of debentures comes to ₹ 1,60,000 (8% of ₹ 20,00,000). Since the debentures are redeemable at different dates, the total amount of discount is to be written off in the proportion to the amount outstanding against debentures.

Calculation of amount of discount to be written-off

At the end of	Debentures Outstanding (₹)	Ratio of Benefits Derived	Amount of Discount to be written-off
1st year	20,00,000	10	10/40 of ₹ 1,60,000 = ₹ 40,000
2nd year	20,00,000	10	10/40 of ₹ 1,60,000 = ₹ 40,000
3rd year	18,00,000	9	9/40 of ₹ 1,60,000 = ₹ 36,000
4th year	14,00,000	7	7/40 of ₹ 1,60,000 = ₹ 28,000
5th year	8,00,000	4	4/40 of ₹ 1,60,000 = ₹ 16,000
Total		40	₹ 1,60,000

In the books of X Limited

Dr. **Discount on Issue of Debentures Account** **Cr.**

Date	Particulars	₹	Date	Particulars	₹
Year 1			Year 1		
Jan. 1	To 12% Debentures A/c	1,60,000	Dec. 31	By Statement of Profit and Loss	40,000
			"	By Balance c/d	1,20,000
		1,60,000			1,60,000
Year 2			Year 2		
Jan. 1	To Balance b/d	1,20,000	Dec. 31	By Statement of Profit and Loss	40,000
			"	By Balance c/d	80,000
		1,20,000			1,20,000
Year 3			Year 3		
Jan. 1	To Balance b/d	80,000	Dec. 31	By Statement of Profit and Loss	36,000
			"	By Balance c/d	44,000
		80,000			80,000
Year 4			Year 4		
Jan. 1	To Balance b/d	44,000	Dec. 31	By Statement of Profit and Loss	28,000
			"	By Balance c/d	16,000
		44,000			44,000
Year 5			Year 5		
Jan. 1	To Balance b/d	16,000	Dec. 31	By Statement of Profit and Loss	16,000
		16,000			16,000

Illustration 7

X Limited issued 6,000, 12% Debentures of ₹ 100 each at a discount of 6% on 1.1.2006. The debentures were payable in instalments of ₹ 2,00,000 starting from 31.12.2008.

Show the Discount on Issue of Debentures Account for the year 2006 to 2013.

Solution

The total amount of discount on issue of debentures comes to ₹ 36,000 (6% of ₹ 6,00,000). Since the debentures are redeemed at different dates, the total amount of discount is to be written-off in the proportion to the amount outstanding against debentures.

Calculation of amount of discount to be written-off

At the end of	Debentures Outstanding (₹)	Ratio of Benefits Derived	Amount of Discount to be written-off
2006	6,00,000	3	3/12 of ₹ 36,000 = ₹ 9,000
2007	6,00,000	3	3/12 of ₹ 36,000 = ₹ 9,000
2008	6,00,000	3	3/12 of ₹ 36,000 = ₹ 9,000
2009	4,00,000	2	2/12 of ₹ 36,000 = ₹ 6,000
2013	2,00,000	1	1/12 of ₹ 36,000 = ₹ 3,000
Total		12	₹ 36,000

In the books of X Limited

Dr. **Discount on Issue of Debentures Account** **Cr.**

Date	Particulars	₹	Date	Particulars	₹
2006			2006		
Jan. 1	To 12% Debentures A/c	36,000	Dec. 31	By Statement of Profit and Loss	9,000
			"	By Balance c/d	27,000
		36,000			36,000
2007			2007		
Jan. 1	To Balance b/d	27,000	Dec. 31	By Statement of Profit and Loss	9,000
			"	By Balance c/d	18,000
		27,000			27,000
2008			2008		
Jan. 1	To Balance b/d	18,000	Dec. 31	By Statement of Profit and Loss	9,000
			"	By Balance c/d	9,000
		18,000			18,000
2009			2009		
Jan. 1	To Balance b/d	9,000	Dec. 31	By Statement of Profit and Loss	6,000
			"	By Balance c/d	3,000
		9,000			9,000
2013			2013		
Jan. 1	To Balance b/d	3,000	Dec. 31	By Statement of Profit and Loss	3,000
		3,000			3,000

Debentures Payable By Instalments

Like shares, company may issue debentures payable by instalments, for example, 20% with application; 30% with allotment; and balance in final call. Prospectus contains the details of money payable (both amount and date). In this case also debentures may be issued: (i) at par, (ii) at a discount; or (iii) at a premium. The accounting entries are similar to that of issue of shares.

Debentures Issued at par

Accounting Entries

(a) When application money is received

Bank Account Dr.

To Debentures Application Account

(b) When excess application money is refunded

Debentures Application Account Dr.

To Bank Account

(Being the refund of excess application money on ... debentures as per Board's Resolution No ... dated ...)

(c) When the debentures are allotted

(i) Debentures Application Account Dr.
To Debentures Account
(Being the allotment of .....debentures as per Board's Resolution No... dated...)

(ii) Debentures Allotment Account Dr.
To Debentures Account
(Being allotment money due on.....debentures @ ₹ ....each as per Board's Resolution No... dated...)

(d) When allotment money is received

Bank Account Dr.
To Debentures Allotment Account
(Being allotment money received)

(e) When call money is due

Debentures Call Account Dr.
To Debentures Account
(Being call money due on... debentures @ ₹ ... each as per Board's Resolution No... dated...)

(f) When call money is received

Bank Account Dr.
To Debentures Call Account
(Being call money received on... debentures @ ₹ ...each)

Illustration 8

AB Ltd issued 20,000, 14% Debentures of ₹ 100 each at par on 1st January, 2014, payable on the following terms :

On application —₹ 40; On allotment —₹ 40; and On final call —₹ 20

Applications were received for 22,000 debentures and all the application money was received by 15th January, 2014. Allotment was made on 1st February 2014, and allotment money was received in full on 20th February, 2014. The call was made on 1st March, 2014 and fully paid on 20th March, 2014. Pass necessary journal enries (including cash transactions).

Solution

In the books of AB Limited

Journal

Date	Particulars	L.F.	Dr. ₹	Cr. ₹
2014 Jan. 15	Bank A/c Dr. To Debentures Application A/c (Being the application money received for 22,000 debentures @ ₹ 40 each)		8,80,000	8,80,000
Feb. 1	Debentures Application A/c Dr. To Bank A/c (Being excess application money on 2,000 debentures @ ₹ 40 each refunded as per Board's Resolution No. . . . dated . . .)		80,000	80,000
	Debentures Application A/c Dr. To 14% Debentures A/c (Being the allotment of 20,000 debentures as per Board's Resolution No. . . . dated . . .)		8,00,000	8,00,000
	Debentures Allotment A/c Dr. To 14% Debentures A/c (Being the allotment money due on 20,000 debentures @ ₹ 40 each as per Board's Resolution No. . . . dated . . .)		8,00,000	8,00,000

Feb. 20	Bank A/c Dr. To Debentures Allotment A/c (Being allotment received on 20,000 debentures @ ₹ 40 each)		8,00,000	8,00,000
March 1	Debentures Final Call A/c Dr. To 14% Debentures A/c (Being final call money due on 20,000 debentures @ ₹ 20 each as per Board's Resolution No. . . . dated . . .)		4,00,000	4,00,000
March 20	Bank A/c Dr. To Debentures Final Call A/c (Being final call money received on 20,000 debentures @ ₹ 20 each)		4,00,000	4,00,000

Debentures Issued at a Discount

Debentures can also be issued at a discount just like shares. Generally, discount is adjusted with the allotment (it can also be adjusted with the application as per the terms and conditions of the issue).

Debentures Account is shown in the Balance Sheet at ***nominal value.*** Discount on issue of debentures will be shown in the Balance Sheet under ***Reserve and Surplus*** (as a negative figure) to the extent it is not written-off.

Accounting Entries

(a) When application money is received

Bank Account Dr.
To Debentures Application Account
(Being application money received on . . . debentures @ ₹ . . . each)

(b) When excess application money is refunded

Debentures Application Account Dr.
To Bank Account
(Being the refund of excess application money on ... debentures as per Board's Resolution No ... dated ...)

(c) When the debentures are allotted

(i) Debentures Application Account Dr.
To Debentures Account
(Being the allotment of .....debentures as per Board's Resolution No..... dated.....)

(ii) Debentures Allotment Account Dr.
Discount on Issue of Debentures Account Dr.
To Debentures Account
(Being allotment money due on...debentures @ ₹ ...each as per Board's Resolution No.. dated...)

(d) When allotment money is received

Bank Account Dr.
To Debentures Allotment Account
(Being allotment money received)

(e) When call money is due

Debentures Call Account Dr.
To Debentures Account
(Being call money due on........ debentures @ ₹ .... each as per Board's Resolution No....dated....)

(f) When call money is received

Bank Account Dr.

To Debentures Call Account

(Being call money received on........ debentures @ ₹ ......each)

Illustration 9

XY Ltd issued 2,000, 12% Debentures of ₹ 100 each at a discount of 10% on 1st April, 2014 payable on the following terms:

On application	₹ 50
On allotment	₹ 30 (after adjusting discount)
On final call	₹ 10

The issue was fully subscribed and all money received in full by 30th June, 2014.

Pass necessary journal entries (including cash transactions) and also show the relevant portion of the Balance Sheet after issue of debentures.

Solution

In the books of XY Ltd

Journal

Date	Particulars	L.F.	Dr. ₹	Cr. ₹
2014 April 1	Bank A/c Dr. To Debentures Application A/c (Being the application money received on 2,000 debentures @ ₹ 50 each)		1,00,000	1,00,000
?	Debentures Application A/c Dr. To 12% Debentures A/c (Being the allotment of 2,000 debentures of ₹ 100 each as per Board's Resolution No. . . . dated . . .)		1,00,000	1,00,000
?	Debentures Allotment A/c Dr. Discount on Issue of Debentures A/c Dr. To 12% Debentures A/c (Being allotment money due on 2,000 debentures @ ₹ 30 each after adjusting discount of ₹ 10 per debenture as per Board's Resolution No. . . . dated . . .)		60,000 20,000	80,000
?	Bank A/c Dr. To Debentures Allotment A/c (Being allotment money received on 2,000 debentures @ ₹ 30 each)		60,000	60,000
?	Debentures Final Call A/c Dr. To 12% Debentures A/c (Being the final call money due on 2,000 debentures @ ₹ 10 each as per Board's Resolution No. . . . dated . . .)		20,000	20,000
June 30	Bank A/c Dr. To Debentures Final Call A/c (Being final call money received on 2,000 debentures @ ₹ 10 each)		20,000	20,000

Balance Sheet of XY Ltd. as at 30th June, 2014 [Extract],

Particulars (1)	Note No. (2)	Amount (₹) (3)
I. EQUITY AND LIABILITIES		
(1) Shareholders' Funds :		
(a) Share Capital		?
(b) Reserves and Surplus	(1)	(20,000)
(c) Money Received against Share Warrants		?
(2) Share Application Money Pending Allotment :		

(3) Non-current Liabilities :		
(a) Long-term Borrowings	(2)	2,00,000
(b) Deferred Tax Liabilities (Net)		?
(c) Other Long-term Liabilities		?
(d) Long-term Provisions		?
(4) Current Liabilities :		?
(a) Short-term Borrowings		?
(b) Trade Payables		?
(c) Other Current Liabilities		?
(d) Short-term Provisions		?
TOTAL		
II. ASSETS		
(1) Non-current Assets :		
(a) Fixed Assets		
(i) Tangible Assets		?
(ii) Intangible Assets		?
(iii) Capital Work-in-progress		?
(iv) Intangible Assets under Development		?
(b) Non-current Investments		?
(c) Deferred Tax Assets (Net)		?
(d) Long-term Loans and Advances		?
(e) Other Non-current Assets		?
(2) Current Assets :		
(a) Current Investments		?
(b) Inventories		?
(c) Trade Receivables		?
(d) Cash and Cash Equivalents		1,80,000
(e) Short-term Loans and Advances		?
(f) Other Current Assets		?
TOTAL		

Notes to Accounts :

(1) Reserve and Surplus

Particulars	₹
Discount on Issue of Debentures	(20,000)
(3) Cash and Cash Equivalents	
Cash at Bank	1,80,000

(2) Long-term Borrowings (Secured)

Particulars	₹
2,000, 12% Debentures of ₹ 100 each	2,00,000

Debentures Issued at a Premium

Debentures can be issued at a premium if the rate of interest payable on debenture is very attractive. Premium on Debenture is shown in the Company Balance Sheet under "***Reserve and Surplus***". It is generally used for writing off debenture issue expenses, discount on issue of shares etc. However, Debenture Account is shown in the company Balance Sheet at nominal value. Debenture premium can be collected with application or allotment as per the terms and conditions of the issue.

Accounting Entries [Assuming premium is payable on application]

(a) When application money is received

Bank Account	Dr.	[Including premium]
To Debentures Application Account		

(b) When excess application money is refunded

Debentures Application Account	Dr.	
To Bank Account		[Including premium]

(c) When the debentures are allotted

(i) Debentures Application Account	Dr.
To Debentures Account	
To Securities Premium Account	
(ii) Debentures Allotment Account	Dr.
To Debentures Account	

(d) When allotment money is received

Bank Account	Dr.
To Debentures Allotment Account	

(e) When call money is due

Debentures Call Account	Dr.
To Debentures Account	

(f) When call money is received

Bank Account	Dr.
To Debentures Call Account	

Accounting Entries [Assuming premium is payable on *allotment*]

(a) When application money is received

Bank Account	Dr.
To Debentures Application Account	

(b) When excess application money is refunded

Debentures Application Account	Dr.
To Bank Account	

(c) When debentures are allotted

(i) Debentures Application Account	Dr.
To Debentures Account	
(ii) Debentures Allotment Account	Dr.
To Debentures Account	
To Securities Premium Account	

(d) When allotment money is received

Bank Account	Dr.
To Debentures Allotment Account	

(e) When call money is due

Debentures Call Account	Dr.
To Debentures Account	

(f) When call money is received

Bank Account Dr.

To Debentures Call Account

Illustration 10

XYZ Company Limited issued 10,000, 10% Debentures of ₹ 100 each at a premium of ₹ 5, payable as follows :

On application ₹ 40 (including premium)

On allotment ₹ 65

All the debentures were subscribed for and the money was duly received. Pass necessary journal entries to record the above issue of debentures.

Solution

In the books of XYZ Company Limited

Journal

Date	Particulars		L.F.	Dr. ₹	Cr. ₹
	Bank A/c	Dr.		4,00,000	
	To Debentures Application A/c				4,00,000
	(Being the application money received on 10,000, 10% debentures of ₹ 100 each @ ₹ 40 per debenture including premium)				
	10% Debenturse Application A/c	Dr.		4,00,000	
	To Debentures A/c				3,50,000
	To Securities Premium A/c				50,000
	(Being the allotment of 10,000 debentures as per Board's Resolution No. . . . dated . . .)				
	10% Debentures Allotment A/c	Dr.		6,50,000	
	To Debentures A/c				6,50,000
	(Being the allotment money due on 10,000 debentures @ ₹ 65 each as per Board's Resolution No. . . . dated . . .)				
	Bank A/c	Dr.		6,50,000	
	To Debentures Allotment A/c				6,50,000
	(Being the allotment money received in full)				

Issue of Debentures for Consideration other than Cash

A company may purchase assets from vendors on the condition that the price of assets to be paid not in cash but by issuing debentures of the company. This type of debenture issue is called '***Issue of Debenture for Consideration Other than Cash***'.

The debentures may be issued at par or at a discount or at a premium.

Accounting Entries

(i) When assets are purchased

Assets Account Dr.

To Vendor Account

(ii) When debentures are issued at par

Vendor Account Dr.

To Debentures Account

OR

(iii) When debentures are issued at a discount

Vendor Account   Dr.
Discount on Issue of Debentures Account   Dr.
    To Debentures Account

OR

(iv) When debentures are issued at a premium

Vendor Account   Dr.
    To Debentures Account
    To Securities Premium Account

Illustration 11

A B Ltd purchased building costing ₹ 4,05,000. It was agreed that the purchase consideration be paid by issue of 12% debentures of ₹ 100 each. Assuming that debentures have been issued (i) at par and (ii) at a discount of 10%, pass necessary journal entries.

Solution

In the books of AB Ltd
Journal

Date	Particulars		L.F.	Dr. ₹	Cr. ₹
	Building A/c	Dr.		4,05,000	
	To Vendor A/c				4,05,000
	(Being the purchase of building from the vendor)				
	Debentures Issued at Par				
	Vendor A/c	Dr.		4,05,000	
	To 12% Debentures A/c				4,05,000
	(Being the issue of debentures of ₹ 4,05,000 to the vendor to satisfy his dues)				
	Debentures Issued at a Discount				
	Vendor A/c	Dr.		4,05,000	
	Discount on Issue of Debentures A/c	Dr.		45,000	
	To 12% Debentures A/c				4,50,000
	(Being the issue of debentures of ₹ 4,50,000 at 10% discount to the vendor to satisfy his dues)				

Illustration 12

Y Ltd. purchased machinery for ₹ 90,000. Half of the amount was paid in cash and the remaining half by issue of 12% debentures of ₹ 100 each at a discount of ₹ 10 each.

Pass necessary journal entries.

Solution

In the books of Y Ltd
Journal

Date	Particulars		L.F.	Dr. ₹	Cr. ₹
	Machinery A/c	Dr.		90,000	
	To Vendor A/c				90,000
	(Being the purchase of machinery from the vendor)				
	Vendor A/c	Dr.		90,000	
	Discount on Issue of Debentures A/c	Dr.		5,000	
	To Bank A/c				45,000
	To 12% Debentures A/c				50,000
	(Being the payment of cash and issue of debentures of ₹ 50,000 to vendor to satisfy his dues)				

Illustration 13

Naresh & Co. Limited purchased a building worth ₹ 1,41,000. It issued 15% debentures of ₹ 100 each at a discount of 6% in satisfaction of the purchase price.

Pass necessary journal entries.

Solution **In the books of Naresh & Co. Limited**

Journal

Date	Particulars		L.F.	Dr. ₹	Cr. ₹
	Building A/c	Dr.		1,41,000	
	To Vendor A/c				1,41,000
	(Being the purchase of building from the vendor)				
	Vendor A/c	Dr.		1,41,000	
	Discount on Issue of Debentures A/c	Dr.		9,000	
	To 15% Debentures A/c				1,50,000
	(Being the issue of debentures of ₹ 1,50,000 to the vendor to satisfy his dues)				

Illustration 14

M Limited issues debentures of ₹ 80 each at a premium of ₹ 10 per debenture for satisfying the purchase price of machinery at ₹ 45,000. Pass journal entries for the same.

Solution **In the books of M Limited**

Journal

Date	Particulars		L.F.	Dr. ₹	Cr. ₹
	Machinery A/c	Dr.		45,000	
	To Vendor A/c				45,000
	(Being the purchase of machinery from the vendor)				
	Vendor A/c	Dr.		45,000	
	To Debentures A/c				40,000
	To Premium on Issue of Debentures A/c				5,000
	(Being the issue of 5,000 debentures of ₹ 80 each at a premium of ₹ 10 per debenture to the vendor to satisfy his dues)				

Illustration 15

X Ltd. purchased machinery for ₹ 5,50,000 from Y Ltd. ₹ 55,000 were paid by X Ltd. in cash and the balance was paid by issue of 9% debentures of ₹ 1,000 each at 10% premium redeemable after three years. Pass necessary journal entries in the books of the company.

[CBSE (Delhi) — 2008]

Solution **In the books of X Limited**

Journal

Date	Particulars		L.F.	Dr. ₹	Cr. ₹
	Machinery A/c	Dr.		5,50,000	
	To Bank A/c				55,000
	To Y Ltd A/c				4,95,000
	(Being the purchase of machinery from Y Ltd)				
	Y Ltd A/c	Dr.		4,95,000	
	To 9% Debentures A/c				4,50,000
	To Securities Premium A/c				45,000
	(Being the payment of dues to Y Ltd by issuing 450, 9% debentures of ₹ 1,000 each at a premium of 10%)				

Working Note ; Number of debentures issued = 4,95,000 ÷ 1100 = 450 debentures.

Sometimes a company may purchase different assets and take over different liabilities for some agreed value — called Purchase Consideration. The purchase consideration is satisfied by issuing debentures. In this case the entries will be :

(i) When assets are and liabilities are taken over

Sundry Assets Account	Dr.	[Individually]
To Sundry Liabilities Account		[Individually]
To Vendor Account		[Purchase consideration]

(ii) When debentures are issued at par

Vendor Account	Dr.
To Debentures Account	

OR

(iii) When debentures are issued at a discount

Vendor Account	Dr.
Discount on Issue of Debentures Account	Dr.
To Debentures Account	

OR

(iv) When debentures are issued at a premium

Vendor Account	Dr.
To Debentures Account	
To Securities Premium Account	

Students should note the following :

(i) Purchase Consideration < (Assets – Liabilities taken over) = Capital Reserve

(ii) Purchase Consideration > (Assets – Liabilities taken over) = Goodwill

Illustration 16

Mohit Ltd. took over assets of ₹ 8,40,000 and liabilities of ₹ 80,000 of Ram Ltd. at an agreed value of ₹ 7,20,000. Mohit Ltd. paid to Ram Ltd. by issue of 9% debentures of ₹ 100 each at a premium of 20%. Pass necessary journal entries to record the above transactions in the books of Mohit Ltd.

[CBSE (Delhi) — 2009]

Solution

In the books of Mohit Ltd

Journal

Date	Particulars		L.F.	Dr. ₹	Cr. ₹
	Sundry Assets A/c	Dr.		8,40,000	
	To Sundry Liabilities A/c				80,000
	To Capital Reserve A/c (Note 1)				40,000
	To Ram Ltd A/c				7,20,000
	(Being the assets and liabilities taken over from Ram Ltd)				
	Ram Ltd A/c	Dr.		7,20,000	
	To 9% Debentures A/c				6,00,000
	To Securities Premium A/c				1,20,000
	(Being the issue of 6,000*, 9% debentures of ₹ 100 each at a premium of 20%)				

*Number of debentures issued = 7,20,000 ÷ 120 = 6,000 debentures.

Working Note :

		₹
(1) Purchase consideration		7,20,000
Net assets taken over :		
Sundry assets	8,40,000	
Sundry liabilities	(80,000)	7,60,000
Capital Reserve (being negative)		(40,000)

Illustration 17

X Ltd. purchased the following assets of Y Ltd :

Land — ₹ 30,00,000; Building — ₹ 10,00,000; Furniture — ₹ 5,00,000.

X Ltd. has also taken over the following liabilities :

Long-term Bank Loan — ₹ 10,00,000; Sundry Creditors — ₹ 5,00,000.

The purchase consideration was agreed at ₹ 33,00,000.

X Ltd. paid the purchase consideration by issuing 10% Debentures of ₹ 100 each at a premium of 10%. You are required to pass necessary journal entries in the books of X Ltd.

Solution

In the books of X Ltd.
Journal

Date	Particulars		L.F.	Dr. ₹	Cr. ₹
	Land A/c	Dr.		30,00,000	
	Building A/c	Dr.		10,00,000	
	Furniture A/c	Dr.		5,00,000	
	Goodwill A/c (Note 1)	Dr.		3,00,000	
	To Long-term Bank Loan A/c				10,00,000
	To Sundry Creditors A/c				5,00,000
	To Y Ltd A/c				33,00,000
	(Being the acquisition of different assets and liabilities)				
	Y Ltd A/c	Dr.		33,00,000	
	To 10% Debentures A/c				30',00,000
	To Securities Premium A/c				3,00,000
	(Being the issue of 30,000, 10% debentures of ₹ 100 each at a premium of 10%)				

Working Notes :

		₹
(1) Purchase consideration		33,00,000
Net assets taken over :		
Sundry assets	45,00,000	
Sundry liabilities	(15,00,000)	30,00,000
Goodwill		3,00,000

Issue of Debenture with Terms of Redemption

In many cases, debentures are issued with the terms of redemption. ***For example***, it may happen that debentures are issued at par but as per the terms of issue, the debentures are to be redeemed at a premium. Similarly, debentures may be issued at par but to be redeemed at par or at a discount.

Basic accounting entries for issue of debentures at par / at a discount / at a premium will be made in the usual manner. However, ***extra entries*** are to be passed (***at the time of issue***) if the debentures are to be redeemed at a premium as per the 'terms of issue'.

In the following diagram, the different situations have been shown. ***Students should carefully study the diagram before going through the entries under different situations.***

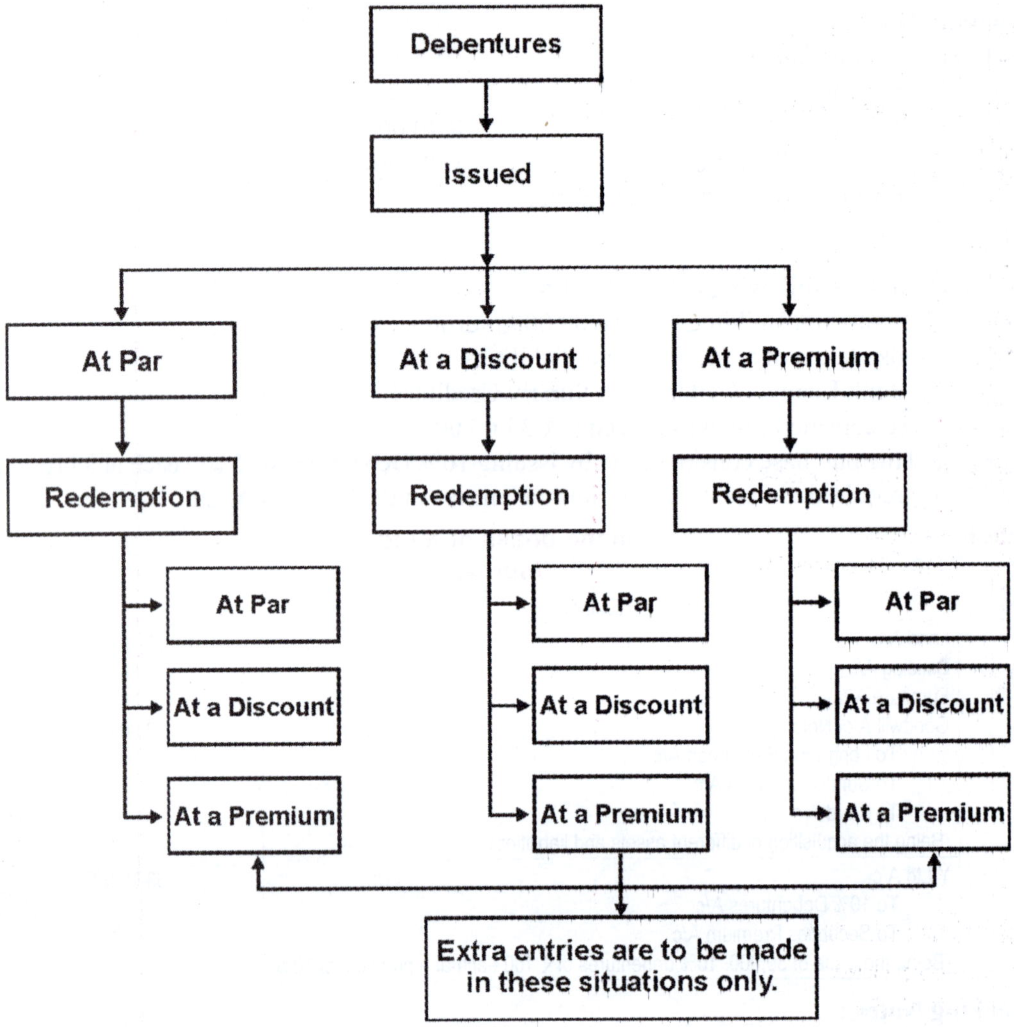

Where debentures are to be redeemed at par or at a discount (rare in practice), no extra entry is to be made ***at the time of issue and allotment of debentures.***

Case 1: When debentures are issued at par and redeemable at par or at a discount

(a) Bank Account Dr.
  To Debentures Application Account

(b) Debentures Application Account Dr.
  To Debentures Account

Case 2: When debentures are issued at a discount and redeemable at par or at a discount

(a) Bank Account Dr.
  To Debentures Application Account

(b) Debentures Application Account Dr.
 Discount on Issue of Debentures Account Dr.
  To Debentures Account

Case 3: When debentures are issued at a premium but redeemable at par or at a discount

(a) Bank Account Dr.
  To Debentures Application Account
(b) Debentures Application Account Dr.
  To Debentures Account
  To Securities Premium Account

Where debentures are to be redeemed at a premium, an extra entry is to be made at the time of issue and allotment of debentures. This extra entry is to be passed for providing premium payable on redemption. Remember that this extra entry is to be made at the time of issue.

Accounting Entries

Case 1 : When debentures are issued at par but redeemable at a premium

(a) Bank Account Dr.
  To Debentures Application Account
(b) Debentures Application Account Dr.
  To Debentures Account
(c) Loss on Issue of Debentures Account Dr. [For providing premium
  To Premium on Redemption of Debentures Account on redemption]

Students should note that, instead of passing the separate entries as above, a combined entry can be passed.

Bank Account Dr.
Loss on Issue of Debentures Account Dr.
  To Debentures Account
  To Premium on Redemption of Debentures Account

Case 2 : When debentures are issued at a discount but redeemable at a premium

(a) Bank Account Dr.
  To Debentures Application Account
(b) Debentures Application Account Dr.
  Discount on Issue of Debentures Account Dr.
  To Debentures Account
(c) Loss on Issue of Debentures Account Dr. [For providing premium
  To Premium on Redemption of Debentures Account on redemption]

Alternatively :

Bank Account Dr.
Discount on Issue of Debentures Account Dr.
Loss on Issue of Debentures Account Dr.
  To Debentures Account
  To Premium on Redemption of Debentures Account

Case 3 : When debentures are issued at a premium and redeemable at a premium

(a) Bank Account Dr.
  To Debentures Application Account
(b) Debentures Application Account Dr.
  To Debentures Account
  To Securities Premium Account

(c) Loss on Issue of Debentures Account Dr.
To Premium on Redemption of Debentures Account

Alternatively :

Bank Account Dr.
Loss on Issue of Debentures Account Dr.
To Debentures Account
To Premium on Redemption of Debentures Account
To Securities Premium Account

In this case, debentures premium can be adjusted with the loss on issue of debentures at the year-end.

Presentation in the Balance Sheet

'***Loss on Issue of Debentures***' and '***Discount on Issue of Debentures***' are written-off systematically over the life of the debentures. Many companies, in practice, are adjusting these items against Securities Premium depending upon the amount. In some cases, companies are showing the amount under '***Reserve and Surplus***' as negative figures to the extent not yet written-off. In the pre-revised Schedule VI these items used to be shown under 'Miscellaneous Expenditure' on the assets side. These items are not assets because the definition and measurement criteria does not support it.

Conceptual Framework for Preparation and presentation of Finance Statements has defined assets as follows :

'***An asset is a resource controlled by the enterprise as a result of past events from which future economic benefits are expected to flow to the enterprise.***'

The criteria for recognition of assets has been stated that :

'***An asset is recognised in the Balance Sheet when it is possible that the future economic benefits associated with it will flow to the enterprise and the asset has a cost or value that can be measured reliably.***'

It is clear from the above that these items can not be recognised as ***an asset*** in the Balance Sheet. It should be written off over the years based on the amount.

'***Premium on Redemption of Debentures***' is payable to the debentureholders at the time of redemption of these debentures. Till the date of redemption, such premium is to be shown in the Balance Sheet as a line item — '***Long-term Provisions***'.

Example

On 1st July, 2014 RPL Ltd. issued 2,000, 10% debentures of ₹ 100 each @ ₹ 95. The debentures will be redeemed after 5 years from the date of issue. The debentures money was received in full on time.

You are required to show the relevant items in the Balance Sheet of RPL Ltd. as at 1st July, 2014.

Balance Sheet of RPL Ltd. as at 1st July, 2014 [Extract],

Particulars	Note No.	Amount (₹)
(1)	(2)	(3)
I. EQUITY AND LIABILITIES		
(1) Shareholders' Funds :		
(a) Share Capital		?
(b) Reserves and Surplus	(1)	(20,000)
(c) Money Received against Share Warrants		?

	Note	₹
(2) Share Application Money Pending Allotment :		
(3) Non-current Liabilities :		
(a) Long-term Borrowings	(2)	2,00;000
(b) Deferred Tax Liabilities (Net)		?
(c) Other Long-term Liabilities		?
(d) Long-term Provisions	(3)	10,000
II. ASSETS		
(2) Current Assets :		
(d) Cash and Cash Equivalents	(4)	1,90,000

Notes to Accounts :

(1) Reserve and Surplus

Particulars	₹
Discount on Issue of Debentures	(10,000)
Loss on Issue of Debentures	(10,000)
	(20,000)

(3) Long-term Provisions

Particulars	₹
Premium on Redemption of Debentures	10,000

(2) Long-term Borrowings (Secured)

Particulars	₹
2,000, 10% Debentures of ₹ 100 each	2,00,000

(4) Cash and Cash Equivalent

Particulars	₹
Cash at bank (2,000 x ₹ 95)	1,90,000

Illustration 18

Give journal entries for issuing of 2,000, 10% Debentures of ₹ 100 each in the following cases : (i) Issued at ₹ 100 and redeemable at ₹ 110 and (ii) Issued at ₹ 95 and redeemable at ₹ 105.

Solution

(i) Journal

Date	Particulars		L.F.	Dr. ₹	Cr. ₹
	Bank A/c	Dr.		2,00,000	
	To Debentures Application A/c				2,00,000
	(Being application money received for 2,000, 10% debentures of ₹ 100 each)				
	Debentures Application A/c	Dr.		2,00,000	
	To 10% Debentures A/c				2,00,000
	(Being the issue of 2,000, 10% debentures at par and redeemable at a premium of 10% as per Board's Resolution No. . . . dated . . .)				
	Loss on Issue of Debentures A/c	Dr.		20,000	
	To Premium on Redemption of Debentures A/c				20,000
	(Being the provision for premium payable on redemption)				
	Alternative entry may be :				
	Bank A/c	Dr.		2,00,000	
	Loss on Issue of Debentures A/c	Dr.		20,000	
	To 10% Debentures A/c				2,00,000
	To Premium on Redemption of Debentures A/c				20,000
	(Being the issue of 2,000, 10% debentures @ 100 each at par and redeemable at 10% premium)				

(ii) Journal

Date	Particulars		L.F.	Dr. ₹	Cr. ₹
	Bank A/c	Dr.		1,90,000	
	To Debentures Application A/c				1,90,000
	(Being application money received for 2,000, 10% debentures of ₹ 95 each)				
	Debentures Application A/c	Dr.		1,90,000	
	Discount on Issue of Debentures A/c	Dr.		10,000	
	To 10% Debentures A/c				2,00,000
	(Being the issue of 2,000, 10% debentures of ₹ 100 each at 5% discount and redeemable at 5% premium as per Board's Resolution No. . . . dated . . .)				

	Particulars	L.F.	₹	₹
	Loss on Issue of Debentures A/c Dr. To Premium on Redemption of Debentures A/c (Being the provision for premium payable on redemption)		10,000	10,000

Illustration 19

Pass the necessar journal entries for issue of 1,000, 7% Debentures of ₹ 100 each in the following cases :

(a) Issued at 5% premium redeemable at a premium of 10%.

(b) Issued at a discount of 5% redeemable at par.

[CBSE (Delhi) — 2013]

Journal

Date	Particulars	L.F.	Dr. ₹	Cr. ₹
(a)	Bank A/c (1,000 x ₹ 105) Dr. To 7% Debentures Application A/c (Being application money received for 1,000 of ₹ 100 each. It is to be issued at 5% premium)		1,05,000	1,05,000
	7% Debentures Application A/c Dr. To 7% Debentures A/c To Securities Premium A/c (Being the issue of 1,000 of ₹ 100 each at premium of 5% as per Board's Resolution No. . . . dated . . .)		1,05,000	1,00,000 5,000
	Loss on Issue of Debentures A/c Dr. To Premium on Redemption of Debentures A/c (Being the provision for premium payable on redemption)		10,000	10,000

Alternatively

Date	Particulars	L.F.	Dr. ₹	Cr. ₹
	Bank A/c Dr. Loss on Issue of Debentures A/c Dr. To 7% Debentures A/c To Securities Premium A/c To Premium on Redemption of Debentures A/c (Being issue of 1,000, 7% debentures of ₹ 100 each at a premium of 5% as per Board's Resolution No. ... dated .... The debentures are to be redeemed at a premium of 10%)		1,05,000 10,000	1,00,000 5,000 10,000
	Tutorial Note : Loss on issue of debentures can be adjusted against Debenture premium received at the time of issue of debentures			
	Securities Premium A/c Dr. To Loss on Issue of Debentures A/c (Being the adjustment of loss on issue against securities premium))		5,000	5,000
(b)	Bank A/c Dr. To 7% Debentures Application A/c (Being application money received on 1,000 debentures @ ₹ 95 each)		95,000	95,000
	7% Debentures Application A/c Dr. Discount on Issue of Debentures A/c Dr. To 7% Debentures A/c (Being the issue of 1,000 debentures of ₹ 100 each at a 5% discount as per Board's Resolution No. ... dated ...)		95,000 5,000	1,00,000

Illustration 20

Give journal entries in each of the following cases if the face value of a Debenture is ₹ 100 :

(i) A debenture issued at ₹ 110 repayable at ₹ 100.

(ii) A debenture issued at ₹ 100 repayable at ₹ 105.

(iii) A debenture issued at ₹ 105 repayable at ₹ 105.

[CBSE (Delh) — 2009]

Solution

(i) Journal

Date	Particulars	L.F.	Dr. ₹	Cr. ₹
	Bank A/c Dr.		110	
	To Debentures Application A/c			110
	(Being application money received)			
	Debentures Application A/c Dr.		110	
	To ...% Debentures A/c			100
	To Securities Premium A/c			10
	(Being the issue of debentures at a premium of 10% as per Board's Resolution No. . . . dated . . .)			

(ii) Journal

Date	Particulars	L.F.	Dr. ₹	Cr. ₹
	Bank A/c Dr.		100	
	To Debentures Application A/c			100
	(Being application money received)			
	Debentures Application A/c Dr.		100	
	To ...% Debentures A/c			100
	(Being the issue of debentures at a par as per Board's Resolution No. ... dt . . .)			
	Loss on Issue of Debentures A/c Dr.		5	
	To Premium on Redemption of Debentures A/c			5
	(Being the amount provided for premium on redemption of debentures)			
	Alternative entry may be :			
	Bank A/c Dr.		100	
	Loss on Issue of Debentures A/c Dr.		5	
	To Debentures A/c			100
	To Premium on Redemption of Debentures A/c			5
	(Being the issue of debentures at par and redeemable at a premium of 5% as per Board's Resolution No. ... dated ...)			

(iii) Journal

Date	Particulars	L.F.	Dr. ₹	Cr. ₹
	Bank A/c Dr.		105	
	To Debentures Application A/c			105
	(Being application money received)			
	Debentures Application A/c Dr.		105	
	To ...% Debentures A/c			100
	To Securities Premium A/c			5
	(Being the issue of debentures at a premium of 5% as per Board's Resolution No. ... dt . . .)			
	Loss on Issue of Debentures A/c Dr.		5	
	To Premium on Redemption of Debentures A/c			5
	(Being the premium on redemption provided)			

	Securities Premium A/c Dr. To Loss on Issue of Debentures A/c (Being the loss on issue of debentures adjusted against securities premium)		5	5

Illustration 21

Journalise the transactions given below :

(i) A debenture issued at ₹ 95 repayable at ₹ 100.

(ii) A debenture issued at ₹ 95 repayable at ₹ 105.

(iii) A debenture issued at ₹ 100 repayable at ₹ 105.

(iv) A debenture issued at ₹ 105 repayable at ₹ 100.

[Note : Face value of each debenture is ₹ 100] *[CBSE — Adapted]*

Solution

(i) Journal

Date	Particulars	L.F.	Dr. ₹	Cr. ₹
	Bank A/c Dr. To Debentures Application A/c (Being application money received)		95	95
	Debentures Application A/c Dr. Discount on Issue of Debentures A/c Dr. To Debentures A/c (Being the issue of debentures at a discount of 5% as per Board's Resolution No. ... dated ...)		95 5	100
	Alternative entry may be : Bank A/c Dr. Discount on Issue of Debentures A/c Dr. To Debentures A/c (Being the issue of debentures at a discount of 5% as per Board's Resolution No. . . . dated . . .)		95 5	100

(ii) Journal

Date	Particulars	L.F.	Dr. ₹	Cr. ₹
	Bank A/c Dr. To Debentures Application A/c (Being application money received)		95	95
	Debentures Application A/c Dr. Discount on Issue of Debentures A/c Dr. To Debentures A/c (Being the issue of debentures at a discount of 5% as per Board's Resolution No. . . . dated . . .)		95 5	100
	Loss on Issue of Debentures A/c Dr. To Premium on Redemption of Debentures A/c (Being the amount provided for premium on redemption of debentures)		5	5
	Alternative entry may be : Bank A/c Dr. Loss on Issue of Debentures A/c Dr. To Debentures A/c To Premium on Redemption of Debentures A/c (Being the issue of debentures at a discount of 5% and redeemable at a premium of 5% as per Board's Resolution No. . . . dated . . .)		95 10	100 5

(iii) Journal

Date	Particulars		L.F.	Dr. ₹	Cr. ₹
	Bank A/c To Debentures Application A/c (Being application money received)	Dr.		100	100
	Debentures Application A/c To Debentures A/c (Being the issue of debentures at par as per Board's Resolution No... dated ...)	Dr.		100	100
	Loss on Issue of Debentures A/c To Premium on Redemption of Debentures A/c (Being the amount provided for premium on redemption of debentures)	Dr.		5	5
	Alternative entry may be : Bank A/c Loss on Issue of Debentures A/c To Debentures A/c To Premium on Redemption of Debentures A/c (Being the issue of debentures at par and redeemable at a premium of 5% as per Board's Resolution No. . . . dated . . .)	 Dr. Dr.		 100 5	 100 5

(iv) Journal

Date	Particulars		L.F.	Dr. ₹	Cr. ₹
	Bank A/c To Debentures Application A/c (Being application money received)	Dr.		105	105
	Debentures Application A/c To Debentures A/c To Securities Premium A/c (Being the issue of debentures at a premium of 5% as per Board's Resolution No. ... dated . . .)	Dr.		105	 100 5
	Alternative entry may be : Bank A/c To Debentures A/c To Securities Premium A/c (Being the issue of debentures at a premium of 5% as per Board's Resolution No. ... dated ...)	 Dr.		 105	 100 5

Illustration 22

What journal entries will be made in the following cases :

(i) A company issued ₹ 40,000 12% Debentures at a discount of 10% redeemable at par;

(ii) A company issued ₹ 40,000, 12% Debentures at a premium of 5% redeemable at par;

(iii) A company issued ₹ 40,000, 12% Debentures at par redeemable at 10% premium; and

(iv) A company issued ₹ 40,000, 12% Debentures at discount of 5% and redeemable at 5% premium.

[Note : The face value of a 12% Debenture is ₹ 100.] *[CBSE — Adapted]*

Solution

(i) Journal

Date	Particulars		L.F.	Dr. ₹	Cr. ₹
	Bank A/c To Debentures Application A/c (Being application money received for 400 debentures @ ₹ 90 each)	Dr.		36,000	36,000
	Debentures Application A/c Discount on Issue of Debentures A/c To 12% Debentures A/c (Being the issue of 400, 12% debentures of ₹ 100 each @ ₹ 90 each as per Board's Resolution No. ... dated ...)	Dr. Dr.		36,000 4,000	 40,000

Date	Particulars	L.F.	Dr. ₹	Cr. ₹
	Alternative entry may be :			
	Bank A/c Dr.		36,000	
	Discount on Issue of Debentures A/c Dr.		4,000	
	To 12% Debentures A/c			40,000
	(Being the issue of 400, 12% debentures of ₹ 100 each @ ₹ 90 each as per Board's Resolution No. . . . dated . . .)			

(ii) Journal

Date	Particulars	L.F.	Dr. ₹	Cr. ₹
	Bank A/c Dr.		42,000	
	To Debentures Application A/c			42,000
	(Being application money received for 400 debentures @ ₹ 105 each)			
	Debentures Application A/c Dr.		42,000	
	To 12% Debentures A/c			40,000
	To Securities Premium A/c			2,000
	(Being the issue of 400, 12% debentures of ₹ 100 each at a premium of 5% as per Board's Resolution No. ... dated ...)			
	Alternative entry may be :			
	Bank A/c Dr.		42,000	
	To 12% Debentures A/c			40,000
	To Securities Premium A/c			2,000
	(Being the issue of 400, 12% debentures of ₹ 100 each at a premium of 5% as per Board's Resolution No. . . . dated . . .)			

(iii) Journal

Date	Particulars	L.F.	Dr. ₹	Cr. ₹
	Bank A/c Dr.		40,000	
	To Debentures Application A/c			40,000
	(Being application money received for 400 debentures @ ₹ 100 each)			
	Debentures Application A/c Dr.		40,000	
	To 12% Debentures A/c			40,000
	(Being the issue of 400, 12% debentures of ₹ 100 each as per Board's Resolution No. ... dated ...)			
	Loss on Issue of Debentures A/c Dr.		4,000	
	To Premium on Redemption of Debentures A/c			4,000
	(Being the amount provided for premium on redemption of debentures)			
	Alternative entry may be :			
	Bank A/c Dr.		40,000	
	Loss on Issue of Debentures A/c Dr.		4,000	
	To 12% Debentures A/c			40,000
	To Premium on Redemption of Debentures A/c			4,000
	(Being the issue of 400, 12% debentures of ₹ 100 each at par and redeemable at a premium of 10% as per Board's Resolution No. . . . dated . . .)			

(iv) Journal

Date	Particulars	L.F.	Dr. ₹	Cr. ₹
	Bank A/c Dr.		38,000	
	To Debentures Application A/c			38,000
	(Being application money received for 400 debentures @ ₹ 95 each)			
	Debentures Application A/c Dr.		38,000	
	Discount on Issue of Debentures A/c Dr.		2,000	
	To 12% Debentures A/c			40,000
	(Being the issue of 400, 12% debentures of ₹ 100 each at a discount of 5% as per Board's Resolution No. ... dated ...)			

	Particulars		L.F.	Dr. ₹	Cr. ₹
	Loss on Issue of Debentures A/c	Dr.		2,000	
	To Premium on Redemption of Debentures A/c				2,000
	(Being the amount provided for premium payable on redemption of debentures)				
	Alternative entry may be :				
	Bank A/c	Dr.		38,000	
	Loss on Issue of Debentures A/c	Dr.		4,000	
	To 12% Debentures A/c				40,000
	To Premium on Redemption of Debentures A/c				2,000
	(Being the issue of 400, 12% debentures of ₹ 100 each at a discount of 5% and redeemable at a premium of 5% as per Board's Resolution No. . . . dated . . .)				

Illustration 23

Pass journal entries to record the following issues of debentures :

(i) 400, 8% debentures of ₹ 100 each issued at a discount of 5% repayable at par.

(ii) 400, 8% debentures issued at par repayable at a premium of 5%. Each debenture is of ₹ 100.

(iii) 600, 7% debentures of ₹ 100 each issued at a discount of 5% and repayable at a premium of 4%.

(iv) 700, 7% debentures of ₹ 100 each issued at a premium of 5% and repayable at par.

Solution **In the books of . . .**

(i) **Journal**

Date	Particulars		L.F.	Dr. ₹	Cr. ₹
?	Bank A/c	Dr.		38,000	
	To Debentures Application A/c				38,000
	(Being application money received for 400, 8% debentures @ ₹ 95 each)				
?	Debentures Application A/c	Dr.		38,000	
	Discount on Issue of Debentures A/c	Dr.		2,000	
	To 8% Debentures A/c				40,000
	(Being the issue of 400 debentures of ₹ 100 each at a discount of 5% and redeemable at par as per Board's Resolution No ... dated ...)				

(ii) **Journal**

Date	Particulars		L.F.	Dr. ₹	Cr. ₹
	Bank A/c	Dr.		40,000	
	To Debentures Application A/c				40,000
	(Being application money received for 400, 8% debentures @ ₹ 100 each)				
	Debentures Application A/c	Dr.		40,000	
	To 8% Debentures A/c				40,000
	(Being the issue of 400, 8% debentures at par and redeemable at a premium of 5% as per Board's Resolution No. ... dated ...)				
	Loss on Issue of Debentures A/c	Dr.		2,000	
	To Premium on Redemption of Debentures A/c				2,000
	(Being the provision for premium payable on redemption)				

(iii) **Journal**

Date	Particulars		L.F.	Dr. ₹	Cr. ₹
	Bank A/c	Dr.		57,000	
	To Debentures Application A/c				57,000
	(Being application money received for 600 @ ₹ 95 each)				
	Debentures Application A/c	Dr.		57,000	
	Discount on Issue of Debentures A/c	Dr.		3,000	
	To 7% Debentures A/c				60,000
	(Being the issue of 600, 7% debentures of ₹ 100 each at 5% discount and redeemable at 4% premium as per Board's Resolution No. ... dated ...)				

Date	Particulars	L.F.	Dr. ₹	Cr. ₹
	Loss on Issue of Debentures A/c Dr. To Premium on Redemption of Debentures A/c (Being the provision for premium payable on redemption)		2,400	2,400

(iv) **Journal** **Dr.** **Cr.**

Date	Particulars	L.F.	₹	₹
	Bank A/c Dr. To Debentures Application A/c (Being application money received for 700 @ ₹ 105 each)		73,500	73,500
	Debentures Application A/c Dr. To 7% Debentures A/c To Debentures Premium A/c (Being the issue of 700, 7% debentures of ₹ 100 each at 5% premium as per Board's Resolution No. ... dated ...)		73,500	70,000 3,500

Ilustration 24

Show by means of journal entries, how would you record the following issues. Also show how would they appear in their respective Balance Sheets.

(i) B Ltd. issues 30,000, 12% debentures of ₹ 100 each at a discount of 5% to be repaid at par at the end of 5 years.

(ii) C Ltd. issues 12% debentures of the total face value of ₹ 40,00,000 at a premium of 5% to be redeemed at par.

(iii) D Ltd. issues ₹ 50,00,000, 12% debentures at par but redeemable at the end of 10 years at 105%.

(iv) E Ltd. issues ₹ 60,00,000, 12% debentures at a discount of 5% repayable at a premium of 10% at the end of 5 years.

Solution

In the books of B Ltd.

(i) **Journal** **Dr.** **Cr.**

Date	Particulars	L.F.	₹	₹
?	Bank A/c Dr. To Debentures Application A/c (Being application money received for 30,000 debentures @ ₹ 95 each)		28,50,000	28,50,000
?	Debentures Application A/c Dr. Discount on Issue of Debentures A/c Dr. To 12% Debentures A/c (Being the issue of 30,000, 12% debentures of ₹ 100 each at a discount of 5% as per Board's Resolution No ... dated ...)		28,50,000 1,50,000	30,00,000

Balance Sheet of B Ltd. as at ... [Extract],

Particulars (1)	Note No. (2)	Amount (₹) (3)
I. EQUITY AND LIABILITIES		
(1) Shareholders' Funds :		
(a) Share Capital		?
(b) Reserves and Surplus	(1)	(1,50,000)
(c) Money Received against Share Warrants		?
(2) Share Application Money Pending Allotment :		
(3) Non-current Liabilities :		
(a) Long-term Borrowings	(2)	30,00,000
(b) Deferred Tax Liabilities (Net)		?
(c) Other Long-term Liabilities		?
(d) Long-term Provisions		?
TOTAL		

II. ASSETS		
(2) Current Assets :		
(d) Cash and Cash Equivalents	(3)	28,50,000
TOTAL		

Notes to Accounts :

(1) Reserve and Surplus

Particulars	₹
Discount on Issue of Debentures	(1,50,000)

(2) Long-term Borrowings (Secured)

Particulars	₹
30,000, 12% Debentures of ₹ 100 each	30,00,000

(3) Cash and Cash Equivalents

Particulars	₹
Cash at Bank	28,50,000

In the books of C Ltd.

(ii) Journal

Date	Particulars	L.F.	Dr. ₹	Cr. ₹
?	Bank A/c Dr. To Debentures Application A/c (Being application money received for 40,000 debentures @ ₹ 105 each)		42,00,000	 42,00,000
?	Debentures Application A/c Dr. To 12% Debentures A/c To Securities Premium A/c (Being the issue of 40,000, 12% debentures of ₹ 100 each at a premium of 5% as per Board's Resolution No ... dated ...)		42,00,000	 40,00,000 2,00,000

Balance Sheet of C Ltd. as at ... [Extract],

Particulars (1)	Note No. (2)	Amount (₹) (3)
I. EQUITY AND LIABILITIES		
(1) Shareholders' Funds :		
(a) Share Capital		?
(b) Reserves and Surplus	(1)	2,00,000
(c) Money Received against Share Warrants		?
(2) Share Application Money Pending Allotment :		
(3) Non-current Liabilities :		
(a) Long-term Borrowings	(2)	40,00,000
(b) Deferred Tax Liabilities (Net)		?
(c) Other Long-term Liabilities		?
(d) Long-term Provisions		?
TOTAL		
II. ASSETS		
(2) Current Assets :		
(d) Cash and Cash Equivalents	(3)	42,00,000
TOTAL		

Notes to Accounts :

(1) Reserve and Surplus

Particulars	₹
Securities Premium	2,00,000

(2) Long-term Borrowings (Secured)

Particulars	₹
40,000, 12% Debentures of ₹ 100 each	40,00,000

(3) Cash and Cash Equivalents

Particulars	₹
Cash at Bank	42,00,000

In the books of D Ltd.

(iii) **Journal**

Date	Particulars	L.F.	Dr. ₹	Cr. ₹
?	Bank A/c Dr.		50,00,000	
	To Debentures Application A/c			50,00,000
	(Being application money received for 50,000 debentures @ ₹ 100 each)			
?	Debentures Application A/c Dr.		50,00,000	
	To 12% Debentures A/c			50,00,000
	(Being the issue of 50,000, 12% debentures of ₹ 100 each and redeemable at 105% as per Board's Resolution No ... dated ...)			
	Loss on Issue of Debentures A/c Dr.		2,50,000	
	To Premium on Redemption of Debentures A/c			2,50,000
	(Being the provision for premium payable on redemption)			

Balance Sheet of D Ltd. as at ... [Extract],

Particulars	Note No.	Amount (₹)
(1)	(2)	(3)
I. EQUITY AND LIABILITIES		
(1) Shareholders' Funds :		
(a) Share Capital		?
(b) Reserves and Surplus	(1)	(2,50,000)
(c) Money Received against Share Warrants		?
(2) Share Application Money Pending Allotment :		
(3) Non-current Liabilities :		
(a) Long-term Borrowings	(2)	50,00,000
(b) Deferred Tax Liabilities (Net)		?
(c) Other Long-term Liabilities		?
(d) Long-term Provisions	(3)	2,50,000
TOTAL		
II. ASSETS		
(2) Current Assets :		
(d) Cash and Cash Equivalents	(4)	50,00,000
TOTAL		

Notes to Accounts :

(1) Reserve and Surplus

Particulars	₹
Loss on Issue of Debentures	(2,50,000)

(2) Long-term Borrowings (Secured)

Particulars	₹
50,000, 12% Debentures of ₹ 100 each	50,00,000

(4) Cash and Cash Equivalents

Particulars	₹
Cash at Bank	50,00,000

(3) Long-term Provisions

Particulars	₹
Premium on Redemption of Debentures	2,50,000

In the books of E Ltd.

(iv) **Journal**

Date	Particulars	L.F.	Dr. ₹	Cr. ₹
?	Bank A/c Dr.		57,00,000	
	To Debentures Application A/c			57,00,000
	(Being application money received for 60,000, debentures @ ₹ 95 each)			

?	Debentures Application A/c Dr.		57,00,000	
	Discount on Issue of Debentures A/c Dr.		3,00,000	
	To 12% Debentures A/c			60,00,000
	(Being the issue of 60,000, 12% debentures of ₹ 100 each at a discount of 5% and redeemable at a premium of 10% as per Board's Resolution No ... dated ...)			
	Loss on Issue of Debentures A/c Dr.		6,00,000	
	To Premium on Redemption of Debentures A/c			6,00,000
	(Being the provision for premium payable on redemption)			

Balance Sheet of E Ltd. as at ... [Extract],

Particulars	Note No.	Amount (₹)
(1)	(2)	(3)
I. EQUITY AND LIABILITIES		
(1) Shareholders' Funds :		
(a) Share Capital		?
(b) Reserves and Surplus	(1)	(9,00,000)
(c) Money Received against Share Warrants		?
(2) Share Application Money Pending Allotment :		
(3) Non-current Liabilities :		
(a) Long-term Borrowings	(2)	60,00,000
(b) Deferred Tax Liabilities (Net)		?
(c) Other Long-term Liabilities		?
(d) Long-term Provisions	(3)	6,00,000
TOTAL		
II. ASSETS		
(2) Current Assets :		
(d) Cash and Cash Equivalents	(4)	57,00,000
TOTAL		

Notes to Accounts :

(1) Reserve and Surplus

Particulars	₹
Discount on Issue of Debentures	(3,00,000)
Loss on Issue of Debentures	(6,00,000)
	(9,00,000)

(2) Long-term Borrowings (Secured)

Particulars	₹
60,000, 12% Debentures of ₹ 100 each	60,00,000

(4) Long-term Provisions

Particulars	₹
Premium on redemption of debentures	6,00,000

(4) Cash and Cash Equivalents

Particulars	₹
Cash at Bank	57,00,000

Illustration 25

Show by means of journal entries how will you record the following issues. Also show how they will appear in the respective Balance Sheets:

(a) P Ltd issues 5,000, 10% Debentures of ₹ 100 each at a discount of 5% redeemable at the end of 5 years at par.

(b) Q Ltd issues 5,000, 11% Debentures of ₹ 100 each at par, redeemable at the end of 5 years at a premium of 5%.

(c) R Ltd issues 5,000, 12% Debentures of ₹ 100 each at a discount of 5%, redeemable at the end of 5 years at a premium of 5%.

(d) S Ltd issues 5,000, 13% Debentures of ₹ 100 each at a premium of 5%, redeemable at the end of 5 years at a premium of 5%.

Solution

(a)

In the books of P Limited

Journal

Date	Particulars	L.F.	Dr. ₹	Cr. ₹
?	Bank A/c Dr. To Debentures Application A/c (Being application money received for 5,000, 10% debentures @ ₹ 95 each)		4,75,000	4,75,000
?	Debentures Application A/c Dr. Discount on Issue of Debentures A/c Dr. To 10% Debentures A/c (Being the issue of 5,000 debentures of ₹ 100 each at a discount of 5% and redeemable at par as per Board's Resolution No ... dated ...)		4,75,000 25,000	5,00,000

Balance Sheet of P Ltd. as at ... [Extract],

Particulars (1)	Note No. (2)	Amount (₹) (3)
I. EQUITY AND LIABILITIES		
(1) Shareholders' Funds :		
(a) Share Capital		?
(b) Reserves and Surplus	(1)	(25,000)
(c) Money Received against Share Warrants		?
(2) Share Application Money Pending Allotment :		
(3) Non-current Liabilities :		
(a) Long-term Borrowings	(2)	5,00,000
(b) Deferred Tax Liabilities (Net)		?
(c) Other Long-term Liabilities		?
(d) Long-term Provisions		?
TOTAL		
II. ASSETS		
(2) Current Assets :		
(d) Cash and Cash Equivalents	(3)	4,75,000
TOTAL		

Notes to Accounts :

(1) Reserve and Surplus

Particulars	₹
Discount on Issue of Debentures	(25,000)

(3) Cash and Cash Equivalents

Particulars	₹
Cash at Bank	4,75,000

(2) Long-term Borrowings (Secured)

Particulars	₹
5,000, 10% Debentures of ₹ 100 each	5,00,000

(b)

In the books of Q Limited

Journal

Date	Particulars	L.F.	Dr. ₹	Cr. ₹
?	Bank A/c Dr. To Debentures Application A/c (Being application money received for 5,000, 11% debentures @ ₹ 100 each)		5,00,000	5,00,000
?	Debentures Application A/c Dr. To 11% Debentures A/c (Being the issue of 5,000, 11% debentures at par and redeemable at a premium of 5% as per Board's Resolution No ... dated ...)		5,00,000	5,00,000

?	Loss on Issue of Debentures A/c Dr. To Premium on Redemption of Debentures A/c (Being the provision for premium payable on redemption)		25,000	25,000
	Alternative entry may be : Bank A/c Dr. Loss on Issue of Debentures A/c Dr. To 11% Debentures A/c To Premium on Redemption of Debentures A/c (Being the issue of 5,000, 11% debentures of ₹ 100 each at par and redeemable at a premium of 5%)		5,00,000 25,000	5,00,000 25,000

Balance Sheet of Q Ltd. as at ... [Extract],

Particulars	Note No.	Amount (₹)
(1)	(2)	(3)
I. EQUITY AND LIABILITIES		
(1) Shareholders' Funds :		
(a) Share Capital		?
(b) Reserves and Surplus	(1)	(25,000)
(c) Money Received against Share Warrants		?
(2) Share Application Money Pending Allotment :		
(3) Non-current Liabilities :		
(a) Long-term Borrowings	(2)	5,00,000
(b) Deferred Tax Liabilities (Net)		?
(c) Other Long-term Liabilities		?
(d) Long-term Provisions	(3)	25,000
TOTAL		
II. ASSETS		
(2) Current Assets :		
(d) Cash and Cash Equivalents	(4)	5,00,000
TOTAL		

Notes to Accounts :

(1) Reserve and Surplus

Particulars	₹
Loss on Issue of Debentures	(25,000)

(4) Cash and Cash Equivalents

Particulars	₹
Cash at Bank	5,00,000

(2) Long-term Borrowings (Secured)

Particulars	₹
5,000, 11% Debentures of ₹ 100 each	5,00,000

(3) Long-term Provisions

Particulars	₹
Premium on Redemption of Debentures	25,000

(c)

In the books of R Limited

Journal

Date	Particulars	L.F.	Dr. ₹	Cr. ₹
?	Bank A/c Dr. To Debentures Application A/c (Being application money received for 5,000, 12% debentures @ ₹ 95 each)		4,75,000	4,75,000
?	Debentures Application A/c Dr. Discount on Issue of Debentures A/c Dr. To 12% Debentures A/c (Being the issue of 5,000, 12% debentures of ₹ 100 each at 5% discount and redeemable at 5% premium as per Board's Resolution No ... dated ...)		4,75,000 25,000	5,00,000

?	Loss on Issue of Debentures A/c	Dr.	25,000	
	To Premium on Redemption of Debentures A/c			25,000
	(Being the provision for premium payable on redemption)			
	Alternative (1) entry may be :			
	Bank A/c	Dr.	4,75,000	
	Discount on Issue of Debentures A/c	Dr.	25,000	
	Loss on Issue of Debentures A/c	Dr.	25,000	
	To 12% Debentures A/c			5,00,000
	To Premium on Redemption of Debentures A/c			25,000
	(Being the issue of 5,000, 12% debentures of ₹ 100 each at a discount of 5% and redeemable at a premium of 5% as per Board's Resolution No ... dated ,..)			
	Alternative (2) entry may be :			
	Bank A/c	Dr.	4,75,000	
	Loss on Issue of Debentures A/c	Dr.	50,000	
	To 12% Debentures A/c			5,00,000
	To Premium on Redemption of Debentures A/c			25,000
	(Being the issue of 5,000, 12% debentures of ₹ 100 each at a discount of 5% and redeemable at a premium of 5% as per Board's Resolution No ... dated ...)			

Balance Sheet of R Ltd. as at ... [Extract],

Particulars	Note No.	Amount (₹)
(1)	(2)	(3)
I. EQUITY AND LIABILITIES		
(1) Shareholders' Funds :		
(a) Share Capital		?
(b) Reserves and Surplus	(1)	(50,000)
(c) Money Received against Share Warrants		?
(2) Share Application Money Pending Allotment :		
(3) Non-current Liabilities :		
(a) Long-term Borrowings	(2)	5,00,000
(b) Deferred Tax Liabilities (Net)		?
(c) Other Long-term Liabilities		?
(d) Long-term Provisions	(3)	25,000
TOTAL		
II. ASSETS		
(2) Current Assets :		
(d) Cash and Cash Equivalents	(4)	4,75,000
TOTAL		

Notes to Accounts :

(1) Reserve and Surplus

Particulars	₹
Loss on Issue of Debentures	(50,000)

(2) Long-term Borrowings (Secured)

Particulars	₹
5,000, 12% Debentures of ₹ 100 each	5,00,000

(3) Long-term Provisions

Particulars	₹
Premium on Redemption of Debentures	25,000

(4) Cash and Cash Equivalents

Particulars	₹
Cash at Bank	4,75,000

(d) **In the books of S Limited**

Journal

Date	Particulars		L.F.	Dr. ₹	Cr. ₹
?	Bank A/c	Dr.		5,25,000	
	To Debentures Application A/c				5,25,000
	(Being application money received for 5,000, 13% debentures @ ₹ 105 each)				
?	Debentures Application A/c	Dr.		5,25,000	
	To 13% Debentures A/c				5,00,000
	To Securities Premium A/c				25,000
	(Being the issue of 5,000, 13% debentures of ₹ 100 each at a premium of 5% and redeemable at 5% premium as per Board's Resolution No ... dated ...)				
?	Loss on Issue of Debentures A/c	Dr.		25,000	
	To Premium on Redemption of Debentures A/c				25,000
	(Being the provision for premium payable on redemption)				
	Alternative entry may be :				
	Bank A/c	Dr.		5,25,000	
	Loss on Issue of Debentures A/c	Dr.		25,000	
	To 13% Debentures A/c				5,00,000
	To Securities Premium A/c				25,000
	To Premium on Redemption of Debentures A/c				25,000
	(Being the issue of 5,000, 13% debentures of ₹ 100 each at a premium of 5% and redeemable at a premium of 5% as per Board's Resolution No ... dated ...)				
	Securities Premium A/c	Dr.		25,000	
	To Loss on Issue of Debentures A/c				25,000
	(Being the adjustment for premium received on issue with the premium payable on redemption)				

Balance Sheet of S Ltd. as at ... [Extract],

Particulars (1)	Note No. (2)	Amount (₹) (3)
I. EQUITY AND LIABILITIES		
(1) Shareholders' Funds :		
(a) Share Capital		?
(b) Reserves and Surplus		Nil
(c) Money Received against Share Warrants		?
(2) Share Application Money Pending Allotment :		
(3) Non-current Liabilities :		
(a) Long-term Borrowings	(1)	5,00,000
(b) Deferred Tax Liabilities (Net)		?
(c) Other Long-term Liabilities		?
(d) Long-term Provisions	(2)	25,000
TOTAL		
II. ASSETS		
(2) Current Assets :		
(d) Cash and Cash Equivalents	(3)	5,25,000
TOTAL		

Notes to Accounts :

(1) Long-term Borrowings (Secured)

Particulars	₹
5,000, 13% Debentures of ₹ 100 each	5,00,000

(2) Long-term Provisions

Particulars	₹
Premium on Redemption of Preference Shares	25,000

(3) Cash and Cash Equivalents

Particulars	₹
Cash at Bank	5,25,000

Issue of Debentures as Collateral Security for Loan

Secondary or supporting security is called ***collateral security***. The lender realises this security when the original security is insufficient to cover the loan.

Sometimes companies issue their own debentures as collateral security for a loan or a fluctuating overdraft. When the loan is repaid on the due date, these debentures are at once released with the main security. In case, the company cannot repay its loan and the interest thereon on the due date, the lender becomes the debentureholder who can exercise all the rights of a debentureholder. The holder of such debentures is entitled to interest only on the ***amount of loan, but not on the debentures***.

Accounting Method

There are two methods of showing these types of debentures in the accounts of a company.

Method 1

Under this method, no entry is made in the books of account of the company at the time of making issue of such debentures. In the Balance Sheet, the fact of the debentures being issued and outstanding is not shown. The fact is disclosed in the '***Notes to Accounts***'.

Illustrative Example

X Ltd obtains a loan from ICICI of ₹ 20,00,000, giving as collateral security of ₹ 25,00,000, 14%, First Mortgage Debentures. In the Balance Sheet of X Ltd, it is shown as follows :

Balance Sheet of Y Ltd. as at ... [Extract],

Particulars (1)	Note No. (2)	Amount (₹) (3)
I. EQUITY AND LIABILITIES		
(1) Shareholders' Funds :		
(a) Share Capital		?
(b) Reserves and Surplus		?
(c) Money Received against Share Warrants		?
(2) Share Application Money Pending Allotment :		
(3) Non-current Liabilities :		
(a) Long-term Borrowings	(1)	20,00,000
(b) Deferred Tax Liabilities (Net)		?
(c) Other Long-term Liabilities		?
(d) Long-term Provisions		?
(4) Current Liabilities :		?
(a) Short-term Borrowings		?
(b) Trade Payables		?
(c) Other Current Liabilities		?
(d) Short-term Provisions		?
TOTAL		

Notes to Accounts :

(1) Long-term Borrowings (Secured)

Particulars	₹
ICICI Loan (colaterally secured by issue of ₹ 25,00,000, 14% First Mortgage Debentures)	20,00,000

Method 2

Under this method, the following entry is made to record the issue of such debentures:

Debentures Suspense Account Dr.

To Debentures Account

(Being the issue of...debentures collaterally... as per Board's Resolution No ....dated)

It is to be noted that Debenture Suspense Account or Debenture Account will not be shown in the Balance Sheet. However, in the Notes to Account it is disclosed showing the details.

Illustrative Example

Taking the same information of the above example, the entry on issue will be as follows:

Solution

In the books of X Limited

Journal

Date	Particulars	Dr. ₹	Cr. ₹
	Debentures Suspense A/c Dr.	25,00,000	
	To 14% First Mortgage Debentures A/c		25,00,000
	(Being the issue of ₹ 25,00,000 debentures collaterally as per Board's Resolution No. ... dtd. ...)		

Balance Sheet of Y Ltd. as at ... [Extract],

Particulars	Note No.	Amount (₹)
(1)	(2)	(3)
I. EQUITY AND LIABILITIES		
(1) Shareholders' Funds :		
(a) Share Capital		?
(b) Reserves and Surplus		?
(c) Money Received against Share Warrants		?
(2) Share Application Money Pending Allotment :		
(3) Non-current Liabilities :		
(a) Long-term Borrowings	(1)	20,00,000
(b) Deferred Tax Liabilities (Net)		?
(c) Other Long-term Liabilities		?
(d) Long-term Provisions		?
(4) Current Liabilities :		?
(a) Short-term Borrowings		?
(b) Trade Payables		?
(c) Other Current Liabilities		?
(d) Short-term Provisions		?
TOTAL		

Notes to Accounts :

(2) Long-term Borrowings (Secured)

Particulars	₹
ICICI Loan	20,00,000

14% First Mortgage Debentures have been issued as collateral securities which has been shown as follows:

25,000, 14% First Mortgage Debentures :	25,00,000
Less: Debenture Suspense Account	25,00,000
	Nil

Students should note that the Method 1 is much more logical from the accounting point of view. Therefore, we advise to follow Method 1.

Illustration 26

A Ltd issued 5,000, 13% Debentures of ₹ 100 each at par and raised a loan of ₹ 80,000 from bank, collaterally secured by ₹ 1,00,000, 13% Debentures.

How will you show the debentures in the Balance Sheet of the company assuming that the company has recorded the issue of debentures as collateral security in the books ?

Balance Sheet of A Ltd. as at ... [Extract],

Particulars	Note No.	Amount (₹)
(1)	(2)	(3)
I. EQUITY AND LIABILITIES		
(1) Shareholders' Funds :		
(a) Share Capital		?
(b) Reserves and Surplus		?
(c) Money Received against Share Warrants		?
(2) Share Application Money Pending Allotment :		
(3) Non-current Liabilities :		
(a) Long-term Borrowings	(1)	5,80,000
(b) Deferred Tax Liabilities (Net)		?
(c) Other Long-term Liabilities		?
(d) Long-term Provisions		?
II. ASSETS		
(2) Current Assets :		
(d) Cash and Cash Equivalents		?

Notes to Accounts :

(1) Long-term Borrowings (Secured)

Particulars	₹
5,000, 13% Debentures of ₹ 100 each	5,00,000
Bank Loan	80,000
	5,80,000
13% Debentures have been issued as collateral security which has been shown as follows :	
1,000, 13% Debentures	1,00,000
Less: Debenture Suspense Account	1,00,000
	Nil

Special Problem

Illustration 27

BA Limited made an issue, which was fully subscribed, of 1,000 debentures of ₹ 100 each at ₹ 97. The debentures were allotted on 31st July, 2013, subscriptions being payable 10% on application, 40% on allotment, 25% on first call on 30th September and the balance on final call on 30th November, 2013.

Under the terms of the issue, payment could be made in full on 31st July, 2013. Interest on any amounts prepaid being allowable at the rate of 10% p.a.; such interest was not deductible from the subscriber's payment, but was payable by the company on 30th November, 2013.

The alloter of 300 debentures took advantage of the pre-paid terms, while others paid on the due date.

Journalise the entries to be made in the company's books (ignore debenture interest).

Solution

In the books of BA Ltd

Journal

Date	Particulars		L.F.	Dr. ₹	Cr. ₹
2013	Bank A/c	Dr.		10,000	
	To Debentures Application A/c				10,000
	(Being application money received on 1,000 debentures @ ₹ 10 each)				
July 31	Debentures Application A/c	Dr.		10,000	
	To Debentures A/c				10,000
	(Being the allotment of 1,000 debentures as per Board's Resolution No. . . . dated. . .)				
	Debentures Allotment A/c	Dr.		40,000	
	Discount on Issue of Debentures A/c	Dr.		3,000	
	To Debentures A/c				43,000
	(Being allotment money due on 1,000 debentures @ ₹ 40 each and discount @ ₹ 3 per debenture has been adjusted as per Board's Resolution No. ... dated...)				
	Bank A/c	Dr.		40,000	
	To Debentures Allotment A/c				40,000
	(Being the allotment money received on 1,000 debentures @ ₹ 40 each)				
	Bank A/c	Dr.		14,100	
	To Calls-in-Advance A/c				14,100
	(Being the amount received in advance in respect of 300 debentures @ ₹ 47 each)				
	Debentures First Call A/c	Dr.		25,000	
	To Debentures A/c				25,000
	(Being first call money due on 1,000 debentures @ ₹ 25 each as per Board's Resolution No. . . . dated . . .)				
Sept. 30	Bank A/c	Dr.		17,500	
	Calls-in-Advance A/c	Dr.		7,500	
	To Debentures First Call A/c				25,000
	(Being the amount received on first call after adjustment of calls-in-advance @ ₹ 25 each on 300 debentures)				
	Debentures Final Call A/c	Dr.		22,000	
	To Debentures A/c				22,000
	(Being final call money due on 1,000 debentures @ ₹ 22 each as per Board's Resolution No. . . . dated . . .)				

Date	Particulars		L.F.	Dr. (₹)	Cr. (₹)
Nov. 30	Bank A/c	Dr.		15,400	
	Calls-in-Advance A/c	Dr.		6,600	
	To Debentures Final Call A/c				22,000
	(Being the amount received on final call after adjustment of calls-in-advance @ ₹ 22 each on 300 debentures)				
	Interest on Calls-in-Advance A/c (Note 1)	Dr.		345	
	To Bank A/c				345
	(Being interest on calls-in-advance paid @ 10% on ₹ 7,500 for 2 months and on ₹ 6,600 for 4 months)				

Working Notes :

(1) Calculation of Interest on Calls-in-Advance

	₹
(a) ₹ 7,500 × 10% × 2/12	125
(b) ₹ 6,600 × 10% × 4/12	220
	345

Interest on Debentures

Debenture interest is payable at regular intervals at a fixed percentage on the face value of the debenture. It is payable to the debentureholders whether profits are earned or not. The rate of interest paid by the company on its debentures depends on the following factors :

(i) the market rate of interest;
(ii) the security that the company agrees;
(iii) the terms of conversion into shares; and
(iv) the credit rating of the company.

Debenture interest is paid to debentureholders after deducting tax at source (where applicable).

Debenture interest is treated as operating expenses and it is charged to Statement of Profit & Loss.

Accounting Entries

(a) Debenture Interest Account Dr. [Gross interest]
    To Debentureholders Account [Net amount]
    To Tax Deducted at Source Account [Tax deducted]
(Being the interest payable to debentureholders after tax deducted at source).

(b) Debentureholders Account Dr.
    To Bank Account
(Being interest paid to debentureholders)

Alternatively

Debenture Interest Account Dr.
    To Bank Account
    To Tax Deducted at Source Account

(c) Statement of Profit and Loss Dr.
    To Debenture Interest Account

Tax deducted at source must be deposited to the Government (through prescribed banks) within a specified period. When it is deposited to the bank, the following entry is made :

Tax Deducted at Source Account Dr.
    To Bank Account

Illustration 28

ABC Ltd issues 1,000, 14% debentures of ₹ 100 each at par on January 1, 2012.

Under the terms of issue:

(a) Debenture interest is annually payable on 31st December every year; and

(b) 1/5th of the debentures are annually redeemable by drawings, the 1st redemption occurring on 31st December, 2014.

Pass necessary journal entries for the year 2012 and 2013.

Solution

In the books of ABC Ltd

Journal

Date	Particulars	L.F.	Dr. ₹	Cr. ₹
2012 Jan. 1	Bank A/c Dr. To Debenture Application A/c (Being application money received for 1,000 debentures of ₹ 100 each)		1,00,000	1,00,000
	Debenture Application A/c Dr. To 14% Debentures A/c (Being the allotment of 1,000 debentures of ₹ 100 each, as per Board's Resolution No. ... dated ...)		1,00,000	1,00,000
Dec. 31	Debenture Interest A/c Dr. To Bank A/c (Being the debenture interest paid for the year)		14,000	14,000
	Statement of Profit and Loss Dr. To Debenture Interest A/c (Being the debenture interest transferred to Statement of Profit and Loss)		14,000	14,000
2013 Dec. 31	Debenture Interest A/c Dr. To Bank A/c (Being the debenture interest paid for the year)		14,000	14,000
	Statement of Profit and Loss Dr. To Debenture Interest A/c (Being the debenture interest transferred to Statement of Profit and Loss)		14,000	14,000

Illustration 29

Lotus Ltd issued 2,000, 15% debentures of ₹ 100 each at a premium of 10% on 1st January, 2013. Under the terms of issue:

(a) Entire money is payable on application.

(b) Debenture interest is payable half-yearly on 30th June and 31st December.

(c) Tax to be deducted at source @ 10%.

(d) Debentures are to be redeemed after 5 years from the date of issue.

Pass necessary journal entries for the year 2013.

Solution

In the books of Lotus Ltd

Journal

Date	Particulars	L.F.	Dr. ₹	Cr. ₹
2013 Jan. 1	Bank A/c Dr. To Debenture Application A/c (Being application money received for 2,000 debentures of ₹ 100 each, issued at a premium of 10%)		2,20,000	2,20,000

	Debenture Application A/c Dr. To 15% Debentures A/c To Securities Premium A/c (Being the allotment of 2,000 debentures of ₹ 100 each, at a premium of 10% p.a. as per Board's Resolution No. ... dated ...)	2,20,000	 2,00,000 20,000
June 30	Debenture Interest A/c Dr. To Debentureholders A/c To Tax Deducted at Source A/c (Being the interest payable to debentureholders after tax deducted at source for 6 months)	15,000	 13,500 1,500
	Debentureholders A/c Dr. To Bank A/c (Being the interest paid to debentureholders)	13,500	 13,500
	Tax Deducted at Source A/c Dr. To Bank A/c (Being the amount deposited from tax deducted at source)	1,500	 1,500
Dec. 31	Debenture Interest A/c Dr. To Debentureholders A/c To Tax Deducted at Source A/c (Being the interest payable to debentureholders after tax deducted at source for 6 months)	15,000	 13,500 1,500
	Debentureholders A/c Dr. To Bank A/c (Being the interest paid to debentureholders)	13,500	 13,500
	Tax Deducted at Source A/c Dr. To Bank A/c (Being the amount deposited for tax deducted at source)	1,500	 1,500
	Statement of Profit and Loss (Note 1) Dr. To Debenture Interest A/c (Being the amount transferred to Statement of Profit and Loss)	30,000	 30,000

Tutorial Note : Debenture interest of the whole year is transferred to Statement of Profit and Loss at the end of the accounting year.

Chapter Summary

- **Debenture** is a certificate issued by the company, stamped with official seal, which contains the details of an interest-bearing loan made by the company on long term basis.
- **Some of the features of a Debenture are the following** :
  1. It is a document which evidences a loan made by a company.
  2. It is a fixed interest-bearing security where interest falls due on specific dates.
  3. Interest is payable at a predetermined fixed rate, regardless of the level of profit.
  4. It is repaid at a specified future date or it is converted into shares or other debentures
- As per 'Schedule III' the debentures are shown under main heading — '***Non-Current Liabilities***' and sub-heading '***Long-term Borrowings***'.
- The Companies Act does not impose any restriction on the price at which debentures can be issued. Unlike shares, there is no maximum limit for discount on issue of debenture. This is why it is very common for debentures to be issued at a discount.

Chapter Summary (contd.)

- Discount on issue of debentures is written off over a period of time by debiting Statement of Profit and Loss and crediting Discount on Issue of Debenture Account. Amount to be written-off every year will depend upon the terms of redemption.
- A company may purchase assets from vendors on the condition that the price of assets to be paid not in cash but by issuing debentures of the company. This type of debenture issue is called '***Issue of Debenture for Consideration Other than Cash***'.
- '***Premium on Redemption of Debentures***' is payable to the debentureholders at the time of redemption of these debentures. Till the date of redemption, such premium is to be shown in the Balance Sheet as a line item — '***Long-term Provisions***'.

THEORETICAL QUESTIONS

A. Multiple Choice

[1 Mark each]

Select the best choice to answer the following questions :

1. When debentures are issued at a discount, it is shown in the Balance Sheet at
   A net of discount under 'Shareholders' Funds'
   B net of discount under 'Long-term Borrowings'
   C face value under 'Shareholders' Funds'
   D face value under 'Long-term Borrowings'
2. Premium on Issue of Debentures are shown in the Balance Sheet under
   A long-term provisions
   B short-term provisions
   C reserve and surplus
   D none of the above
3. Interest on debenture is
   A a charge against profit
   B an appropriation of profit
   C an item of Balance Sheet
   D none of the above
4. Debentureholders are
   A the co-owner of the company
   B the creditors of the company
   C the debtors of the company
   D none of the above
5. Debenture interest is paid
   A at a variable rate which is dependent upon the profits of a particular year
   B at a fixed rate, irrespective of profits earned by the company
   C as per the decision of the Board of Directors
   D none of the above

6. Debenture is a certificate
   - **A** issued by the managing director
   - **B** issued by the company
   - **C** issued by the bankers of the company
   - **D** issued to the trade creditors
7. Debentures can be issued
   - **A** at par only
   - **B** at a discount only
   - **C** at a premium only
   - **D** at par, at a discount or at a premium
8. Discount on issue of debentures is
   - **A** an expense of the year in which debtentures are issued
   - **B** an intangible asset shown in the asset section of the Balance Sheet
   - **C** written off over the life of the debentures
   - **D** none of the above
9. Debentures
   - **A** can not be forfeited for non-payment of call money
   - **B** can be forfeited for non-payment of call money
   - **C** can be forfeited for any reason
   - **D** none of the above
10. Premium on issue of debentures can
    - **A** be used for payment of dividend
    - **B** be used for writing off discount on issue of debentures
    - **C** be transferred to capital reserve
    - **D** none of the above
11. Premium for Redemption of Debentures is shown in the Balance Sheet as
    - **A** other long-term liabilities
    - **B** short-term provisions
    - **C** long-term provisions
    - **D** other current liabilities
12. 'Loss on Issue of Debentures' is shown in the Balance Sheet
    - **A** in the assets section
    - **B** in the equity and liabilities section as a deduction from share capital
    - **C** in the equity and liabilities section under reserve and surplus (negative figure)
    - **D** none of the above

B. Short Answer Questions : Type I

[3 Marks each]

1. What do you mean by debenture ?
2. State two features of debenture.
3. What do you mean by issue of debentures at par ?
4. What do you mean by issue of debentures at a discount ?
5. What do you mean by issue of debentures at a premium ?
6. How is 'discount on issue of debentures' shown in the Balance Sheet ?

7. Under which heading debenture is shown in the Balance Sheet ?
8. Why debenture is called 'loan capital' ?

C. Short Answer Questions : Type II

[4 Marks each]

1. What do you mean by debenture ? What are the features of a debenture ? What are the factors to be considered for the issue of debentures ?
2. Distinguish between debentures and shares. What are the different types of debentures ?
3. How the discount on issue of debentures are treated in accounts ?
4. Distinguish between debentureholders and shareholders.
5. Distinguish between equity shares and debentures.

PRACTICAL QUESTIONS

Issue of Debentures for Cash

1. X Ltd. issued 20,000, 14% debentures of ₹ 100 each, at par payable in full on application by 1st April, 2015. Applications were received for 24,000 debentures. Debentures were allotted on 9th April, 2015. Excess application money were refunded on the same date.
   You are required to pass necessary journal entries (including cash transactions) in the books of the company and also show ledger accounts and the Balance Sheet.
2. Y Ltd. issued 12,000, 14% debentures of ₹ 100 each at a premium of 10% payable in full on application by 5th May, 2015. The issue was fully subscribed and debentures were allotted on 10th May, 2015. Pass necessary journal entries (including cash transactions) in the books of the company and also show the Balance Sheet.
3. Z Ltd. issued 20,000, 12% debentures of ₹ 100 each at a discount of 10% payable in full on application by 31st May, 2015. Applications were received for 22,000 debentures. Debentures were allotted on 9th June, 2015. Excess monies were refunded on the same date. Pass necessary journal entries and show ledger accounts and the Balance Sheet after issue.
4. XYZ Company Limited issued 10,000, 10% debentures of ₹ 100 each at a premium of ₹ 5, payable as follows : On application ₹ 40 (including premium); On allotment ₹ 65. All debentures were subscribed for and the money was duly received. Pass necessary journal entries to record the above issue of debentures.
5. B Ltd. issued ₹ 10,00,000, 12% debentures of ₹ 100 each at a discount of 10% payable as follows: On application 10%; On allotment 40%; On final call — balance The debentures were duly taken up by the public and the money were received in full. Pass necessary journal entries and show the Cash Book.
6. R Ltd. issued 20,000, 14% debentures of ₹ 100 each at a premium of 10%, payable as follows: On application ₹ 30; On allotment ₹ 50 (including premium); On final call ₹ 30
   All the debentures were subscribed for and the money was duly received.
   Pass necessary journal entries to record the above transactions.
7. Kitply Ltd. issued 10,000, 12% debentures of ₹ 100 each, at par, on the following terms :
   ₹ 20 on application; ₹ 50 on allotment; ₹ 30 on first and final call
   Applications were received for 12,000 debentures. Application for 9,000 debentures were accepted in full. Applications for 2,000 debentures were allotted 1,000 debentures and the balance applications were rejected. All the amount was duly received. Pass necessary journal entries.

8. A limited company made an issue of 10,000, 14% debentures of ₹ 100 each at par, which was fully subscribed. The debentures were allotted on July 31, 2015, subscription being payable 10% on application, 40% on allotment, 25% on September 30, 2015, and the balance on November 30, 2015. Under the terms of the issue, payment could be made in full on July 31, 2015. Interest on any such prepayment at the rate of 12% p.a. Such interest is not deductible from the subscribers' payment, but is payable by the company on November 30, 2015. One allottee of 500 debentures took advantage of the prepayment terms, while others paid on the due dates.
   Journalise the entries to be made in the books of the company.
9. Journalise the following transactions :
   (a) X Ltd. issues ₹ 2,00,000, 12% debentures at a discount of 5%, redeemable at par.
   (b) Y Ltd issues ₹ 5,00,000 debentures at a discount of 5%, redeemable at a premium of 7%.
10. Show by means of journal entries, the following at the time of issue on 1st January, 2008 and redemption after 6 years on 31st December, 2014 :
   (i) A Ltd issues 20,000, 13% debentures of ₹ 100 each at a discount of 3% to be redeemed at par at the end of 6th year.
   (ii) B Ltd issues 10,000, 13% debentures of ₹ 100 each at a discount of 3% to be redeemed at a premium of 3% at the end of 6th year.
   (iii) C Ltd issues 15,000 14% debentures of ₹ 100 each at par to be redeemed at a premium of 4% at the end of 6th year.
   (iv) D Ltd issues 12,000, 15% debentures of ₹ 100 each at a premium of 3%, to be redeemed at par at the end of 6th year. *[CBSE — Adapted]*
11. A company issues the following debentures :
   (i) 10,000, 12% debentures of ₹ 100 each at par but redeemable at a premium of 5% after 5 years.
   (ii) 10,000, 12% debentures of ₹ 100 each at a discount of 5%, but redeemable at a premium of 5% after 5 years.
   (iii) 5,000, 12% debentures of ₹ 1,000 each at a premium of 10% but redeemable at par after 5 years.
   (iv) 1,000, 14% debentures of ₹ 100 each issued to a supplier of machinery costing ₹ 95,000. The debentures are repayable after 5 years; and
   (v) 300, 13% debentures of ₹ 10 each as a collateral security to a bank who has advanced a loan of ₹ 25,000 to the company for a period of 5 years.
   Pass the journal entries to record the issue of debentures. *[CBSE — Adapted]*
12. Show by means of journal entries how will you record the following issues. Also, show how they will appear in the respective Balance Sheets :
   (a) A Ltd issues 10,000, 16% debentures of ₹ 100 each at a discount of 5%, redeemable at the end of 6 years at par.
   (b) B Ltd issues 10,000, 14% debentures of ₹ 100 each at a discount of 5%, redeemable at the end of 5 years at a premium of 5%.
   (c) C Ltd issues 10,000, 15% debentures of ₹ 100 each at par, redeemable at the end of 5 years at a premium of 5%. *[CBSE — Adapted]*
13. You are required to show the journal entries necessary to record the issue of 10,000, 12% debentures of ₹ 100 each by X and Co. Ltd under the following cases separately :
   (i) At par and were also redeemable at par;

(ii) At a discount of 5% but were redeemable at par;
(iii) At a premium of 5%, but were redeemable at par;
(iv) At a discount of 5% but were redeemable at a premium of 5%; and
(v) At par, but were redeemable at a premium of 5%.

Show also how the Debenture Account and the accounts representing premium received on the issue of debenture, premium payable on the redemption of debentures and losses incurred on the issue of debentures be shown in the Balance Sheet of the company. (Figures should be ignored, only the Account Headings should be shown in a single Balance sheet.)

Treatment of Discount on Issue of Debentures

14. X Ltd issues 20,000, 12% debentures of ₹ 100 each at ₹ 94 on 1st January, 2015. Under the terms of issue, the debentures are redeemable at the end of 8 years from the date of the issue. Calculate the amount of discount to be written-off in each of the 8 years.

15. Y Ltd issues 30,000, 12% debentures of ₹ 100 each at ₹ 94 on 1st January, 2009. Under the terms of issue, 1/5th of the debentures are annually redeemable by drawings, the first redemption occurring on 31st December, 2009. Calculate the amount of discount to be written-off in 2009 to 2013.

16. Z Ltd issues 10,000, 12% debentures of ₹ 100 each at ₹ 98 on 1st January, 2012.
Under the terms of issue:
(a) debenture interest is annually payable on 31st December every year; and
(b) 1/5th of the debentures are annually redeemable by drawings, the 1st redemption occurring on 31st December, 2013.

Calculate the amount of discount to be written-off each year and also show the Discount on Issue of Debentures Account.

17. X Limited issued 12% debentures of ₹ 10,00,000 at 8% discount redeemable at par. Assume that the debentures are redeemed by drawings method in the following manner :

Year end	Face value (₹)
2	1,00,000
3	2,00,000
4	3,00,000
5	4,00,000

Prepare Discount on Issue of Debentures Account.

18. A company issued debentures of the face value of ₹ 1,00,000 at a discount of 6% on 1st January, 2014. These debentures are redeemable by annual drawings of ₹ 20,000 made on 31st December each year. The directors decided to write off discount based on the debentures outstanding each year. Calculate the amount of discount to be written off each year. Give journal entries also.

19. On 1st January, 2012 a limited company issued ₹ 2,00,000 debentures at 6% discount repayable by draw of lots starting from 31st December, 2013 of ₹ 40,000 every year. Show Discount on Issue of Debentures Account till all debentures are redeemed.

20. A company issued 10% debentures of the face value of ₹ 1,20,000 at a discount of 6% on 1st January, 2014. The debentures are repayable by annual drawings of ₹ 40,000 commencing from the end of the third year. How will you deal with discount on debentures ?

Show the Discount on Debentures Account in the company's ledger for the period of duration of debentures. Assume accounts are closed on 31st December.

21. A company issued ₹ 1,00,000, 10% debentures on 1st April, 2014 at a discount of 5 per cent repayable in annual drawings of ₹ 25,000 each 31st March every year. Calculate the amount of discount to be written off each year. The financial year of the company ends on 31st December each year.

Issue of Debenture for Consideration Other than Cash

22. Make journal entries for the following transactions :
Z Ltd purchased plant and machinery for ₹ 2,00,000 payable as to ₹ 65,000 in cash and the balance by an issue of 6% debentures of ₹ 1,000 each at a discount of 10%.

23. Reliance Ltd purchased building costing ₹ 5,60,000. It was agreed that the purchase consideration be paid by issue of 14% debentures of ₹ 100 each. Assuming that debentures have been issued: (i) at par; and (ii) at a discount of 10%.
Pass necessary journal entries in the books of the company.

24. Z Ltd purchased building for ₹ 2,20,000. Half the payment was made in cash and the remaining half by issue of 12% debentures at a premium of 10%. Pass the necessary journal entries.

25. X Company Limited issued 14% debentures of nominal value of ₹ 10,00,000 as follows :
(a) to sundry persons for cash at 90% — ₹ 5,00,000 nominal; (b) to a vendor for ₹ 4,50,000 for purchase of fixed assets — ₹ 5,00,000 nominal.
Pass necessary journal entries.

Miscellaneous Problems

26. Y Ltd issued ₹ 2,00,000 debentures as follows :
    (a) to sundry applicants for cash at 95% — ₹ 1,00,000 (nominal)
    (b) to a creditor for ₹ 40,000 capital expenditure in satisfaction of his claim — ₹ 50,000 (nominal)
    (c) to bankers as collateral security — ₹ 50,000 (nominal).

    The issues (a) and (b) are redeemable at the end of 10 years at par. How should the debentures be dealt with in preparing the Balance Sheet of the company ?

27. Max Ltd issued 2,500, 12% debentures of ₹ 100 each on 1st January, 2013. the interest is paid half-yearly on 30th June and 31st December every year. Tax deducted at source @ 20%. Pass necessary journal entries in the books of the company for the year 2013.

28. (a) X Ltd issued 3,000, 12% debentures of ₹ 100 each at ₹ 95 on 1st January, 2013. As per the terms of issue, debentures are to be redeemed at the end of five years. Show the amount of the discount to be written off to the Statement of Profit and Loss every year.
    (b) Y Ltd purchased assets of ₹ 3,00,000 and liabilities of ₹ 70,000 for a sum of ₹ 2,20,000. The purchase consideration is satisfied by the issue of 10% debentures of ₹ 100 each at par. Pass necessary journal entries.

29. X Limited issued for subscription 5,000 debentures of ₹ 100 each at a discount of 3%. The whole of the issue offered was underwritten by Pal & Co., commission being 2.5% on nominal value. The public subscribed ₹ 4,00,000 worth of debentures balance being allotted to Pal & Co., who on subsequent date released their holdings in the market. The company took power to issue

additional debentures worth ₹ 50,000 which were issued to its bank as collateral security against a loan of ₹ 40,000. Show the entries in the Cash Book and Ledger of the company and show how the entries would appear in the Balance Sheet.

GUIDE TO ANSWERS

Check Your Progress

1. B **2.** C **3.** C **4.** A **5.** B **6.** B **7.** C

Multiple Choice

1. D **2.** C **3.** A **4.** B **5.** B **6.** B **7.** D **8.** C **9.** A **10.** B **11.** C **12.** C

Practical Questions

8. Interest on calls-in-advance — ₹ 750.
14. Discount to be written off ₹ 15,000 every year.
15. Discount to be written off : 2009—₹ 60,000; 2010—₹ 48,000; 2011—₹ 36,000; 2012—₹ 24,000; 2013 — ₹ 12,000.
16. Discount to be written off : 2012 — ₹ 10,000; 2013 — ₹ 10,000; 2014 — ₹ 8,000; 2012 — ₹ 6,000; 2013 — ₹ 4,000; 2014 — ₹ 2,000.
17. Discount to be written off : 1st year — ₹ 20,000; 2nd year — ₹ 20,000; 3rd year — ₹ 18,000; 4th year — ₹ 14,000; 5th year — ₹ 8,000.
18. Discount to be written off : 1st year — ₹ 2,000; 2nd year — ₹ 1,600; 3rd year — ₹ 1,200; 4th year — ₹ 800; 5th year — ₹ 400.
19. Discount to be written off : 2012 — ₹ 3,000; 2013 — ₹ 3,000; 2014 — ₹ 2,400; 2015 — ₹ 1,800; 2016 — ₹ 1,200; 2017 — ₹ 600.
20. Discount to be written off : 2014 — ₹ 1,800; 2015— ₹ 1,800; 2016 — ₹ 1,800; 2017 — ₹ 1,200; 2018 — ₹ 600.
21. Discount to be written off : 2014 — ₹ 1,500; 2012 — ₹ 1,625; 2013 — ₹ 1,125; 2014 — ₹ 625; 2018 — ₹ 125.
22. Discount on issue of debentures — ₹ 15,000; Face value of debentures issued — ₹ 1,50,000.
23. Discount on issue of debentures — ₹ 60,000; Face value of debentures issued — ₹ 6,00,000.

Section B : Redemption of Debentures

Meaning of Redemption of Debentures

Redemption of debentures is a process of repayment of loan taken by issue of debentures. Most debentures are issued with the notice that they may be redeemed at the option of the company within a specified period and at a specified price. The terms of redemption are clearly mentioned in the debenture certificate. By the process of redemption, a company can adjust its capital structure.

Rules for Redemption of Debentures

Rule 18 of the Companies (Share Capital and Debenture) Rules, 2014 states that :

A company can issue secured debentures, provided the date of redemption shall not exceed ***10 years*** from the date of issue.

However, a company engaged in the setting up of infrastructure projects may issue secured debentures for a period exceeding ***ten years*** but not exceeding ***thirty years.***

It is clear from the above rules that the company will have to redeem the debentures within a certain period. Hence, it is important to note that the company must redeem the debentures in accordance with terms and conditions of their issue.

The provision of ***Section 71(10) and (11) of the Companies Act, 2013*** states that :

(1) Where a company fails to redeem the debentures on the date of their maturity or fails to pay interest on the debentures when it is due, the Tribunal may, on the application of any or all of the debentureholders, or debenture trustee and, after hearing the parties concerned, direct by order, the company to redeem the debentures forthwith on payment of principal and interest due thereon.

(2) If any default is made in complying with the order of the Tribunal under this section, every office of the company who is in default shall be punished with imprisonment for a term which may extend to three years or with a fine which shall not be less than ₹ ***two lakh*** but which may extend to ₹ ***five lakh*** or ***with both***.

It is important to note that the provisions of the Companies Act, 2013 regarding the redemption of debentures are very strict. Therefore, every company chalks out the plan in advance for the redemption of the debentures.

Sources of Redemption of Debentures

Debentures can be redeemed by utilising any of the following sources :

(a) From the proceeds of the fresh issue of share capital and debentures;

(b) Out of profit.

Methods of Redemption of Debentures

The debentures can be redeemed in one of the following ***four*** ways :

(a) In lump sum at the end of the stipulated period;

(b) By draw of lots;

(c) By purchasing in the open market;

(d) By conversion into new debentures or shares.

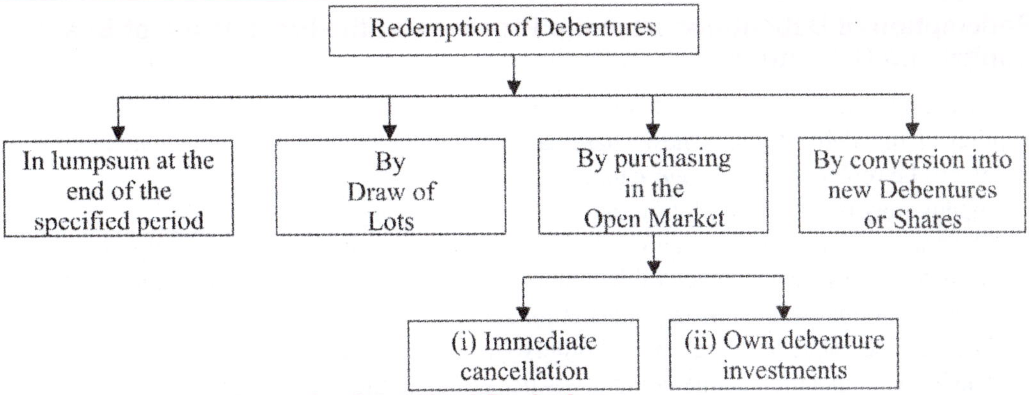

In Lump Sum at the End of a Specified Period

In this case, all debentures are redeemed at a time at the end of a specified period. The accounting entries are:

(a) When debentures are redeemed at par

Particulars		
(i) Debentures Account	Dr.	
To Debentureholders Account		
(ii) Debentureholders Account	Dr.	
To Bank Account		

(b) When debentures are redeemed at a premium

Particulars		
(i) Debentures Account	Dr.	[Nominal value]
Premium on Redemption of Debentures Account	Dr.	[Premium]
To Debentureholders Account		
(ii) Debentureholders Account	Dr.	
To Bank Account		

(c) When debentures are redeemed at a discount

Particulars		
(i) Debentures Account	Dr.	[Nominal value]
To Debentureholders Account		[Actual amount]
To Profit on Redemption of Debentures Account		[Discount]
(ii) Debentureholders Account	Dr.	
To Bank Account		

In fact, premium paid on redemption is a loss. Generally, at the time of issue of debentures, a provision is made for the premium payable on redemption by debiting "Loss on Issue of Debentures Account" and crediting "Premium on Redemption Debentures Account". Till the date of redemption, it is shown in the '***Equity and Liabilities***' section of the Balance Sheet. However, a portion of "loss on issue of debentures" is written-off every year by debiting Statement of Profit and Loss.

Where no provision was made, Premium on Redemption of Debentures Account is closed by passing the following entry :

Particulars	
Securities Premium Account	Dr.
Statement of Profit and Loss	Dr.
To Premium on Redemption of Debentures Account	

(a) Redemption of Debentures from the Proceeds of the Fresh Issue of Share Capital and Debentures

A company can issue new shares / debentures and the proceeds from such new issue can be used for redemption of old debentures. If new shares are issued for this purpose, the ***loan capital*** of the company will be replaced by the ***own capital***.

A company may prefer issue of new shares for the following reasons :

(i) The company has come to realise that the capital is needed permanently and it makes more sense to issue shares in place of debentures which carry a fixed rate of interest.

(ii) There is a boom in the primary market for shares.

(iii) The balance of profit, which would otherwise be available for dividend, is insufficient.

(iv) The liquidity position of the company is not good enough.

If new debentures are issued for this purpose, the ***old debentures*** will be replaced by the new debentures.

A company may prefer issue of new debentures when :

(i) company can issue fresh debentures by offering ***lower*** rate of interest.

(ii) the primary market for share is very dull.

(iii) the capital is not needed permanently.

(iv) the liquidity position of the company is not good enough.

Illustration 1

X Ltd issued 1,00,000, 12% Debentures of ₹ 100 each at par on 1st January, 2013 with the condition that they will be redeemed after one year.

The interest is payable on 31st December and accounting year closes on the same date.

On 1st January, 2014, the debentures were redeemed by issuing required numbers of equity shares of ₹ 10 each at par.

Pass necessary journal entries for the issue and redemption of these debentures and issue of the equity shares.

Solution

In the books of X Limited

Journal

Date	Particulars		L.F.	Dr. ₹	Cr. ₹
2013 Jan. 1	Bank A/c	Dr.		1,00,00,000	
	To Debentures Application A/c				1,00,00,000
	(Being the amount received on 1,00,000 debentures @ ₹ 100 each)				
	Debentures Application A/c	Dr.		1,00,00,000	
	To 12% Debentures A/c				1,00,00,000
	(Being the allotment of 1,00,000, 12% debentures of ₹ 100 each as per Board's Resolution No. . . . dated . . .)				
Dec. 31	Debenture Interest A/c	Dr.		12,00,000	
	To Bank A/c				12,00,000
	(Being interest paid for the year)				
	Statement of Profit and Loss	Dr.		12,00,000	
	To Debenture Interest A/c				12,00,000
	(Being the interest on debentures transferred to Statement of Profit and Loss)				
2014 Jan. 1	Bank A/c	Dr.		1,00,00,000	
	To Equity Share Application A/c				1,00,00,000
	(Being the application money received on 10,00,000 equity shares of ₹ 10 each)				

Equity Share Application A/c Dr. To Equity Share Capital A/c (Being the issue of 10,00,000 equity shares of ₹ 10 each at par as per Board's Resolution No. . . . dated . . .)		1,00,00,000	1,00,00,000
12% Debenture A/c Dr. To Debentureholders A/c (Being the amount payable to debentureholders)		1,00,00,000	1,00,00,000
Debentureholders A/c Dr. To Bank A/c (Being the amount paid to debentureholders)		1,00,00,000	1,00,00,000

(b) Redemption of Debenture out of Profit

When debentures are to be redeemed after the expiry of 18 months from the date of issue, an adequate amount is to be transerred to Debenture Redemption Reserve out of profit of the company. It should be noted that after providing for DRR, divisible profits will go down. Hence, reward to shareholders would be diminished. However, after redemption of debentures, the balance of Debenture Redemption Reserve is transferred to ***General Reserve***.

The amount set aside may be employed in the business or may be invested outside the business in gilt-edged securities and allowed to accummulate at compound interest, so as to produce the amount required to repay the debentureholders on the date of redemption.

Accounting Entries

(i) For transfer of amount to Debenture Redemption Reserve

Statement of Profit and Loss Dr.
To Debenture Redemption Reserve Account

(ii) For redemption of Debentures

(a) ***When debentures are redeemed at par***

(i) Debentures Account Dr. [Nominal value]
To Debentureholders Account

(ii) Debentureholders Account Dr.
To Bank Account

(b) ***When debentures are redeemed at a premium***

(i) Debentures Account Dr. [Nominal value]
Premium on Redemption of Debentures Account Dr. [Premium]
To Debentureholders Account [Total amount]

(ii) Debentureholders Account Dr.
To Bank Account

(c) ***When debentures are redeemed at a discount***

(i) Debentures Account Dr. [Nominal value]
To Debentureholders Account [Actual amount]
To Profit on Redemption of Debentures Account [Discount]

(ii) Debentureholders Account Dr.
To Bank Account

(iii) For transfer to General Reserve

Debenture Redemption Reserve Account Dr.
To General Reserve Account

Illustration 2

On 1 January, 2013, X Ltd issued 1,000, 12% Debentures of ₹ 100 each at par. These are repayable on 1st January, 2015 at par. X Ltd. transferred ₹ 25,000 every year to Debenture Redemption Reserve account to comply with the provision of the Act. Interest is payable on 31st December every year. The accounting year closes on 31st December.

You are required to pass necessary journal entries for the ***first year***.

Solution

In the books of X Ltd

Journal

Date	Particulars	L.F.	Dr. ₹	Cr. ₹
2013 Jan. 1	Bank A/c Dr. To Debentures Application A/c (Being the application money received on 1,000 debentures @ ₹ 100 each)		1,00,000	1,00,000
?	Debentures Application A/c Dr. To 12% Debentures A/c (Being the allotment of 1,000, 12% debentures of ₹ 100 each as per Board's Resolution No. . . . dated . . .)		1,00,000	1,00,000
Dec. 31	Debenture Interest A/c Dr. To Bank A/c (Being interest paid for the year)		12,000	12,000
	Statement of Profit and Loss Dr. To Debenture Interest A/c (Being the interest on debentures transferred to Statement of Profit and Loss)		12,000	12,000
	Statement of Profit and Loss Dr. To Debenture Redemption Reserve A/c (Being the necessary amount transferred to Debenture Redemption Reserve)		25,000	25,000

Illustration 3

N Limited issues 10,000 debentures of ₹ 100 each at a discount of 10% with the condition that they will be redeemed at a premium of 5% after the expiry of three years.

Pass the necessary journal entries only for the issue and redemption of these debentures after the expiry of three years.

[CBSE — Adapted]

Solution

In the books of N Limited

Journal

Date	Particulars	L.F.	Dr. ₹	Cr. ₹
Year 1	**On Issue of Debentures** Bank A/c Dr. To Debentures Application A/c (Being the amount received on 10,000 debentures @ ₹ 90 each)		9,00,000	9,00,000
	Debentures Application A/c Dr. Loss on Issue of Debentures A/c Dr. To Debentures A/c To Premium on Redemption of Debentures A/c (Being the allotment of 10,000 debentures of ₹ 100 each at a discount of 10%, redeemable at a premium of 5% as per Board's Resolution No. . . . dated . . .)		9,00,000 1,50,000	10,00,000 50,000
Year 3	**On Redemption of Debentures** Debentures A/c Dr. Premium on Redemption of Debentures A/c Dr. To Debentureholders A/c (Being the amount payable on redemption, transferred to Debentureholders' Account)		10,00,000 50,000	10,50,000

Date	Particulars		L.F.	Dr. ₹	Cr. ₹
	Debentureholders A/c To Bank A/c (Being the amount paid to debentureholders on redemption)	Dr.		10,50,000	10,50,000
	Debentures Redemption Reserve A/c To General Reserve A/c (Being the transfer of Debentures Redemption Reserve to General Reserve after redemption of debentures)	Dr.		10,00,000	10,00,000

Tutorial Note: Every year a portion of 'Loss on issue of debentures' will be written off by debiting Statement of Profit and Loss. It is assumed that N Ltd transferred adequate amount to Debentures Redemption Reserve as per the requirement of the Companies Act.

Illustration 4

X Ltd. has ₹ 8,00,000, 9% debentures due to be redeemed out of profits on 1st October, 2009 at a premium of 5%. The company had a Debenture Redemption Reserve of ₹ 4,14,000.

Pass necessary journal entries at the time of redemption.

[CBSE (Delhi) — 2010]

Solution

The company has already transferred ₹ 4,14,000 to Debenture Redemption Reserve which is more than 50% of the debentures outstanding. Therefore, company can redeem debentures as the requirement of SEBI guidelines — 2000 has been fulfilled.

In the books of X Ltd

Journal

Date	Particulars		L.F.	Dr. ₹	Cr. ₹
	9% Debentures A/c Premium on Redemption of Debentures A/c To Debentureholders A/c (Being the amount payable to the debentureholders)	Dr. Dr.		8,00,000 40,000	8,40,000
	Debentureholders A/c To Bank A/c (Being the amount paid to debentureholders)	Dr.		8,40,000	8,40,000
	Statement of Profit and Loss To Premium on Redemption of Debentures A/c (Being the amount of premium payable on redemption transferred to Statement of Profit and Loss)	Dr.		40,000	40,000
	Debenture Redemption Reserve A/c To General Reserve A/c (Being the balance of Debenture Redemption Reserve transferred to General Reserve)	Dr.		4,14,000	4,14,000

Illustration 5

On 1.1.2007, a public limited company issued 5,000, 10% Debentures of ₹ 100 each at par which were repayable at a premium of 10% on 31.12.2011. On the date of maturity, the company decided to redeem the above mentioned 10% Debentures as per the terms of issue, out of profits. the Profit and Loss Account shows a credit balance of ₹ 6,00,000 on this date. The offer was accepted by all the Debentureholders and all the Debentures were redeemed.

Pass the necessary journal entries in the books of the Company only for the redemption of Debentures, if the Company follows Section 117C of the Companies Act.

[CBSE (Foreign) — 2011]

Solution

In the books of ...
Journal

Date	Particulars		L.F.	Dr. ₹	Cr. ₹
2011 Dec. 31	Statement of Profit and Loss	Dr.		5,00,000	
	To Debenture Redemption Reserve A/c (Note 1)				5,00,000
	(Being creation of Debenture Redemption Reserve out of Profit and Loss balance)				
	10% Debentures A/c	Dr.		5,00,000	
	Premium on Redemption of Debentures A/c (Note 2)	Dr.		50,000	
	To Debentureholders A/c				5,50,000
	(Being the amount payable to debentureholders for redemption of 5,000, 10% Debentures of ₹ 100 each at a premium of 10%)				
	Debentureholders A/c	Dr.		5,50,000	
	To Bank A/c				5,50,000
	(Being the amount paid to debentureholdres)				
	Debenture Redemption Reserve A/c	Dr.		5,00,000	
	To General Reserve A/c				5,00,000
	(Being the balance of Debenture Redemption Reserve transferred to General Reserve)				

Working Notes :

(1) It is assumed that the company had not created DRR in previous years.

(2) It is assumed that the company provided for Premium on Redemption of Debentures at the time of issue of debentures. The loss on issue of debentures has thus been written off.

Illustration 6

MMTC Limited issued 500, 12% Debentures of ₹ 100 each at a discount of 5%, repayable after 5 years at a premium of 5%.

You are required to show the journal entries at the time of issue and redemption of debentures. Also show the Loss on Issue of Debentures Account over the period.

Solution

In the books of MMTC Limited
Journal

Date	Particulars		L.F.	Dr. ₹	Cr. ₹
Year 1	**On Issue of Debentures**				
	Bank A/c	Dr.		47,500	
	To Debentures Application A/c				47,500
	(Being the amount received on 500 debentures @ ₹ 95 each)				
	Debentures Application A/c	Dr.		47,500	
	Loss on Issue of Debentures A/c	Dr.		5,000	
	To 12% Debentures A/c				50,000
	To Premium on Redemption of Debentures A/c				2,500
	(Being the allotment of 500, 12% debentures of ₹ 100 each at a discount of 10%, redeemable at a premium of 5% as per Board's Resolution No. . . . dated . . .)				
Year 5	**On Redemption of Debentures**				
	12% Debentures A/c	Dr.		50,000	
	Premium on Redemption of Debentures A/c	Dr.		2,500	
	To Debentureholders A/c				52,500
	(Being the amount payable on redemption, transferred to Debentureholders' Account)				
	Debentureholders A/c	Dr.		52,500	
	To Bank A/c				52,500
	(Being the amount paid to debentureholders on redemption)				

Debenture Redemption Reserve A/c To General Reserve A/c (Being the transfer of Debentures Redemption Reserve to General Reserve after redemption of debentures)	Dr.	50,000	50,000

Tutorial Note : It is assumed that N Ltd transferred adequate amount to Debentures Redemption Reserve as per the requirement of the Companies Act.

Dr. **Loss on Issue of Debentures Account** **Cr.**

Date	Particulars	₹	Date	Particulars	₹
Year 1 Jan. 1	To 12% Debentures A/c	2,500	Year 1 Dec. 31	By Statement of Profit and Loss (Note 1)	1,000
	To Premium on Red. of Debentures A/c	2,500		By Balance c/d	4,000
		5,000			5,000
Year 2 Jan. 1	To Balance b/d	4,000	Year 2 Dec. 31	By Statement of Profit and Loss	1,000
				By Balance c/d	3,000
		4,000			4,000
Year 3 Jan. 1	To Balance b/d	3,000	Year 3 Dec. 31	By Statement of Profit and Loss	1,000
				By Balance c/d	2,000
		3,000			3,000
Year 4 Jan. 1	To Balance b/d	2,000	Year 4 Dec. 31	By Statement of Profit and Loss	1,000
				By Balance c/d	1,000
		2,000			2,000
Year 5 Jan. 1	To Balance b/d	1,000	Year 5 Dec. 31	By Statement of Profit and Loss	1,000
		1,000			1,000

Working Note :

(1) Since the debentures are redeemable after 5 years, the Loss on Issue of Debentures is written off equally throughout the life of the debentures.

By Draw of Lots

In this case, debentures to be redeemed are selected by lottery or drawings. The accounting entries are simple. When debentures are redeemed, Debentures Account is debited with the face value of debentures and Debentureholders Account is credited. On actual payment, Debentureholders Account is debited and Bank Account is credited. If the debentures are redeemed at a premium, the Debentureholders Account is credited with the premium and Premium on Redemption of Debentures Account is debited.

Accounting Entries

(a) When debentures are redeemed at par

(i) Debentures Account	Dr.	[Nominal value]
To Debentureholders Account		[Actual amount]
(ii) Debentureholders Account	Dr.	[Actual amount paid]
To Bank Account		

(b) When debentures are redeemed at a premium

(i) Debentures Account	Dr.	[Nominal value]
Premium on Redemption of Debentures Account	Dr.	[Premium]
To Debentureholders Account		
(ii) Debentureholders Account	Dr.	[Actual amount paid]
To Bank Account		

(c) When debentures are redeemed at a discount

(i) Debentures Account Dr. [Nominal value]
  To Debentureholders Account [Actual amount]
  To Profit on Redemption of Debentures Account [Discount]
(ii) Debentureholders Account Dr. [Actual amount paid]
  To Bank Account

Illustration 7

Reliance Limited issues 500, 12% debentures of ₹ 100 each at par on 1st January 2011. Under the terms of issue: (a) Debenture Interest is annually payable on 31st December every year, and (b) 1/5th of the debentures are annually redeemable by drawings, the 1st redemption occurring on 31st December 2013. The company transferred ₹ 15,000 every year to Debenture Redemption Reserve Account as per the requirement of the Companies Act, 2000 (Amended).

Pass necessary journal entries for 2011, 2012 and 2013.

Solution

In the books of Reliance Limited

Journal

Date	Particulars	L.F.	Dr. ₹	Cr. ₹
2011 Jan. 1	Bank A/c Dr. To Debentures Application A/c (Being the amount received on 500 debentures @ ₹ 100 each)		50,000	50,000
Jan. 1	Debentures Application A/c Dr. To 12% Debentures A/c (Being the issue of 500 debentures of ₹ 100 each at par as per Board's Resolution No. ... dated ...)		50,000	50,000
Dec. 31	Debenture Interest A/c Dr. To Bank A/c (Being the debenture interest paid for the year)		6,000	6,000
Dec. 31	Statement of Profit and Loss Dr. To Debenture Interest A/c (Being the debenture interest transferred to Statement of Profit and Loss)		6,000	6,000
Dec. 31	Statement of Profit and Loss Dr. To Debenture Redemption Reserve A/c (Being the amount transferred to Debenture Redemption Reserve Account)		15,000	15,000
2012 Dec. 31	Debenture Interest A/c Dr. To Bank A/c (Being the debenture interest paid for the year)		6,000	6,000
Dec. 31	Statement of Profit and Loss Dr. To Debenture Interest A/c (Being the debenture interest transferred to Statement of Profit and Loss)		6,000	6,000
Dec. 31	Statement of Profit and Loss Dr. To Debenture Redemption Reserve A/c (Being the amount transferred to Debenture Redemption Reserve Account)		15,000	15,000
2013 Dec. 31	Debenture Interest A/c Dr. To Bank A/c (Being the debenture interest paid for the year)		6,000	6,000
Dec. 31	12% Debentures A/c Dr. To Debentureholders A/c (Being the amount payable on redemption, transferred to Debentureholders Account)		10,000	10,000
Dec. 31	Debentureholders A/c Dr. To Bank A/c (Being the amount paid to Debentureholders on redemption)		10,000	10,000

Dec. 31	Statement of Profit and Loss Dr. To Debenture Interest A/c (Being the debenture interest transferred to Statement of Profit and Loss)		6,000	6,000
Dec. 31	Statement of Profit and Loss Dr. To Debenture Redemption Reserve A/c (Being the amount transferred to Debenture Redemption Reserve Account)		15,000	15,000

Tutorial Note : After redemption of all the debentures, the balance of Debenture Redemption Reserve Account will be closed by transferring to General Reserve.

By Purchasing in the Open Market

If the debentures are listed in the stock market, they can be easily purchased and sold. A company may purchase its own debentures from stock market either :

(i) for immediate cancellation; or (ii) as an investment (to be cancelled when required)

Generally, the company is interested to purchase its own debentures for redemption when the interest rate on the debentures is considerably higher than the current market interest rate.

When debentures are not listed on the stock exchange and issued privately, the company may negotiate a price with the debentureholders to buy back the debentures for cancellation.

Purchase of Debentures for Immediate Cancellation — On the Date of Interest

A Company may purchase its own debentures at any date for immediate cancellation. If the date of purchase of debentures and the date for payment of interest on debentures are the same, interest upto the date of purchase will be paid to the (old) debentureholders.

The entries for purchase and cancellation of debentures will be as follows:

(a) When debentures are purchased

Debentures Redemption Account Dr. [Quoted price x No. of debentures purchased]
To Bank Account

(b) When expenses are incurred for purchase of debentures from market

Debenture Redemption Account Dr.
To Bank Account

(c) When debentures are cancelled

(i) Debentures Account Dr. [Face value]
To Debentures Redemption Account [Purchase price]
To Profit on Cancellation of Debentures Account [Profit]

(ii) If there is a loss on cancellation, it is transferred to Statement of Profit and Loss.
Statement of Profit and Loss Dr. [Loss]
To Debentures Redemption Account

(d) When profit on cancellation of debentures is transferred to Capital Reserve

Profit on Cancellation of Debentures Account Dr.
To Capital Reserve Account*

*Profit on cancellation is a capital profit, it should be transferred to capital reserve.

Illustration 8

Z Limited purchased its own debentures of the face value of ₹ 20,000 from the open market for immediate cancellation at ₹ 92. Pass necessary journal entries.

Solution

In the books of Z Limited

Journal

Date	Particulars		L.F.	Dr. ₹	Cr. ₹
	Debentures Redemption A/c (Note 1) To Bank A/c (Being the purchase of 200 own debentures of ₹ 100 each @ ₹ 92 each for immediate cancellation)	Dr.		18,400	 18,400
	Debentures A/c To Debentures Redemption A/c To Profit on Cancellation of Debentures A/c (Being cancellation of 200 debentures as per Board's Resolution No. ... dt ...)	Dr.		20,000	 18,400 1,600
	Profit on Cancellation of Debentures A/c (Note 2) To Capital Reserve A/c (Being the profit on cancellation transferred to Capital Reserve)	Dr.		1,600	 1,600

Tutorial Note : After redemption of all the debentures, the balance of Debenture Redemption Reserve Account will be closed by transferring to General Reserve.

Working Notes :

(1) Debentures Purchase Account can be debited in place of Debentures Redemption Account.

(2) Profit on redemption of debentures is a capital profit. Therefore, it should be transferred to Capital Reserve.

(3) It is assumed that the redemption has been done out of profit.

Illustration 9

Shakti Ltd. decided to redeem its 750, 12% Debentures of ₹ 100 each. The company purchased 500 Debentures at ₹ 94 per debenture from the open market. The remaining debentures were redeemed out of profits. The company had already made a provision for Debenture Redemption Reserve in its books.

Pass necessary journal entries in the books of the company for the above transactions.

[CBSE (Delhi) — 2012]

Solution

In the books of Shakti Limited

Journal

Date	Particulars		L.F.	Dr. ₹	Cr. ₹
	Debentures Redemption A/c To Bank A/c (Being the purchase of 500 debentures of ₹ 100 each @ ₹ 94 each for cancellation)	Dr.		47,000	 47,000
	12% Debentures A/c To Debentures Redemption A/c To Profit on Cancellation of Debentures A/c (Being the cancellation of 500 debentures as per Board's Resolution No. ... dt ...)	Dr.		50,000	 47,000 3,000
	12% Debentures A/c To Debentureholders A/c (Being the amount payable to debentureholders for redemption of 250 debentures of ₹ 100 each)	Dr.		25,000	 25,000
	Debentureholders A/c To Bank A/c (Being amount paid for redemption of 250 debentures)	Dr.		25,000	 25,000
	Debenture Redemption Reserve A/c (Note 1) To General Reserve A/c (Being the balance of Debenture Redemption Reserve A/c transferred to General Reserve A/c)	Dr.		75,000	 75,000

Particulars		L.F.	Dr. ₹	Cr. ₹
Profit on Cancellation of Debentures A/c Dr. To Capital Reserve A/c (Being the profit on cancellation of 500 debentures @ ₹ 6 each transferred to Capital Reserve)			3,000	3,000

Working Notes :

(1) It is assumed that the company has created Capital Redemption Reserve for the entire debentures, i.e., ₹ 75,000.

Illustration 10

On 1st January 2013, X Limited had 10,000, 12% Debentures of ₹ 100 each. As per the provision of the deed, the directors acquired in the open market the following debentures for immediate cancellation: June 30, 2013 debentures @ ₹ 98; December 31, 4,000 debentures @ ₹ 96. Debentures interest is payable half-yearly, on 30th June and 31st December.

Pass necessary Journal Entries (ignore interest and tax).

Solution

In the books of X Limited

Journal

Date	Particulars	L.F.	Dr. ₹	Cr. ₹
2013 June 30	Debentures Redemption A/c (Note 1) Dr. To Bank A/c (Being the purchase of 2,000 debentures of ₹ 100 each @ ₹ 98 each for immediate cancellation)		1,96,000	1,96,000
June 30	12% Debentures A/c Dr. To Debentures Redemption A/c To Profit on Cancellation of Debentures A/c (Being the cancellation of 2,000 deben. as per Board's Resolution No. ... dt ...)		2,00,000	1,96,000 4,000
Dec. 31	Debentures Redemption A/c Dr. To Bank A/c (Being the purchase of 4,000 debentures of ₹ 100 each @ ₹ 96 each for immediate cancellation)		3,84,000	3,84,000
Dec. 31	12% Debentures A/c Dr. To Debentures Redemption A/c To Profit on Cancellation of Debentures A/c (Being the cancellation of 4,000 debentures as per Board's Resolution No. ... dated ...)		4,00,000	3,84,000 16,000
Dec. 31	Profit on Cancellation of Debentures A/c (₹ 4,000 + 16,000) Dr. To Capital Reserve A/c (Note 2) (Being the profit on cancellation transferred to Capital Reserve)		20,000	20,000

Tutorial Notes :

(1) Debentures Purchase Account can be debited in place of Debentures Redemption Account;

(2) Profit on cancellation of debentures is a capital profit. Therefore, it should be transferred to Capital Reserve Account;

(3) No entry is required to be passed for interest on debentures as per the requirement of the problem.

(4) After redemption of all the debentures, the balance of Debenture Redemption Reserve Account will be closed by transferring to General Reserve.

Illustration 11

At the commencement of 2012 Y Limited made an issue of 1,000, 10% Debentures of ₹ 100 each at par. The terms of issue provided for the redemption of ₹ 10,000 annually, commencing from the end of 2013, either by drawings at par or by purchase in the market at the company's option. Interest is payable on 31st December every year.

At the end of 2013, the company purchased for cancellation ₹ 5,000 of its Debentures at ₹ 96 each, ₹ 3,000 at ₹ 98 each and ₹ 2000 at ₹ 98.50 each. The expenses of purchase amounted to ₹ 40. The Board of Directors decided to redeem the debentures out of profits. Pass necessary journal entries for the year 2013.

Solution

In the books of Y Limited
Journal

Date	Particulars	L.F.	Dr. ₹	Cr. ₹
2012 Jan. 1	Bank A/c Dr. To Debentures Application A/c (Being the amount received on 1,000 debentures @ ₹ 100 each)		1,00,000	1,00,000
Jan. 1	Debentures Application A/c Dr. To 10% Debentures A/c (Being the allotment of 1,000, 10% debentures of ₹ 100 each as per Board's Resolution No. ... dated ...)		1,00,000	1,00,000
Dec. 31	Debenture Interest A/c Dr. To Bank A/c (Being the debenture interest paid for the year)		10,000	10,000
"	Statement of Profit and Loss Dr. To Debenture Redemption Reserve A/c (Being the necessary amount transferred to Debenture Redemption Reserve Account)		1,00,000	1,00,000
2013 Dec. 31	Debentures Redemption A/c (Note 1) Dr. To Bank A/c (Being the purchase of 50 debentures @ ₹ 96 each, 30 debentures @ ₹ 98 each and 20 debentures @ ₹ 98.50 each for immediate cancellation)		9,710	9,710
"	Debentures Redemption A/c Dr. To Bank A/c (Being expenses for purchase of debentures paid)		40	40
"	10% Debentures A/c Dr. To Debenture Redemption A/c (₹ 9,710 + 40) To Profit on Cancellation of Debentures A/c (Note 2) (Being the redemption of 100 debentures purchased as per Board's Resolution No. . .. dated . . .)		10,000	9,750 250
"	Debentures Interest A/c Dr. To Bank A/c (Being debenture interest paid for the year)		10,000	10,000
Dec. 31	Statement of Profit and Loss Dr. To Debenture Interest A/c (Being the debenture interest transferred to Statement of Profit and Loss)		10,000	10,000

Tutorial Note : After redemption of all the debentures, the balance of Debenture Redemption Reserve Account will be closed by transferring to General Reserve.

Working Notes :

(1) Cost of Debentures Purchased

Particulars	₹
50 Debentures @ ₹ 96	4,800
30 Debentures @ ₹ 98	2,940
20 Debentures @ ₹ 98.50	1,970
	9,710

(2) Calculation of Profit on Cancellation

Particulars	₹
Face value of debentures redeemed (100 x ₹ 100)	10,000
Less: Cost of investment (Note 1)	9,710
	290
Less : Expenses on purchase of debentures	40
	250

Illustration 12

On 1.1.2012 a company issued 10,000, 9% Debentures of ₹ 100 each at a discount of 5%. The terms of issue provide for redemption of ₹ 90,000 worth of Debentures every year commencing from the end of 2013 either by purchasing in the open market or by draw of lots at the company's option. The company also wrote off ₹ 10,000 during the years 2012 and 2013 from the Debentures Discount Account. The company transferred ₹ 3,00,000 to Debenture Redemption Reserve Account as per the requirement of the Act in 2012 and 2013 respectively. During the year 2013 the company purchased 400 Debentures @ ₹ 95 each and 500 Debentures @ ₹ 96 each for cancellation. Journalise these transactions and also show how you will deal with the profit on redemption of debentures.

Solution

In the books of the Company

Journal

Date	Particulars	L.F.	Dr. ₹	Cr. ₹
2012 Jan. 1	Bank A/c Dr. To Debentures Application A/c (Being the amount received on 10,000 debentures @ ₹ 95 each)		9,50,000	9,50,000
Jan. 1	Debentures Application A/c Dr. Discount on Issue of Debentures A/c Dr. To 9% Debentures A/c (Being the allotment of 10,000 debentures of ₹ 100 each @ ₹ 95 each as per Board's Resolution)		9,50,000 50,000	10,00,000
Dec. 31	Debenture Interest A/c (Note 2) Dr. To Bank A/c (Being the debenture interest paid for the year)		90,000	90,000
Dec. 31	Statement of Profit and Loss Dr. To Debenture Interest A/c (Being the debenture interest transferred to Statement of Profit and Loss)		90,000	90,000
Dec. 31	Statement of Profit and Loss Dr. To Discount on Issue of Debentures A/c (Being ₹ 10,000 discount on issue of debentures written off)		10,000	10,000
Dec 31	Statement of Profit and Loss Dr. To Debenture Redemption Reserve A/c (Being the amount transferred to Debenture Redemption Reserve A/c)		3,00,000	3,00,000
2013 Dec. 31	Debenture Interest A/c (Note 2) Dr. To Bank A/c (Being the debenture interest paid for the year)		90,000	90,000
Dec. 31	Statement of Profit and Loss Dr. To Debenture Interest A/c (Being the debenture interest transferred to Statement of Profit and Loss)		90,000	90,000
Dec 31	Statement of Profit and Loss Dr. To Debenture Redemption Reserve A/c (Being the amount transferred to Debenture Redemption Reserve A/c)		3,00,000	3,00,000

Dec. 31	Debentures Redemption A/c Dr. To Bank A/c (Being the purchase of 400 debentures of ₹ 100 each @ ₹ 95 each for immediate cancellation)		38,000	 38,000
Dec. 31	9% Debentures A/c Dr. To Debenture Redemption A/c To Profit on Cancellation of Debentures A/c (Being the cancellation of 400 debentures as per Board's Resolution No. . . . dated . . .)		40,000	 38,000 2,000
Dec. 31	Debentures Redemption A/c Dr. To Bank A/c (Being the purchase of 500 debentures of ₹ 100 each @ ₹ 96 each for immediate cancellation)		48,000	 48,000
Dec. 31	9% Debentures A/c Dr. To Debenture Redemption A/c To Profit on Cancellation of Debentures A/c (Being the cancellation of 500 debentures as per Board's Resolution No. . . . dated . . .)		50,000	 48,000 2,000
Dec. 31	Profit on Cancellation of Debentures A/c (₹ 2,000 + 2,000) Dr. To Capital Reserve A/c (Note 1) (Being the profit on cancellation transferred to Capital Reserve)		4,000	 4,000
Dec. 31	Statement of Profit and Loss Dr. To Discount on Issue of Debentures A/c (Being ₹ 10,000 discount on issue of debentures written off)		10,000	 10,000

Tutorial Note : After redemption of all the debentures, the balance of Debenture Redemption Reserve Account will be closed by transferring to General Reserve.

Working Notes :

(1) Profit on cancellation of debentures is a ***capital profit***. Therefore, it should be transferred to Capital Reserve Account.

(2) It is assumed that interest on debentures is payable on 31st December every year.

(3) It is assumed that debentures were purchased for cancellation at the end of the year and interest thereon was paid for the entire debentures.

Illustration 13

Z Limited has an outstanding liability of 10%, ₹ 100 debentures amounting to ₹ 1,00,000 redeemable at the option of the company by drawing at par, or by purchase in the open market. It decides to redeem ₹ 25,000 debentures, and purchase ₹ 20,000 debentures in the open market at ₹ 99 each and draw ₹ 5,000 debentures.

Show the necessary Ledger Accounts.

Solution

In the books of Z Limited

Dr. 10% Debentures Account Cr.

Date	Particulars	₹	Date	Particulars	₹
	To Bank A/c (Note 1)	5,000		By Balance b/d	1,00,000
	To Debenture Redemption A/c	20,000			
	To Balance c/d	75,000			
		1,00,000			1,00,000

Dr. **Debenture Redemption Account** **Cr.**

Date	Particulars	₹	Date	Particulars	₹
	To Bank A/c (₹ 20,000 at 99%)	19,800		By 10% Debentures A/c	20,000
	To Profit on Cancellation of Debentures A/c	200			
		20,000			20,000

Working Notes :

(1) Total debentures are to be redeemed for ₹ 25,000. Debentures purchased from the open market for ₹ 20,000. Therefore, Debentures of ₹ 5,000 is to be redeemed by drawings.

Illustration 14

On 1st January, 2013, ABC Ltd had outstanding in its books 1,500, 12% debentures of ₹ 100 each. On the same date the balance of Debenture Redemption Reserve was ₹ 1,50,000. The interest is payable on 30th June and 31st December every year. In accordance with the power in the deed, the directors acquired in the open market debentures for immediate cancellation as follows :

On 1st July, 2013, 200 debentures @ ₹ 98 each.

On 31st December, 2013, 300 debentures @ ₹ 96 each.

Pass necessary journal entries in the books of the company (ignore income tax).

Solution

In the books of ABC Ltd

Journal

Date	Particulars	L.F.	Dr. ₹	Cr. ₹
2013 June 30	Debenture Interest A/c Dr. To Bank A/c (Being the interest paid on 1,500 debentures @ 12% p.a. for 6 months ending on 30th June)		9,000	9,000
July 1	Debentures Redemption A/c Dr. To Bank A/c (Being the purchase of 200, 12% debentures @ ₹ 98 each for immediate cancellation)		19,600	19,600
	12% Debentures A/c Dr. To Debenture Redemption A/c To Profit on Cancellation of Debentures A/c (Being the cancellation of 200 debentures purchased as per Board's Resolution No. . . . dated . . .)		20,000	19,600 400
Dec. 31	Debenture Interest A/c (Note 1) Dr. To Bank A/c (Being the interest paid on 1,300 debentures @ 12% p.a. for 6 months ending on 31st December)		7,800	7,800
"	Debentures Redemption A/c Dr. To Bank A/c (Being the purchase of 300, 12% debentures @ ₹ 96 each for immediate cancellation)		28,800	28,800
	12% Debentures A/c Dr. To Debenture Redemption A/c To Profit on Cancellation of Debentures A/c (Being the cancellation of 300 debentures purchased as per Board's Resolution No. . . dated . . .)		30,000	28,800 1,200
"	Statement of Profit and Loss (₹ 9,000 + 7,800) Dr. To Debenture Interest A/c (Being the interest on debentures for the year transferred to Statement of Profit and Loss)		16,800	16,800

Particulars		L.F.	Dr.	Cr.
Profit on Cancellation of Debentures A/c (Note 3) To Capital Reserve A/c (Being the profit on cancellation of debentures transferred to Capital Reserve)	Dr.		1,600	1,600

Working Notes :

(1) Out of 1,500 debentures, 200 debentures were redeemed on 1st July. Therefore, interest from July to December will be paid on 1,300 debentures only. The interest will be :₹ 1,30,000 × 12/100 × 6/12 = ₹ 7,800.

(2) After redemption of all debentures, the balance of Debenture Redemption Reserve will be transferred to General Reserve.

(3) Total profit on cancellation will be ₹ 400 + ₹ 1,200 = ₹ 1,600.

Purchase of Debentures as Investment — On the Date of Interest

It is not necessary that a company purchases its own debentures from the market only for cancellation purposes. Sometimes a company may purchase its own debentures for the purpose of investment. These debentures are kept alive. In future, it can be sold in the market again or it can be cancelled.

When debentures are purchased for the purpose of investment, an account called 'Own Debentures Account' or 'Investment in Own Debentures Account' is debited with the cost and Bank Account is credited for the same. Till the debentures are cancelled, these are shown in the Balance Sheet (on the assets side) just like any other investment.

Interest on own debentures for the post-purchase period will be treated as income and credited to Statement of Profit and Loss. However, Debenture Interest Account is debited with the total interest of that period (payable to outside debentureholders plus interest on own debentures held as investment).

The accounting entries will be as follows:

(a) When debentures are purchased

Investment in Own Debentures Account Dr. [Quotation price x No. of debentures purchased]
To Bank Account
(Being the purchase of ... debentures @ ₹ ..... each as investment)

(b) When interest on debentures is due and paid

Debenture Interest Account Dr. [Total interest]
To Bank Account [Interest paid to outside debentureholders]
To Interest on Own Debentures Account [Own Debentures]
(Being the interest on debentures paid and adjusted)

(c) When debentures are cancelled

Debentures Account Dr. [Face value]
To Investment in Own Debentures Account [Purchase price]
To Profit on Cancellation of Debentures Account [Profit]
(Being the cancellation of ... debentures)

(d) When profit on cancellation of debentures is transferred to Capital Reserve

Profit on Cancellation of Debentures Account Dr.
To Capital Reserve Account
(Being profit on cancellation is transferred to Capital Reserve Account)

(e) When interest on own debentures is transferred

Interest on Own Debentures Account Dr.
  To Statement of Profit and Loss
(Being the interest on own debentures is transferred to Statement of Profit and Loss)

(f) When debentures interest (paid during the year) is transferred to Statement of Profit and Loss

Statement of Profit and Loss Dr.
  To Debenture Interest Account
(Being interest charged to Statement of Profit and Loss)

Treatment of Interest on Own Debentures

When debentures are purchased as investment, the interest of the post-purchase period is calculated and credited to "Interest on Own Debentures Account". Debenture Interest Account is debited with the ***full interest*** (whether held by the company or outsiders). At the end of the accounting period, Statement of Profit and Loss is debited with the full amount of "Debenture Interest". "Interest on Own Debentures" is credited to Statement of Profit and Loss.

Illustration 15

On 1st January, 2013, HP Limited had 10,000, 12% Debentures of ₹ 100 each. On the same date the balance of Debenture Redemption Reserve was ₹ 10,00,000. The company purchased in the open market 2,000 debentures @ ₹ 98 each on 1st July, 2013as investment. Debenture interest is payable on 30th June and 31st December. The company cancelled all the debentures (purchased on 1st July, 2013) on 31st December, 2013, the date of the year ending.

Pass necessary journal entries in the books of the company (ignore income tax).

Solution

In the books of HP Limited

Journal

Date	Particulars	L.F.	Dr. ₹	Cr. ₹
2013				
June 30	Debenture Interest A/c Dr.		60,000	
	To Bank A/c			60,000
	(Being int. paid on 10,000 deben. @ 12% p.a. for 6 months ending on 30th June)			
July 1	Investment in Own Debentures A/c Dr.		1,96,000	
	To Bank A/c			1,96,000
	(Being the purchase of 2.000, 12% debentures @ ₹ 98 each as investment)			
Dec. 31	Debenture Interest A/c Dr.		60,000	
	To Bank A/c			48,000
	To Interest on Own Debentures A/c			12,000
	(Being the interest on 8,000 debentures @ 12% p.a. for 6 months ending on 31st December paid to outside Debentureholders and interest on 2000 debentures @ 12% p.a. for 6 months credited to Interest on Own Debenture Account)			
"	12% Debentures A/c Dr.		2,00,000	
	To Investment in Own Debentures A/c			1,96,000
	To Profit on Cancellation of Debentures A/c			4,000
	(Being the cancellation of 2,000, 12% debentures purchased on 1st July, 2010)			

Date	Particulars	L.F.	Dr. ₹	Cr. ₹
"	Statement of Profit and Loss Dr. To Debenture Interest A/c (Being the debenture interest for the year transferred to Statement of Profit and Loss)		1,20,000	1,20,000
"	Interest on Own Debentures A/c Dr. To Statement of Profit and Loss (Being the interest on own debentures credited to Statement of Profit and Loss)		12,000	12,000
"	Profit on Cancellation of Debentures A/c Dr. To Capital Reserve A/c (Being the profit on cancellation of debentures transferred to Capital Reserve)		4,000	4,000

Tutorial Note : After redemption of all the debentures, the balance of Debenture Redemption Reserve Account will be closed by transferring to General Reserve.

Illustration 16

Draft journal entries in respect of the following : In 2010, Z Limited had issued 5,000, 10% Debentures of ₹ 100 each. On 1st July, 2012 the company purchased 500 of its own 10% debentures at ₹ 48,000. On the same date the balance of Debenture Redemption Reserve was ₹ 5,00,000. The debentures were held as investment until 30th June, 2013 when it was decided to cancel them.

Interest is payable half-yearly on 31st December and 30th June and the books are closed on 30th June each year.

Solution

In the books of Z Limited

Journal

Date	Particulars	L.F.	Dr. ₹	Cr. ₹
2012 July 1	Investment in Own Debentures A/c Dr. To Bank A/c (Being the purchase of 500, 10% debentures at ₹ 48,000 as investment)		48,000	48,000
Dec. 31	Debenture Interest A/c Dr. To Bank A/c To Interest on Own Debentures A/c (Being the interest paid on 4,500 debentures @ 10% p.a. for 6 months ending on 31st December paid to outside debentureholders and interest on 500 debentures @ 10% p.a. for 6 months credited to Interest on Own Debentures Account)		25,000	22,500 2,500
2013 June 30	Debenture Interest A/c Dr. To Bank A/c To Interest on Own Debentures A/c (Being the interest paid on 4,500 debentures @ 10% p.a. for 6 months ending on 30th June paid to outside debentureholders and interest on 500 debentures @ 10% p.a. for 6 months credited to Interest on Own Debentures Account)		25,000	22,500 2,500
June 30	10% Debentures A/c Dr. To Investment in Own Debentures A/c To Profit on Cancellation of Debentures A/c (Being the cancellation of 500, 10% debentures purchased on 1st July, 2010)		50,000	48,000 2,000
"	Interest on Own Debenture A/c Dr. To Statement of Profit and Loss (Being the interest on own debentures credited to Statement of Profit and Loss)		5,000	5,000
	Statement of Profit and Loss Dr. To Debenture Interest A/c (Being the interest on debentures for the year transferred to Statement of Profit and Loss)		50,000	50,000

"	Profit on Cancellation of Debentures A/c Dr. To Capital Reserve A/c (Being the profit on cancellation of debentures transferred to Capital Reserve)		2,000	 2,000

Tutorial Note : After redemption of all the debentures, the balance of Debenture Redemption Reserve Account will be closed by transferring to General Reserve.

Redemption of Debentures by Conversion into Shares

Debentures can be redeemed by conversion into shares. A convertible debenture gives the holder the option to convert it into shares at a later date and also at a fixed price. A company may issue two types of convertible debentures :

(i) Partly convertible debentures (PCD); and

(ii) Fully convertible debentures (FCD)

When the entire amount of the debenture is convertible, it is called a fully convertible debenture. On the other hand, when only a part of the debenture is convertible, it is called a partly convertible debenture.

A company may not find it advantageous to raise additional capital by the issue of shares; it might also feel that debentures can only sold at a higher rate of interest. The issue of convertible debentures is the answer to these problems.

When the debentures are converted into shares, the fixed interest charges of the company are to that extent reduced. If a part of the total convertible debentures are not converted (some debentureholders do not exercise their option of converting), these debentures are redeemed in the usual way as per the terms of the agreement and debentureholders are paid-off accordingly.

Accounting Entries for Issue of Debentures

1. On receipt of application money

Cash/Bank Account Dr.
    To Debentures Application Account

---

2. For allotment of debentures

Debentures Application Account Dr.
    To Convertible Debentures Account

Accounting Entries for Conversion of Debentures at Par

For conversion of the debentures into equity/preference shares

Convertible Debentures Account Dr.
    To Equity/Preference Share Capital Account

OR

(i) Convertible Debentures Account Dr.
    To Debentureholders Account

(ii) Debentureholders Account Dr.
    To Equity/Preference Share Capital Account

Illustration 17

TCS Limited made a public issue of 15% fully convertible debenture (FCD) of ₹ 100 each for cash at par aggregating ₹ 10 lakhs. Issue opened on 1st June, 20103 issue closed on 15th June, 2013. Allotment made on 1st July, 2013.

The terms and conditions of the issue are :

(a) Full amount payable on application;

(b) Each FCD will be automatically converted into 10 equity shares of ₹ 10 each at par on 31st December, 2013. Debenture interest were paid upto 31st December.

You are required to pass necessary journal entries assuming that the accounting year closes on 31st December, every year.

Solution

In the books of TCS Limited

Journal

Date	Particulars	L.F.	Dr. ₹	Cr. ₹
2013 June 15	Bank A/c Dr.		10,00,000	
	To Debentures Application A/c			10,00,000
	(Being application money received on 10,000 debentures @ ₹ 100 each)			
July 1	Debentures Application A/c Dr.		10,00,000	
	To 15% Fully Convertible Debentures A/c			10,00,000
	(Being the allotment of 10,000, 15% fully convertible debentures)			
Dec. 31	15% Fully Convertible Debenture A/c Dr.		10,00,000	
	To Equity Share Capital A/c			10,00,000
	(Being the conversion of 10,000 15% FCD into 1,00,000 equity shares of ₹ 10 each as per Board's Resolution No. . . . dated . . .)			
Dec. 31	Debenture Interest A/c Dr.		75,000	
	To Bank A/c			75,000
	(Being debenture interest paid for 6 months ending on 31st December)			
Dec. 31	Statement of Profit and Loss Dr.		75,000	
	To Debenture Interest A/c			75,000
	(Being the debenture interest transferred to Statement of Profit and Loss)			

For calculating number of shares to be issued at the time of conversion is to be calculated as follows:

Accounting Entries for Conversion of Debentures at a Premium

For conversion of the debentures into Equity / Preference Shares at a Premium

Convertible Debentures Account Dr.
Premium on Redemption Account Dr. (If payable)
  To Equity / Preference Shares Account
  To Securities Premium Account

OR

(i) Convertible Debentures Account Dr.
  Premium on Redemption Account Dr. (If payable)
  To Debentureholders Account

(ii) Debentureholders Account Dr.
  To Equity Share Capital Account
  To Securities Premium Account

Step 1 : Calculate the amount payable to the debentureholders as follows :

Face Value of Debentures to be Converted	***
Add: Premium on Redemption (if any)	***
Total amount to be Converted	***

Step 2 : Calculate the value of shares to be issued for conversion of debentures as follows :

Face Value of Shares	***
Add: Securities Premium	***
OR	
Less : Discount on Shares	***
Net Value of each Share	***

Step 3 : Calculate the number of Shares to be issued :

$$\text{No. of Shares to be Issued} = \frac{\text{Total Amount to be Converted}}{\text{Net Value of Each Share}}$$

Illustration 18

On 1st June, 2013 Hindustan Computers Limited made a public issue of 10,000, 14% fully convertible debentures of ₹ 100 each for cash at par. The entire amount is payable on application. Allotment was made on 1st July, 2013. The entire face value of ₹ 100 of each debenture would be compulsorily and automatically converted into five equity shares of ₹ 10 each in the company credited as fully paid-up at a premium of ₹ 10 per share on the expiry of six months from the date of allotment. On 31.12.2013 half-yearly interest had accrued on debentures and paid on that date.

Pass necessary journal entries assuming that accounting year closing on 31st December every year.

Solution **In the books of Hindustan Computers Limited**

Journal

Date	Particulars	L.F.	Dr. ₹	Cr. ₹
2013 June 1	Bank A/c Dr. To Debentures Application A/c (Being application money received on 10,000 debentures @ ₹ 100 each)		10,00,000	10,00,000
July 1	Debentures Application A/c Dr. To 14% Fully Convertible Debentures A/c (Being the allotment of 10,000, 14% fully convertible debentures of ₹ 100 each at par as per Board's Resolution No. . . . dated . . .)		10,00,000	10,00,000
Dec. 31	Debenture Interest A/c Dr. To Bank A/c (Being half-yearly interest on debentures paid)		70,000	70,000
Dec. 31	Statement of Profit and Loss Dr. To Debenture Interest A/c (Being the debenture interest transferred to Statement of Profit and Loss)		70,000	70,000
Dec. 31	14% Fully Convertible Debentures A/c Dr. To Equity Share Capital A/c To Securities Premium A/c (Being the conversion of 10,000, 14% FCD into 50,000 equity shares of ₹ 10 each at a premium of ₹ 10 per share as per Board's Resolution No. ... dated ...)		10,00,000	5,00,000 5,00,000

Illustration 19

Taneja Construction Ltd. has an outstanding balance of ₹ 5,00,000, 7% debentures of ₹ 100 each redeemable at a premium of 10%. According to the terms of redemption, the company redeemed 30% of the above debentures by converting them into shares of ₹ 50 each at a premium of 20%.

Record the entries for redemption of debentures in the books of Taneja Construction Ltd.

[CBSE (Delhi) — 2013]

Solution

(i) Amount payable to Debentureholders

	₹
Face value (30% of ₹ 5,00,000)	1,50,000
Add: Premium on Redemption (10%)	15,000
	1,65,000

(ii) Value of each Share

Face value	50
Add: 20% Premium	10
	60

$$\textbf{(iii) No. of Shares} = \frac{\text{Amount Payable to the Debentureholders}}{\text{Value of Each Share}}$$

= 1,65,000 ÷ 60 = **2,750 Shares**

In the books of Taneja Construction Ltd

Journal

Date	Particulars		L.F.	Dr. ₹	Cr. ₹
	7% Debentures A/c	Dr.		1,50,000	
	Premium on Redemption of Debentures A/c	Dr.		15,000	
	To Debentureholders A/c				1,65,000
	(Being the amount due to holders of 1,500 debentures)				
	Debentureholders A/c	Dr.		1,65,000	
	To Equity Shares Capital A/c				1,37,500
	To Securities Premium A/c				27,500
	(Being the issue of 2,750 equity shares of ₹ 50 each to the debentureholders on account of conversion of 1,500 debentures of ₹ 100 each at a premium of 10%)				

Illustration 20

X Ltd. redeemed 100, 6% Debentures of ₹ 100 each by converting them into equity shares of ₹ 100 each. The 6% debentures were redeemable at 10% premium for which the equity shares were issued at 25% premium.

Pass the necessary journal entries for the redemption of above mentioned debentures in the books of X Ltd. *[CBSE (Delhi) — 2011]*

Solution

(i) Amount payable to Debentureholders

	₹
Face value (100 × ₹ 100)	10,000
Add: Premium on Redemption (10%)	1,000
	11,000

(ii) Value of each Share

Face value	100
Add: 25% Premium	25
	125

$$\textbf{(iii) No. of Shares} = \frac{\text{Amount Payable to the Debentureholders}}{\text{Value of Each Share}}$$

= 11,000 ÷ 125 = **88 Shares**

In the books of X Ltd
Journal

Date	Particulars		L.F.	Dr. ₹	Cr. ₹
	6% Debentures A/c	Dr.		10,000	
	Premium on Redemption of Debentures A/c	Dr.		1,000	
	To Debentureholders A/c				11,000
	(Being the amount due to holders of 100 debentures of ₹ 100 each)				
	Debentureholders A/c	Dr.		11,000	
	To Equity Shares Capital A/c				8,800
	To Securities Premium A/c				2,200
	(Being the issue of 88 equity shares of ₹ 100 eachat a premium of 25% to the debentureholders on account of conversion of 100 debentures)				

Redemption of Debentures by Conversion into New Debentures

Debentures can be redeemed by conversion into new series of debentures. Generally new series of debentures are issued at a higher rate of interest. It is done when the existing debentures are due for redemption but the company is not in a position to pay the debentureholders in cash. In this case, the following journal entries are passed :

A. When Conversion is at Par

1. Convertible Debentures Account Dr.
   To New Debentures

OR

(i) Convertible Debentures Account Dr.
   To Debentureholders Account
(ii) Debentureholders Account Dr.
   To New Debentures Account

B. When Conversion is at a Premium

Convertible Debentures Account Dr.
   To New Debentures Account
   To Securities Premium Account

OR

(i) Convertible Debentures Account Dr.
   To Debentureholders Account
(ii) Debentureholders Account Dr.
   To New Debentures Account
   To Securities Premium Account

Illustration 21

Pass necesary journal entries for the following transactions in the books of Sudarshan Ltd. :

(i) Redeemed 750, 12% Debentures of ₹ 75 each by converting into equity shares of ₹ 100 each. The equity shares were issued at a discount of 10%.

(ii) Converted 550, 12% Debentures of ₹ 1,000 each into new 13% Debentures of ₹ 100 each. The new debentures were issued at a premium of 10%. *[CBSE (Delhi) — 2012]*

Solution

In the books of Sudarshan Ltd
Journal

Date	Particulars		L.F.	Dr. ₹	Cr. ₹
(i)	12% Debentures A/c	Dr.		56,250	
	To Debentureholders A/c				56,250
	(Being the amount payable to debentureholders for redemption of 750 debentures of ₹ 75 each)				
	Debentureholders A/c	Dr.		56,250	
	Discount on Issue of Equity Shares A/c	Dr.		6,250	
	To Equity Share Capital A/c (Note 1)				62,500
	(Being the issue of 625 equity shares of ₹ 100 each at a discount of 10% as per Board's Resolution No. ... dated ...)				
(ii)	12% Debentures A/c	Dr.		5,50,000	
	To Debentureholders A/c				5,50,000
	(Being the amount payable to debentureholders for redemption of 550 debentures of ₹ 1,000 each)				
	Debentureholders A/c	Dr.		5,50,000	
	To 13% Debentures A/c (Note 2)				5,00,000
	To Securities Premium A/c				50,000
	(Being the issue of 5,000, 13% debentures of ₹ 100 each at a premium of 10% as per Board's Resolution No. ... dated ...)				

Working Notes :

(1) No. of Equity Shares Issued $= \dfrac{\text{Amount Due to the Debentureholders}}{\text{Value of Each Equity Share}}$

$= ₹\ 56{,}250 \div ₹\ 110 =$ **625 Equity Shares**

(2) No. of Debentures Issued $= \dfrac{\text{Amount Due to the Debentureholders}}{\text{Value of Each Debenture}}$

$= ₹\ 5{,}50{,}000 \div ₹\ 110 =$ **5,000 Debentures**

Illustration 22

Pass necessary journal entries in the books of Maharaja Ltd for the redemption of 20,000, 10% Debentures of ₹ 50 each issued at par to be redeemed as :

(i) Redeemable at a premium of 10% by conversion into equity shares of ₹ 10 each at par.

(ii) Redeemable at a premium of 10% by conversion into 8% preference shares of ₹ 100 each issued at a premium of 25%.

(iii) Redeemable at a premium of 8% by conversion into 8% preference shares of ₹ 100 each issued at a discount of 10%.

(iv) 50% of the redemption is to be made in cash and the balance to be redeemed at a premium of 20% through the issue of fresh 12% debentures. *[CBSE — Adapted]*

In the books of Maharaja Ltd
Journal

Date	Particulars		L.F.	Dr. ₹	Cr. ₹
(i)	10% Debentures A/c	Dr.		10,00,000	
	Premium on Redemption of Debentures A/c (Note 1)	Dr.		1,00,000	
	To Debentureholders A/c				11,00,000
	(Being the amount payable to debentureholders for redemption of 20,000, 10% debentures of ₹ 50 each at a premium of 10%				

	Particulars		L.F.	Dr.	Cr.
	Debentureholders A/c	Dr.		11,00,000	
	To Equity Shares Capital A/c				11,00,000
	(Being the issue of 1,10,000 equity shares of ₹ 10 each at par as per Board's Resolution No. ... dated ...)				
(ii)	10% Debentures A/c	Dr.		10,00,000	
	Premium on Redemption of Debentures A/c	Dr.		1,00,000	
	To Debentureholders A/c				11,00,000
	(Being the amount payable to debentureholders for redemption of 20,000, 10% debentures of ₹ 50 each at a premium of 10%)				
	Debentureholders A/c	Dr.		11,00,000	
	To 8% Preference Shares Capital A/c (Note 1)				8,80,000
	To Securities Premium A/c				2,20,000
	(Being the amount payable to debentureholders for redemption of 20,000, 10% debentures of ₹ 50 each at a premium of 25%)				
(iii)	10% Debentures A/c	Dr.		10,00,000	
	Premium on Redemption of Debentures A/c	Dr.		80,000	
	To Debentureholders A/c				10,80,000
	(Being the amount payable to debentureholders for redemption of 20,000, 10% debentures of ₹ 50 each at a premium of 8%)				
	Debentureholders A/c	Dr.		10,80,000	
	Discount on Issue of Preference Shares A/c	Dr.		1,20,000	
	To 8% Preference Shares Capital A/c (Note 2)				12,00,000
	(Being the issue of 13,200, 8% preference shares of ₹ 100 each at a discount of 10% as per Board's Resolution No. ... dated ...)				
(iv)	10% Debentures A/c	Dr.		10,00,000	
	Premium on Redemption of Debentures A/c (Note 3)	Dr.		1,00,000	
	To Debentureholders A/c				11,00,000
	(Being the amount payable to debentureholders for redemption of 20,000, 10% debentures of ₹ 50 each)				
	Debentureholders A/c	Dr.		5,00,000	
	To Bank A/c)				5,00,000
	(Being the amount paid to debentureholders in cash)				
	Debentureholders A/c	Dr.		6,00,000	
	To 12% Debentures A/c				6,00,000
	(Being the issue of new debentures)				

Working Notes :

(1) It is assumed that the company had provided for 'Premium on Redemption of Debentures' at the time of issue of the debentures.

(2) Amount payable to debentureholders = ₹ 10,80,000. 8% Preference Shares are to be issued at a discount of 10%. Therefore, the number of preference shares to be issued = ₹ 10,80,000 ÷ ₹ 90 = **12,000.**

(3) Premium on redemption is to be paid for 50% debentures which are to be converted into 12% Debentures (New). Therefore, premium on redemption will be :
1/2 × ₹ 10,00,000 × 20% = ₹ 1,00,000.

Students should note that there is no prohibition to issue debentures at a discount. But when such debentures are converted into shares, the amount to be converted will be equal to net proceeds received from such debentureholders.

In this case, ***journal entry for conversion*** will be :

(a) Convertible Debentures Account	Dr.	[Face value]
To Debentureholders Account		[Net proceeds received]
To Discount on Issue of Debentures Account		[Cancellation of discount on issue of debentures converted]
(b) Debentureholders Account	Dr.	[Net proceeds]
To Equity/Preference Share Capital Account		
To Securities Premium Account		[if converted at a premium]

At the time of conversion, if the Discount on Issue of Debentures Account is not showing any balance (because it has already been written off by debiting Statement of Profit and Loss of the earlier years) then the credit balance of Discount on Issue of Debentures Account [arising from entry (a) above] will be closed by crediting Statement of Profit and Loss and debiting Discount on Issue of Debentures Account.

If any balance left in the Discount on Issue of Debentures Account after passing entry (a) above, then such balance will be written-off by debiting Statement of Profit and Loss and crediting Discount on Issue of Debentures Account in the future years.

When conversion is done at a premium, such premium can be adjusted against the debit balance (not yet written off) of the Discount on Issue of Debentures Account to the extent possible.

Illustration 23

On 1.1.2013, J K Limited issued 3,000, 12% fully convertible debentures of ₹ 100 each at a discount of 10%. Holders of these debentures have an option to convert their holding into equity shares of ₹ 10 each at par at any time within 3 years. On 31.12.2013, yearly interest had accrued and paid.

It has been decided to write-off discount on issue of debentures of ₹ 10,000 in the year 2013. On 31.12.2013 a holder of 100 debentures notified his decision to exercise his option.

Pass necessary journal entries for the year 2013 (including cash transactions).

Solution

In the books of J K Limited

Journal

Date	Particulars		L.F.	Dr. ₹	Cr. ₹
2013 Jan. 1	Bank A/c	Dr.		2,70,000	
	To Debentures Application A/c				2,70,000
	(Being application money received on 3,000 debentures @ ₹ 90 each)				
"	Debentures Application A/c	Dr.		2,70,000	
	Discount on Issue of Debentures A/c	Dr.		30,000	
	To 12% Fully Convertibble Debentures A/c				3,00,000
	(Being the issue of 3,000 debentures of ₹ 100 each at 10% discount as per Board's Resolution)				
Dec. 31	Debenture Interest A/c	Dr.		36,000	
	To Bank A/c				36,000
	(Being debenture interest paid for the whole year)				
"	Statement of Profit and Loss	Dr.		36,000	
	To Debenture Interest A/c				36,000
	(Being the debenture interest transferred to Statement of Profit and Loss)				

"	Statement of Profit and Loss Dr. To Discount on Issue of Debenture A/c (Being the amount written off)		10,000	10,000
"	12% Fully Convertibble Debentures A/c Dr. To Debentureholders A/c (Note1) To Discount on Issue of Debentures A/c (Being the amount to be converted into equity shares after adjustment of discount on issue of debentures		10,000	9,000 1,000
"	Debentureholders A/c Dr. To Equity Shares Capital A/c (Being the issue of 900 equity shares of ₹ 10 each at par as per Board's Resolution No. ... dated . . .)		9,000	9,000

Working Note :

(1) When debentures (which were issued at a discount) are to be converted into new shares, the amount to be converted will be equal to net proceeds received from the debentureholders, i.e., face value of debentures issued *less* discount on issue of debentures.

Illustration 24

Pass the necessary journal entries in the books of AB Ltd for the following transactions :

(i) Issued 1,000, 12% debentures of ₹ 100 each at a discount of 6%, repayable at a premium of 6%.

(ii) Converted 100, 12% debentures of ₹ 100 each into 9% preference shares of ₹ 100 each issued at a premium of 25%.

(iii) Converted 100, 12% debentures of ₹ 100 each issued at a discount of 10% into equity shares of ₹ 10 each.

Solution

In the books of AB Ltd
Journal

Date	Particulars	L.F.	Dr. ₹	Cr. ₹
(i)	Bank A/c Dr. To Debentures Application A/c (Being application money received on 1,000 debentures @ ₹ 94 each)		94,000	94,000
	Debentures Application A/c Dr. Loss on Issue of Debentures A/c Dr. To 12% Debentures A/c To Premium on Redemption of Debentures A/c (Being the allotment of 1,000, 12% debentures of ₹ 100 each at a discount of 6% and redeemable at a premium of 6% as per Board's Resolution No. . . . dated . . .)		94,000 12,000	1,00,000 6,000
(ii)	12% Debentures A/c Dr. To 9% Preference Share Capital A/c (₹ 10,000/125 x 100) To Securities Premium A/c (₹ 10,000 / 125 x 25) (Being the conversion of 100, 12% debentures of ₹ 100 each into 9% preference shares of ₹ 100 each at a premium of 25% as per Board's Resolution No. . . . dated . . .)		10,000	8,000 2,000
(iii)	12% Debentures A/c Dr. To 12% Debentureholders A/c To Discount on Issue of Debentures A/c (Note 1) (Being the amount payable to debentureholders on conversion)		10,000	9,000 1,000

	Particulars	L.F.	Dr.	Cr.
	12% Debentureholders A/c Dr. To Equity Shares Capital A/c (Note 2) (Being the issue of 900 equity shares of ₹ 10 each to holders of 100 debentures as per Board's Resolution No. ... dated ...)		9,000	9,000

Working Notes :

(1) When debentures (which were issued at a discount) are to be converted into new shares, the amount to be converted will be equal to net proceeds received from the debentureholders, i.e., face value of debenture issued *less* discount on issue of debentures.

(2) Face value of debentures converted 10,000
Less : Discount allowed 10% 1,000
Net Proceeds received 9,000
Number of equity shares to be issued ₹ 9,000 / ₹ 10 = 900 shares.

Illustration 25

Magnificient Finance Ltd had issued 10,000, 12% debentures in 2007, each ₹ 100, interest payable on June 30 and December 31, every year, till the date of redemption.

It redeemed 1,000 debentures by paying back the money on 31st December, 2010. On the same date, it also converted 2,000 debentures into 19,800 equity shares of ₹ 10 each at par.

Give journal entries for recording these transactions on December 31, 2010 in the books of Magnificient Finance Ltd.

Solution

In the books of Magnificient Finance Ltd

Journal

Date	Particulars	L.F.	Dr. ₹	Cr. ₹
2010 Dec. 31	Debenture Interest A/c Dr. To Bank A/c (Being the debenture interest paid for 6 months ending on 31st December)		60,000	60,000
	12% Debentures A/c Dr. To Debentureholders A/c (Being the amount payable on redemption, transferred to Debentureholders' Account)		1,00,000	1,00,000
	Debentureholders A/c Dr. To Bank A/c (Being the amount paid to debentureholders on redemption)		1,00,000	1,00,000
	12% Debentures A/c Dr. To Equity Share Capital A/c (19,800 x ₹ 10) To Discount on Issue of Debentures A/c (Being the conversion of 2,000, 12% debentures of ₹ 100 each into 19,800 equity shares of ₹ 10 each at par as per Board's Resolution No... dated ...)		2,00,000	1,98,000 2,000
"	Statement of Profit and Loss Dr. To Debenture Interest A/c (Being the debenture interest for the whole year transferred to Statement of Profit and Loss)		1,20,000	1,20,000
"	Statement of Profit and Loss Dr. To General Reserve A/c (Being the amount equal to face value of debentures redeemed out of profit transferred to General Reserve)		1,00,000	1,00,000

Illustration 26

On 1st January, 2013, a company issued 1,000 12% debentures of ₹ 500 each at ₹ 450 each. Debentureholders were given an option to get their debentures converted into equity shares of ₹ 100 each at a premium of ₹ 50 per share.

On 31st December, 2013, one year's interest had accrued on these debentures, which was not paid. A holder of 100 debentures informed that he wanted to exercise the option of conversion of debentures into equity shares.

The company, therefore, accepted his request and redeemed these 100 debentures by issuing him equity shares.

The interest, however, on these 100 debentures was paid to the debentureholder.

Pass the necessary journal entries to record the above transactions in the books of the Company.

[CBSE — Adapted]

Solution

In the books of the Company

Journal

Date	Particulars		L.F.	Dr. ₹	Cr. ₹
2013 Jan. 1	Bank A/c	Dr.		4,50,000	
	To Debentures Application A/c				4,50,000
	(Being the application money received for 1,000 debentures @ ₹ 450 each)				
	Debentures Application A/c	Dr.		4,50,000	
	Discount on Issue of Debentures A/c	Dr.		50,000	
	To 12% Debentures A/c				5,00,000
	(Being the issue of 1,000, 12% debentures of ₹ 500 each at a discount of ₹ 50 as per Board's Resolution No. . . . dated . . .)				
Dec. 31	Debenture Interest A/c	Dr.		60,000	
	To Bank A/c				6,000
	To Outstanding Debenture Interest A/c				54,000
	(Being the debenture interest @ 12% p.a. for 1 year, but paid only in respect of 100 debentures)				
"	Statement of Profit and Loss	Dr.		60,000	
	To Debenture Interest A/c				60,000
	(Being the debenture interest for the whole year transferred to Statement of Profit and Loss)				
	12% Debentures A/c	Dr.		50,000	
	To Debentureholders A/c				45,000
	To Discount on Issue of Debentures A/c				5,000
	(Being the amount to be converted into equity shares after adjustment of discount on issue of debentures)				
"	Debentureholders A/c	Dr.		45,000	
	To Equity Share Capital A/c (Note 2)				30,000
	To Securities Premium A/c				15,000
	(Being 100, 12% debentures of ₹ 500 each, issued at discount of ₹ 50, converted into 300 equity shares of ₹ 100 each at a premium of ₹ 50 per share as per Board's Resolution No. . . . , dated . . .)				
"	Securities Premium A/c	Dr.		15,000	
	To Discount on Issue of Debentures A/c				15,000
	(Being the adjustment of Securities Premium Account against Discount on Issue of Shares Account)				

Working Notes :

(1) No entry for writing off discount on issue of debentures could be passed, for lack of information.

(2) Face value of debentures converted ₹ 50,000

Less : Discount allowed (100 × ₹ 50) 5,000

Net Proceeds received 45,000

Equity shares of ₹ 100 each is to be issued at a premium of ₹ 50 per share.

Therefore, number of equity shares to be issued = ₹ 45,000 / 150 = 300.

Illustration 27

On 1st January, 2012, a company issued 1,000, 12% debentures of ₹ 500 each at ₹ 450. Debentures are redeemable after 5 years. However, the company gave an option to debentureholders to get their debentures converted into equity shares of ₹ 100 each at a premium of ₹ 50 any time after the expiry of one year.

Reena, holder of 120 debentures, informed on January 1, 2013 that she wanted to exercise the option for conversion of debentures into equity shares. The company accepted her request and converted the debentures into shares.

Pass the necessary journal entries to record the above transactions in the books of the company for the year 2012 and 2013.

Give workings also. Ignore tax. *[CBSE — Adapted]*

Solution

In the books of the Company
Journal

Date	Particulars		L.F.	Dr. ₹	Cr. ₹
2012 Jan. 1	Bank A/c	Dr.		4,50,000	
	To Debentures Application A/c				4,50,000
	(Being the application money received for 1,000 debentures @ ₹ 450 each)				
	Debentures Application A/c	Dr.		4,50,000	
	Discount on Issue of Debentures A/c	Dr.		50,000	
	To 12% Debentures A/c				5,00,000
	(Being the issue of 1,000, 12% debentures of ₹ 500 each at a discount of ₹ 50 each as per Board's Resolution No. . . . dated . . .)				
Dec. 31	Debenture Interest A/c	Dr.		60,000	
	To Bank A/c				60,000
	(Being the debenture interest paid)				
"	Statement of Profit and Loss	Dr.		60,000	
	To Debenture Interest A/c				60,000
	(Being the debenture interest transferred to Statement of Profit and Loss)				
	Statement of Profit and Loss (Note 1)	Dr.		10,000	
	To Discount on Issue of Debentures A/c				10,000
	(Being ₹ 10,000 discount on issue of debentures written-off)				
2013 Jan. 1	12% Debentures A/c	Dr.		60,000	
	To 12% Debentureholder A/c (Note 3)				54,000
	To Discount on Issue of Debentures A/c				6,000
	(Being the amount payable to the holder of 120 debentures on conversion)				
"	12% Debentureholder A/c	Dr.		54,000	
	To Equity Share Capital A/c (Note 4)				36,000
	To Securities Premium A/c				18,000
	(Being the isuue of 360 equity shares of ₹ 100 at a premium of ₹ 50 per share to a holder of 120 debentures as per Board's Resolution No. . . dated ...)				

"	Securities Premium A/c Dr. To Discount on Issue of Debentures A/c (Being the premium adjusted against discount on issue of debentures)		18,000	18,000
Dec. 31	Debenture Interest A/c (Note 2) Dr. To Bank A/c (Being the debenture interest paid)		52,800	52,800
"	Statement of Profit and Loss Dr. To Debenture Interest A/c (Being the debenture interest transferred to Statement of Profit and Loss)		52,800	52,800
"	Statement of Profit and Loss (Note 5) Dr. To Discount on Issue of Debentures A/c (Being discount on issue of debentures written-off)		4,000	4,000

Working Notes :

(1) Total discount on issue of debentures is ₹ 50,000. Debentures are redeemable after 5 years. Therefore, 1/5th is to be written- off every year, i.e., ₹ 50,000 / 5 = ₹ 10,000.

(2) Debentures outstanding after conversion is ₹ 4,40,000. Interest on debentures = ₹ 4,40,000 × 12% = ₹ 52,800.

(3) When debentures (which were issued at a discount) are to be converted into new shares, the amount to be converted will be equal to net proceeds received from the debentureholders, i.e., face value of debentures issued, *less* discount on issue of debentures.

	₹
(4) Face value of debentures converted	60,000
Less : Discount allowed @ 10%	6,000
Net Proceeds received	54,000

Equity shares of ₹ 100 is to be issued at a premium of ₹ 50 each.
Therefore, number of equity shares to be issued = ₹ 54,000 / 150 = 360.

(5) Discount on Issue of Debentures to be written-off in 2013

	₹
Total discount on issue of debentures on 1.1.2012	50,000
Less : Amount written-off in 2012 (1/5th of ₹ 50,000)	10,000
	40,000
Less : Amount adjusted in respect of converted debentures	6,000
	34,000
Less : Adjustment of securities premium on conversion debentures	18,000
Amount to be written-off in 4 years (i.e., 2013 to 2016)	16,000

Therefore, in 2013 ₹ 4,000 (1/4th of ₹ 16,000) is to be written-off.

Creation of Debenture Redemption Reserve

As per the Rule 18 of The Companies (Share Capital and Debentures) Rules 2014], the company shall create a Debenture Redemption Reserve for the purpose of redemption of debentures, in accordance with the conditions given below-

(a) the Debenture Redemption Reserve shall be created out of the profits of the company ***available for payment of dividend***;

(b) the company shall create Debenture Redemption Reserve (DRR) in accordance with following conditions:-

(i) No DRR is required for debentures issued by All India Financial Institutions (AIFIs) regulated by Reserve Bank of India and Banking Companies for both public as well as privately placed debentures. For other Financial Institutions (FIs) within the meaning of clause (72) of section 2 of the Companies Act, 2013, DRR will be as applicable to NBFCs registered with RBI.

(ii) For NBFCs registered with the RBI under Section 45-IA of the RBI (Amendment) Act, 1997, 'the adequacy' of DRR will be 25% of the value of debentures issued through public issue as per present SEBI (Issue and Listing of Debt Securities) Regulations, 2008, and no DRR is required in the case of privately placed debentures.

(iii) For other companies including manufacturing and infrastructure companies, the adequacy of DRR will be 25% of the value of debentures issued through public issue as per present SEBI (Issue and Listing of Debt Securities), Regulations 2008 and also 25% DRR is required in the case of ***privately placed debentures by listed companies***. For unlisted companies issuing debentures on private placement basis, the DRR will be 25% of the value of debentures.

(c) every company required to create Debenture Redemption Reserve shall on or before the 30th day of April in each year, invest or deposit, as the case may be, a sum which shall not be less than fifteen percent, of the amount of its debentures maturing during the year ending on the 31st day of March of the next year, in any one or more of the following methods, namely;-

(i) in deposits with any scheduled bank, free from any charge or lien;

(ii) in unencumbered securities of the Central Government or of any State Government;

(iii) in unencumbered securities mentioned in sub-clauses (a) to (d) and (ee) of section 20 of the Indian Trusts Act, 1882;

(iv) in unencumbered bonds issued by any other company which is notified under sub-clause (f) of section 20 of the Indian Trusts Act, 1882;

(v) the amount invested or deposited as above shall not be used for any purpose other than for redemption of debentures maturing during the year referred above:

Provided that the amount remaining invested or deposited, as the case may be, shall not at any time fall below fifteen per cent of the amount of the debentures maturing during the year ending on the 31st day of March of that year;

(d) in case of partly convertible debentures, Debenture Redemption Reserve shall be created in respect of non-convertible portion of debenture issue in accordance with this sub-rule.

(e) the amount credited to the Debenture Redemption Reserve shall not be utilised by the company except for the purpose of redemption of debentures.

Points to be Noted

- ***No DRR is required for debentures issued by All India Financial Institutions (AIFI).***
- ***DRR to the extent of 25% of the value of Debentures issued to be creased by NBFCs registered with RBI. However, no DRR is required for privately placed debentures issued by the NBFCs.***
- ***All companies (except AIFI and NBFCs) will have to create DRR to the extent of 25% of the value of debentures issued.***

Chapter Summary

- Redemption of debentures is a process of repayment of loan taken by issue of debentures.
- Debentures can be redeemed by utilising any of the following sources :
  (a) From the proceeds of the fresh issue of share capital and debentures;
  (b) Out of profit.
- The **debentures can be redeemed** in one of the following four ways :
  (a) In lump sum at the end of the stipulated period;
  (b) By draw of lots;
  (c) By purchasing in the open market;
  (d) By conversion into new debentures or shares.
- After redemption of all the debentures, the balance of Debenture Redemption Reserve Account will be closed by transferring to General Reserve.
- Profit or loss on redemption of debentures arises only on cancellation or sale.
- A company may issue two types of convertible debentures :
  (i) Partly convertible debentures (PCD); and (ii) Fully convertible debentures (FCD)
- When the entire amount of the debenture is convertible, it is called a **fully convertible debenture**.
- When only a part of the debenture is convertible, it is called a **partly convertible debenture**.

THEORETICAL QUESTIONS

Multiple Choice

[1 Mark each]

Select the best choice to answer the following questions :

1. Profit on cancellation of debentures is transferred to
   A General Reserve Account
   B Securities Premium Reserve Account
   C capital Reserve Account
   D none of the above
2. Loss on cancellation of debentures is transferred to
   A General Reserve
   B Statement of Profit and Loss
   C Securities Premium
   D none of the above
3. When all debentures are redeemed, the balance of Debenture Rdemption Reserve is transferred to
   A Capital Reserve Account
   B General Reserve Account
   C Statement of Profit and Loss
   D none of the above

4. When own debentures are purchased for the purpose of investment, it is
   A credited to Debentures Account
   B debited to Debentured Account
   C debited to Own Debentures Account
   D credited to Own Debentures Account
5. Interest related to 'Investment in Own Debentures' is
   A debited to Statement of Profit and Loss
   B credited to Statement of Profit and Loss
   C credited to Debentures Account
   D none of the above
6. After providing for Debenture Redemption Reserve (DRR), the divisible profit
   A will remain same
   B will go up
   C will go down
   D none of the above
7. In case of partly convertible debentures, DRR shall be created in respect of
   A convertible portion of debentures
   B non-convertible portion of debentures
   C both convertible and non-convertible portions of debentures
   D none of the above
8. In the case of privately placed debentures
   A the DRR will be 25% of the value of debentures
   B no DRR is required
   C the DRR will be 50% of the value of debentures
   D none of the above
9. The Debenture Redemption Reserve shall be created
   A out of both capital and revenue profit of the company
   B out of profit of the company available for issue of bonus shares
   C out of profit of the company available for payment of dividend
   D none of the above
10. Debenture Redemption Reserve should be treated as part of
   A capital reserve
   B securities premium
   C general reserve
   D none of the above

Short Answer Questions : Type I

[3 Marks each]

1. What is convertible debenture ?
2. What are the various sources from which the debentures may be redeemed by a company ?
3. Enumerate and explain very briefly the various ways of redemption of debentures.
4. What do you mean by Redemption of Debentures ?
5. What do you mean by Redemption of Debentures out of profit ?

Short Answer Questions : Type II

[4 Marks each]

1. What do you mean by redemption of debentures ? What are the different sources of redemption of debentures ?
2. State the provision of Section 117C of The Companies (Amendment) Act, 2000 in respect of redemption of debentures.
3. State SEBI guidelines 2000 in respect of redemption of debentures.
4. How is premium on redemption of debenture shown in the Balance Sheet ? How is loss on issue of debentures shown in the Balance Sheet as per Revised Schedule - VI ?

PRACTICAL QUESTIONS

Redemption of Debenture — Payment in Lumpsum

1. X Ltd issues 20,000 debentures of ₹ 100 each at a discount of 10% with the condition that they will be redeemed at a premium of 5% after the expiry of three years.
   Pass the necessary journal entries for the issue and redemption of these debentures after the expiry of three years.
2. B Ltd issued 10,000 debntures of ₹ 100 each at a discount of 10% on the condition that the same will be redeemed at a premium of 10% after two years.
   Pass the necessary journal entries for the issue and redemption of these debentures after the expiry of two years.
3. P Ltd issues 7,000 debentures of ₹ 100 each at a discount of 10% with the condition that these will be redeemed at a premium of 5% after the expiry of three years.
   Pass the necessary journal entries for the issue and the redemption of these debentures after the expiry of three years.

Redemption of Debentures — Out of Profit

4. A company made an issue of 1,000, 15% debentures of ₹ 100 each. Of these, debentures of the face value of ₹ 10,000 are to be redeemed annually commencing from 2012, either by drawings at par or by purchase in the market at the company's option.
   During 2015, the company purchased for cancellation ₹ 6,000 debentures at ₹ 95 and ₹ 4,000 debentures at ₹ 98. The expenses of purchase amounted to ₹ 50. The Board of Directors decided to redeem debentures out of profits but without building up a sinking fund. Record the above transactions in company's ledger.
5. A Limited issues 10,000, 14% debentures of ₹ 100 each at par on January 1, 2013. Under the terms of issue (a) debentures interest is annually payable on 31st December every year, and (b) one-fifth of the debentures are annually redeemable by drawings, the first redemption occurring on 31st December, 2015.
   Pass necessary journal entries upto 31st December, 2015, asuming that
   (i) the company's accounting date to 31st December;
   (ii) all the terms of the debenture issue are compiled with; and
   (iii) adequate amount is transferred to Debenture Redemption Reserve Account every year.

Redemption of Debentures — Purchase from Open Market

6. On 1st January, 2014 a company made an issue of 5,000, 5% debentures of ₹ 100 each at ₹ 94 per debenture. The terms of issue provided for redemption of ₹ 20,000 debentures every year commencing from 2015 either by purchase or by drawing at par at the company's option. ₹ 5,000 was written-off the Debenture Discount Account in 2014 and 2015. During the year 2015, the company purchased for cancellation debentures of the face value of ₹ 6,000 at ₹ 94 per debenture and ₹ 14,000 at ₹ 92 per debenture. Pass journal entries recording issue and redemption.

7. On 1st January, 2014, a company made an issue of 10,000, 6% debentures of ₹ 100 each at ₹ 96 per debenture. The terms of issue provided for the redemption of ₹ 20,000 debentures every year commencing from 2015 either by purchase or by drawings at par at the companies' option. ₹ 10,000 was also written-off the Debenture Discount Account in each of the year 2014 and 2015. During 2015, the company purchased for cancellation debentures of the face value of ₹ 8,000 at ₹ 95 per debenture and of ₹ 12,000 at ₹ 90 per debenture.
   Journalise the above transactions and show how the profits on redemption would be treated.

8. Sure Limited made an issue of 10,000, 12% debentures of ₹ 100 each on 1.1.2013 at the issue price of ₹ 96. The terms of issue provided that begining with 2010, ₹ 40,000 debentures should be redeemed either by purchase in the market or by a lot at par. The expenses of the issue amounted to ₹ 8,000 which were written-off in 2013. In 2014 and 2015, the discount on issue of debentures were written-off equally. On 31st December, 2010 the debentures necessarily to be redeemed were purchased from the market @ ₹ 98 each. Assuming that the interest is payable on 30th June and 31st December every year. Pass necessary journal entries to record the above transactions.

Convertible Debentures

9. On 1.1.2014 Jamurki Ltd issued 2,000, 15% debentures of ₹ 100 each at 5% discount. Holders of these debentures have an option to convert their holdings into 18% preference shares of ₹ 100 each at ₹ 125 at any time within 3 years.
   On 31.12.2014 yearly interest had accrued on the debentures and remained outstanding and a holder of 500 debentures notified his decision to exercise his option. Pass the necessary journal entries.

10. X Limited had 4,800, 12% Convertible Debentures of ₹ 100 each. On 1.4.2010 the company according to the power of articles, made a notice for getting one of the following options to the debentureholders :
    (i) 10% Cumulative Preference Shares at a premium of 10% of ₹ 100 each; (ii) New 12% Debentures at ₹ 100 each at a discount of 10%; (iii) cash at par value. Debentureholders holding 2,200 debentures took the first option, 1,800 debentureholders the second option and the balance third option. Show journal entries to record the above transactions.

11. Tata Press Limited made a public issue of 15% Partly Convertible Debentures (PCD) of ₹ 150 each for cash at par aggregating ₹ 300 lakhs. Issue opened on 1st June, 2014; issue closed on 15th June. Allotment made on 1st July, 2014.
    Principal terms of PCD :
    1. Entire amount is payable on application.

2. Each PCD will have a face value of ₹ 150 and shall consist of two parts—
   Part A : Convertible portion of ₹ 50.
   Part B : Non-convertible portion of ₹ 100.
3. Part A of each PCD will be automatically converted into 5 equity shares of ₹ 10 each at par on 31st December, 2014.
4. Part B of each PCD will be non-convertible.

Interest on all debentures were paid upto 31st December, 2014. You are required to pass necessary journal entries assuming that the accounting year closes on 31st December, every year.

12. Pass necessary journal entries for the following transactions in the books of Jay Ltd. :
    (i) Redeemed 1,500, 9% Debentures of ₹ 150 each by converting into equity shares of ₹ 10 each. The equity shares were issued at a discount of 10%.
    (ii) Converted 1,100, 8% Debentures of ₹ 1,000 each into 12% New Debentures of ₹ 100 each. The new Debentures were issued at a premium of 10%.

GUIDE TO ANSWERS

Multiple Choice

1. C **2.** B **3.** B **4.** C **5.** B **6.** C **7.** B **8.** A **9.** C **10.** A

Practical Questions

4. Profit on redemption ₹ 330.
6. Profit on cancellation of debentures ₹ 1,480.
7. Profit on cancellation of debentures ₹ 1,600 (₹ 400 + ₹ 1,200).
8. Profit on cancellation of debentures ₹ 800.
9. Discount on issue of debentures ₹ 10,000; Number of equity shares issued 380 at a premium of ₹ 25 each for conversion of 500 debentures of ₹ 100 each issued at a discount of 5%.
10. (i) 10% Cumulative Preference Shares issued 2,000.
    (ii) New 12% Debentures issued 2,000.
    (iii) Cash paid ₹ 80,000.
11. Debenture interest paid upto 31st December ₹ 22,50,000.

15% Partly Convertible Debentures Account	Dr.	₹ 100,00,000	
To Equity Share Capital Account			₹ 100,00,000

CBSE Accountancy — 2014 (Delhi)

Time allowed : 3 hours | **Maximum marks : 80**

General Instructions

(i) This Question Paper contains three parts : A, B and C.

(ii) Part A is compulsory for all candidates.

(iii) Candidates can attempt only one part of the remaining parts B and C.

Set 1

Part A

ACCOUNTING FOR PARTNERSHIP FIRMS AND COMPANIES

Q.1. What is meant by 'Reconstitution of a Partnership Firm' ? ***1***

Answer

When there is a change in the profit-sharing ratio between the existing partners or there is a change in composition of partners due to admission or retirement or death of a partner, it is called 'Reconstitution of a Partnership Firm'. The existing agreement is replaced by the new agreement between the partners.

Q.2. X, Y and Z are partners sharing profits in the ratio of 1/2, 2/5 and 1/10. Find the new ratio of remaining partners if Z retires. ***1***

Answer

At present, X, Y and Z are sharing profits and losses in the ratio of 1/2, 2/5 and 1/10 or $\frac{5}{10}, \frac{4}{10}$ and $\frac{1}{10}$. *After Z's retirement, the profit-sharing ratio of X and Y will be 5 : 4.*

Points to be Noted

If nothing is mentioned, the continuing partners will share the profits and losses in future in the old ratio only.

Q.3. Distinguish between 'Dissolution of Partnership' and 'Dissolution of Partnership Firm' on the basis of closure of books. ***1***

Answer

The distinction between Dissolution of the Partnership and Dissolution of the Firm are given below:

Sl. No.	Dissolution of the Partnership	Sl. No.	Dissolution of the PartneshipFirm
1.	A partnership is dissolved when a new partner is admitted or an old partner retires or dies.	1.	A firm is dissolved by the partners mutually or by the Court.
2.	The dissolution of the partnership does not necessarily mean the termination of the business of the partnership.	2.	The dissolution of the partnership firm means the termination of partnership business.
3.	The dissolution of the partnership will not lead to disposal of assets of the firm and settlement of liabilities of the third parties.	3.	The dissolution of the partnership firm will lead to disposal of partnership assets and settlement of liabilities of the third parties as well as of the partners.
4.	The dissolution of a partnership will create a new partnership.	4.	The dissolution of a partnership firm will not create a new partnership.

Q.4. Why are heirs of a retiring / deceased partner entitled to a share of goodwill of the firm ? *1*

Answer

The retiring partner(s) / heir(s) of deceased partners are entitled to get the share of goodwill because it is a common property of all the partners. The retiring partner(s) / heir(s) of deceased partner will not continue as partner in future. Therefore, they must be compensated for goodwill.

Q.5. Give the meaning of 'Debenture'. *1*

Answer

Debenture is a certificate issued by the company, stamped with official seal, which contains the details of an interest-bearing loan made by the company on long term basis.

It is a document which either creates a debt or acknowledges it. Debentures include stock, bonds and any other securities of the company, which may or may not contain a charge on the assets of the company.

Q.6. What is the maximum amount of discount at which forfeited shares can be re-issued ? *1*

Answer

The discount on re-issue of shares can not exceed the amount forfeited in respect of those shares.

For example : Issue price = ₹ 10, amount paid = ₹ 6. Final call ₹ 4 was not paid. The shares were forfeited. At the time of re-issue maximum discount cannot exceed ₹ 6 — the forfeited amount.

Q.7. Give any one purpose for which the amount receied as 'Securities Premium' may be utilised. *1*

Answer

Securities premium may be utilised for :

(i) issuing full paid-up bonus shares

(ii) payment of premium on buy-back of shares.

Q.8. Saloni and Shrishti were partners in a firm sharing profits in the ratio of 7 : 3. Their capitals were ₹ 2,00,000 and ₹ 1,50,000 respectively. They admitted Aditi on 1st April, 2013 as a new partner for 1/6th share in future profits. Aditi brought ₹ 1,00,000 as her capital. Calculate the value of goodwill of the firm and record necessary journal entry for the above transaction on Aditiri's admission. *3*

Answer

Total capital of the firm based on Aditi's share of profit:

Aditi's share of profit = 1/6. Capital brought-in by her = ₹ 1,00,000. Therefore, total capital of the firm = ₹ 1,00,000 × 6/1 = ₹ 6,00,000.

Combined capital of Saloni and Shrishti = ₹ **6,00,000** × 5/6 (1 – 1/6) = ₹ **5,00,000.**

Goodwill = New combined capital – Old combined capital
= ₹ 5,00,000 – (2,00,000 + 1,50,000)
= ₹ 5,00,000 – 3,50,000
= ₹ **1,50,000**

In the books of the firm

Journal

Date	Particulars		L.F.	Dr. ₹	Cr. ₹
2013 April 1	Bank / Cash A/c	Dr.		1,00,000	
	To Aditi's Capital A/c				1,00,000
	(Being capital brought-in by Aditi)				
	Goodwill A/c	Dr.		1,50,000	
	To Saloni Capital A/c				1,05,000
	To Shristi Capital A/c				45,000
	(Being goodwill raised in the books of accounts in old ratio 7 : 3)				
	Saloni Capital A/c	Dr.		87,500	
	Shristi Capital A/c	Dr.		37,500	
	Aditi Capital A/c	Dr.		25,000	
	To Goodwill A/c				1,50,000
	(Being goodwill written-off in the new ratio, 7 : 3 : 2- Note 1)				

Working Notes :

(1) Calculation of New Profit Sharing-ratio :

Saloni's share of profit = 5/6 × 7/10 = 35/60
Shristi's share of profit = 5/6 × 3/10 = 15/60
Aditi's share of profit = 1/6 = 10/60
Therefore, new profit sharing ratio = 35 : 15 : 10 or 7 : 3 : 2.

Q.9. BG Ltd. issued 2,000, 12% debentures of ₹ 100 each on 1st April, 2012. The issue was fully subscribed. According to the terms of issue, interest on the debentures is payable half-yearly on 30th September and 31st March and the tax deducted at source is 10%. Pass necessary journal entries related to the debenture interest for the half-yearly ending 31st March, 2013 and transfer of interest on debentures of the year to the Statement of Profit and Loss. **3**

Answer

In the books of BG Ltd.

Journal

Date	Particulars		L.F.	Dr. ₹	Cr. ₹
2013 March, 31	Interest on Debentures A/c	Dr.		12,000	
	To Debentureholders A/c				10,800
	To Tax Deducted at Source A/c				1,200
	(Being the interest payable for 6 months on ₹ 2,00,000 @ 12%)				
	Debentureholders A/c	Dr.		10,800	
	To Bank A/c				10,800
	(Being the interest on debentures paid after TDS of ₹ 1,200)				

Particulars		Dr. ₹	Cr. ₹
Tax Deducted at Source A/c Dr. To Bank A/c (Being the amount deposited in Government Account in respect of TDS)		1,200	1,200
Statement of Profit and Loss A/c Dr. To Interest on Debentures A/c (Being the interest on debentures of ₹ 2,00,000 @ 12% for full year charged to Statement of Profit and Loss)		24,000	24,000

Q.10. Not in Syllabus.

Q.11. Satnam and Qureshi after doing their MBA decided to start a partnership firm to manufacture ISI marked electronic goods for economically weaker section of the society. Satnam also expressed his willingness to admit Juliee as a partner without capital who is specially abled but a very creative and intelligent friend of his. Qureshi agreed to this. They formed a partnership on 1st April, 2012 on the following terms :

(i) Satnam will contribute ₹ 4,00,000 and Qureshi will contribute ₹ 2,00,000 as capitals.

(ii) Satnam, Qureshi and Juliee will share profits in the ratio of 2 : 2 : 1.

(iii) Interest on capital will be allowed @ 6% p.a.

Due to shortage of capital Satnam contributed ₹ 50,000 on 30th September, 2012 and Qureshi contributed ₹ 20,000 on 1st January, 2013 as adiditional capitals. The profit of the firm for the year ended 31st March, 2013 was ₹ 3,37,800.

(i) Identify any two values which the firm wants to communicate to the society.

(ii) Prepare Profit & Loss Appropriation Account for the year ending 31st March, 2013. 4

Answer

(i) The values that the firm wants to communicate to the Society are :

(a) Encourage differently-abled person to become entrepreneur and contribute to the Society.

(b) Manufacture quality products to get ISI mark. Manufacture only safe electronic products.

(ii)

Satnam, Qureshi and Juliee

Dr. Profit and Loss Appropriation Account for the year ended 31st March, 2013 Cr.

Particulars		₹	Particulars	₹
To Interest on Capital :			By Profit and Loss A/c — Net Profit	3,37,800
Satnam (Note 1)	25,500			
Qureshi (Note 1)	12,300	37,800		
To Partners' Capital / Current A/cs :				
Satnam	1,20,000			
Qureshi	1,20,000			
Juliee	60,000	3,00,000		
		3,37,800		3,37,800

Working Notes :

(1) Calculation of Interest on Capital : ₹

Satnam :

	₹
On ₹ 4,00,000 @ 6% for one year	24,000
On ₹ 50,000 @ 6% for 1/2 year	1,500
	25,500

Qureshi :

	₹
On ₹ 2,00,000 @ ₹ 6% for one year	12,000
On ₹ 20,000 @ ₹ 6% for 1/4th year	300
	12,300

Q.12. Virad, Vishad and Roma were partners in a firm sharing profits in the ratio of 5 : 3 : 2 respectively. On March 31, 2013 their Balance Sheet was as under :

Liabilities		₹	Assets	₹
Capitals :			Buildings	2,00,000
Virad	3,00,000		Machinery	3,00,000
Vishad	2,50,000		Patents	1,10,000
Roma	1,50,000	7,00,000	Stock	1,00,000
Reserve Fund		60,000	Debtors	80,000
Creditors		1,10,000	Cash	80,000
		8,70,000		8,70,000

Virad died on October 1, 2013. It was agreed between his executors and the remaining partners that :

(i) Goodwill of the firm be valued at $2^1/_2$ years' purchase of average profits for the last three years. The average profits were ₹ 1,50,000.

(ii) Interest on capital be provided at 10% p.a.

(iii) Profit for the year 2013-14 be taken as having accrued at the same rate as that of the previous year which was ₹ 1,50,000.

Prepare Virad's Capital Account to be presented to his Executors as on October 1, 2013. **4**

Answer

In the books of the Firm

Dr. Virad Capital Account Cr.

Date	Particulars	₹	Date	Particulars	₹
	To Virad's Executors A/c	5,52,500	2013		
			April 1	By Balance b/d	3,00,000
			Oct 1	By Reserve Fund A/c (Note 1)	30,000
				By Interest on Capital A/c (Note 3)	15,000
				By Vishad Capital A/c (Note 2)	1,12,500
				By Roma Capital A/c (Note 2)	75,000
				By Profit and Loss Suspense A/c (Note 4)	20,000
		5,52,500			5,52,500

Working Notes :

(1) Reserve Fund will be distributed in the profit-sharing ratio, i.e., 5 : 3 : 2. Virad's share of Reserve Fund = ₹ 60,000 × 5/10 = ₹ 30,000.

(2) Valuation of Goodwill :

Goodwill = 2.5 × ₹ 1,50,000 = ₹ 3,75,000.

Particulars	Virad (₹)	Vishad (₹)	Roma (₹)
Right of goodwill before death (5 : 3 : 2)	1,87,500	1,12,500	75,000
Right of goodwill after death (3 : 2)	—	2,25,000	1,50,000
(Sacrifice) / Gain	(-)1,87,500 (Cr.)	(+)1,12,500 (Dr.)	(+) 75,000 (Dr.)

(3) Calculation of Interest on Capital :

Virad's Capital = ₹ 3,00,000. Interest is payable @ 10% p.a.

Therefore, Interest = ₹ 3,00,000 × 10% × 6/12 = ₹ **15,000.**

(4) Calculation of Virad's Share of Profit :

Average Profit = ₹ 1,50,000 for the year 2012-13.

Average Profit of 6 months (1.4.2013 to 30.9.2013) = ₹ 75,000 (1/2 of ₹ 1,50,000).

Average Profit of the Firm:	75,000
Less: Interest on Capital of all partners for 6 months (₹ 7,00,000 × 10% × 1/2)	35,000
Divisible Profit	40,000

Virad's share of profit = 5/10 of ₹ 40,000 = ₹ **20,000.**

Q.13 On 1st April, 2012 Vivek Ltd. was formed with an aiuthorised capital of ₹ 1,00,00,000 divided into 2,00,000 equity shares of ₹ 50 each. The company issued prospectus inviting applications for 1,80,000 shares. The issue price was payable as under :

On Application : ₹ 15

On Allotment : ₹ 20

On Call : balance amount

The issue was fully subscribed and the company allotted shares to all the applicants. The company did not make the call during the year.

Show the following :

(a) Share capital in the Balance Sheet of the company as per revised Schedule - VI – Part-I of the Companies Act, 1956.

(b) Also prepare 'Notes to Accounts' for the same. **4**

Answer

Vivek Ltd.
Balance Sheet as at 31st March, 2013

I. Equity and Liabilities	Note No.	₹
(a) Shareholders' Fund :		
(i) Share Capital	(1)	63,00,000

Notes to Accounts	₹
Share Capital	
Authorised Capital :	
2,00,000 Equity Shares of ₹ 50 each	1,00,00,000
Issued Capital :	
1,80,000 Equity Shares of ₹ 50 each	90,00,000
Subscribed Capital :	
Subscribed but not fully paid :	
1,80,000 Equity Shares of ₹ 50 each, 35 called-up and paid in full	63,00,000

Q.14. Pass necessary journal entries for the following transactions in the books of Rajan Ltd. : **4**

(a) Rajan Ltd. purchased machinery of ₹ 7,20,000 from Kundan Ltd. The payment was made to Kundan Ltd. by issue of equity shares of 100 each at 10% discount.

(b) Rajan Ltd. purchased a running business from Vikas Ltd. for a sum of ₹ 2,50,000 payable as ₹ 2,20,000 in fully paid equity shares of ₹ 10 each and balance by a bank draft. the assets and liabilities consisted of the following :

Plant and Machinery ₹ 90,000; Building ₹ 90,000; Sundry Debtors ₹ 30,000; Stock ₹ 50,000; Cash ₹ 20,000; Sundry Creditors ₹ 20,000.

Answer

In the books of Rajan Ltd.
Journal

Date	Particulars		L.F.	Dr. ₹	Cr. ₹
(a)	Machinery A/c	Dr.		7,20,000	
	To Kundan Ltd. A/c				7,20,000
	(Being purchase of machinery from Kundan Ltd.)				
	Kundan Ltd. A/c	Dr.		7,20,000	
	Discount on Issue of Shares A/c	Dr.		80,000	
	To Equity Share Capital A/c				8,00,000
	(Being the issue of 8,000 equity shares of ₹ 100 each at 10% discount for purchase of machinery as per Board's Resolution No. ... dated ...)				
(b)	Plant and Machinery A/c	Dr.		90,000	
	Building A/c	Dr.		90,000	
	Sundry Debtors A/c	Dr.		30,000	
	Stock A/c	Dr.		50,000	
	Cash A/c	Dr.		20,000	
	To Sundry Creditors A/c				20,000
	To Liquidators of Vikas Ltd. A/c				2,50,000
	To Capital Reserve A/c (Note 1)				10,000
	(Being the acquisition of different assets and liabilities of Vikas Ltd.)				
	Liquidators of Vikas Ltd. A/c	Dr.		2,50,000	
	To Equity Share Capital A/c				2,20,000
	To Bank A/c				30,000
	(Being the purchase consideration paid by issuing 22,000 equity shares of ₹ 10 each at par and the balance by bank draft)				

Q.15. Naveen, Seerat and Hina were partners in a firm manufacturing blankets. They were sharing profits in the ratio of 5 : 3 : 2. Their capitals on 1st April, 2012 were ₹ 2,00,000, ₹ 3,00,000 and ₹ 6,00,000 respectivley. After the floods in Uttarakhand all partners decided to help the flood victims personally.

For this Naveen withdrew ₹ 10,000 from the firm on 1st September, 2012. Seerat instead of withdrawing cash from the firm took blankets amounting to ₹ 12,000 from the firm and distributed to the flood victims. On the other hand, Hina withdrew ₹ 2,00,000 from her capital on 1st January, 2013 and set up a centre to provide medical facilities in the flood affected area.

The partnership deed provides for charging interest on drawings @ 6% p.a. After the Final Accounts were prepared, it was discovered that interest on drawings had not been charged. Give the necessary adjusting journal entry and show the workings clearly.

Also state any two values that the partners wanted to communicate to the society. **6**

Answer

Calculation of Interest on Drawings :

Naveen's drawing = ₹ 10,000.

Interest on drawings = ₹ 10,000 × 6/100 × 7/12 (for 7 months) = ₹ 350.

Seerat's drawings = ₹ 12,000.

Interest on drawings = ₹ 12,000 × 6/100 × 6/12 (Note 1) = ₹ 360

Hina's drawings is Nil. She has withdrawn her capital. Therefore, the question of interest on drawings does not arise.

Working Notes :

(1) Date of withdrawal of blanket has not been given. Therefore, interest has been charged for 6 months.

Total interest on drawings = ₹ 350 + ₹ 360 = ₹ 710.

It is the income of the firm. Therefore, it is to be distributed among the partners in the profit-sharing ratio, i.e., 5 : 3 : 2.

The share of interest on drawings will be :

Naveen : 5/10 × 7/10	355
Seerat : 3/10 × 7/10	213
Hina : 2/10 × 7/10	142
	710

Statement Showing the Adjustment for Interest on Capital

Particulars	Naveen (₹)	Seerat (₹)	Hina (₹)
Interest on Drawings to be charged (debited)	350	360	Nil
Interest on Drawings to be credited (share)	355	213	142
	5 (Cr.)	147 (Dr.)	142 (Cr.)

Journal

Date	Particulars	L.F.	Dr. ₹	Cr. ₹
	Seerat Capital A/c Dr.		147	
	To Naveen Capital A/c			5
	To Hina Capital A/c			142
	(Being the necessary adjustment for interest on Drawings)			

The partners wanted to communicate the values :

(i) Contribute generously to help the victims of natural calamity.

(ii) Discourage division of society on the basis of religion / caste / colour, etc. Secular face of the firm has been demonstrated.

Q.16. Shanti and Satya were partners in a firm sharing profits in the ratio of 4 : 1. On 31st March, 2013 their Balance Sheet was as follows :

Balance Sheet of Shanti and Satya as on 31st March, 2013

Liabilities	₹	Assets	₹
Creditors	45,000	Bank	55,000
Workmen's Compensation Fund	40,000	Debtors	60,000
Satya's Current Account	65,000	Stock	85,000
Capitsl :		Furniture	1,00,000
Shanti	2,00,000	Machinery	1,30,000
Satya	1,00,000	Shanti's Current Account	20,000
	4,50,000		4,50,000

On the above date the firm was dissolved :

(i) Shanti took over 40% of the stock at 10% less than its book value and the remaining stock was sold for ₹ 40,000. Furniture realised ₹ 80,000.

(ii) An unrecorded investment was sold for ₹ 20,000. Machinery was sold at a loss of ₹ 60,000.

(iii) Debtors realised ₹ 55,000.

(iv) There was an outstanding bill for repairs for which ₹ 19,000 were paid.

Prepare Realisation Account

Answer

In the books of the Firm
Realisation Account

Dr. Cr.

Date	Particulars	₹	Date	Particulars	₹
2013			2013		
March 31	To Debtors A/c	60,000	March 31	By Creditors A/c	45,000
	To Stock A/c	85,000		By Bank A/c (Assets realised) :	
	,To Furniture A/c	1,00,000		Stock	40,000
	To Machinery A/c	1,30,000		Furniture	80,000
	To Bank A/c (Payment) :			Investment	20,000
	Creditors	45,000		Machinery (1,30,000 -60,000)	70,000
	Outstanding Expenses	19,000		Debtors	55,000
				By Shanti Capital A/c (Assets taken over) (85,000 x 40% x 30%)	30,600
				By Partners Capital A/cs :	
				Shanti	78,720
				Satya (Note 3)	19,680
		4,39,000			4,39,000

Turotial Notes :

(1) Bank balance will not be transferred to Realisation Account.

(2) Workmen's compensation fund will be credited to Partners' Capital Accounts in the profit-sharing ratio.

(3) Loss on realistion ₹ 98,400 will be shared by Shanti and Satya in the ratio of 4 : 1. Shanti's share of loss = ₹ 98,400 × 4/5 = ₹ **78,720**; Satya's share of loss = 1/5 of ₹ 98,400 = ₹ **19,680.**

Q.17. Mohan and Mahesh were partners in a firm sharing profits in the ratio of 3 : 2. On 1st April, 2012 they admitted Nusrat as a partner in the firm. the Balance Sheet of Mohan and Mahesh on that date was as under :

Balance Sheet of Mohan and Mahesh as on 1st April, 2012

Liabilities		₹	Assets	₹
Creidtors		2,10,000	Cash in Hand	1,40,000
Workmen's Compensation Fund		2,50,000	Debtors	1,60,000
General Reserve		1,60,000	Stock	1,20,000
Mohan	1,00,000		Machinery	1,00,000
Mahesh	80,000	1,80,000	Building	2,80,000
		8,00,000		8,00,000

It was agreed that :

(i) The value of Building and Stock be appreciated to ₹ 3,80,000 and ₹ 1,60,000 respectively.

(ii) The liabilities of workmen's compensation fund was determined at ₹ 2,30,000.

(iii) Nusrat brought in her share of goodwill ₹ 1,00,000 in cash.

(iv) Nusrat was to bring further cash as would make her capital equal to 20% of the combined capital of Mohan and Mahesh after above revaluation and ajdustments are carried out.

(v) The future profit sharing ratio will be Mohan 2/5, Maesh 2/5 and Nusrat 1/5.

Prepare Revaluation Account, Partners' Capital Accounts and Balance Sheet of the new firm. Also show clearly the calculation of Capital brought in by Nusrat.

Answer

In the books of the Firm

Realisation Account

Dr. Cr.

Date	Particulars	₹	Date	Particulars	₹
2012 April 1	To Partners' Capital A/cs :		2012 April 1	By Stock A/c	40,000
	Mohan (3/5 of ₹ 1,40,000)	84,000		By Building A/c	1,00,000
	Mahesh : (2/5 of ₹ 1,40,000)	56,000			
		1,40,000			1,40,000

Partners' Capital Accounts

Dr. Cr.

Particulars	Mohan (₹0	Mahesh (₹)	Nusrat (₹)	Particulars	Mohan (₹)	Mahesh (₹)	Nusrat (₹)
To Balance c/d	3,92,000	2,08,000	1,20,000	By Balance b/d	1,00,000	80,000	—
				By Bank A/c (Note 4)	—	—	1,20,000
				By General Reserve A/c (Note 1)	96,000	64,000	—
				By Workmen Compensation Fund A/c (Note 2)	12,000	8,000	—
				By Revaluation A/c	84,000	56,000	—
				By Premium for Goodwill A/c (Note 3)	1,00,000	—	—
	3,92,000	2,08,000	1,20,000		3,92,000	2,08,000	1,20,000

Balance Sheet as at 1st April, 2012

Liabilities	₹	Assets	₹
Partners' Capital A/cs :		Building	3,80,000
Mohan	3,92,000	Machinery	1,00,000
Mahesh	2,08,000	Debtors	1,60,000
Nusrat	1,20,000	Stock	1,60,000
Creditors	2,10,000	Cash in Hand (Note 5)	3,60,000
Workmen Compensation Fund	2,30,000		
	11,60,000		11,60,000

Working Notes :

(1) General Reserve of ₹ 1,60,000 will be distributed between the old partners in the old ratio :

Mohan's share : 3/5 of ₹ 1,60,000 = ₹ 96,000

Mahesh's share : 2/5 of ₹ 1,60,000 = ₹ 64,000.

(2) After providing workmen compensation of ₹ 2,30,000, the balance ₹ 20,000 (2,50,000 – 2,30,000), will be shared by old partners in the old ratio :

Mohan's share = 3/5 of ₹ 20,000 = ₹ 12,000.

Mahesh's share = 2/5 of ₹ 20,000 = ₹ 8,000.

(3) **Adjustment for Goodwill :**

Particulars	Mohan (₹)	Mahesh (₹)	Nusrat (₹)
Right of goodwill before admission (3 : 2 : 0)	*3,00,000	*2,00,000	—
Right of goodwill after admission (2 : 2 : 1)	2,00,000	2,00,000	1,00,000
	1,00,000 (Sacrifice)	—	1,00,000 (Gain)

* Total value of Goodwill = ₹ 1,00,000 × 5/1 = ₹ **5,00,000.**

The amount of ₹ 1,00,000 brought-in by Nusrat will be credited to Mohan in full as Mahesh is not sacrificing anything.

(4) Calculation of Capital to be brought-in by Nusrat :

	₹
Combined Capital of Mohan and Mahesh	1,80,000
Add : Premium for Goodwill	1,00,000
Add : General Reserve	1,60,000
Add : Surplus of Workmen Compensation	20,000
Add : Revaluation Profit	1,40,000
	6,00,000

Nusrat will bring 20% of ₹ 6,00,000 = ₹ **1,20,000.**

(5) Cash after Admission

	₹
Opening balance	1,40,000
Add : Goodwill Premium	1,00,000
Add : Capital brought-in by Nusrat	1,20,000
	3,60,000

OR

Kushal, Kumar and Kavita were partners in a firm sharing profits in the ratio of 3 : 1 : 1. On 1st April, 2012 their Balance Sheet was as follows :

Balance Sheet of Kushal, Kumar and Kavita as on 1st April, 2012

Liabilities		₹	Assets		₹
Creditors		1,20,000	Cash		
Bills Payable		1,80,000	Debtors	2,00,000	
General Reserve		1,20,000	Less: Provision	10,000	
Capitals :			Stock		
Kushal	3,00,000		Furniture		
Kumar	2,80,000		Building		
Kavita	3,00,000	8,80,000	Land		
		13,00,000			13,00,000

On the above date, Kavita retired and the following was agreed :

(i) Goodwill of the firm was valued at ₹ 40,000.

(ii) Land was to be appreciated by 30% and building was to be depreciated by ₹ 1,00,000.

(iii) Value of furniture was to be reduced by ₹ 20,000.

(iv) Bad debts reserve is to be increased to ₹ 15,000.

(v) 10% of the amount payable to Kavita was paid in cash and the balance was transferred to her Loan Account.

(vi) Capitals of Kushal and Kumar will be in proportion to their new profit sharing ratio. The surplus / deficit, if any, in their Capital Accounts will be adjusted through Current Accounts.

Prepare Revaluation Account, Partners' Capital Accounts and Balance Sheet of Kushal and Kumar after Kvita's retirement.

Answer

In the books of the Firm

Revaluation Account

Dr. **Cr.**

Date	Particulars	₹	Date	Particulars	₹
	To Building A/c	1,00,000		By Land A/c	1,20,000
	To Furniture A/c	20,000		By Partners' Capital A/cs (Loss on Revaluation)	

To Bad Debts Reserve A/c	5,000	Kushal (3/5 of ₹ 5,000) Kumar (1/5 of ₹ 5,000) Kavita (1/5 of ₹ 5,000)	3,000 1,000 1,000
	1,25,000		1,25,000

Dr. **Partners' Capital Accounts** **Cr.**

Particulars	Kushal (₹0	Kumar (₹)	Kavita (₹)	Particulars	Kushal (₹)	Kumar (₹)	Kavita (₹)
To Revaluation A/c	3,000	1,000	1,000	By Balance b/d	3,00,000	2,80,000	3,00,000
To Kavita Capital A/c (Note 1)	6,000	2,000	—	By Kushal Capital A/c	—	—	6,000
To Cash A/c				By Kumar Capital A/c (Note 1)	—	—	2,000
(10% of amount due)	—	—	33,100	By General Reserve A/c	72,000	24,000	24,000
To Kavita Loan A/c	—	—	2,97,900				
To Balance c/d	3,63,000	3,01,000	—				
	3,72,000	3,04,000	3,32,000		3,72,000	3,04,000	3,32,000
To Kumar Current A/c (Note 2)	—	1,35,000	—	By Balance b/d	3,63,000	3,01,000	—
To Balance c/d	4,98,000	1,66,000	—	By Kushal Current A/c (Note 2)	1,35,000	—	—
	4,98,000	3,01,000	—		4,98,000	3,01,000	—

Kushal and Kumar
Balanec Sheet as at 1st April, 2012

Liabilities	₹	Assets		₹
Creditors	1,20,000	Cash (Note 3)		36,900
Bills Payable	1,80,000	Debtors	2,00,000	
Kavita Loan	2,97,900	Less : Provision	15,000	1,85,000
Capital Accounts :		Stock		2,20,000
Kushal	4,98,000	Furniture		1,00,000
Kumar	1,66,000	Building		2,00,000
Current Accounts :		Land		5,20,000
Kumar	1,35,000	Current Account : Kushal		1,35,000
	13,96,900			13,96,900

Working Notes :

(1) Adjustment for Goodwill :

Particulars	Kushal (₹)	Kumar (₹)	Kavita (₹)
Right of goodwill before retirement (3 : 1 : 1)	24,000	8,000	8,000
Right of goodwill after retirement (3 : 1)	30,000	10,000	—
	(+) 6,000	(+) 2,000	(–) 8,000

(2) Calculation of Proportionate Capital of Kushal and Kumar :

Total Capital after retirement (₹ 3,63,000 + ₹ 3,01,000) = ₹ 6,64,000.

Kushal's Capital in the new profit-sharing ratio : ₹ 6,64,000 / 4 × 3	4,98,000
Less: Present Capital balance	3,63,000
Amount to be Debited to Kushal's Current Account	1,35,000
Kumar's Capital in the new profit-sharing ratio = ₹ 6,64,000 / 4	1,66,000
Less: Present Capital balance	3,01,000
Amount to be Credited to Kumar's Current Account	(1,35,000)

(3) Cah Balance after retirment:

Opening Balance of Cash	70,000
Less: Paid to Kavita (10% of ₹ 3,31,000)	33,100
	36,900

Q.18. XYZ Ltd. invited applications for 40,000 equity shares of ₹ 100 each at a discount of 6%. The amount was payable as follows :
On application and allotment — ₹ 90 per share
On first and final call — the balance amount
*Applications for 60,000 shares were received. Applications for 10,000 shares were rejected and shares were alloted on pro-rata basis to remaining applicants. Excess application money received on application and allotment was refunded in cash to rejected applicants as well as pro-rata allottes. the call was made. A shareholder, who had applied for 50 shares, failed to pay the first and final call money. His shares were forfeited. All the forfeited shares were re-issued at ₹ 97 per share fully paid up,. **[As the question was incorrect, it has been modified.]***
Pass necessary journal entries for the above transactions in the books of XYZ Ltd. **8**

Answer

In the books of the Firm

Journal

Date	Particulars	L.F.	Dr. ₹	Cr. ₹
	Bank A/c Dr. To Application and Allotment A/c (Being application money received on 60,000 shares @ ₹ 90 each)		54,00,000	 54,00,000
	Application and Allotment A/c Dr. Discount on Issue of Shares A/c Dr. To Equity Share Capital A/c (Being application and allotment money on 40,000 shares @ ₹ 90 each transferred to Equity Share Capital Account. Discount on issue of shares @ ₹ 6 adjusted, as per Board's Resolution No. ... dated ...)		36,00,000 2,40,000	 38,40,000
	Application and Allotment A/c Dr. To Bank A/c (Being application and allotment money on 20,000 shares @ ₹ 90 each refunded as per Board's Resolution No. ... dated ...)		18,00,000	 18,00,000
	First and Final Call A/c Dr. To Equity Share Capital A/c (Being first and final call money due on 40,000 shares @ ₹ 4 each as per Board's Resolution No. ... dated ...)		1,60,000	 1,60,000
	Bank A/c Dr. Calls-in-Arrear A/c Dr. To First and Final Call A/c (Being first and final call money)		1,59,840 160	 1,60,000
	Equity Share Capital A/c (40 x 100) Dr. To Calls-in-Arrear A/c To Discount on Issue of Shares A/c (40 x 6) To Forfeited Shares A/c (Being the forfeiture of 40 equity shares for non-payment of first and final call money @ ₹ 4 each as per Board's Resolution No. ... dated ...)		4,000	 160 240 3,600
	Bank A/c (40 x 97) Dr. Discount on Issue of Shares A/c (Note 2) To Equity Share Capital A/c (Being the re-issue of 40 equity shares @ ₹ 97 as per Board's Resolution No. ... dated ...)		3,880 120	 4,000
	Forfeited Shares A/c Dr. To Capital Reserve A/c (Being profit on re-issue transferred to Capital Reserve)		3.600	 3.600

Tutorial Notes :

(1) No. of shares allotted to defaulter shareholder $= \frac{40,000}{60,000} \times 60 =$ **40 Shares**

(2) When shares are originally issued at discount, at the time of re-issue, the discount to be debited first. In this case, original discount was ₹ 6 per share. The shares were issued @ ₹ 97. Therefore, ₹ 3 discount per share is to be debited to Discount on Issue of Shares.

OR

AB Ltd. invited applications for issuing 75,000 equity shares of ₹ 100 each at a premium of ₹ 30 per share. the amount was payable as follows :
On application and allotment — ₹ 85 per share (including premium)
On first and final call — the balance amount
Applications for 1,27,500 were received. Applications for 27,500 shares were rejected and shares were allotted on pro-rata basis to the remaining applicnts. Excess money received on application and allotment was refunded in cash to rejected applicants as well as pro-rata allottees. The calls were made. A shareholders, who had applied for 1,000 shares failed to pay the first and final call money. His shares were forfeited. All the forfeited shares were re-issued at ₹ 150 per share fully paid up.
Pass necessary journal entries for the above transactions in the books of AB Ltd.

Answer

In the books of AB Ltd.
Journal

Date	Particulars		L.F.	Dr. ₹	Cr. ₹
	Bank A/c	Dr.		1,08,37,500	
	To Equity Share Application and Allotment A/c				1,08,37,500
	(Being application money received for 1,27,500 equity shares @ ₹ 85 each including premium of ₹ 30 per share)				
	Equity Share Application and Allotment A/c	Dr.		1,08,37,500	
	To Equity Shares Capital A/c (75,000 x ₹ 55)				41,25,000
	To Securities Premium Reserve A/c (75,000 x ₹ 30)				22,50,000
	To Bank A/c				44,62,500
	(Being adjustment of application money. Application money on 75,000 shares @ ₹ 55 transferred to Equity Share Capital Account and the balance amount refunded, as per Board's Resolution No. ... dated ...)				
	Equity Shares First and Final Call A/c (75,000 x ₹ 45)	Dr.		33,75,000	
	To Equity Shares Capital A/c				33,75,000
	(Being first and final call money due on 75,000 equity shares @ ₹ 45 each as per Board's Resolution No. ... dated ...)				
	Bank A/c	Dr.		33,41,250	
	Calls-in-Arrear A/c	Dr.		33,750	
	To Equity Share First and Final Call A/c				33,75,000
	(Being the first and final call money received on 47,250 shares @ ₹ 45)				
	Equity Share Capital A/c (750 x ₹ 100)	Dr.		75,000	
	To Calls-in-Arrear A/c				33,750
	To Forfeited Shares A/c				41,250
	(Being the forfeiture of 750 equity shares for non-payment of first and final call money @ ₹ 45 each as per Board's Resolution No. ... dated ...)				

	Bank A/c (750 x ₹ 150) Dr. To Equity Share Capital A/c To Securities Premium A/c (Being the re-issue of 750 shares @ ₹ 150 each as per Board's Resolution No. ... dated ...)		1,12,500	 75,000 37,500
	Forfeited Shares A/c (750 x ₹ 55) Dr. To Capital Reserve A/c (Being the profit on re-issue transferred to Capital Reserve)		41,250	 41,250

Working Notes :

(1) Number of Shares Allotted to Defaulted Shareholder

$$= \frac{75,000}{1,00,000} \times 100 = \textbf{750 Shares}$$

CBSE Accountancy — 2015 (Delhi)

Time allowed : 3 hours **Maximum marks : 80**

General Instructions

(i) This Question Paper contains three parts : A, B and C.

(ii) Part A is ***compulsory*** for all candidates.

(iii) There are two parts. Part B – Financial Statement Analysis and Part C – Computerised Accounting. Attempt only one Part.

(iv) All parts of a question should be attempted at one place..

Set 1

Part A

ACCOUNTING FOR PARTNERSHIP FIRMS AND COMPANIES

Q.1. In the absence of partnership deed the profits of a firm are divided among the partners : *1*

(a) in the ratio of capital

(b) equally

(c) in the ratio of time devoted for the firm's business

(d) according to the managerial abilities of the partners

Answer

(b) Equally.

Q.2. A, B, C and D were partners in a firm sharing profits in the ratio of 4 : 3 : 2 : 1. On 1.1.2015 they admitted E as a new partner for $\frac{1}{10}$ share in the profits. E brought ₹ 10,000 for his share of goodwill premium which was correctly recorded in the books by the accountant. The accountant showed goodwill at ₹ 1,00,000 in the books. Was the accountant correct in doing so ? Give reason in support of your answer. *1*

Answer

No. The accountant was not correct.

Reason : The premium for goodwill was brought in cash by E. Therefore, the Goodwill Account will not be shown in the books of accounts.

Q.3. On the retirement of Hari from the firm of 'Hari, Ram and Sharma', the Balance sheet showed a debit balance of ₹ 12,000 in the Profit and Loss Account. For calculating the amount payable to Hari this balance will be transferred

(a) to the credit of the Capital Accounts of Hari, Ram and Sharma equally

(b) to the debit of the Capital Accounts of Hari, Ram and Sharma equally **1**
(c) to the debit of the Capital accounts of Ram and Sharma equally
(d) to the credit of the Capital Acounts of Ram and Sharma equally.

Answer

(b) to the debit of Capital Accounts of Hari, Ram and Sharma equally.

Q.4. Kumar, Verma and Naresh were partners in a firm sharing profit and loss in the ratio of 3 : 2 : 2. On 23rd January, 2015 Verma died. Verma's share of profit till the date of his death was calculated at ₹ 2,350.
Pass necessary journal entry for the same in the books of the firm. **1**

Answer

In the books of the Firm
Journal

Date	Particulars	L.F.	Dr. ₹	Cr. ₹
2015 Jan. 23	Profit and Loss Suspense A/c Dr. To Verma Capital A/c (Being Verma's share of profit upto the date of death credited to his Capital Account)		2,350	2,350

Q.5. Give the meaning of 'forfeiture of shares'. **1**

Answer

Forfeiture of Share means the cancellation of shares allotted to a shareholder. The shares are forfeited for non-payment of money payable on allotment or call or both. The amount of money paid is not refunded but forfeited by the company.

Q.6. Joy Ltd. issued 1,00,000 equity shares of ₹ 10 each. The amount was payable as follows :
On application — ₹ 3 per share
On allotment — ₹ 4 per share
On 1st and final call — balance
Applications for 95,000 shares were received and shares were allotted to all the applicants. Sonam to whom 500 shares were allotted failed to pay allotment money and Gautam paid his entire amount due including the amount due on first and final call on the 750 shares allotted to him along with allotment. The amount received on allotment was **1**
(a) ₹ 3,80,000
(b) ₹ 3,78,000
(c) ₹ 3,80,250
(d) ₹ 4,00,250

Answer

(c) ₹ 3,80,250.

Hint : (i) (95,000 – 500) × ₹ 4 = 3,78,000
(ii) 750 × ₹ 3 = 2,250
3,80,250

Q.7. State any three purposes other than 'issue of bonus shares' for which securities premium can be utilised. *1*

Answer

Securities premium may be utilised for :

(i) Buy-back of its own equity shares.

(ii) Payment of premium on redemption of preference shares.

(iii) Adjustment of preliminary expenses, commission and issue of shares or debentures.

Q.8. On 1.4.2013 Jay and Vijay entered into partnership for supplying laboratory equipments to government schools situated in remote and backward areas. They contributed capitals of ₹ 80,000 and ₹ 50,000 respectively and agreed to share the profits in the ratio of 3 : 2. The partnership deed provided that interest on capital shall be allowed at 9% per annum. During the year the firm earned a profit of ₹ 7,800.

Showing your calculations, prepare Profit and Loss Appropriation Account of Jay and Vijay for the year ended 31.3.2014. *3*

Answer

In the books of Jay and Vijay

Dr. **Profit and Loss Account for the year ended 31st March, 2014** **Cr.**

Particulars	₹	Particulars	₹
To Interest on Capital :		By Profit for the year	7,800
Jay (Note 1)	4,800		
Vijay (Note 1)	3,000		
	7,800		7,800

Working Notes :

(1) Interest on Capital (Actual)

	₹
Vijay : 80,000 × 9%	7,200
Vijay : 50,000 × 9%	4,500
	11,700

Actual interest on capital is ₹ 11,700 but the profit is not sufficient to pay the entire amount of interest on capital. Therefore, the total amount of ₹ 7,800 will be distributed between Jay and Vijay in the ratio of 7200 : 4500 or 8 : 5.

Jay's amount — $\frac{7,800}{13} \times 8$ 4,800

Vijay's amount — $\frac{7,800}{13} \times 5$ 3,000

7,800

Q.9. Tractors India Ltd. is registered with an authorised capital of ₹ 10,00,000 divided into 1,00,000 equity shares of ₹ 10 each. The company issued 50,000 equity shares at a premium of ₹ 5 per share. ₹ 2 per share were payable with application, ₹ 8 per share including premium on allotment and the balance amount on first and final call. The issue was fully subscribed and all the amount due was received except the first and final call money on 500 shares allotted to Balaram.

Present the Share Capital in the Balance Sheet of Tractors India Ltd. as per Schedule VI Part I of the Companies Act, 1956. Also prepare Notes to Accounts for the same. *3*

Answer

Tractors India Ltd.
Balance Sheet as at . . .

Particulars	Note No.	Figures as at the end of current reporting period ₹
I. **EQUITY AND LIABILITIES**		
1. Shareholders' funds :		
(a) Share Capital	(1)	4,97,500
(b) Reserve and Surplus		—
(c) Money received against share warrants		—

Notes to Accounts :
Share Capital

Particulars			₹
Authorised Capital :			
1,00,000 Equity Shares of ₹ 10 each			10,00,000
Issued Capital :			
50,000 Equity Shares of ₹ 10 each			5,00,000
Subscribed Capital and Fully Paid			
49,500 Equity Shares of ₹ 10 each		4,95,000	
Subscribed but not Fully Paid :			
500 Equity Shares of ₹ 10 each	5,000		
Less: Calls-in-Arrear (500 x ₹ 5)	2,500	2,500	4,97,500

Q.10. Sangam Woollens Ltd., Ludhiana, are the manufacturers and exporters of woollen garments. The company decided to distribute free of cost woollen garments to 10 villages of Lahaul and Spiti District of Himachal Pradesh. The company also decided to employ 50 young persons from these villages in its newly established factory. The company issued 40,000 equity shares of ₹ 10 each and 1,000, 9% debentures of ₹ 100 each to the vendors for the purchase of machinery of ₹ 5,00,000.
Pass necessary journal entries. Also identify any one value that the company wants to communicate to the society. *3*

Answer

In the books of Sangam Woollens Ltd.
Journal

Date	Particulars		L.F.	Dr. ₹	Cr. ₹
	Machinery A/c	Dr.		5,00,000	
	To Vendors A/c				5,00,000
	(Being the purchase of machinery)				
	Vendors A/c	Dr.		5,00,000	
	To Equity Share Capital A/c				4,00,000
	To 9% Debentures A/c				1,00,000
	(Being the issue of 40,000 equity shares of ₹ 10 each and issue of 1,000, 9% Debentures of ₹ 100 each to the Vendors for purchase of machinery)				

Values which the company wants to communicate :

(i) Discharging of corporate social responsibility and promoting inclusive growth.

(ii) Generation of employment for youth of rural India.

Q.11. Dev, Swati and Sanskar were partners in a firm sharing profits in the ratio of 2 : 2 : 1. On 31.3.2014 their Balance Sheet was as follows :

Liabilities		₹	Assets	₹
Trade Payables		17,000	Building	1,04,000
Bank Loan		13,000	Inventory	16,000
Capitals :			Trade Receivables	23,000
Dev	77,000		Cash	40,000
Swati	87,000		Profit and Loss A/c	57,000
Sanskar	46,000	2,10,000		
		2,40,000		2,40,000

On 30th June, 2014 Dev died. According to partnership agreement Dev was entitled to interest on capital @ 12% per annum. His share of profit till the date of his death was to be calculated on the basis of the average profits of last four years. the profits of the last four years were :

Years	*Profit (₹)*
2010-11	*2,04,000*
2011-12	*1,80,000*
2012-13	*90,000*
2013-14 (Loss)	*57,000*

On 1.4.2014, Dev withdrew ₹ 15,000 to pay for his medical bills.

Prepare Dev' Account to be presented to his executors. *4*

Answer

In the books of the Firm
Dev Capital Account

Dr. **Cr.**

Particulars	₹	Particulars	₹
To Drawings A/c	15,000	By Balance b/d	77,000
To Profit and Loss A/c (carried forward loss) (Note 3)	22,800	By Profit and Loss Suspense A/c (Note 1)	10,425
To Dev's Executors A/c	51,935	By Interest on Capital A/c (Note 2)	2,310
	89,735		89,735

Working Notes :

(1) Calculation of Average Profit

$$\frac{2,04,000 + 1,80,000 + 90,000 - 57,000}{4} = ₹\ \mathbf{1,04,250}.$$

Dev's share of profit = ₹ 1,04,250 × 2/5 × 3/12 = ₹ **10,425.**

(2) Interest on Capital of Dev

77,000 × 12% × 3/12 = ₹ **2,310.**

(3) Dev's share of carried forward loss

2/5 × ₹ 57,000 = ₹ **22,800.**

Q.12. Kumar, Gupta and Kavita were partners in a firm sharing profits and losses equally. The firm was engaged in the storage and distribution of canned juice and its godowns were located at three different places in the city. Each godown was being managed individually by Kumar, Gupta and Kavita. Because of increase in business activities at the godown managed by Gupta, he had to devote more time. Gupta demanded that his share in the profits of the firm be increased, to which Kumar and Kavita agreed. The new profit sharing ratio was agreed to

1 : 2 : 1. For this purpose the goodwill of the firm was valued at two years purchase of the average profits of last five years. The profits of the last five years were as follows :

Year	*Profit (₹)*
I	*4,00,000*
II	*4,80,000*
III	*7,33,000*
IV (Loss)	*33,000*
V	*2,20,000*

You are required to :

(i) Calculate the goodwill of the firm.

(ii) Pass necessary journal entry for the treatment of goodwill on change in profit sharing ratio of Kumar, Gupta and Kavita. **4**

Answer

(i) Calculation of Goodwill

$$\text{Average Profit} = \frac{4,00,000 + 4,80,000 + 7,33,000 - 33,000 + 2,20,000}{5} = ₹\ \mathbf{3,60,000}$$

Value of Goodwill = 2 years' purchase of Average Profit

= 2 × ₹ 3,60,000

= **₹ 7,20,000**

(ii) Statement Showing the Adjustment for Goodwill

Particulars	Kumar (₹)	Gupta (₹)	Kavita (₹)
Right of goodwill before change in the profit sharing ratio (1 : 1 : 1)	2,40,000	2,40,000	2,40,000
Right of goodwill after change in the profit sharing ratio (1 : 2)	1,80,000	3,60,000	1,80,000
(Sacrifice) / Gain	(60,000) (Cr.)	1,20,000 (Dr.)	(60,000) (Cr.)

In the books of Firm

Journal

Date	Particulars	L.F.	Dr. ₹	Cr. ₹
	Gupta Capital A/c Dr.		1,20,000	
	To Kumar Capital A/c			60,000
	To Kavita Capital A/c			60,000
	(Being the necessary adjustments for changes in the profit sharing ratio)			

Q.13 On 1.4.2010 Sahil and Charu entered into partnership for sharing profits in the ratio of 4 : 3. They admitted Tanu as a new partner on 1.4.2012 for $\frac{1}{5}$th share which she acquired equally from Sahil and Charu. Sahil, Charu and Tanu earned profits at a higher rate than the normal rate of return for the year ended 31.3.2013. Therefore, they decided to expand their business. To meet the requirements of additional capital they admitted Puneet as a new partner on 1.4.2013 for $\frac{1}{7}$th share in profits which he acquired from Sahil and Charu in 7 : 3 ratio.

Calculate :

(i) New profit sharing ratio of Sahil, Charu and Tanu for the year 2012-13.

(ii) New profit sharing ratio of Sahil, Charu, Tanu and Puneet on Puneet's admission. **6**

Answer

(i) Calculation of New Profit Sharing Ratio of Sahil, Charu and Tanu

Sahil's share of profit — 4/7

Charu's share of profit — 3/7

Tanu is admitted for 1/5 share which she acquired ***equally*** from Sahil and Charu.

(a) **Sahil's New Share of Profit**

$$4/7 - 1/10 = \frac{40 - 7}{70} = \frac{33}{70}$$

(b) **Charu's New Share of Profit**

$$3/7 - 1/10 = \frac{30 - 7}{70} = \frac{23}{70}$$

(c) **Tanu's Share of Profit** — 1/5 or $\frac{14}{70}$.

The profit sharing ratio among Sahil, Charu and Tanu

$= \frac{33}{70} : \frac{23}{70} : \frac{14}{70}$ or **33 : 23 : 14**

(ii) Calculation of New Profit Sharing Ratio of Sahil, Charu, Tanu and Puneet

(a) Sahil's Share of Profit = 33/70.

Sahil surrendered 7/10 of 1/7 or 7/70

$\therefore$ Sahil's new share of profit $= \frac{33}{70} - \frac{7}{70} = \frac{26}{70}$

(b) Charu's Share of Profit = 23/70

Charu surrendered 3/10 of 1/7 = 3/70

$\therefore$ Charu's new share of profit $= \frac{23}{70} - \frac{3}{70} = \frac{20}{70}$

(c) Tanu's Share of Profit $= \frac{14}{70}$

(d) Puneet's Share of Profit = 1/7 or 10/70

The new profit sharing ratio among Sahil, Charu, Tanu and Puneet :

$\frac{26}{70} : \frac{20}{70} : \frac{14}{70} : \frac{10}{70}$ or 26 : 20 : 14 : 10 or **13 : 10 : 7 : 5**

Q.14. Bharat Ltd. had an authorised capital of ₹ 20,00,000 divided into 2,00,000 equity shares of ₹ 10 each. The company issued 1,00,000 shares and the dividend paid per share was ₹ 2 for the year ended 31.3.2008. The management of the company decided to export its products to the neighbouring countries Nepal, Bhutan, Sri Lanka and Bangladesh. To meet the requirement of additional funds the financial manager of the company put up the following three alternatives before its Board of Directors :

(i) Issue 54,000 equity shares.

(ii) Obtain a loan from Import and Export Bank of India. the loan was available at 12% per annum interest.

(iii) To issue 9% Debentures at a discount of 10%.

After comparing the available alternatives the company decided on 1.4.2008 to issue 6,000, 9% Debentures of ₹ 100 each at a discount of 10%. These debentures were redeemable in four instalments starting from the end of third year. The amount of debentures to be redeemed at the end of third, fourth, fifth and sixth year was as follows :

Year	*Profit (₹)*
III	*1,00,000*
IV	*1,00,000*
V	*2,00,000*
VI	*2,00,000*

Prepare 9% Debentures Account for the years 2008-09 to 2013-14. **6**

Answer

In the books of Bharat Ltd.

Dr. 9% Debentures Account Cr.

Date	Particulars	₹	Date	Particulars	₹
2009 Mar 31	To Balance c/d	6,00,000	2008 April 1	By Debenture Application & Allotment A/c	5,40,000
				By Discount on Issue of Debentures A/c	60,000
		6,00,000			6,00,000
2010 Mar 31	To Balance c/d	6,00,000	2009 April 1	By Balance b/d	6,00,000
2011 Mar 31	To Sundry Debentureholders A/c	1,00,000	2010 April 1	By Balance b/d	6,00,000
	To Balance c/d	5,00,000			
		6,00,000			6,00,000
2012 Mar 31	To Sundry Debentureholders A/c	1,00,000	2011 April 1	By Balance b/d	5,00,000
	To Balance c/d	4,00,000			
		5,00,000			5,00,000
2013 Mar 31	To Sundry Debentureholders A/c	2,00,000	2012 April 1	By Balance b/d	4,00,000
	To Balance c/d	2,00,000			
		4,00,000			4,00,000
2014 Mar 31	To Sundry Debentureholders A/c	2,00,000	2013 April 1	By Balance b/d	2,00,000

Q.15 Bora, Singh and Ibrahim were partners in a firm sharing profits in the ratio of 5 : 3 : 1. On 2.3.2015, their firm was dissolved. The assets were realised and the liabilities were paid off. Given below are the Realisation Account, Partners' Capital Accounts and Bank Account of the firm. The accountant of the firm left a few amounts unposted in these accounts. You are required to complete these accounts by posting the correct amounts.

Dr. Realisation Account Cr.

Particulars		₹	Particulars		₹
To Stock		10,000	By Provision for Bad Debts		5,000
To Debtors		25,000	By Sundry Creditors		16,600
To Plant and Machinery		40,000	By Bills Payable		3,400
To Bank :			By Mortgage Loan		15,000
Sundry Creditors	16,000		By Bank — assets realised :		
Bills Payable	3,400		Stock	6,700	
Mortgage Loan	15,000	34,400	Debtors	12,500	
To Bank (Outstanding repairs)		400	Plant and Machinery	36,000	55,200

	₹		₹
To Bank (Expenses)	620	By Bank (unrecorded assets realised)	6,220
		By ________________	—
	1.10.420		1.10.420

Dr. **Capital Accounts** **Cr.**

Particulars	Bora (₹0	Singh (₹)	Ibrahim (₹)	Particulars	Bora (₹)	Singh (₹)	Ibrahim (₹)
—	—	—	—	By Balance b/d	22,000	18,000	10,000
—	—	—	—	By General Reserve A/c	2,500	1,500	500
	24,500	19,500	10,500		24,500	19,500	10,500

Dr. **Bank Account** **Cr.**

Particulars	₹	Particulars	₹
To Balance b/d	19,500	By Realisation (liabilities)	34,400
To Realisation (assets realised)	55,200	By Realisation (unrecorded liabilities)	400
________________		By ________________	
		By ________________	
	80,920		80,920

6

Answer

In the books of the Firm

Dr. **Realisation Account** **Cr.**

Particulars		₹	Particulars		₹
To Stock		10,000	By Provision for Bad Debts		5,000
To Debtors		25,000	By Sundry Creditors		16,600
To Plant and Machinery		40,000	By Bills Payable		3,400
To Bank :			By Mortgage Loan		15,000
Sundry Creditors	16,000		By Bank — assets realised :		
Bills Payable	3,400		Stock	6,700	
Mortgage Loan	15,000	34,400	Debtors	12,500	
To Bank (Outstanding repairs)		400	Plant and Machinery	36,000	55,200
To Bank (Expenses)		620	By Bank (unrecorded assets realised)		6,220
			By Partners' Capital A/cs :(Loss on revaluation)		
			Bora	5,000	
			Singh	3,000	
			Ibrahim	1,000	9,000
		1.10.420			1.10.420

Dr. **Capital Accounts** **Cr.**

Particulars	Bora (₹0	Singh (₹)	Ibrahim (₹)	Particulars	Bora (₹)	Singh (₹)	Ibrahim (₹)
To Realisation A/c	5,000	3,000	1,000	By Balance b/d	22,000	18,000	10,000
To Bank A/c	19,500	16,500	9,500	By General Reserve A/c	2,500	1,500	500
	24,500	19,500	10,500		24,500	19,500	10,500

Dr. **Bank Account** **Cr.**

Particulars	₹	Particulars	₹
To Balance b/d	19,500	By Realisation (liabilities)	34,400
To Realisation (Assets Realised)	55,200	By Realisation (unrecorded liabilities)	400
To Realisation A/c (Unrecorded Assets)	6.220	By Realisation A/c (Expenses)	620

		By Partners' Capital A/cs :	
		Bora	19,500
		Singh	16,500
		Ibrahim	9,500
	80,920		80,920

Q.16. Alfa Ltd. invited applications for issuing 75,000 equity shares of ₹ 10 each. The amount was payable as follows :

On application and allotment — ₹ 4 per share.

On first call — ₹ 3 per share.

On second and final call — balance.

Applications for 1,00,000 shares were received. Shares were allotted to all the applicants on pro-rata basis and excess money received with applications was transferred towards sums due on first call. Vibha who was allotted 750 shares failed to pay the first call. Her shares were immediately forfeited. Afterwards the second call was made. The amount due on second call was also received except on 1,000 shares, applied by Monika. Her shares were also forfeited. all the forfeited shares were re-issued to Mohit for ₹ 9,000 as fully paid-up.

Pass necessary journal entries in the books of Alfa Ltd. for the above transactions. ***8***

Answer

In the books of Alfa Ltd.

Journal

Date	Particulars		L.F.	Dr. ₹	Cr. ₹
	Bank A/c	Dr.		4,00,000	
	To Equity Share Application and Allotment A/c				4,00,000
	(Being application money received for 1,00,000 equity shares @ ₹ 4 per share)				
	Equity Share Application and Allotment A/c	Dr.		4,00,000	
	To Equity Share Capital A/c				3,00,000
	To Calls-in-Advance A/c				1,00,000
	(Being the allotment of 75,000 shares. The application and allotment money transferred to Equity Share Capital Account @ ₹ 4 per share and the balance amount transferred to Calls-in-Advance Account as per Board's Resolution No. ... dated ...)				
	Equity Share First Call A/c	Dr.		2,25,000	
	To Equity Share Capital A/c				2,25,000
	(Being the first call money due on 75,000 shares @ ₹ 3 each as per Board's Resolution No. ... dated ...)				
	Bank A/c (Note 2)	Dr.		1,23,750	
	Calls-in-Advance A/c	Dr.		1,00,000	
	Calls-in-Arrear A/c (Note 1)	Dr.		1,250	
	To Equity Share First Call A/c				2,25,000
	(Being first call money received on all shares except on 750 shares and the advance adjusted)				
	Equity Share Capital A/c (750 x 7)	Dr.		5,250	
	To Calls-in-Arrear A/c				1,250
	To Forfeited Shares A/c				4,000
	(Being the forfeiture of 750 equity shares for non-payment of first call money as per Board's Resolution No. ... dated ...)				
	Equity Share Second and Final Call A/c	Dr.		2,22,750	
	To Equity Share Capital A/c				2,22,750
	(Being second and final call due on 74,250 shares @ ₹ 3 each as per Board's Resolution No. ... dated ...)				

Particulars		Dr. (₹)	Cr. (₹)
Bank A/c Dr. Calls-in-Arrear A/c Dr. To Equity Share Second and Final Call A/c (Being second and final call money received on 73,500 shares @ ₹ 3 each)		2,20,500 2,250	 2,22,750
Equity Share Capital A/c (750 x 10) Dr. To Calls-in-Arrear A/c To Forfeited Shares A/c (Being the forfeiture of 750 shares of ₹ 10 each for non-payment of second and final call as per Board's Resolution No. ... dated ...)		7,500	 2,250 5,250
Bank A/c Dr. Forfeited Shares A/c Dr. To Equity Share Capital A/c (Being the re-issue of 1,500 equity shares of ₹ 10 each for ₹ 9,000 as fully paid as per Board's Resolution No. ... dated ...)		9,000 6,000	 15,000
Forfeited Shares A/c Dr. To Capital Reserve A/c (Being profit on re-issue transferred to Capital Reserve)		3,250	 3,250

Working Notes :

(1) Calculation of Money Not Received on First Call

75,000 Shares were allotted to applicant of 1,00,000 shares

1 Share was allotted to applicant of 1,00,000 / 75,000 shares

750 Shares were allotted to applicant of $\frac{1,00,000 \times 750}{75,000}$ shares= **1,000 shares**

Vibha applied for 1,000 shares. She paid 1,000 × ₹ 4 = ₹ 4,000.

The amount not paid by Vibha on first call has been calculated as follows :

	₹
Application money paid	4,000
Less: Application and Allotment money adjusted (750 × 4)	3,000
Excess application money	1,000
Money due on first call (750 × 3)	2,250
Less: Excess application money adjusted	1,000
Money not received on first call from Vibha	1,250

(2) Money Received on First Call

Amount due (75,000 × 3)	2,25,000
Less: Calls-in-Advance	1,00,000
	1,25,000
Less: Amount not received on first call (Note 1)	1,250
	1,23,750

OR

Jeevan Dhara Ltd. invited applications for issuing 1,20,000 equity shares of ₹ 10 each at a premium of ₹ 2 per share. the amount was payable as follows :

On application — ₹ 2 per share.

On allotment — ₹ 5 per share (including premium)

On first and final call — balance.

Applications for 1,50,000 shares were received. Shares were allotted to all the applicants on pro-rata basis. Excess money received on applications was adjusted towards sums due on

allotment. all calls were made. Manu who had applied for 3,000 shares failed to pay the amount due on allotment and first and final call. Madhur who was allotted 2,400 shares failed to pay the first and final call. Shares of both Manu and Madhur were forfeited. The forfeited shares were re-issued at ₹ 9 per share as fully paid-up.

Pass necessary journal entries for the above transations in the books of Jeevan Dhara Ltd.

Answer

In the books of Jeevan Dhara Ltd.

Journal

Date	Particulars		L.F.	Dr. ₹	Cr. ₹
	Bank A/c	Dr.		3,00,000	
	To Equity Share Application A/c				3,00,000
	(Being application money received for 1,50,000 equity shares @ ₹ 2 per share)				
	Equity Share Application A/c	Dr.		3,00,000	
	To Equity Share Capital A/c				2,40,000
	To Equity Share Allotment A/c				60,000
	(Being the allotment of 1,20,000 shares as per Board's Resolution No. ... dt ...)				
	Equity Share Allotment A/c	Dr.		6,00,000	
	To Equity Share Capital A/c				3,60,000
	To Securities Premium Reserve A/c				2,40,000
	(Being the allotment money due on 1,20,000 shares @ ₹ 5 per share as per Board's Resolution No... dated ...)				
	Bank A/c (Note 1)	Dr.		5,29,200	
	Calls-in-Arrear A/c	Dr.		10,800	
	To Equity Share Allotment A/c				5,40,000
	(Being allotment money received on 1,17,600 shares after adjusting excess money received on application)				
	Equity Share First and Final Call A/c	Dr.		6,00,000	
	To Equity Share Capital A/c				6,00,000
	(Being first and final call money due on 1,20,000 equity shares @ ₹ 5 each as per Board's Resolution No. ... dated ...)				
	Bank A/c	Dr.		5,76,000	
	Calls-in-Arrear A/c	Dr.		24,000	
	To Equity Share First and Final Call A/c				6,00,000
	(Being first and final call money received on 1,15,200 shares)				
	Equity Share Capital A/c	Dr.		48,000	
	Securities Premium Reserve A/c	Dr.		4,800	
	To Calls-in-Arrear A/c				34,800
	To Forfeited Shares A/c (Note 3)				18,000
	(Being the forfeiture of 4,800 equity shares for non-payment of allotment money on 2,400 shares and first and final call money on 4,800 shares as per Board's Resolution No. ... dated ...)				
	Bank A/c (4,800 x ₹ 9)	Dr.		43,200	
	Forfeitured Shares A/c	Dr.		4,800	
	To Equity Share Capital A/c				48,000
	(Being the re-issue of 4,800 equity shares @ ₹ 9 each as per Board's Resolution No. ... dated ...)				
	Forfeited Shares A/c	Dr.		13,200	
	To Capital Reserve A/c				13,200
	(Being the profit on re-issue transferred to Capital Reserve)				

Working Notes :

(1) Calculation of Money Received on Allotment

	₹
Money due on allotment	6,00,000
Less: Excess application money adjusted	60,000
	5,40,000
Less: Money not paid by Manu (Note 2)	10,800
	5,29,200

(2) Money Not Paid by Manu

Money paid on application (3,000 × 2)	6,000
Less: Money adjusted for shares allotted ($\frac{1,20,000}{1,50,000}$ × 3,000) × ₹ 2	4,800
Excess application money	1,200
Money due on allotment (2,400 × ₹ 5)	12,000
Less: Excess application money	1,200
Amount not paid	10,800

(3) Amount Forfeited

Manu paid (3,000 × ₹ 2)	6,000
Madhu paid (2,400 × ₹ 5)	12,000
	18,000

Q.17. Charu and Harsha were partners in a firm sharing profits in the ratio of 3 : 2. On 1.4.2014 their Balance sheet was as follows :

Balance Sheet of Charu and Harsha as on 1st April, 2014

Liabilities		₹	Assets	₹
Creidtors		17,000	Cash	6,000
General Reserve		4,000	Debtors	15,000
Workmen Compensation Fund		9,000	Investments	20,000
Investment Fluctuation Fund		11,000	Plant	14,000
Provision for Bad Debts		2,000	Land and Building	38,000
Capitals :				
Charu	30,000			
Harsha	20,000	50,000		
		93,000		93,000

On the above date Vaishali was admitted for 1/4th share in the profits of the firm on the following terms :

(i) Vaishali will bring ₹ 20,000 for her capital and ₹ 4,000 for her share of goodwill premium.

(ii) All debtors were considered good.

(iii) The market value of investments was ₹ 15,000.

(iv) There was a liability of ₹ 6,000 for workmen compensation.

(v) Capital Accounts of Charu and Harsha are to be adjusted on the basis of Vasihali's capital by opening Current Accounts.

Prepare Revaluation Account and Partners' Capital Accounts. ***8***

Answer

In the books of the Firm

Dr. Revaluation Account Cr.

Date	Particulars	₹	Date	Particulars	₹
	To Partners' Capital A/cs :			By Provision for Bad Debts A/c	2,000
	Charu	1,200			
	Harsha	800			
		2,000			2,000

Dr. Partners' Capital Accounts Cr.

Particulars	Charu (₹0	Harsha (₹)	Vaishali (₹)	Particulars	Charu (₹)	Harsha (₹)	Vaishali (₹)
To Current A/c (Balancing figure)	5,400	3,600	—	By Balance b/d	30,000	20,000	—
To Balance c/d (Note 1)	36,000	2,400	20,000	By General Reserve	2,400	1,600	—
				By Cash A/c	—	—	20,000
				By Premium for Goodwill A/c	2,400	1,600	—
				By Revaluation A/c	1,200	800	—
				By Workmen Compensation Fund	1,800	1,200	—
				By Investment Fluctuation Fund	3,600	2,400	—
	41,400	27,600	20,000		41,400	27,600	20,000

Working Note :

(1) Calculation of New Profit Sharing Ratio

Vaishali's share 1/4.

The balance 3/4 is to be shared by Charu and Harsha in the ratio of 3 : 2.

(i) Charu's share of profit $= \frac{3}{5} \times \frac{3}{4} = \frac{9}{20}$

(ii) Harsha's share of profit $= \frac{2}{5} \times \frac{3}{4} = \frac{6}{20}$

(iii) Vaishali's share of profit $= \frac{1}{4}$ or $\frac{5}{20}$

The new ratio of profit is **9 : 6 : 5**.

New Capital of Partners

Charu : $\frac{20,000}{5} \times 9 =$ ₹ 36,000;

Harsha : $\frac{20,000}{5} \times 6 =$ ₹ 24,000;

Vaishali : ₹ 20,000

OR

Amit, Balan and Chander were partners in a firm sharing profits in the proportion of $\frac{1}{2}, \frac{1}{3}$ and $\frac{1}{6}$ respectively. Chander retired on 1.4.2014. The Balance Sheet of the firm on the date of Chander's retirement was as follows :

Balance Sheet of Amit, Balan and Chander as on 1st April, 2014

Liabilities		₹	Assets		₹
Sundry Creditors		12,600	Bank		4,100
Provident fund		3,000	Debtors	30,000	
General Reserve		9,000	Less: Provision	1,000	29,000
Capitals :			Stock		25,000
Amit	40,000		Investments		10,000
Balan	36,500		Patents		5,000
Chander	20,000	96,500	Machinery		48,000
		1,21,100			1,21,100

It was agreed that :

(a) Goodwill will be valued at ₹ 27,000.

(b) Depreciation of 10% was to be provided on machinery.

(c) Patents were to be reduced by 20%.

(d) Liability on account of Provident fund was estimated at ₹ 2,400.

(e) Chander took over investments for ₹ 15,800.

(f) Amit and Balan decided to adjust their capitals in proportion of their profit sharing ratio by opening Current Accounts.

Prepare Revaluation Account and Partners' Capital Accounts on Chander's retirement.

Answer

In the books of the Firm

Dr. Revaluation Account Cr.

Date	Particulars	₹	Date	Particulars	₹
2014			2014		
April 1	To Machinery A/c	4,800	April 1	By Liability for Provident Fund A/c	600
	To Patents A/c	1,000		By Investments A/c	5,800
	To Partners' Capital A/cs :				
	Amit	300			
	Balan	200			
	Chander	100			
		6,400			6,400

Dr. Partners' Capital Accounts Cr.

Particulars	Amit (₹0	Balan (₹)	Chander (₹)	Particulars	Amit (₹)	Balan (₹)	Chander (₹)
To Partners' Capital A/cs :				By Balance b/d	40,000	36,500	20,000
Chander	2,700	1,800	—	By General Reserve A/c	4,500	3,000	1,500
To Investment A/c	—	—	15,800	By Revaluation A/c	300	200	100
To Chander's Loan A/c	—	—	10,300	By Partners' Capital A/cs :			
To Balan's Current A/c	—	5,900	—	Amit	—	—	2,700
To Balance c/d	48,000	32,000	—	Balan	—	—	1,800
				By Amit's Current A/c	5,900	—	—
	50,700	39,700	26,100		50,700	39,700	26,100

(Outside Delhi)

Time allowed : 3 hours **Maximum marks : 80**

General Instructions

(i) This Question Paper contains three parts : A and B.

(ii) Part A is ***compulsory*** for all candidates.

(iii) Part B has two options – Analysis of Financial Statements and Computerised Accounting.

(iv) Attempt only one option of Part B.

(v) All parts of a question should be attempted at one place.

Set I

Part A

ACCOUNTING FOR PARTNERSHIP FIRMS AND COMPANIES

Q.1. In the absence of Partnership Deed, interest on loan of a partner is allowed :

(i) at 8% per annum

(ii) at 6% per annum

(iii) no interest is allowed

(iv) at 12% per annum *1*

Answer

(ii) at 6% per annum.

Q.2. Geeta, Sunita and Anita were partners in a firm sharing profits in the ratio of 5 : 3 : 2. On 1.1.2015 they admitted Yogita as a new partner for 1/10th share in the profits. On Yogita's admission, the Profit and Loss Account of the firm was showing a debit balance of ₹ 20,000 which was credited by the accountant of the firm to the Capital Accounts of Geeta, Sunita and Anita in their profit sharing ratio. Did the accountant give correct treatment ? Give reason in support of your answer. *1*

Answer

No, the accountant's treatment was not correct because the debit balance of Profit and Loss Account will be written-off by debiting Partners' Capital Accounts and crediting Profit and Loss Account.

Q.3. On the death of a partner, his share in the profits of the firm till the date of his death is transferred to the :

(i) Debit of Profit and Loss Account

(ii) Credit of Profit and Loss Account

(iii) Debit of Profit and Loss Suspense Account

(iv) Credit of Profit and Loss Suspense Account *1*

Answer

(iii) Debit of Profit and Loss Suspense Account.

Q.4. Anant, Gulab and Khushbu were partners in a firm sharing profits in the ratio of 5 : 3 : 2. From 1.4.2014, they decided to share the profits equally. For this purpose the goodwill of the firm was valued at ₹ 2,40,000.

Pass necessary journal entry for the treatment of goodwill on change in the profit sharing ratio of Anant, Gulab and Khushbu. **1**

Answer

In the books of the Firm

Journal

Date	Particulars		L.F.	Dr. ₹	Cr. ₹
2014 April 1	Gulab Capital A/c (Note 1) Khusbu Capital A/c To Anant Capital A/c (Being the adjustment for goodwill due to change in the profit sharing ratio)	Dr. Dr.		8,000 32,000	 40,000

Working Note : (1) Statement Showing the Adjustment for Goodwill

Particulars	Anant (₹)	Gulab (₹)	Khusbu (₹)
Right of goodwill before change in the profit sharing ratio (5 : 3 : 2)	1,20,000	72,000	48,000
Right of goodwill after change in the profit sharing ratio (1 : 1 : 1)	80,000	80,000	80,000
Change in the Share of Goodwill	40,000 (Cr.)	8,000 (Dr.)	32,000 (Dr.)

Q.5. Give the meaning of forfeiture of shares. **1**

Answer

Forfeiture of Share means the cancellation of shares allotted to a shareholder. The shares are forfeited for non-payment of money payable on allotment or call or both. The amount of money paid is not refunded but forfeited by the company.

Q.6. Nirman Ltd. issued 50,000 equity shares of ₹ 10 each. The amount was payable as follows :

On application — ₹ 3 per share

On allotment — ₹ 2 per share

On first and final call — the balance

Applications for 45,000 shares were received and shares were allotted to all the applicants. Pooja, to whom 500 shares were allotted, paid her entire share money at the time of allotment, whereas Kundan did not pay the first and final call on his 300 shares. The amount received at the time of making first and final calls was :

(i) ₹ 2,25,000

(ii) ₹ 2,20,000

(iii) 2,21,000

(iv) ₹ 2,19,500 **1**

Answer

(iii) 2,21,000

Hints :

(45,000 – 500 – 300) × ₹ 5 = ₹ **2,21,000.**

Q.7. Guru Ltd. invited applications for issuing 5,00,000 equity shares of ₹ 10 each at a premium of ₹ 5 per share. Because of favourable market conditions the issue was over-subscribed and applications for 15,00,000 shares were received.
Suggest the alternatives available to the Board of Directors for the allotment of shares. ***3***

Answer

The issue has been oversubscribed by 3 times. The alternatives to Board of Directors are :

(1) Reject the excess application for 10,00,000 shares. The remaining applicants should be allotted in full.

(2) The shares may be allotted to all applicants on pro-rata basis.

(3) Applications for small number of shares may be rejected and shares may be allotted to the remaining applicants on pro-rata basis.

Q.8. On 1.4.2013, Brij and Nandan entered into partnership to construct toilets in government girls schools in the remote areas of Uttarakhand. They contributed capitals of ₹ 10,00,000 and ₹ 15,00,000 respectively. Their profit sharing ratio was 2 : 3 and interest allowed on capital as provided in the Partnership Deed was 12% per annum. During the year ended 31.3.2014, the firm earned a profit of ₹ 2,00,000.
Prepare Profit and Loss Appropriation Account of Brij and Nandan for the year ended 31.3.2014. ***3***

Answer

In the books of Brij and Nandan
Profit and Loss Appropriation A/c for the year ended on 31st March, 2014

Particulars	₹	Particulars	₹
To Interest on Capital A/c :		By Profit for the year	2,00,000
Brij (Note 1)	80,000		
Nandan (Note 1)	1,20,000		
	2,00,000		2,00,000

Working Note :

(1) Interest on Capital (Actual) :

	₹
Brij : 10,00,000 × 12%	1,20,000
Nandan : 15,00,000 × 12%	1,80,000
	3,00,000

Actual interest payable on capital is ₹ 3,00,000 but the profit is only ₹ 2,00,000 which is insufficient to pay interest on capital fully.

Therefore, ₹ 2,00,000 will be distributed between Brij and Nandan in the ratio of 2 : 3 (capital ratio).

	₹
Brij's amount of interest = ₹ 2,00,000 × 2/5	80,000
Nandan's amount of interest = ₹ 2,00,000 × 3/5	1,20,000
	2,00,000

Q.9. Suvidha Ltd. is registered with an authorised capital of ₹ 10,00,00,000 divided into 10,00,000 equity shares of ₹ 100 each. The company issued 1,00,000 shares for public subscription. A shareholder holding 100 shares failed to pay the final call of ₹ 20 per share. His shares were forfeited. The forfeited shares were re-issued at ₹ 90 per share as fully paid-up.
Prepare the Share Capital in the Balance Sheet of the company as per Schedule VI Part I of the Companies Act, 1956. Also prepare 'Notes to Accounts'. ***3***

Answer

Suvidha Ltd.
Balance Sheet as at . . .

Particulars	Note No.	Figures as at the end of current reporting period ₹
I. **EQUITY AND LIABILITIES**		
1. Shareholders' funds :		
(a) Share Capital	(1)	1,00,00,000
(b) Reserve and Surplus		?
(c) Money received against share warrants		?

Notes to Accounts :
Share Capital

Particulars	₹
Authorised Capital :	
10,00,000 Equity Shares of ₹ 100 each	10,00,00,000
Issued Capital :	
1,00,000 Equity Shares of ₹ 100 each	1,00,00,000
Subscribed Capital and Fully Paid	
1,00,000 Equity Shares of ₹ 100 each	1,00,00,000

Q.10. Good Blankets Ltd. are the manufacturers of woollen blankets. Blankets of the company are exported to many countries. The company decided to distribute blankets free of cost to five villages of Kasmir Valley destroyed by the recent floods. It also decided to employ 100 young persons from these villages in their newly established factory at Solan in Himachal Pradesh. To meet the requirements of funds for starting its new factory, the company issued 50,000 equity shares of ₹ 10 each and 2,000, 8% debentures of ₹ 100 each to the vendors of machinery purchased for ₹ 7,00,000.

Pass necessary journal entries for the above transactions in the books of the company.

Also identify any one value which the company wants to communicate to the society. 3

Answer

In the books of Good Blankets Ltd.
Journal

Date	Particulars		L.F.	Dr. ₹	Cr. ₹
	Machinery A/c	Dr.		7,00,000	
	To Vendors A/c				7,00,000
	(Being purchase of machinery)				
	Vendors A/c	Dr.		7,00,000	
	To Equity Share Capital A/c				5,00,000
	To 8% Debentures A/c				2,00,000
	(Being the issue of 50,000 equity shares of ₹ 10 each and issue of 2,000, 8% Debentures of ₹ 100 each to the Vendors for purchase of machinery)				

Values which the company wants to communicate :

(i) Discharging of corporate social responsibility and promoting inclusive growth.

(ii) Generation of employment for youth of rural India.

Q.11. Arun, Varun and Karan were partners in a firm, sharing profits in the ratio of 4 : 3 : 3. On 31.3.2014, their Balance sheet was as follows :

Liabilities		₹	Assets	₹
Creditors		17,000	Cash	8,000
Bills Payable		12,000	Debtors	13,000
Karan's Loan		28,000	Bills Receivables	9,000
Capitals :			Furniture	27,000
Arun	70,000		Machinery	1,25,000
Varun	68,000	1,38,000	Karan's Capital	13,000
		1,95,000		1,95,000

On 30.9.2014, Karan died. The Partnership Deed provided for the following to the executors of the deceased partner :

(a) His share in the goodwill of the firm calculated on the basis of three years' purchase of the average profits of the last four years. The profits of the last four years were ₹ 1,90,000; ₹ 1,70,000; ₹ 1,80,000; and ₹ 1,60,000 respectively.

(b) His share in the profits of the firm till the date of his death calculated on the basis of the average profits of the last four years.

(c) Interest @ 8% p.a. on the credit balance, if any, in his Capital Account.

(d) Interest on his loan @ 12% p.a.

Prepare Karan's Capital Account to be presented to his executors, assuming that his loan and interest on loan were transferred to his Capital Account. **4**

Answer

In the books of the Firm

Karan's Capital Account

Dr. **Cr.**

Particulars	₹	Particulars	₹
To Balance b/d	13,000	By Arun Capital A/c (Note 1)	90,000
To Karan's Executors A/c	2,00,430	By Varun Capital A/c (Note 1)	67,500
		By Profit and Loss Suspense A/c (Note 2)	26,250
		By Karan's Loan A/c (Note 3)	28,000
		By Interest on Loan A/c	1,680
	2,13,430		2,13,430

Working Notes :

(1) Calculation of Average Profit

$$\frac{1,90,000 + 1,70,000 + 1,80,000 + 1,60,000}{4} = ₹\ \mathbf{1,75,000.}$$

Value of Goodwill = ₹ 1,75,000 × 3 = **₹ 5,25,000.**

Karan's share of Goodwill = ₹ 1,57,500 (3/10 of ₹ 5,25,000) which should be provided by Arun and Varun in the ratio of 4 : 3.

Arun;s Share = ₹ 1,57,500 × 4/7 = ₹ 90,000

Varun's Share = ₹ 1,57,500 × 3/7 = ₹ 67,500

(2) Calculation of Share of Profit of Karan

1,75,000 × 6/12 × 3/10 = **₹ 26,250.**

(3) Interest on Loan of Karan

= ₹ 28,000 × 12% × 1/2 = **₹ 1,680.**

Q.12. Prem, Param and Priya were partners in a firm. Their fixed capitals were Prem —₹ 2,00,000; Param —₹ 3,00,000; and Priya —₹ 5,00,000. They were sharing profits in the ratio of their capitals. The firm was engaged in the sale of ready-to-eat food packets at three different locations in the city, each being managed by Prem, Param and Priya. The outlet managed by Prem was doing more business than the outlets managed by Param and Priya. Prem requested Param and Priya for a higher share in the profits of the firm which Param and Priya accepted. It was decided that the new profit sharing ratio will be 2 : 1 : 2 and its effect will be introduced respectively for the last four years. The profits of the last four years were ₹ 2,00,000; ₹ 3,50,000; ₹ 4,75,000 and ₹ 5,25,000 respectively.
Showing your calculations clearly, pass a necessary adjustment entry to give effect to the new agreement between Prem, Param and Priya. 4

Answer

Total Profit of last 4 years = ₹ 2,00,000 + 3,50,000 + 4,75,000 + 5,25,000 = ₹ **15,50,000**

Statement Showing the Adjustment for Profit already Distributed

Particulars	Prem (₹)	Param (₹)	Priya (₹)
Share of Profit as per new agreement (2 : 1 : 2)	6,20,000	3,10,000	6,20,000
Share of Profit already Credited (2 : 3 : 5)	3,10,000	4,65,000	7,75,000
	3,10,000 (Cr.)	(1,55,000) (Dr.)	(1,55,000) (Dr.)

In the books of Firm
Journal

Date	Particulars		L.F.	Dr. ₹	Cr. ₹
	Param Current A/c	Dr.		1,55,000	
	Priya Current A/c	Dr.		1,55,000	
	To Prem Current A/c				3,10,000
	(Being the adjustment for changes in the profit sharing ratio)				

Q.13 On 1.1.2008, Uday and Kaushal entered into partnership with fixed capitals of ₹ 7,00,000 and ₹ 3,00,000 respectively. They were doing good business and were interested in its expansion but could not do the same because of lack of capital. Therefore, to have more capital, they admitted Govind as a new partner on 1.1.2010. Govind brought ₹ 10,00,000 as capital and the new profit sharing ratio decided was 3 : 2 : 5. On 1.1.2012, another new partner Hari was admitted with a capital of ₹ 8,00,000 for 1/10th share in the profits, which he acquired equally from Uday, Kaushal and Govind. On 1.4.2014, Govind died and his share was taken over by Uday and Hari equally.
Calculate :
(i) The sacrificing ratio of Uday and Kaushal on Govind's admission/
(ii) New profit sharing ratio of Uday, Kaushal, Govind and Hari on Hari's admission.
(iii) New profit sharing ratio of Uday, Kaushal and Hari on Govind's death. 6

Answer

(i) Calculation of Sacrificing Ratio :

Uday : $\frac{1}{2} - \frac{3}{10} = \frac{5-3}{10} = \frac{2}{10}$;   Kushal : $\frac{1}{2} - \frac{2}{10} = \frac{5-2}{10} = \frac{3}{10}$

Therefore, sacrificing ratio = **2 : 3**

(ii) Profit sharing ratio of Uday, Kushal and Govind — 3 : 2 : 5. 1/10th share were acquired by Hari from all the partners equally. It means, each partner sacrificed $\frac{1}{30}$th share of profit. The new profit sharing ratio will be :

$$\text{Uday} : \frac{3}{10} - \frac{1}{30} = \frac{9-1}{30} = \frac{8}{30}$$

$$\text{Kushal} : \frac{2}{10} - \frac{1}{30} = \frac{6-1}{30} = \frac{5}{30}$$

$$\text{Govind} : \frac{5}{10} - \frac{1}{30} = \frac{15-1}{30} = \frac{14}{30}$$

$$\text{Hari} : \frac{1}{10} \text{ or } \frac{3}{30}$$

Therefore, new profit-sharing ratio = **8 : 5 : 14 : 3**

(iii) New profit sharing ratio of Uday, Kushal and Hari after Govind's death :

$$\text{Uday} : \frac{8}{30} + \frac{7}{30} = \frac{15}{30}$$

$$\text{Kushal} : \frac{5}{30}$$

$$\text{Hari} : \frac{3}{30} + \frac{7}{30} = \frac{10}{30}$$

Therefore, new profit sharing ratio of Uday, Kushal and Hari : 15 : 5 : 10 or **3 : 1 : 2**.

Q.14. Ananya Ltd. had an authorised capital of ₹ 10,00,00,000 divided into 10,00,000 equity shares of ₹ 100 each. The company had already issued 2,00,000 shares. The dividend paid per share for the year ended 31.3.2007 was ₹ 30. The management decided to export its products to African countries. To meet the requirements of additional funds, the finance manager put up the following three alternative proposals before the Board of Directors :

(i) Issue 47,500 equity shares at a premium of ₹ 100 per share.

(ii) Obtain a long-term loan from bank which was available at 12% per annum.

(iii) Issue 9% debentures at a discount of 5%.

After evaluating these alternatives, the company decided to issue 1,00,000, 9% debentures on 1.4.2008. the face value of each debentures was ₹ 100. These debentures were redeemable in four instalments starting from the end of third year, which was as follows :

Year	*Amount (₹)*
II	*10,00,000*
III	*20,00,000*
IV	*30,00,000*
V	*40,00,000*

Prepare 9% Debenture Account from 1.4.2008 till all the debentures were redeemed. **6**

Answer

In the books of Ananya Ltd.

Dr. **9% Debentures Account** Cr.

Date	Particulars	₹	Date	Particulars	₹
2009 Mar 31	To Balance c/d	100,00,000	2008 April 1	By Debenture Application & Allotment A/c By Discount on Issue of Debentures A/c	95,00,000 5,00,000
		100,00,000			100,00,000
2010 Mar 31	To Balance c/d	100,00,000	2009 April 1	By Balance b/d	100,00,000
2011 Mar 31	To Debentureholders A/c To Balance c/d	10,00,000 90,00,000	2010 April 1	By Balance b/d	100,00,000
		100,00,000			100,00,000
2012 Mar 31	To Debentureholders A/c To Balance c/d	20,00,000 70,00,000	2011 April 1	By Balance b/d	90,00,000
		90,00,000			90,00,000
2013 Mar 31	To Debentureholders A/c To Balance c/d	30,00,000 40,00,000	2012 April 1	By Balance b/d	70,00,000
		70,00,000			70,00,000
2014 Mar 31	To Debentureholders A/c	40,00,000	2013 April 1	By Balance b/d	40,00,000

Q.15. Mala, Neela and Kala were partners sharing profits in the ratio of 3 : 2 : 1. On 1.3.2015 their firm was dissolved. The assets were realised and liabilities were paid off. The accountant prepared Realisation Account, Partners' Capital Accounts and Cash Account, but forgot to post few amounts in these accounts.

You are required to complete these below given amounts by posting correct amounts.

Dr. **Realisation Account** Cr.

Particulars		₹	Particulars		₹
To Sundry Assets :			By Provision for Bad Debts		1,000
Machinery	10,000		By Sundry Creditors		15,000
Stock	21,000		By Sheela's Loan		13,000
Debtors	20,000		By Repairs and Renewals Reserve		1,200
Prepaid Insurance	400		By Cash — Assets sold :		
Investments	3,000	54,400	Machinery	8,000	
To Mala's Capital A/c (Sheela's Loan)		13,000	Stock	14,000	
To Cash — Creditors Paid		15,000	Debtors	16,000	38,000
To Cash — Dishonoured Bill Paid		5,000	By Mala's Capital (Investments)		2,000
To Cash Expenses		800	....		
		88,200			88,200

Dr. **Capital Accounts** Cr.

Particulars	Mala (₹0	Neela (₹)	Kala (₹)	Particulars	Mala (₹)	Neela (₹)	Kala (₹)
—	—	—	—	—	—	—	—
—	—	—	—	—	—	—	—
To Cash	12,000	9,000	—	By Cash	—	—	1,000
	23,000	15,000	3,000		23,000	15,000	3,000

Dr. Cash Account Cr.

Particulars	₹	Particulars	₹
To Balance b/d	2,800	By Realisation A/c (Creditors Paid)	15,000
To Realisation A/c (Sale of Assets)	38,000	By Dishonoured Bill	5,000
To Kala's Capital A/c	1,000	By ____________	
		By Mala's Capital A/c	12,000
		By Neela's Capital A/c	9,000
	41,800		41,800

6

Answer

In the books of the Firm

Dr. Realisation Account Cr.

Particulars		₹	Particulars		₹
To Sundry Assets :			By Provision for Bad Debts		1,000
Machinery	10,000		By Sundry Creditors		15,000
Stock	21,000		By Sheela's Loan		13,000
Debtors	20,000		By Repairs and Renewals Reserve		1,200
Prepaid Insurance	400		By Cash — Assets sold :		
Investments	3,000	54,400	Machinery	8,000	
To Mala's Capital A/c (Sheela's Loan)		13,000	Stock	14,000	
To Cash — Creditors Paid		15,000	Debtors	16,000	38,000
To Cash — Dishonoured Bill Paid		5,000	By Mala's Capital (Investments)		2,000
To Cash Expenses		800	By Partners' Capital A/cs (Loss) :		
			Mala		9,000
			Neela		6,000
			Kala		3,000
		88,200			88,200

Dr. Capital Accounts Cr.

Particulars	Mala (₹0	Neela (₹)	Kala (₹)	Particulars	Mala (₹)	Neela (₹)	Kala (₹)
To Realisation A/c (Sh. of Loss)	9,000	6,000	3,000	By Balance b/d (balancing fig.)	10,000	15,000	2,000
To Realisation A/c	2,000	—	—	By Realisation A/c	13,000	—	—
To Cash	12,000	9,000	—	By Cash	—	—	1,000
	23,000	15,000	3,000		23,000	15,000	3,000

Dr. Cash Account Cr.

Particulars	₹	Particulars	₹
To Balance b/d	2,800	By Realisation A/c (Creditors Paid)	15,000
To Realisation A/c (Sale of Assets)	38,000	By Dishonoured Bill	5,000
To Kala's Capital A/c	1,000	By Realisation A/c (Expenses)	800
		By Mala's Capital A/c	12,000
		By Neela's Capital A/c	9,000
	41,800		41,800

Q.16. BMY Ltd. invited applications for issuing 1,00,000 equity shares of ₹ 10 each at a premium of ₹ 10 per share. The amount was payable as follows :

On application — ₹ 10 per share (including ₹ 5 premium)

On allotment — The balance

The issue was fully subscribed. A shareholder holding 300 shares paid the full share money with application. Another shareholder holding 200 shares failed to pay the allotment money. His shares were forfeited. Later on these shares were re-issued for ₹ 4,000 as fully paid up. Pass necessary journal entries for the above transactions in the books of BMY Ltd. **8**

Answer

In the books of BMY Ltd.
Journal

Date	Particulars		L.F.	Dr. ₹	Cr. ₹
	Bank A/c	Dr.		10,00,000	
	To Equity Share Application A/c				10,00,000
	(Being application money received for 1,00,000 equity shares @ ₹ 10 each)				
	Bank A/c (Note 1)	Dr.		3,000	
	To Advance for Shares A/c				3,000
	(Being advance amount received with application money)				
	Equity Share Application A/c	Dr.		10,00,000	
	To Equity Shares Capital A/c				5,00,000
	To Securities Premium A/c				5,00,000
	(Being the application money @ ₹ 5 on 1,00,000 shares transferred to Equity Share Capital Account. ₹ 5 on 1,00,000 shares transferred to Securities Premium Account as per Board's Resolution No. ... dated ...)				
	Equity Shares Allotment A/c	Dr.		10,00,000	
	To Equity Shares Capital A/c				5,00,000
	To Securities Premium A/c				5,00,000
	(Being the allotment money due on 1,00,000 equity shares @ ₹ 10 each including premium of ₹ 5 per share as per Board's Resolution No. ... dated ...)				
	Bank A/c	Dr.		9,95,000	
	Advance for Shares A/c	Dr.		3,000	
	Calls-in-Arrear A/c	Dr.		2,000	
	To Equity Share Allotment A/c				10,00,000
	(Being the allotment money received on 99,500 shares @ ₹ 10 per share)				
	Equity Share Capital A/c	Dr.		2,000	
	Securities Premium A/c (Note 2)	Dr.		1,000	
	To Calls-in-Arrear A/c				2,000
	To Forfeited Shares A/c				1,000
	(Being the forfeiture of 200 equity shares for non-payment of allotment money @ ₹ 10 each along with premium of ₹ 5 each as per Board's Resolution No. ... dated ...)				
	Bank A/c	Dr.		4,000	
	To Equity Share Capital A/c				2,000
	To Securities Premium A/c				2,000
	(Being the re-issue of 200 shares @ ₹ 20 each as per Board's Resolution No. ... dated ...)				
	Forfeited Shares A/c	Dr.		1,000	
	To Capital Reserve A/c				1,000
	(Being the profit on re-issue transferred to Capital Reserve)				

Working Note :

(1) It has been given in the problem that one shareholder holding 300 shares paid the full share money with the application. In our opinion, legally and practically it is not possible. Therefore, the money paid should be transferred to a separate account called 'Advance for Shares Account'. It should not be treated as part of the application money.

OR

Blue Star Ltd. was registered with an authorised capital of ₹ 2,00,000 divided into 20,000 shares of ₹ 10 each. 6,000 of these shares were issued to the vendor for building purchased. 8,000 shares were issued to the public and ₹ 5 per share were called up as follows :

On application — ₹ 2 per share

On allotment — ₹ 1 per share

On first call — Balance of the called up amount.

The amounts received on these shares were as follows :

On 6,000 shares — Full amount called

On 1,250 shares — ₹ 3 per share

On 750 shares — ₹ 2 per share

The directors forfeited 750 shares on which ₹ 2 per share were received. Pass necessary journal entries for the above transactions in the books of Blue Star ltd.

Answer

In the books of Blue Star Ltd.

Journal

Date	Particulars		L.F.	Dr. ₹	Cr. ₹
	Building A/c	Dr.		60,000	
	To Vendor A/c				60,000
	(Being the purchase of building from the vendor)				
	Vendor A/c	Dr.		60,000	
	To Equity Share Capital A/c				60,000
	(Being the issue of shares to the Vendor for the purchase of the building)				
	Bank A/c	Dr.		16,000	
	To Equity Share Application A/c				16,000
	(Being application money received for 8,000 shares @ ₹ 2 each)				
	Equity Share Application A/c	Dr.		16,000	
	To Equity Share Capital A/c				16,000
	(Being the application money transferred to Equity Share Capital Account, as per Board's Resolution No. ... dated ...)				
	Equity Share Allotment A/c	Dr.		8,000	
	To Equity Share Capital A/c				8,000
	(Being allotment money due on 8,000 shares @ ₹ 1 as per Board's Resolution No. ... dated ...)				
	Bank A/c	Dr.		7,250	
	Calls-in-Arrear A/c	Dr.		750	
	To Equity Share Allotment A/c				8,000
	(Being allotment money received on 7,250 shares @ ₹ 1 each)				
	Equity Share First Call A/c	Dr.		16,000	
	To Equity Share Capital A/c				16,000
	(Being first call money due on 8,000 shares @ ₹ 2 each as per Board's Resolution No. ... dated ...)				
	Bank A/c	Dr.		12,000	
	Calls-in-Arrear A/c	Dr.		4,000	
	To Equity Share First Call a/c				16,000
	(Being first call money received on 6,000 shares @ ₹ 2 each)				

Equity Share Capital A/c (750 x ₹ 5) Dr.		3,750	
To Calls-in-Arrear A/c (750 x ₹ 3)			2,250
To Forfeited Shares A/c (750 x ₹ 2)			1,500
(Being the forfeiture of 750 equity shares for non-payment of allotment money and first call money as per Board's Resolution No. ... dated ...)			

Q.17. Om, Ram and Shanti were partners in a firm sharing profits in the ratio of 3 : 2 : 1. On 1st April, 2014 their Balance Sheet was as follows :

Liabilities		₹	Assets	₹
Capital Accounts :			Land and Building	3,64,000
Om	3,58,000		Plant and Machinery	2,95,000
Ram	3,00,000		Furniture	2,33,000
Shanti	2,62,000	9,20,000	Bills Receivable	38,000
General Reserve		48,000	Sundry Debtors	90,000
Creditors		1,60,000	Stock	1,11,000
Bills Payable		90,000	Bank	87,000
		12,18,000		12,18,000

On the above date, Hanuman was admitted on the following terms :

(i) He will bring ₹ 1,00,000 for his capital and will get 1/10th share in the profits.

(ii) He will bring necessary cash for his share of goodwill premium. The goodwill of the firm was valued at ₹ 3,00,000.

(iii) A liability of ₹ 18,000 will be created against bills receivables discounted.

(iv) The value of stock and furniture will be reduced by 20%.

(v) The value of land and building will be increased by 10%.

(vi) Capital Accounts of the partners will be adjusted on the basis of Hanuman's capital in their profit sharing ratio by opening current accounts.

Prepare Revaluation Account and Partners' Capital Accounts. **8**

Answer

In the books of Om, Ram and Shanti

Realisation Account

Dr. Cr.

Date	Particulars	₹	Date	Particulars	₹
2014 April 1	To Liability for Bills Discounted A/c	18,000	2010 April 1	By Land and Building A/c	36,400
	To Stock A/c	22,200		By Partners' Capital A/c (Loss) :	
	To Furniture A/c	46,600		Om	25,200
				Ram	16,800
				Shanti	8,400
		86,800			86,800

Partners' Capital Accounts

Dr. Cr.

Particulars	Om (₹0	Ram (₹)	Shanti (₹)	Hanuman (₹)	Particulars	Om (₹)	Ram (₹)	Shanti (₹)	Hanuman (₹)
To Revaluation A/c (Loss)	25,200	16,800	8,400	—	By Balance b/d	3,58,000	3,00,000	2,62,000	—
					By Bank A/c	—	—	—	1,00,000
To Current A/cs (Balancing fig.)	—	9,200	1,16,600	—	By Premium for Goodwill A/c	15,000	10,000	5,000	—
To balance c/d (Note 1)	4,50,000	3,00,000	1,50,000	1,00,000	By General Reserve A/c	24,000	16,000	8,000	—
					By Current A/c (Balancing fig.)	78,200	—	—	—
	4,75,200	3,26,000	2,75,000	1,00,000		4,75,200	3,26,000	2,75,000	1,00,000

Working Notes :

(1) Calculation of Capital of Partners :

New profit sharing ratio of Om, Ram and Shanti have been calculated as follows :

Om's share of profit : $\frac{3}{6}$ of $\frac{9}{10} = \frac{27}{60}$

Ram's share of profit : $\frac{2}{6}$ of $\frac{9}{10} = \frac{18}{60}$

Shanti's share of profit : $\frac{1}{6}$ of $\frac{9}{10} = \frac{9}{60}$

Hanuman's share of profit : 1/10 or $\frac{6}{60}$

New Profit Sharing Ratio :
Om : Ram : Shanti : Hanuman = 27 : 18 : 9 : 6 or **9 : 6 : 3 : 2**

Hanuman brought in ₹ 1,00,000 as capital for 1/10th share of profit. Therefore the total capital of the new firm will be ₹ 10,00,000.

Om's Capital : $\frac{10,00,000}{20} \times 9 =$ ₹ 4,50,000

Ram's Capital : $\frac{10,00,000}{20} \times 6 =$ ₹ 3,00,000

Shanti's Capital : $\frac{10,00,000}{20} \times 3 =$ ₹ 1,50,000

OR

Xavier, Yusuf and Zaman were partners in a firm sharing profits in the ratio of 4 : 3 : 2. On 1.4.2014 their Balance Sheet was as follows :

Liabilities		₹	Assets		₹
Sundry Creditors		41,400	Cash at Bank		33,000
Capital Accounts :			Sundry Debtors	30,450	
Xavier	1,20,000		Less: Provision for Bad Debts	1,050	29,400
Yusuf	90,000		Stock		48,000
Zamani	60,000	2,70,000	Plant and machinery		51,000
			Land and Building		1,50,000
		3,11,400			3,11,400

Yusuf had been suffering from ill health and thus gave notice of retirement from the firm. An agreement was, therefore, entered into as on 1.4.2014, the terms of which were as follows :

(i) That Land and Building be appreciated by 10%.
(ii) The provision for Bad Debts is no longer necessary.
(iii) That Stock be appreciated by 20%.
(iv) That Goodwill of the firm be fixed at ₹ 54,000. Yusuf's share of the same be adjusted into Xavier's and Zaman's Capital Accounts, who are going to share future profits in the ratio of 2 : 1.
(v) The entire capital of the newly constituted firm be readjusted by bringing in or paying necessary cash so that the future capitals of Xavier and Zaman will be in their profit sharing ratio.

Prepare Revaluation Account and Partners' Capital Accounts.

Answer

In the books of the Firm

Revaluation Account

Dr. Cr.

Date	Particulars	₹	Date	Particulars	₹
2014			2014		
April 1	To Partners' Capital A/c (Note 1)		April 1	By Land and Building A/c	15,000
	Xavier (4/9)	11,400		By Provision for Bad Debt A/c	1,050
	Yusuf (3/9)	8,550		By Stock A/c	9,600
	Zaman (2/9)	5,700			
		25,650			25,650

Partners' Capital Accounts

Dr. Cr.

Particulars	Xavier (₹)	Yusuf (₹)	Zaman (₹)	Particulars	Xavier (₹)	Yusuf (₹)	Zaman (₹)
To Yusuf Capital A/c (Note 1)	12,000	—	6,000	By Balance b/d	1,20,000	90,000	60,000
To Yusuf Loan A/c	—	1,16,550	—	By Realisation A/c	11,400	8,550	5,700
To Balance c/d	1,19,400	—	59,700	By Xavier Capital A/c	—	12,000	—
				By Zaman Capital A/c	—	6,000	—
	1,31,400	1,16,550	65,700		1,31,400	1,16,550	65,700
				By Balance b/d	1,19,400	—	59,700

Working Notes : (1) Statement Showing the Adjustment for Goodwill

Particulars	Xavier (₹)	Yusuf (₹)	Zaman (₹)
Right of goodwill before retirement (4 : 3 : 2)	24,000	18,000	12,000
Right of goodwill after retirement (2 : 1)	36,000	—	18,000
(Sacrifice) / Gain	12,000 (Dr.)	18,000 Cr.	6,000 (Dr.)

(2) Total Capital of the new firm = ₹ 1,19,400 + 59,700 = ₹ 1,79,100.

Xavier's share of capital : $\frac{1,79,100}{3} \times 2 =$ ₹ 1,19,400

Zaman's share of capital : $\frac{1,79,100}{3} \times 1 =$ ₹ 59,700

The partners capital is already in their profit sharing ratio. Therefore, no cash is to be paid / brought in by any partner.

(Foreign)

Time allowed : 3 hours | **Maximum marks : 80**

General Instructions

(i) This Question Paper contains three parts : A and B.

(ii) Part A is *compulsory* for all candidates.

(iii) Part B has two options – Analysis of Financial Statements and Computerised Accounting.

(iv) Attempt only one option of Part B.

(v) All parts of a question should be attempted at one place.

Set I

Part A

ACCOUNTING FOR PARTNERSHIP FIRMS AND COMPANIES

Q.1. In the absence of Partnership Agreement, interest on drawings of a partner is charged :

(i) at 6% per annum

(ii) at 9% per anum

(iii) at 12% per annum

(iv) no interest is charged **1**

Answer

(iv) no interest is charged

Q.2. Kamal and Vimal were partners in a firm sharing profits in the ratio of 3 : 2. Ghosh was admitted as a new partner for $\frac{1}{5}$th share in the profits. On Ghosh's admission the Balance Sheet of the firm showed a credit balance of ₹ 10,000 in its Profit and Loss Account which was debited by the accountant of the firm in the accounts of Kamal and Vimal. Did the accountant give correct treatment to the balance of Profit and Loss Account ? If yes, give the reason and if 'not' give the correct treatment. **1**

Answer

No, the accountant's accounting treatment for credit balance in the Profit and Loss Account was not correct.

Reason : The credit balance of Profit and Loss Account should be distributed among the old partners by crediting their capital in the profit sharing ratio.

Q.3. Anurag and Bhawana entered into partnership on 1.4.2014. On 1.1.2015 they admitted Monika as a new partner for $\frac{3}{10}$th share in the profits which she acquired equally from Anurag and Bhawana. The new profit sharing ratio of Anurag, Bhawana and Monika was 4 : 3 : 3.

Calculate the profit sharing ratio of Anurag and Bhawana at the time of forming the partnership. *1*

Answer

Monika's share of profit in the new firm = 3/10th. She acquired 1/2 from Anurag and 1/2 from Bhawana

$$\text{Anurag's sacrifice} = \frac{3}{10} \times \frac{1}{2} = \frac{3}{20}$$

$$\text{Bhawna's sacrifice} = \frac{3}{10} \times \frac{1}{2} = \frac{3}{20}$$

Calculation of Old Profit Sharing Ratio of Anurag and Bhawna

Old Profit Sharing Ratio = New Profit Sharing Ratio + Share of profit sacrificed

$$\text{Anurag's share of profit} = \frac{4}{10} + \frac{3}{20} = \frac{8+3}{20} = \frac{11}{20}$$

$$\text{Bhawna's share of profit} = \frac{3}{10} + \frac{3}{20} = \frac{6+3}{20} = \frac{9}{20}$$

Profit sharing ratio of Anurag and Bhawna = **11 : 9.**

Q.4. Deepak, Farukh and Lily were partners in a firm sharing profits in the ratio of 3 : 2 : 1. On 28.2.2015 Farukh retired from the firm. On Farukh's retirement, there was a balance of ₹ 12,000 in Workmen's Compensation Reserve which was no more required. On Farukh's retirement this amount will be :

(a) Debited to the Capital Accounts of all the partners in their profit sharing ratio.
(b) Credited to the Capital Accounts of all the partners in their profit sharing ratio.
(c) Credited to the Capital Accounts of Deepak and Lilly in their profit sharing ratio.
(d) Credited to the Capital Accounts of Farukh. *1*

Answer

(b) Credited to the Capital Accounts of all the partners in their profit sharing ratio.

Q.5. Give the meaning of forfeiture of shares. *1*

Answer

Forfeiture of Share means the cancellation of shares allotted to a shareholder. The shares are forfeited for non-payment of money payable on allotment or call or both. The amount of money paid is not refunded but forfeited by the company.

Q.6. 'Samta Limited' invited applications for issuing 6,750 equity shares of ₹ 10 each. The amount was payable as follows :

On application — ₹ 3 per share
On allotment — ₹ 5 per share
On first and final call — ₹ 2 per share

The issue was fully subscribed. Subhash applied for 250 shares and paid his entire share money with application. Moti applied for 175 shares and paid allotment money also with application. The amount received with applications was :

(i) ₹ 16,750
(ii) ₹ 16,000
(iii) ₹ 19,250
(iv) ₹ 22,875 **1**

Answer

(iv) ₹ 22,875.

Hint :	₹
₹ 6,750 × 3	20,250
₹ 250 × 7	1,750
₹ 175 × 5	875
	22,875

Q.7. *State any three purposes other than buy-back of shares for which securities premium can be utilised.* **3**

Answer

Securities Premium can be utilised for the following purposes other than buy-back of shares:

1. Issue of fully paid bonus shares.
2. Writing off the preliminary expenses.
3. Writing off expenses on issue of shares or debentures (e.g., commission, brokerage, etc.)

Q.8. *A And B Are Partners in a firm Sharing Profits In The Ratio Of 3 : 2. On 31.3.2014, The Balance Sheet of the firm was as follows :*

Liabilities		₹	Assets	₹
Capitals :			Sundry Assets	80,000
A	60,000			
B	20,000	80,000		
		80,000		80,000

The profit of ₹ 80,000 for the year ended 31.3.2014 was divided between the partners without allowing interest on capital @ 12% per annum and a salary to A at ₹ 1,000 per month. During the year A withdrew ₹ 10,000 and B ₹ 20,000.

Pass a single journal entry to rectify the error. **3**

Answer

Calculation of Interest on Capital

	₹
A — (60,000 + 10,000) × 12%	8,400
B — (20,000 + 20,000) × 12%	4,800
	13,200

Salary of A ; ₹ 1,000 × 12 = ₹ **12,000.**

Divisible Profit :

Profit for the year	80,000
Less: Interest on Capital	(13,200)
Less: A's Salary	(12,000)
	54,800

A's share of profit = 3/5 of ₹ 54,800	32,880
Add: Interest on Capital	8,400
Add: Salary	12,000
Total amount due	53,280
Less: Amount already distributed $\frac{80,000 \times 3}{5}$	48,000
Amount still due to A	5,280
B's share of profit = 3/5 of ₹ 54,800	21,920
Add: Interest on Capital	4,800
	26,720
Less: Amount already distributed $\frac{2}{5} \times 80,000$	32,000
Excess amount to be adjusted	5,280

B Capital Account	Dr.	5,280	
To A Capital Account			5,280
(Being the adjustment for profit already distributed)			

Q.9. 'Telecom Limited' is registered with an authorised capital of ₹ 8,00,00,000 divided into 80,00,000 equity shares of ₹ 10 each. The company issued 1,00,000 shares at a premium of ₹ 2 per share. The amount was payable as follows :

On application — ₹ 3 per share

On allotment — ₹ 5 per share (including premium)

On first and final call — The balance

All calls were made and were duly received except the first and final call on 1,000 shares held by Asha.

Prepare the Share Capital in the Balance Sheet of the company as per Schedule VI Part I of the Companies Act, 1956. *3*

Answer

Telecom Ltd.
Balance Sheet as at . . .

Particulars	Note No.	Figures as at the end of current reporting period ₹
I. EQUITY AND LIABILITIES		
1. Shareholders' funds :		
(a) Share Capital	(1)	9,96,000

Notes to Accounts :
(1) Share Capital

Particulars	₹
Authorised Capital :	
80,00,000 Equity Shares of ₹ 10 each	8,00,00,000
Issued Capital :	
1,00,000 Equity Shares of ₹ 10 each	10,00,000

Subscribed Capital and Fully Paid			
99,000 Equity Shares of ₹ 10 each		9,90,000	
Subscribed But Not Fully Paid			
1,000 Equity Shares of ₹ 10 each	10,000		
Less: Calls-in-Arrear	4,000	6,000	9,96,000

Q.10. Panipat Blankets Ltd. are the manufacturers and exporters of woollen blankets. The company decided to distribute 1,000 blankets free of cost to five villages of Kasmir which had been damaged by the floods. It also decided to employ 100 young persons from these villages in their newly established factory at Ludhiana in Punjab. To meet the requirements of funds for starting its new factory, the company issued 1,00,000 equity shares of ₹ 10 each and 2,000, 9% debentures of ₹ 100 each to the vendors of machinery purchased for ₹ 12,00,000.
Pass necessary journal entries for the above transactions in the books of the company.
Also identify any one value which the company wants to communicate to the society. **3**

Answer

In the books of Panipat Blankets Ltd.
Journal

Date	Particulars	L.F.	Dr. ₹	Cr. ₹
	Machinery A/c Dr.		12,00,000	
	To Vendors A/c			12,00,000
	(Being purchase of machinery)			
	Vendors A/c Dr.		12,00,000	
	To Equity Share Capital A/c			10,00,000
	To 9% Debentures A/c			2,00,000
	(Being the issue of 1,00,000 equity shares of ₹ 10 each and issue of 2,000, 9% Debentures of ₹ 100 each to the Vendors for purchase of machinery as per Board's resoluation no ......dated........)			

Values which the company wants to communicate :

(i) Discharging of corporate social responsibility and promoting inclusive growth.

(ii) Generation of employment for youth of rural India.

Q.11. Joshi, Pandey and Agarwal were partners in a firm, sharing profits in the ratio of 2 : 2 : 1. On 31.3.2014, their Balance Sheet was as follows :

Liabilities		₹	Assets	₹
Creditors		51,000	Cash	24,000
Bills Payable		36,000	Debtors	39,000
Agarwal's Loan		84,000	Bills Receivables	27,000
Capitals :			Furniture	81,000
Joshi	2,10,000		Machinery	3,75,000
Pandey	2,04,000	4,14,000	Agarwal's Capital	39,000
		5,85,000		5,85,000

On 31.12.2014, Agarwal died. The Partnership Deed provided for the following to the executors of the deceased partner :

(a) His share in the goodwill of the firm calculated on the basis of three years' purchase of the average profits of the last four years. The profits of the last four years were ₹ 2,70,000; ₹ 3,00,000; ₹ 5,40,000; and ₹ 8,10,000 respectively.

(b) *His share in the profits of the firm till the date of his death calculated on the basis of the average profits of the last four years.*

(c) *Interest @ 12% p.a. on the credit balance, if any, in his Capital Account.*

(d) *Interest on his loan @ 12% p.a.*

Prepare Agarwal's Capital Account to be presented to his executors. **4**

Answer

In the books of the Firm

Dr. Agarwal Capital Account Cr.

Particulars	₹	Particulars	₹
To Balance b/d	39,000	By Agarwal Loan A/c	84,000
To Agarwal's Executors A/c	4,12,560	By Profit and Loss Suspense A/c	72,000
		By Joshi Capital A/c (Note 1)	1,44,000
		By Pandey Capital A/c (Note 1)	1,44,000
		By Interest on Loan A/c	7,,560
	4,51,560		4,51,560

Working Notes :

(1) Calculation of Goodwill

$$\text{Average Profit} = \frac{2,77,000 + 3,00,000 + 5,40,000 + 8,10,000}{4} =$$

$$= \frac{19,20,000}{4}$$

$$= ₹\ \mathbf{4,80,000.}$$

Value of Goodwill = 3 year's purchase of Average Profit of four year

= 4,80,000 × 3

= ₹ **14,40,000**

Agarwal's Share of goodwill = ₹ 1/5 of ₹ 14,40,000 = ₹ **2,88,000**

Agarwal's Share of profit = Average Profit × 1/5 × 9/12

= ₹ 4,80,000 × 1/5 × 9/12

= ₹ 72,000

$$\text{Interest on Loan of Agarwal} = 12\% \text{ of } ₹\ 84,000 \times \frac{9}{12} = ₹\ \mathbf{7,560.}$$

Statement Showing the Adjustment for Goodwill

Particulars	Joshi (₹)	Pandey (₹)	Agarwal (₹)
Share of Goodwill before death (2 : 2 : 1)	5,76,000	5,76,000	2,88,000
Share of Goodwill after death (1 : 1)	7,20,000	7,20,000	—
	1,44,000 (Dr.)	1,44,000 (Dr.)	2,88,000 (Cr.)

Q.12. Jain, Gupta and Singh were partners in a firm. Their fixed capitals were : Jain — ₹ 4,00,000; Gupta — ₹ 6,00,000; and Singh — ₹ 10,00,000. They were sharing profits in the ratio of their capitals. The firm was engaged in the processing and distribution of flavoured milk. The partnership deed provided for interest on capital at 10% per annum. During the year ended 31st March, 2014 the firm earned a profit of ₹ 1,47,000.

Showing your working notes clearly, prepare Profit and Loss Appropriation Account of the firm.. **4**

Answer

In the books of Jain, Gupta and Singh

Dr. Profit and Loss Appropriation Account for the year ended 31st March, 2014 Cr.

Particulars	₹	Particulars	₹
To Interest on Capital :		By Profit for the year	1,47,000
Jain (Note 1)	29,400		
Gupta (Note 1)	44,100		
Singh (Note 1)	73,500		
	1,47,000		1,47,000

Working Note :

(1) Interest on Capital (Actual) :

	₹
Jain — ₹ 4,00,000 × 10%	40,000
Gupta — ₹ 6,00,000 × 10%	60,000
Singh — ₹ 10,00,000 × 10%	1,00,000
	2,00,000

Actual interest on capital is ₹ 2,00,000 but the net profit is not sufficient to pay the entire amount of interest on capital. Therefore, the total amount of ₹ 1,47,000 will be distributed in the ratio of interest, i.e., 4 : 6 : 10 or 2 : 3 : 5.

$$\text{Jain's amount of interest} = \frac{1,47,000}{10} \times 2 = ₹\ 29,400$$

$$\text{Gupta's amount of interest} = \frac{1,47,000}{10} \times 3 = ₹\ 44,100$$

$$\text{Singh's amount of interest} = \frac{1,47,000}{10} \times 5 = ₹\ 73,500$$

Q.13 On 1.4.2013, Mohan and Sohan entered into partnership for doing business of dry fruits. Mohan introduced ₹ 1,00,000 as capital and Sohan introduced ₹ 50,000. Since Sohan could introduce only ₹ 50,000 it was further agreed that as and when there will be a need, Sohan will introduce further capital. Sohan was also allowed to withdraw from his capital when the need for the capital was less. During the year ended 31.3.2014, Sohan introduced and withdrew the following amounts of capital :

Date	Capital Introduced	Capital Withdrawn
01.5.2013	10,000	—
30.6.2013	—	5,000
30.9.2013	97,000	—
01.2.2014	—	87,000

The partnership deed provided for interest on capital @ 6% per annum. Calculate interest on capitals of the partners. **6**

Answer

Calculation of Interest of Partners

Mohan — ₹ 1,00,000 × 6/100 = **₹ 6,000**

Sohan — ₹ 10,73,000* × 6/12 × 1/2 = **₹ 5,365.**

***Calculation of Effective Capital**

Date	Amount	Months	Product (₹)
1.4.2013	50,000	1	50,000
1.5.2013	(50,000 + 10,000) = 60,000	2	1,20,000
30.6.2013	(60,000 – 5,000) = 55,000	3	1,65,000
30.9.2013	(55,000 + 97,000) = 1,52,000	4	6,08,000
1.2.2014	(1,52,000 – 87,000) = 65,000	2	1,30,000
	TOTAL		10,73,000

Q.14. Chennai Fibers Limited was registered with an authorised capital of ₹ 40,00,000 divided into 4,00,000 equity shares of ₹ 10 each. The company had issued 1,00,000 shares and the dividend paid per share was ₹ 3 for the year 2007-08. The management of the company decided to export its readymade apparels to European countries. To meet the requirement of additional funds, the finance manager put up before the Board of Directors the following three alternative proposals :

(i) Issue of 1,54,000 equity shares at par

(ii) Obtain a loan of ₹ 15,40,000 from a financial institution for a period of 5 years. The loan was available @ 12% per annum.

(iii) Issue 16,000, 9% debentures of ₹ 100 each at a discount of 10% redeemable in instalments at the end of third, fourth, fifth and sixth year as per details given below :

Year	*Amount (₹)*
III	*2,00,000*
IV	*3,00,000*
V	*4,00,000*
VI	*7,00,000*

After comparing the alternatives, the company decided in favour of the third alternative and issued debentures on 1.4.2008.

Prepare 9% Debenture Account for the years 2008-09 to 2013-14. **6**

Answer

In the books of Chennai Fibres Ltd.

Dr. **9% Debentures Account** **Cr.**

Date	Particulars	₹	Date	Particulars	₹
2009			2008		
Mar 31	To Balance c/d	16,00,000	April 1	By Debenture Application & Allotment A/c	14,40,000
				By Discount on Issue of Debentures A/c	1,60,000
		16,00,000			16,00,000
2010			2009		
Mar 31	To Balance c/d	16,00,000	April 1	By Balance b/d	16,00,000
2011			2010		
Mar 31	To Sundry Debentureholders A/c	2,00,000	April 1	By Balance b/d	16,00,000
	To Balance c/d	14,00,000			
		16,00,000			16,00,000
2012			2011		
Mar 31	To Sundry Debentureholders A/c	3,00,000	April 1	By Balance b/d	14,00,000
	To Balance c/d	11,00,000			
		14,00,000			14,00,000

2013 Mar 31	To Sundry Debentureholders A/c	4,00,000	2012 April 1	By Balance b/d	11,00,000
	To Balance c/d	7,00,000			
		11,00,000			11,00,000
2014 Mar 31	To Sundry Debentureholders A/c	7,00,000	2013 April 1	By Balance b/d	7,00,000

Q.15. Chopra, Shah and Patel were partners sharing profits in the ratio of 3 : 2 : 1. On 31.3.2014 their firm was dissolved. The assets were realised and liabilities were paid off. The accountant prepared Realisation Account, Partners' Capital Accounts and Cash Account, but forgot to post few amounts in these accounts.

You are required to complete the below given amounts by posting correct amounts.

Dr. Realisation Account Cr.

Particulars	₹	Particulars		₹
To Plant and Machinery	1,60,000	By Sundry Creditors		1,50,000
To Stock	1,50,000	By Mrs. Chopra's Loan		1,30,000
To Sundry Debtors	2,00,000	By Repairs and Renewals Reserve		12,000
To Prepaid Insurance	4,000	By Provision for Bad Debts		10,000
To Investments	30,000	By Cash A/c — Assets sold :		
To Chopra's Capital A/c (Mrs. Chopra's Loan)	1,30,000	Plant	1,00,000	
To Cash A/c — Dishonoured Bill	50,000	Stock	1,20,000	
To Cash — Creditors	1,50,000	Debtors	1,60,000	3,80,000
To Cash Expenses	8,000	By Chopra's Capital A/c (Investments)		20,000
		....		
	8,82,000			8,82,000

Dr. Partners' Capital Accounts Cr.

Particulars	Chopra (₹0	Shah (₹)	Patel (₹)	Particulars	Chopra (₹)	Shah (₹)	Patel (₹)
To Realisation (Investments)	20,000	....	....	By Balance b/d	....	....	....
....	....	....	....	By Realisation (Loan)	1,30,000	....	....
....	....	....	....	....	....	....	....
	2,30,000	1,50,000	30,000		2,30,000	1,50,000	30,000

Dr. Cash Account Cr.

Particulars	₹	Particulars	₹
....		By Realisation A/c (Dishonoured Bill)	50,000
....		By Realisation (Sundry Creditors)	1,50,000
To Patel's Capital A/c	10,000	By	
		By Chopra's Capital A/c	1,20,000
		By Shah's Capital A/c	90,000
	4,18,000		4,18,000

6

Answer

Dr. Realisation Account Cr.

Particulars	₹	Particulars	₹
To Plant and Machinery	1,60,000	By Sundry Creditors	1,50,000
To Stock	1,50,000	By Mrs. Chopra's Loan	1,30,000
To Sundry Debtors	2,00,000	By Repairs and Renewals Reserve	12,000

Particulars	₹	Particulars		₹
To Prepaid Insurance	4,000	By Provision for Bad Debts		10,000
To Investments	30,000	By Cash A/c — Assets sold :		
To Chopra's Capital A/c (Mrs. Chopra's Loan)	1,30,000	Plant	1,00,000	
To Cash A/c — Dishonoured Bill	50,000	Stock	1,20,000	
To Cash — Creditors	1,50,000	Debtors	1,60,000	3,80,000
To Cash Expenses	8,000	By Chopra's Capital A/c (Investments)		20,000
		By Partners' Capital A/c (Loss)		
		Chopra		90,000
		Shah		60,000
		Patel		30,000
	8,82,000			8,82,000

Dr. **Partners' Capital Accounts** **Cr.**

Particulars	Chopra (₹0	Shah (₹)	Patel (₹)	Particulars	Chopra (₹)	Shah (₹)	Patel (₹)
To Realisation (Investments)	20,000	—	—	By Balance b/d	1,00,000.	1,50,000	.20,000
To Realisation A/c (Loss)	90,000	60,000	30,000	By Realisation (Loan)	1,30,000	—	—
To Cash A/c	1,20,000	90,000	—	.By Cash A/c	—	—	10,000
	2,30,000	1,50,000	30,000		2,30,000	1,50,000	30,000

Dr. **Cash Account** **Cr.**

Particulars	₹	Particulars	₹
To Balance b/d	28,000	By Realisation A/c (Dishonoured Bill)	50,000
To Realisation A/c (Sale of Assets)	3,80,000	By Realisation (Sundry Creditors)	1,50,000
To Patel's Capital A/c	10,000	By .Realisation A/c (Expenses)	8,000
		By Chopra's Capital A/c	1,20,000
		By Shah's Capital A/c	90,000
	4,18,000		4,18,000

Q.16. 'Nigam Limited'. invited applications for issuing 15,000 equity shares of ₹ 10 each at a discount of ₹ 1 per share. The amount was payable as follows :

On application — ₹ 2 per share

On allotment — ₹ 3 per share

On first and final call — ₹ 4 per share

Applications for 18,000 shares were received. Shares were issued proportionately to all applicants. Excess money received with applications was adjusted towards sums due on allotment. Ramesh who had applied for 360 shares failed to pay allotment, and first and final call money. Naresh to whom 150 shares were allotted failed to pay the first and final call money. Shares of both Ramesh and Naresh were forfeited. Out of the forfeited shares, 200 shares were re-issued at ₹ 9 per share as fully paid-up. The re-issued shares included all the shares of Naresh.

Pass necessary journal entries for the above transactions in the books of Nigam Limited. **8**

Answer

In the books of Nigam Ltd.

Journal

Date	Particulars		L.F.	Dr. ₹	Cr. ₹
	Bank A/c	Dr.		36,000	
	To Equity Share Application A/c				36,000
	(Being application money received for 18,000 equity shares @ ₹ 2 each)				

Particulars		L.F.	Dr. (₹)	Cr. (₹)
Equity Share Application A/c	Dr.		36,000	
To Equity Shares Capital A/c				30,000
To Equity Shares Allotment A/c				6,000
(Being the application money @ ₹ 2 on 15,000 shares transferred to Equity Share Capital Account and the excess money transferred to Equity Shares Allotment Account as per Board's Resolution No. ... dated ...)				
Equity Shares Allotment A/c	Dr.		45,000	
Discount on Issue of Shares A/c	Dr.		15,000	
To Equity Shares Capital A/c				60,000
(Being the allotment money due on 15,000 equity shares @ ₹ 4 each including discount of ₹ 1 per share as per Board's Resolution No. ... dated ...)				
Bank A/c	Dr.		38,220	
Calls-in-Arrear A/c	Dr.		780	
To Equity Share Allotment A/c				39,000
(Being the allotment money received on 14,700 shares after adjusting excess application money)				
First and Final Call A/c	Dr.		60,000	
To Equity Share Capital A/c				60,000
(Being the first and final call money due on 15,000 shares @ ₹ 4 each as per Board's Resolution No. ... dated ...)				
Bank A/c	Dr.		58,200	
Calls-in-Arrear A/c	Dr.		1,800	
To First and Final Call A/c				60,000
(Being the the first and final call money received on 14,550 shares @ ₹ 4 each)				
Equity Share Capital A/c (450 x 10)	Dr.		4,500	
To Discount on Issue of Shares A/c				450
To Calls-in-Arrear A/c (780 + 1,800)				2,580
To Forfeited Shares A/c (720 + 750)				1,470
(Being the forfeiture of 450 equity shares for non-payment of allotment money and first and final call money on 300 shares and final call money on 150 shares as per Board's Resolution No. ... dated ...)				
Bank A/c (200 x 9)	Dr.		1,800	
Discount on Issue of Shares A/c	Dr.		200	
To Equity Share Capital A/c				2,000
(Being the re-issue of 200 equity shares @ ₹ 9 each as fully paid up as per Board's Resolution No. ... dated ...)				
Forfeited Shares A/c (Note 3)	Dr.		870	
To Capital Reserve A/c				870
(Being the profit on re-issue transferred to Capital Reserve)				

Working Notes :

(1) Calculation of Money Received on Allotment

	₹
Amount due on allotment	45,000
Less: Excess application money	6,000
	39,000
Less: Amount not paid by Ramesh (Note 2)	780
	38,220

(2) Amount Not Received from Ramesh

	₹
Application money paid (360 x 2)	720
Less: Application money adjusted $\left(\frac{15,000}{18,000} \times 360\right) \times 2$	600
Excess application money	120
Money due on allotment (300 x 3)	900
Less: Excess application money	120
Money not paid by Ramesh	780

(3) Amount Transferred to Capital Reserve

Ramesh : (720 / 300) × 50	120
Naresh :	750
	870

OR

Guru Limited invited applications for issuing 80,000 equity shares of ₹ 10 each at a premium of ₹ 10 per share. The amount was payable as follows :
On application and allotment — ₹ 10 per share (including ₹ 5 premium)
On first and final call — ₹ 10 per share (including ₹ 5 premium)
Applications for 1,00,000 shares were received. Applications for 10,000 shares were rejected and application money was refunded. Shares were allotted on pro-rata basis to the remaining applicants. Excess application money received from applicants to whom shares were allotted on pro-rata basis was adjusted towards sums due on first and final call. All calls were made and were duly received except the first and final call money from Kumar who had applied for 1,800 shares. His shares were fofeited. The forfeited shares were re-issued at ₹ 9 per share as fully paid-up.
Pass necessary journal entries for the above transactions in the books of 'Guru Limited'.

Answer

In the books of Guru Ltd.
Journal

Date	Particulars	L.F.	Dr. ₹	Cr. ₹
	Bank A/c (1,00,000 x ₹ 10) Dr.		10,00,000	
	To Equity Share Application and Allotment A/c			10,00,000
	(Being the application money received for 1,00,000 equity shares @ ₹ 10 each)			
	Equity Shares Application and Allotment A/c Dr.		10,00,000	
	To Equity Share Capital A/c			4,00,000
	To Securities Premium A/c			4,00,000
	To Bank A/c			1,00,000
	To Equity Shares First and Final Call A/c			1,00,000
	(Being the allotment of 80,000 equity shares. Excess application money on 10,000 shares refunded and excess application money on 10,000 shares adjusted in First and Final Call Account as per Board's Resoluation no..dated....)			
	Equity Share First and Final Call A/c Dr.		8,00,000	
	To Equity Shares Capital A/c			4,00,000
	To Securities Premium A/c			4,00,000
	(Being the first and final call money due on 80,000 equity shares @ ₹ 10 each, including premium of ₹ 5 each as per Board's Resolution No. ... dated...)			

Particulars		Dr. (₹)	Cr. (₹)
Bank A/c (Note 1) Dr. Calls-in-Arrear A/c (Note 2) Dr. To Equity Share First and Final Call A/c (Being the first and final call money received on 78,400 shares @ ₹ 10 each after adjustment of excess application money)		6,86,000 14,000	 7,00,000
Equity Share Capital A/c (1,600 x ₹ 10) Dr. Securities Premium A/c (1,600 x ₹ 5) Dr. To Calls-in-Arrear A/c To Forfeited Shares A/c (Note 3) (Being the forfeiture of 1,600 equity shares for non-payment of first and final call money @ ₹ 10 each including premium of ₹ 5 each, as per Board's Resolution No. ... dated ...)		16,000 8,000	 14,000 10,000
Bank A/c Dr. Forfeited Shares A/c (1,600 x ₹ 1) Dr. To Equity Share Capital A/c (Being the re-issue of 1,600 shares @ ₹ 9 each as per Board's Resolution No. ... dated ...)		14,400 1,600	 16,000
Forfeited Shares A/c Dr. To Capital Reserrve A/c (Being the profit on re-issue of shares transferred to Capital Reserve)		8,400	 8,400

Working Notes :

(1) Amount Received on First and Final Call

	₹
Amount due on first and final call	8,00,000
Less: Excess application money	1,00,000
	7,00,000
Less: Amount not paid by Kumar (Note 2)	14,000
Amount received	6,86,000

(2) Amount Not Paid by Kumar

Amount paid on application (1,800 × ₹ 10)	18,000
Less: amount adjusted $\left(\frac{80,000}{90,000} \times 1,800\right) \times 10$	16,000
Excess application money	2,000
Amount due on first and final call (1,600 × ₹ 10)	16,000
Less: Excess application money	2,000
Amount not paid by Kumar	14,000

(3) Kumar paid ₹ 18,000. The securities premium of ₹ 5 per share on 1,600 shares of Kumar has been credited to Securities Premium Account. Therefore, (1,600 × ₹ 5) = ₹ 8,000 should not be transferred to Forfeited Shares Account. Only (₹ 18,000 – ₹ 8,000) = ₹ ***10,000 will be transferred to Forfeited Shares Account.***

Q.17. A, B and C were partners in a firm sharing profits in the ratio of 3 : 2 : 1. On 1.4.2014 their Balance Sheet was as follows :

Liabilities	₹	Assets		₹
Creditors	25,200	Bank		8,200
Provident Fund	3,000	Debtors	60,000	
General Reserve	21,000	Less: Provision	2,000	58,000

		₹		₹
Capital Accounts :			Stock	50,000
A	80,000		Investments	20,000
B	73,000		Patents	10,000
C	40,000	1,93,000	Machinery	96,000
		2,42,200		2,42,200

On the above date C retired. It was agreed that :

(i) Goodwill of the firm be valued at ₹ 5,400..

(ii) Depreciation of 10% was to be provided on machinery.

(iii) Patents were to be reduced by 20%.

(iv) Liability on account of Provident Fund was estimated at ₹ 2,500.

(v) C took over investments for ₹ 31,700.

(vi) A and B decided to adjust their capitals in proportion to their profit sharing ratio. For this purpose current accounts were opened.

Prepare Revaluation Account and Partners' Capital Accounts on C's retirement. **8**

Answer

In the books of the Firm

Revaluation Account

Dr. Cr.

Date	Particulars	₹	Date	Particulars	₹
2014 April 1	To Machinery A/c	9,600	2014 April 1	By Provident Fund A/c	500
	To Patents A/c	2,000		By Investment A/c	11,700
	To Partners' Capital A/cs (Profit)				
	A	300			
	B	200			
	C	100			
		12,200			12,200

Partners' Capital Accounts

Dr. Cr.

Particulars	A (₹0	B (₹)	C (₹)	Particulars	A (₹)	B (₹)	C (₹)
To C Capital A/c	540	360	—	By Balance b/d	80,000	73,000	40,000
To Investment A/c	—	—	31,700	By A Capital A/c	—	—	540
To C Loan A/c	—	—	12,800	By B Capital A/c	—	—	360
To Current A/c	—	11,800	—	By General Reserve A/c	10,500	7,000	3,500
To Balance c/d	1,02,060	68,040	—	By Revaluation A/c (Profit)	300	200	100
				By Current A/c	11,800	—	—
	1,02,600	80,200	44,500		1,02,600	80,200	44,500

Working Note :

Total capital of the new firm = ₹ 1,70,100 (A — ₹ 90,260; B — ₹ 79,840). A's new capital should be : ₹ 1,70,100 × 3/5 = ₹ **1,02,060**. Therefore, ₹ 1,02,060 – ₹ 90,260 = ₹ 11,800 is to be debited to A's Current Account. B's new capital should be : ₹ 1,70,100 × 2/5 = ₹ **68,040**.

Therefore, ₹ 79,840 – ₹ 68,040 = ₹ 11,800 should be credited to B's Current Account.

OR

O, R and S were partners in a firm sharing profits in the ratio of 3 : 2 : 1. On 1.4.2014 their Balance Sheet was as follows :

Liabilities		₹	Assets	₹
Capital Accounts :			R's Current Account	7,000
O	1,75,000		Land and Building	1,75,000
R	1,50,000		Plant and Machinery	67,500
S	1,25,000	4,50,000	Furniture	80,000

		₹		₹
Current Accounts :			Investments	36,500
O	4,000		Bills Receivable	17,000
S	6,000	10,000	Sundry Debtors	43,500
General Reserve		15,000	Stock	1,37,000
Profit and Loss Account		7,000	Bank	43,500
Creditors		80,000		
Bills Payable		45,000		
		6,07,000		6,07,000

On the above date, H was admitted on the following terms :

(i) H will bring ₹ 50,000 as his capital and will get 1/6th share in the profits.

(ii) He will bring necessary cash for his share of goodwill premium. The goodwill of the firm was valued at ₹ 90,000.

(iii) The new profit sharing ratio will be 2 : 2 : 1 : 1.

(iv) A liability of ₹ 7,004 will be created against bills receivables discounted..

(v) The value of stock, furniture and investments is reduced by 20%, whereas the value of land and building and plant and machinery will be appreciated by 20% and 10% respectively.

(vi) The Capital Accounts of the partners will be adjusted on the basis of H's Capital through their Current Accounts.

Prepare Revaluation Account and Partners' Current Accounts and Capital Accounts.

Answer

In the books of the Firm

Revaluation Account

Dr. Cr.

Date	Particulars	₹	Date	Particulars	₹
	To Liability for Bills Discounted A/c	7,004		By Land and Building A/c	35,000
	To Stock A/c	27,400		By Plant and Machinery A/c	6,750
	To Furniture A/c	16,000		By Partners' Current A/cs (Loss) :	
	To Investments A/c	7,300		O	7,977
				R	5,318
				S	2,659
		57,704			57,704

Partners' Current Accounts

Dr. Cr.

Particulars	O (₹)	R (₹)	S (₹)	Particulars	O (₹)	R (₹)	S (₹)
To Balance b/d	—	7,000	—	By Balance b/d	4,000	—	6,000
To Revaluation A/c (Loss)	7,977	5,318	2,659	By General Reserve A/c	7,500	5,000	2,500
To Balance c/d	97,023	45,015	82,008	By Profit and Loss A/c	3,500	2,333	1,167
				By Premium for Goodwill A/c	15,000	—	—
				By Capital A/cs	75,000	50,000	75,000
	1,05,000	57,333	84,667		1,05,000	57,333	84,667

Partners' Capital Accounts

Dr. Cr.

Particulars	O (₹)	R (₹)	S (₹)	H (₹)	Particulars	O (₹)	R (₹)	S (₹)	H (₹)
To Current A/c	75,000	50,000	75,000	—	By Balance b/d	1,75,000	1,50,000	1,25,000	—
To Balance c/d	1,00,000	1,00,000	50,000	50,000	By Bank A/c —	—	—	—	50,000
	1,75,000	1,50,000	1,25,000	50,000		1,75,000	1,50,000	1,25,000	50,000